5.95
Harlem

GEORGIAN GRACE

PHAETON AND PAIR, SHOWING A LATE EIGHTEENTH CENTURY CURRICLE PHAETON

From the painting by George Stubbs, reproduced by courtesy of the Trustees of the National Gallery.

GEORGIAN GRACE

A Social History of Design
from 1660 to 1830

BY JOHN GLOAG
F.S.A., Hon. A.R.I.B.A., Hon. F.S.I.A.

SPRING BOOKS · LONDON

First published 1956 by A. & C. Black Ltd.
This edition first published 1967 by Spring Books
Drury House · Russell Street · London W.C.2

Printed in Great Britain by Fletcher & Son Ltd, Norwich, and bound by Richard Clay (The Chaucer Press) Ltd, Bungay, Suffolk.

Dedicated to

ROY MURRAY HYSLOP

to record over twenty-one
years of friendship

CONTENTS

ILLUSTRATIONS IN THE TEXT

LIST OF PLATES

REFERENCES

References to authorities, sources of quotations and so forth, are numbered consecutively from 1 to 208, and are set out under their appropriate chapters at the end of the book, beginning on page 349. The sources of the illustrations are acknowledged in the captions. The Index is by Dora Ware.

THE SECRET OF GEORGIAN GRACE

How was it that architects, designers, craftsmen, and their patrons never seemed to put a foot wrong in the Georgian period? What was the secret of their capacity for good design, their sense of style, and their impeccable judgment? This book is an attempt to suggest some answers to these questions. It is not a work of original scholarship; it is a popular work and popular writers are, to some extent, parasitic, depending as they do upon the researches other and better qualified writers have conducted. The social and artistic history of the Georgian period has been covered very thoroughly by such scholars and specialists as Ralph Edwards, Sir Ambrose Heal, Christopher Hussey, Margaret Jourdain, Sir Albert Richardson, Sir John Summerson, and R. W. Symonds.

In this book the period is considered in relation to design, and with particular emphasis upon architectural design and the crafts that serve architecture, such as furniture making, and there is a chapter on vehicles and their architectural affinities. Any attempt to cover all the crafts would have needed an enormous volume, and far more detailed knowledge than the author could ever hope to possess. So textiles, silver, glass and pottery are mentioned only incidentally.

A consistent pattern runs through the design of everything that was made in the hundred and seventy years between 1660 and 1830, and that pattern becomes unmistakably clear during the long Georgian period. Every article and nearly every building then expressed in its form the material significance of the word "grace." It was an age of realism in painting and sculpture, and of superlatively well-handled decoration. The arts reflected the eager and vigorous delight of people in their world. In many ways that age is in painful contrast with our own, for we have passed and are still passing through a major social revolution. When elderly and ageing people speak regretfully about "the old days," as people in their fifties and sixties are apt to in the mid twentieth century, it is obvious that a revolution has come about, for the romantic appellation of "the *good* old days" is still reserved for an imaginary golden age that has not existed in living memory, but is placed at least as far back as the eighteenth century, but generally very much earlier.

The uncertainties and political upheavals of the present century are reflected in painting and architecture and sculpture, and, of course, literature. The popular political creeds of today, which are so often dredged from the shallows of envious minds, have not yet impressed themselves very vividly upon architecture. There is a vogue for plainness and uniformity, attributable partly to the decline of respect for individual liberty and partly to the use of new industrial materials, which are not always employed with imagination. The welfare state, which is inspired by noble aspirations, is probably being recorded far more truthfully than we are aware, by architecture and the ancillary arts. The dumb faceless shapes carved by Henry Moore; the uncouth brutality of the exterior of the Festival Hall, on the South Bank, in London; and the strife and torment of so much contemporary painting, all suggest worship of blind power, and worship, too, of machines, which a civilised age would regard as servants, but a barbaric age of social and economic transition and international tension tends to respect as masters. But already there are indications that fine architecture is being created by men who have not allowed their imagination to be intimidated either by materials or social and economic theories.

Meanwhile consistent propaganda for improvement in design has been going on and gathering strength ever since the end of the 1914–18 war, and after the second war there has been a reaction. This takes the form of a wistfully nostalgic movement, inspired by gifted writers like John Betjeman, who attribute to the architecture and visible character of the Victorian period, virtues which they had never possessed. The Victorians, who had "mistaken comfort for civilisation," seldom liked or produced things of good design except by accident, and even then, hardly anybody appreciated them. Their superb railway locomotives were considered proper objects for the admiration of schoolboys; their great engineering achievements, such as the Forth Bridge, were commended merely as proofs of progress; the Crystal Palace, first of the great modern buildings of Europe, was applauded for its novelty and not for the new constructional technique it demonstrated. Even Paxton, its designer, reverted to a feeble classicism when he attempted to build other structures. The splendid orderliness of the Georgian period was either forgotten or actively disliked by the Victorians; and as jovial specialists in comfort and good living, they left a characteristic mark upon their own period—a thick, smudgy mark. A tenderly unreal picture of mid- and late-Victorian England is now being put together; and it is created by a fashion, largely a literary fashion, cosy and sweet and delicately amusing.

H. G. Wells, in *The Autocracy of Mr. Parham*, described a Victorian room which had "a cottage piano topped with a woollen mat on which were a pot of some fine-leaved fern and a pile of music, a mantel adorned with a large mirror and many ornaments, a central table with a red cloth and some books, a gas pendant, hanging bookshelves, large gilt-framed oleograph landscapes, a small sofa, a brightly burning fire, and a general air of comfort. Cushions, small mats, and antimacassars abounded, and there was an assemblage of stuffed linnets and canaries under a glass shade." He made one comment, condensing with the economy of genius all that it was necessary to say. "It was," he said, "a room to eat muffins in." Precisely. Muffins, crumpets, Pugin, Ruskin, dark red velvet, and Gothic knobs on everything.

How different from the Georgian Age—how different from our own! Compared with the muddled vulgarity of the Victorian period, and our contemporary stridencies, the urbane atmosphere of the eighteenth century seems wholly delightful; but had we lived then we should have been apprehensively aware of much turbulence, of crime and disorder and national disasters, like the loss of the American colonies, and we might have taken for granted the beauty of our environment, as today we are acutely aware of the fears and follies and imperfections of the twentieth century, and tend to ignore the fact that around us a new graceful architecture is arising, which is part of a great pattern of design that before the end of the century may be as easily recognisable and felicitous as the universal system of design which characterises the Georgian period.

INTRODUCTION TO SECOND EDITION

Some minor revisions and corrections have been made in this new edition, but otherwise text and illustrations are the same. The chief alteration is to the caption of plate 29: originally the sitter in Hayman's studio was named as Sir Robert Walpole. Since the first edition was published in 1956 fresh evidence about this picture has suggested that the sitter may be Dr. Martin Folkes (1690–1754), the English antiquary.

JOHN GLOAG
1967

Part One

THE BACKGROUND

KING CHARLES II.
triumphal Entry into the
City of London *at his*
Restoration.

Reproduced from an early eighteenth century print. The decorative musical trophy at the top of the opposite page appeared above this print in the original engraving.

CHAPTER I

THE GROWTH OF EDUCATED PATRONAGE

ENGLAND was herself again; for eleven years she had lost her smile; now she had regained it, and during the next one hundred and seventy years that smile grew more benign and bland with the assured urbanity of a gracious and robust civilisation. The year was 1660. The reign of the bleak, repressive Puritans was over. Men and women could again begin to enjoy life, and to adorn buildings and themselves, purely for pleasure, no man reproving, no saturnine spiritual directors sniffing out sin if they observed exuberant gaiety expressed either in behaviour, by the embellishment of a piece of furniture, or some bright extravagance of costume. Joy at the restoration of Charles II was spontaneous, unrestrained, and in the case of Sir Thomas Urquhart, the masterly translator of Rabelais, fatal, for he is said to have died in a fit of laughing through sheer delight at the news that the king had come into his own again. The prim, Puritan nightmare became an evil memory. The Golden Age was beginning. It was to end only in the nineteenth century, when a new Puritanism arose that found incoherent and emotional expression through the Gothic Revival.

Already in Carolean times, the promise of Georgian grace was discernible. A new architectural orderliness became apparent; and from 1660 until 1830, architects had more opportunities than they ever before enjoyed in Britain; they were the arbiters of taste, they worked for visually educated patrons, and they created that Golden Age of good design, wherein hardly anything was made without the impress of good taste, allied with superlatively competent craftsmanship, and, most important of all, lucid common sense. There were rules for the preservation of this excellence; but they never became restrictive; they supplied a classical framework wherein the ingenuity of artists and craftsmen and the informed taste of the men who commissioned their work, could find unfettered expression. The sense of sight was honoured as it had not been honoured since the age of Pericles; and whatever other senses were neglected—such as the sense of smell—the eye was seldom offended. The architectural achievements of the eighteenth century certainly suggest that England reached a higher level of civilisation between 1700 and 1800 than had ever been attained before—or since. The observance of universal rules of proportion in buildings and in the making of every conceivable article from

a silver cream jug to a sedan chair, placed no restrictive limits upon imagination. Patrons could be as eccentric as they liked, and they were. The eighteenth century was pre-eminently the century of the uncommon man.

The idea of the greatest happiness for the greatest number had not yet
emerged; it was foreshadowed in the Preamble to the Declaration of Independence, when the founders of the American Republic paid their tribute
to democracy, but Dr. Johnson had expressed the general views about the
subject when he composed the doubts of Mrs. Macaulay, who had wondered
how he could reconcile his political with his moral principles, "his notions
of inequality and subordination with wishing well to the happiness of all
mankind, who might live so agreeably, had they all their portions of land,
and none to domineer over another."

To Boswell, Johnson said: "Why, Sir, I reconcile my principles very well,
because mankind are happier in a state of inequality and subordination.
Were they to be in this pretty state of equality, they would soon degenerate
into brutes—they would become Monboddo's nation—their tails would grow.
Sir, all would be losers, were all to work for all—they would have no intellectual
improvement. All intellectual improvement arises from leisure: all leisure arises
from one working for another."

Throughout the Georgian Age the nobility and gentry were happily able
to reconcile their political with their moral principles; and although writers
in our modern democracy may deplore frivolous uses of leisure and condemn
the Georgians for enjoying life without apologising for their frank lust for
living, the by-product of that enjoyment, of that ardent love of pleasure for
its own sake, is an abundance of beauty in the things that were made and used
in England in that period. In the prelude to the Georgian Age, that began
at the Restoration, the love of pleasure and the new, informed delight in
beautiful shapes, was not merely a reaction from Puritanism; it was in part
a visible expression of delight in the new sense of liberty and release, deriving
its animation from a change in the mental tone of England. A new broadening
of the English mind and a brightening of artistic perceptions had occurred
during the reign of the Saints; for then, many Englishmen, to escape from the
spiritual regimentation and restrictions of life at home, had travelled abroad.
Some made their peace with the Puritan Parliament and came home to live,
quietly and inconspicuously, on their estates; some remained permanently
in exile until the king himself returned. These well travelled, observant
Englishmen—of whom, largely because of his Diary, John Evelyn is perhaps
the best known—were eager to encourage all kinds of tastes and fashions and
experiments in the arts. Their artistic education had been amplified; and
among other congenial studies they mastered the precepts of Vitruvius, and
became amateurs of architecture. Sir Henry Wotton's paraphrase of Vitruvius,
which he called *The Elements of Architecture*, had been published as early as
1624, and it was embodied in Izaak Walton's *Reliquiae Wottoniane*, a best seller

in its day, which reached its third edition in 1672. Wren himself was an amateur; a mathematician, a professor of astronomy, and a cultivated gentleman with a bent for science, who had occasionally indulged a taste for architecture. Evelyn himself could produce a plan for the re-building of London; and the noblemen and gentlemen who ornamented and diversified society during the latter part of the seventeenth century supported their taste with technical knowledge and lively imagination, and could meet the specialists upon their own ground. The age when the specialist could be browbeaten by men without knowledge who "knew what they liked" was still far off. Wealth dissociated from culture had not yet created the Philistine; it had merely enlarged the capacity of the wealthy to appreciate beauty and to secure it for their environment. Democratic patronage, working through committees, individually and collectively fearful of offending the taste of the common man, was even farther off. The uncommon man aroused neither envy nor the itch to circumscribe his copious and often socially stimulating forms of self-expression. The dumb, standardised Englishman of the late nineteenth and early twentieth centuries had not yet become God's gift to caricaturists; he was not the inarticulate clod described in Kipling's verse, *The Puzzler*. Of the men of that time it would have been impossible to write, as Kipling did,

"Being void of self-expression they confide their views to none;
But sometimes in a smoking-room, one learns why things were done."

Men were strong, but not silent, and as the habit of reading had not then corrupted the capacity for using words with forcible originality, the art of conversation was practised by all classes, enriched it is true by oaths that derived their violent and picturesque character from religious rather than biological sources, but never degenerating into a pallid interchange of catch phrases and platitudes. Society at all levels was richly diversified, lit and sometimes darkened by great and unusual characters, by men and women whose virtues and beauty were alike astonishing, and whose vices and odd and even alarming eccentricities were multifariously bewildering. For a time the balance of society was nicely adjusted; the island comfortably supported its population; there was peace and plenty and a mounting prosperity; and there was abounding confidence, for Englishmen believed in themselves and their abilities, and in war or peace were people to be reckoned with and respected.

The eighteenth century gentlemen were so much nearer to the Middle Ages than we are—their mediaeval virility and robust appetites had not been debilitated by a civilian century of respectability which separates us from them. In the Georgian Age, a man of war was a man of blood and ravening appetites, and nobody was such a fool as to believe that he was anything else. Soldiers—private soldiers—were scum, out for rape and loot, with glory as an incidental third in their warlike ambitions. Sailors were much more akin to buccaneers than is generally recognised, and the Navy, although efficient, still had something of the happy-go-lucky "privateering" air about it, that made it all too easy for men, and sometimes officers, to take to lawless but transitorily profitable ways of life in the intervals between wars. Not only the Navy gave recruits to dubious careers of adventure; there were cases like that of Major Stede Bonnet, "a gentleman of fortune and distinction in the Island of Barbadoes," who became a pirate, fitted out a sloop with ten guns and sixty men, which he named the *Revenge*, and plundered the merchantmen that sailed to and from the American Colonies, until he was captured, and tried at Charlestown, Carolina, and executed there in November, 1718.

There was always a plentiful supply of adventurers. The great estates and fortunes were preserved in England by the laws of inheritance, and while the eldest son succeeded his father, and lived prudently or extravagantly, according to temperament, a needy brood of younger sons had to provide for themselves. If they were men of spirit they were claimed by adventure or dissipation; few were content to play second fiddle at home, and they went to London or abroad, and sometimes came back with fortunes, or founded cadet branches of their family in those flourishing and spirited colonies on the east coast of North America. And they took their taste for well made, agreeably designed things with them, and helped to impress upon the new towns and cities and country houses of the New World their knowledge of the correct architectural environment. (See Appendix 7.) When they went to other parts of the world, to India and, particularly after Anson's voyage, to the Far East, they brought back with them cargoes of Oriental ideas, which were adopted, adapted, and regularised by those directors of good proportion, the architects and the master craftsmen who worked for them on all the ancillary arts that served architecture, and supplied the background to fashionable life.

The men who stayed at home on their estates were on the whole good landlords, with a sense of social responsibility, and closely and indeed fraternally associated with their tenants in a way that was unknown in European countries, where mediaeval traditions of serfdom long persisted. In many ways they gave substance to the ideal set forth in Pope's *Ode on Solitude*.

> "Happy the man, whose wish and care
>   A few paternal acres bound,
> Content to breathe his native air
>   In his own ground."

Four lines from Lady Winchilsea's *Petition for an Absolute Retreat* might well have followed Pope's verse:

> "Courteous fate! afford me there
>   A table spread, without my care,
>   With what the neighb'ring fields impart,
>   Whose cleanliness be all its art."

The country squire, coarse, frank, equipped with primitive appetites and entertained by rural pastimes, an open-air lover of dogs and horses, would have been quite at home in the company of his mediaeval counterpart, the illiterate lord of the manor; and, in the same way, the fashionable, rakish, cultivated man-about-town would have been perfectly at home with a Roman patrician: but the Roman patrician, well washed and "personally hygienic," in the modern American sense of the words, would have wanted to hold his nose in the proximity of the Georgian exquisite or any of the fine ladies of fashion, for although perfumes struggled for the mastery with what we, with our mawkish delicacy, designate by the initials B.O., the result must usually have been unsavoury. It is, of course, a modern failing to exalt our contemporary standards, and to measure almost any former period, usually to its disadvantage, in olfactory terms, thus assuming that our forbears had noses as sensitive as ours. Our pride in the present is partly sustained by our systematic denigration of the past; we select the dank shadows; we pick out some ugly fact, often the only one, and judge the entire period by that lapse, as though we were to judge, say, the whole of Sir Herbert Read's output of verse by isolating for destructive criticism the coarse descriptive thirty-ninth line that occurs in his poem, *The Execution of Cornelius Vane*. Our Georgian forerunners had faculties that we have lost; and it is at least arguable that they had something much better than our cultivated daintiness: they ignored the natural smells of sweat and dung and dirt, as we ignore the artificial smells of petrol fumes and industrial effluents, but they rejoiced in an unimpaired sense of sight. The visual perfection of their houses and furniture must have supplied supreme compensation for defects that horrify us, defects of which they could not have been wholly unaware, but were stoically endured. The hideous description of Queen Caroline's last illness that Lord Hervey gives in his memoirs—the agony of the patient, the abysmal ignorance and incompetence of the physicians, the clumsy operation, and the squalor of the royal apartments —is revolting to the present-day reader; but the rooms of the royal palace and the furniture that adorned them were a delight to the eye. The queen might die in excessive pain and discomfort—that was accepted as a matter of course; but the intrusion of any ill-formed object or disharmony of colour in the room where she died would have been unthinkable.

The Georgians were ruthlessly realistic about the facts of life and death, for which they were sensibly and spiritually prepared; but they disdained ugliness. The ladies were not squeamish, though to be sure when in *The Way of the World* Millamant's future husband, Mirabell, says: "When you shall be breeding—" she interrupts "Ah! name it not." He continues frankly: "Which may be presumed, with a blessing on our endeavours—" And she interjects: "Odious endeavours!" He proceeds: "I denounce against all strait lacing, squeezing for a shape, 'till you mould my boy's head like a sugar-loaf; and instead of a man-child, make me father of a crooked-billet."

Millamant might protest against this turn of the discussion; but there was no swooning avoidance of the facts of life, no ignorance. The women of the Golden Age lived as ardently as the men; they had a fervent desire for beautiful surroundings, and their taste was elegant without being finical. In pleasing their eyes they exercised a consistent fastidiousness. Their clothes were as lovely as their faces, for unless the portrait painters who flourished between the reigns of Charles II and William IV were lyingly tactful, their subjects possessed beauty lit by a fabulous vitality. From the Restoration to the mincing Victorian period, English women had a voracious appetite for life, as indeed did everybody in the country, and everything that was made and used disclosed something of that robust delight in living life richly day and night.

While it was easy enough for educated and modish people to instruct themselves in the arts, to become fully acquainted with Vitruvian principles of architectural design, and to exercise their personal taste with an informed and critical judgment of shape and colour, how was it possible for the country gentleman, so consistently presented on the stage by Restoration and Georgian dramatists as a bucolic oaf, to acquire such refined sensibilities? By what art or instinct were characters of the type of Sir Wilful Witwould, the rustic squire in *The Way of the World*, able to choose the right forms and ornamental flourishes when they commissioned the country craftsmen who supplied their furniture or made the additions to their houses? *The Way of the World* was first acted

The country gentlemen were lovers of the open air: day after day would be spent in shooting and riding, then home to an enormous meal and perhaps a stupendous debauch, followed by bed in a room with tight-shut windows and with bed curtains closely drawn so that they slept the sleep of the half asphixiated in a stuffy den. (Reproduced from a print of Aston, published in 1744, by Samuel and Nathaniel Buck.)

in 1700, when William Congreve was thirty; and he makes Sir Wilful condemn the modes of the town, and his brother for adopting them: "The fashion's a fool and you're a fop, dear brother. 'Sheart, I've suspected this—By'r Lady I conjectured you were a fop, since you began to change the stile of your letters, and write in a scrap of paper gilt round the edges, no bigger than a subpaena. I might expect this when you left off Honoured Brother; and hoping you are in good health, and so forth—to begin with a Rat me, knight, I'm so sick of a last night's debauch—O'ds heart, and then tell a familiar tale of a cock and a bull, and a whore and a bottle, and so conclude—"

This type of forthright gentleman, devoted to country pursuits and heavy drinking, was constantly appearing on the stage during the eighteenth century: he was a stock figure, aggressively and alcoholically masculine, as indeed Sir Wilful proclaimed when he sang:

> "Prithee fill me the glass
> 'Till it laughs in my face,
> With ale that is potent and mellow;
> He that whines for a lass
> Is an ignorant ass,
> For a *bumper* has not its fellow."

There were exceptions. For instance, in Isaac Bickerstaff's comic opera, *Love in a Village*, which was produced at Covent Garden in 1762, Hawthorne, the sporting squire, was presented on the stage as a very decorative figure, if we may judge from Zoffany's portrait of Charles Reinhold, who played the part. This painting is reproduced on plate 32, but the black and white rendering hardly does justice to Hawthorne's fawn coat and breeches, and the violet, gold-embroidered waistcoat with a turnover disclosing a pale blue lining. The only dull note in his costume is his grey stockings. The portrait suggests that the actor was declaring to Justice Woodcock his satisfaction in a country life, for in Act One, Scene III, he says: "A sportsman! why, there is nothing like it: I would not exchange the satisfaction I feel, while I am beating the lawns and thickets about my little farm, for all the entertainments and pageantry in Christendom." His declaration is followed by this song:

> "Let gay ones and great
> Make the most of their fate,
> From pleasure they run:
> Well, who cares a jot,
> I envy them not,
> While I have my dog and my gun.
>
> For exercise, air,
> To the fields I repair,
> With spirits unclouded and light:

> The blisses I find,
> No stings leave behind,
> But health and diversion unite."

A discerning modern critic, who loved England, once said that the English were a nation of repressed countrymen. When Paul Cohen Portheim wrote that in the nineteen-thirties, he was unfortunately right; but his assessment of our national character would not have applied to the eighteenth century Englishman. The town might set the fashions, delightful conversation might sparkle in the drawing-rooms—malice, wit, and every refinement of social intercourse could have for their background the great town houses and assembly rooms, but everybody loved the country, and even the greatest devotees of fashion frequently withdrew to rural surroundings to repair the ravages of high life. Everyone affected an interest in simplicity; but though some might avow an affection for simple pleasures which they did not sincerely entertain, a basic love of simplicity kept fashion in order. Consequently no mode became too extravagantly remote from reality. This steadying regard for simplicity tamed Rococo, modified and mellowed the Chinese taste, and, to begin with, kept the taste for Gothic forms in a civilised condition. It was a favourite theme for poets, and *The Choice or Wish*, a poem "written by a Person of Quality," that appeared in 1700, epitomises the gentlemanly hedonism which rejected extravagance; and the fact that its author was a clergyman, John Pomfret, the rector of Maulden in Bedfordshire, shows how distant and unreal the sullen, sin-hunting Puritan age had by then become.

> "If Heaven the grateful liberty would give,
> That I might chuse my method how to live,
> And all those hours propitious Fate should lend
> In blissful ease and satisfaction spend:
> Near some fair town I'd have a private seat,
> Built uniform; not little, nor too great;
> Better if on a rising ground it stood,
> On this side fields; on that a neighb'ring wood:
> It should within no other things contain
> But what are useful, necessary, plain:
> Methinks 'tis nauseous, and I'd ne'er endure
> The needless pomp of gaudy furniture.
> A little garden, grateful to the eye,
> And a cool rivulet run murm'ring by,
> On whose delicious banks a stately row
> Of shady limes or sycamores should grow;
> At th' end of which a silent study plac'd,
> Should be with all the noblest authors grac'd."

Those modest desires were echoed during the seventeen-thirties by Matthew Green, in whose poem, *The Spleen*, the following lines occur:

> "Two hundred pounds half-yearly paid,
> Annuity securely made,
> A farm some twenty miles from town,
> Small, tight, salubrious, and my own;
> Two maids, that never saw the town,
> A serving-man not quite a clown,
> A boy to help to tread the mow,
> And drive, while t'other holds the plough;
> A chief, of temper formed to please,
> Fit to converse, and keep the keys;
> And better to preserve the peace,
> Commission'd by the name of niece;
> With understanding of a size
> To think their master very wise.
> May heaven (it's all I wish for) send
> One genial room to treat a friend,
> Where decent cupboard, little plate,
> Display benevolence, not state.
> And may my humble dwelling stand
> Upon some chosen spot of land:
> A pond before full to the brim,
> Where cows may cool, and geese may swim;
> Behind, a green like velvet neat,
> Soft to the eye, and to the feet;
> Where odorous plants in evening fair
> Breathe all around ambrosial air;
> From Eurus, foe to kitchen ground,
> Fenced by a slope with bushes crowned,
> Fit dwelling for the feathered throng,
> Who pay their quit-rents with a song . . . ."

Both verses recall the lines by Pope and Lady Winchilsea quoted earlier; both extol rural surroundings and suggest the rich contentment of the country-man and the satisfactions of country life. The country squire was certainly not insensible to fashion, though the modes of the town were transmitted to him very slowly; and when we ask how these rustic gentlemen could acquire taste and judgment, the answer is that the country squire's taste was formed and guided partly by the surroundings he had inherited—the well-built house, the strong, well-made furniture, exemplifying the good sense and excellent workmanship of the craftsmen of the sixteenth and seventeenth centuries.

Contemporary inventories of the goods in country houses, farms and cottages disclose the abundance and variety of furniture and equipment that was to be found in the homes of the countryside, large or small. For example, in an inventory dated June 4th, 1713, of the goods of Richard Brown of Horsefrith Park, Writtle, Essex, described as a yeoman, the following items are included in the parlour: "Twelve cain chaires, two tables, one looking glass, two brass andirons, & two pair of window curtains." In the hall: "One wanscoat table & four joynt stooles, six leather chaires, one square table, one clock, & 2 andirons."

From the middle of the sixteenth to the end of the eighteenth century, the term wainscot, variously spelt as wanscot or wainscott, was frequently used in country districts to describe any article of furniture of solid construction. Wainscot oak was the term used for the two planks that were cut from the centre of an oak log, and was usually applied to figured oak cut in that way. Deal panelling was also called wainscot, and by the beginning of the nineteenth century Sheraton was defining it in his *Cabinet Dictionary* (1803) as "The wooden work which lines the walls of a room as high up as the surbase." The wainscot table in the hall of Richard Brown's house had probably been in the family for a century or more. In the chamber over the parlour there were: "One old bed & blancketts & other furniture thereunto belonging, one chest of drawers, seven cain chaires, two red chaires & couch, one small table, one pair of andirons, tongs & fire shovell, two pair of window curtaines & hanging of the roome, vjlb. Over the Pantry: One bed, bedstead, curtaines & vallens, boulsters, & blancketts, & coverlid, one square table, & looking glass, six black chaires, vlb. In the Garrett Over the Hall Chamber: One bed, bedstead, curtaines & vallens, blancketts, & coverlid, two small tables, & nine old red chaires, iiijlb. In the Cheese Chamber: All the cheese & rack, ijlb.xs. In the Chamber over the Hall: One bedstead, feather bed, curtains & vallens, blancketts, and coverlid, one chest of drawers, four old chaires, & hanging press, all the linnin & plate, xlb. In the Chamber over the Small Beer Buttery: Two bedsteads, one feather bed, curtains & vallens, blancketts, & coverlid, & one old chair, & one stoole, ijlb. In the Chamber over the Kitchen: One bedstead, bed, curtaines & vallens, blancketts & coverlid, & two old chaires, jlb. Over the Dairy: One half headed bedstead, two flock beds, & blancketts, jlb."[1]

All these things would be of good, lasting quality. Bedsteads and their hangings, for instance, were handed down from generation to generation. Squire or farmer, labourer or artisan, all possessed things that were made to last. The woods of the countryside were used, and they supplied a large choice of appropriate and agreeable materials. Another extract from an early eighteenth century inventory gives a detailed picture of the furnishing of an artisan's home, that of Zachariah Day, of Roxwell in Essex, a blacksmith. It is dated January 22nd, 1705, and the contents of the living-rooms were as

The Parsonage at Woburn, Bedfordshire, attributed to Sir William Chambers and built about 1765. Good architectural manners were exhibited in the houses of the clergy, and when the patron of a living was a man of fashion, the parsonage would often bear the impress of the latest wave of taste, suitably modified. John Pomfret's modest specifications for happiness and contentment might easily have been composed in such agreeable surroundings. (*Drawn by Marcelle Barton.*)

follows: "In the Hall: One ovell table, six rush chaires, three hanging cubbords, a couch, a dresser, and form, a turn spitt jack, three driping pans, three spits, two beefe forkes, two shreding knives, a bras candle stick, and four iron candle stiks, one tin pasty pan, two druging boxes, a candle box, a morter and pessle, a cobiron, two creepers, a fire iron, a paire of bellows, fire shovell and tongs, two paire of tramels, a gridiron, a chaffin dish, a small percell of books, and some other small matters there, 4li.1s.3d. In the Parlor: One feather bedd, two feather bolsters, one pillow, three blankets, a quilt, a sute of curtaines and valence, a chest of drawers, one small ovell table, six rush chaires, a huch, three boxes, a small looking glase, a warmeing pan, and window curtaines there, 7li.5s. In the Chamber over the Parlor: A bedsted, a bolster, two pillows, a trunk, and ten cheeses, 1li. 1s. 9d. In the Chamber over the Hall: Two feather beds, two feather bolsters, two blankets, a rugg, with curtains and valence, four huches, two chaires, with some other small impliments, 5li. 15s."

Other items included: "Eaighteen pewter dishes and a duzen of plates," and under "Linnen about the house" is listed: "Ten paire of sheets, foure paire of pillow beeres, a diaper table cloth, a duzen of diaper napkins and other table linen, with some towels, and a little other small linen, 5li. 5s."[2] A pillow beer or beere, was a pillow case—a mediaeval term that survived until the eighteenth century.

The countryman was well off in goods; and he demanded hard, long service from the things he used. He judged their shape and material with practical common sense; and was suspicious of any fashionable quirks or fantasies if they interfered with utility. Generally the local craftsman preserved a sense of fitness and never presumed to offer his patrons anything but carefully edited versions of town fashions.

Thus metropolitan fashions slowly became a formative influence on the taste of rural patrons; but the principal influence was exerted by the craftsmen they patronised, for they were being educated by the dissemination of the rules for practising the universal system of design represented by the classic orders of architecture. The country craftsman—mason, joiner, carpenter and chairmaker—had access to published plates and copybooks: annotated plates showing the relative proportions of column, capital, and entablature for each order became as much a part of workshop equipment as planes and chisels. So, as the fashions grew up and flourished in London, they were interpreted, simplified, and occasionally improved, at the hands of inventive and highly skilled men who were masters of their materials. To some extent the skill of joiners, furniture makers, and other woodworkers was conditioned by the materials that were available; but it is misleading to take literally that broad classification, "The Age of Oak," which was first adopted by the late Percy Macquoid in *A History of English Furniture*, each of the four volumes being devoted to a period characterised by the extensive use of a particular wood, namely Oak, Walnut, Mahogany and Satinwood.[3] John Evelyn in *Sylva, or a Discourse of Forest Trees and the Propagation of Timber*, which was first published in 1664, had reached a third and enlarged edition by 1679, and was reprinted several times during the eighteenth century, describes the uses of so many home-grown timbers, that although oak was largely employed in building and various industrial arts and crafts it was only one of many woods handled by craftsmen. As a material it had a long life, and many things made of oak have survived to colour our views today about the past. Elm and beech were favoured just as much as oak, and Evelyn commended the use of the former for "*Trunks*, and *Boxes* to be covered with *leather; Coffins*, for *Dressers*, and *Shovelboard-Tables* of great length. . . . also for the *Carver*, by reason of the tenor of the grain, and toughness which fits it for all those curious works of *Frutages, Foleage, Shields, Statues,* and most of the Ornaments appertaining to the *Orders* of *Architecture. . . ."*(4) Of the household uses of beech, Evelyn included *"Dishes, Trays, Rimbs* for *Buckets,* and other Utensils, *Trenchers, Dresser-boards,* &c, likewise for the *Wheeler,* [wheelwright] *Joyner,* for large *Screws,* and *Upholster* for *Sellyes, Chairs, Stools, Bedsteads* &c. . . ."(5)

Ash, sycamore, hornbeam, yew, and the fruit woods, such as apple, cherry, pear and mulberry, were all used by the rural craftsman, who called himself a joiner or a carpenter, for the term cabinet-maker at first denoted only those who practised the elaborate technique of veneering; and the early decades of the eighteenth century had passed before a country workman would identify himself with such ambitious work. By the beginning of the nineteenth century, cabinet making was on the way to becoming, what it has since become, a generic term for the manufacture of furniture generally.

The growth of educated patronage, whether the patron was the man about town or the country gentleman, had by the opening of the eighteenth century established standards of taste that were known and accepted, just as what was correct in manners and forms of address was known and accepted and practised. Everything inside and outside the house was graciously related. The prevailing harmony that characterised the Georgian interior was largely achieved and sustained by the universal respect accorded to the orders of classical architecture, and the rules they provided for attaining good proportions and the examples they supplied for the use of ornament.

It was during the reign of George II that, as Horace Walpole said in his *Anecdotes of Painting in England,* "Architecture resumed all her rights. Noble publications of Palladio, Jones, and the antique, recalled her to true principles and correct taste; she found men of genius to execute her rules, and patrons to countenance their labours. She found more, and what Rome could not boast, men of the first rank who contributed to embellish their country by buildings of their own design in the purest style of antique composition. Before the glorious close of a reign that carried our arms and victories beyond where Roman eagles ever flew, ardour for the arts had led our travellers to explore whatever beauties of Grecian or Latin taste still subsisted in provinces once subjected to Rome; and the fine editions in consequence of those researches have established the throne of architecture in Britain, while it languishes at Rome, wantons in tawdry imitations of the French in other parts of Europe, and struggles in vain at Paris to surmount their prepossession in favour of their own errors—for fickle as we call that nation, their music and architecture prove how long their ears and eyes can be constant to discord and disproportion."

The work and influence of such patrons, and the expeditions of learned travellers to the former provinces of the Roman Empire, are discussed in the next two chapters.

Lady Mary Wortley Montagu on her arrival at Adrianople in the spring of 1717 could write to the Princess of Wales and claim that the journey she had just completed had "not been undertaken by any Christian since the time of the Greek emperors. . . ." Before the end of the eighteenth century many English travellers had ventured far beyond the eastern borders of Europe, to Asia Minor and to North Africa, in their search for remains of the Graeco-Roman civilisation that had inspired and guided so many of the visual achievements of their own. And they would have shared the view expressed by Dr. Johnson when he wrote: "It is by studying at home, that we must obtain the ability of travelling with intelligence and improvement."

CHAPTER II

THE ARCHITECTURAL BONES

FROM Carolean times to the end of the Georgian period, anybody with any pretensions to taste, anybody in fact who considered themselves to be educated, was naturally familiar with the orders of architecture and the system of design to which they supplied the key. The five orders, which enabled everything to be built in what Wren called "a good Roman manner," were Doric, Ionic, Corinthian, Composite and Tuscan. The first three the Romans had derived from the Greek orders of that name; Tuscan and Composite they invented. Tuscan was an agreeable version of Doric; Composite an extravagantly ornamental exaggeration of Corinthian. All were used with characteristic national variations by Renaissance architects, but in England there had been an unfortunate interval of misunderstanding and mishandling during the sixteenth century when the orders often became as bulbous and bloated as the corpulent, self-indulgent gentlemen that so frequently figure in the works of Hogarth and Rowlandson. This was not because English architects and builders were ignorant of their correct proportions; for John Shute's book, *The First and Chief Groundes of Architecture*, published in 1563, contained detailed engravings of the five Roman orders, and three further editions were issued before the end of the sixteenth century; but Elizabethan exuberance, always seeking expression in copious decoration, was not to be restrained by the discipline of the orders, which were treated freely—far too freely. Their rules were deliberately, almost boisterously, flouted. But early in the seventeenth century they were at last soberly and fully comprehended; and

17

through their proper interpretation by the genius of Inigo Jones (1573–1651) gradually gained recognition as the fundamental basis for all architectural design.

This respect for the classic orders implied the total rejection of what Evelyn as early as 1644 had referred to as "the Gotic barbarity."[6] The orders certainly furnished a most flexible method of composing horizontal and vertical elements; and with the Renaissance they had attained a new vigour; fresh life was breathed into the ancient forms, and they were handled with an imaginative daring that had seldom been achieved in Roman civilisation. The Renaissance in architecture was far more than a regurgitation of antique patterns; it was not, like the Gothic Revival of the nineteenth century, a sentimental fashion that became an emotional crusade, hopelessly entangled with moral earnestness; it was a rediscovery of intellectual design, for which the orders supplied a convenient but unlimiting means of expression. It is true that a great Victorian writer like Ruskin could shudder and condemn the whole conception of classical architecture as inimical to spiritual freedom, and that a great archaeologist like Flinders Petrie, intent on observing the symptoms of decline in the eight periods and phases of Mediterranean culture that he recorded in his *Revolutions of Civilisation*, could peremptorily dismiss the Renaissance as "but the resort of copying an earlier period, owing to the decay and loss of the true style of the VIIIth, or Mediaeval, age of Art."[7] But it was not mere copying; it was a continuation and extension of classical architecture, which fertilised the inventive powers of creative minds throughout Europe. The Renaissance architects, Italian, Spanish, German, French and, lastly, English and Scottish, took up the practice of design with the orders at the point where the Romans had left off; or rather at the point where Roman inspiration had ossified.

To the Georgian architects the orders were living guides; innumerable books were printed to expound their regulating virtues and properties; and there was controversy about the purity of the antique sources. Rome was not invariably respected as the provider of the supreme prototypes: for example, in 1728, Robert Morris, of Twickenham—for so he described himself on the title page of his book—wrote *An Essay in Defence of Ancient Architecture*, in which he contended that "The three *Greek* Orders are of themselves sufficient to raise the greatest, noblest, and most magnificent Structure that Mankind can possibly invent, without the least assistance of the *Latin* or *Roman*; which are borrow'd from the Excellencies contain'd in the former, and when compar'd to the Antiquity of the other, but of modern Extraction."[8] Robert Morris was a relative and pupil of Roger Morris, the Master Carpenter to the Office of Ordnance; his *Defence of Ancient Architecture* was his first book, and was a critical attack on the work of Vanbrugh and Hawksmoor. He was, according to Sir John Summerson, "almost the only contemporary theoretical writer," and although he "described himself as a Surveyor . . . no executed works of his are known."[9] Morris published several other books, including the *Architectural*

Remembrancer (1751) and *Select Architecture* (1755). In his chapter "Touching the Orders in general," which has already been quoted, he acknowledges his debt to Roland Fréart's *Parallèle de l'architecture antique avec la moderne*, which Evelyn had translated in 1664, and follows the French writer's observation that there are but three sorts of building by saying "so the three *Greek* Orders furnish us with the three different kinds to execute them; as the Solid with the *Dorick*, the Medium between the Strength of the *Dorick* and the Airiness of the *Corinthian* perform'd with the *Ionick*, the Delicate with the *Corinthian*."[10] Ninety-four years later, during the "Greek Revival," the fourth Earl of Aberdeen in his *Inquiry into the Principles of Beauty in Grecian Architecture*, wrote that "the character of massive and imposing grandeur in the Doric style,—of adorned yet simple majesty in the Ionic,—and of festive sumptuousness in the Corinthian, is preserved throughout the minutest details of these orders."[11] An admirable epitome of their palpable characteristics; but no descriptive phrases, however felicitous, can depict the majestic serenity of the Greek orders. The first and oldest was the Doric, and the Greek prototype is shown on page 20, with the Greek Ionic and Corinthian orders on page 21. These illustrations, which give the bare bones of the Greek orders, are typical of the plates issued throughout the eighteenth and early nineteenth centuries for the guidance of those engaged in building and the crafts that served it, and they are reproduced from a book published in 1823, when the Greek revival was engaging the attention of architects, and the authority of the orders had not yet been disputed by the protagonists of the Gothic revival.[12]

From these three Greek orders sprang the comprehensive system of architectural design that spread over the whole of the Graeco-Roman world, extending in the east to India, following the conquests of Alexander, and in the west to Wales, when Britain became a Roman province. After the Renaissance, the orders marched to the confines of western civilisation, and were transplanted to the New World in the dominions of Spain and Portugal, France and England. The Roman orders achieved that international conquest; and the Roman orders figured chiefly in the books on architecture, from John Shute's in 1563 to such large and detailed works as Isaac Ware's *Complete Body of Architecture*, which first appeared in 1756. It is from the latter work that the illustrations of the five Roman orders are reproduced on pages 22, 23 and 24.

A modern critic of architectural and industrial design, Mr. Paul Reilly, has suggested that the three basic orders, Doric, Ionic, and Corinthian, represent progressive phases of taste; an attractive theory that may be applied broadly to many periods in which architecture and the ancillary arts emerging from archaic origins pass through a stage of sturdy simplicity, the Doric, to a phase of refinement and elegance, the Ionic, finally expressing a confident enjoyment of deliberately contrived decoration, the Corinthian, which may lead disastrously to the use of ornament for its own sake at the expense of structural fitness.[13] After the Corinthian phase anything may happen; a complete

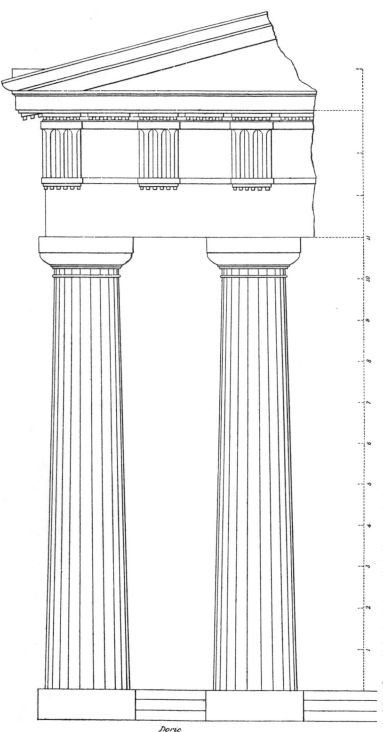

Doric

There were three orders of Greek architecture : the first and oldest, the Doric, is shown on this page. Strong fluted columns, gently diminishing in diameter throughout their height, terminated in broad capitals with very little moulded detail. They supported an entablature that was divided into three horizontal members : architrave, frieze, and cornice. The frieze was vertically divided into triglyph and metope, the latter often bearing sculptured subjects. The Greek Doric order was the progenitor of the system of design that spread through the whole of the Graeco-Roman world, and was revived in Europe at the Renaissance. See opposite page for the Greek Ionic and Corinthian orders, and pages 22, 23 and 24 for the Roman orders. (Reproduced from *The New Practical Builder and Workman's Companion*, by Peter Nicholson. Published by Thomas Kelly, London, 1823.)

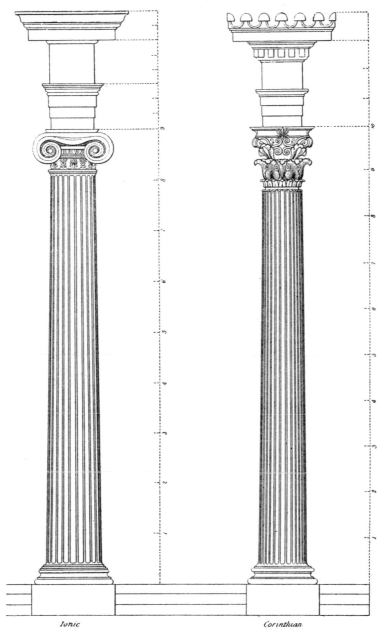

Ionic   Corinthian

The Greek Ionic and Corinthian orders. In both the capitals are elaborately decorative: the Ionic having large spiral ornaments called volutes, smaller volutes and formalised acanthus leaves characterising the Corinthian capital. The entasis on the columns, that is the progressive diminishing along a convex curve of the diameter of the shaft throughout its height, is less marked than in the Doric order. (From *The New Practical Builder and Workman's Companion*, by Peter Nicholson.)

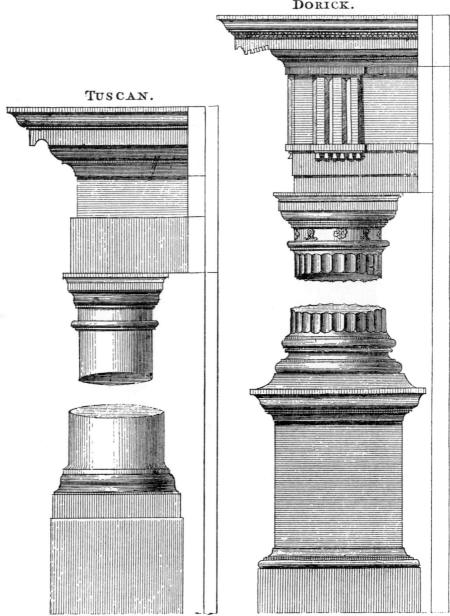

TUSCAN.

DORICK.

Above, the Roman Tuscan and Doric orders. The Romans adapted the Greek Doric order and invented the Tuscan, which was a simplified version of Doric. On the opposite page the Roman Corinthian and Composite orders are shown; the former adapted from the Greek Corinthian order, the latter an over-elaborate and vulgarised rendering of Corinthian which the Romans invented. (The illustrations on both pages are reproduced from plate 2 of *A Complete Body of Architecture*, by Isaac Ware, 1767 edition.)

22

CORINTHIAN.

COMPOSITE.

Cornice.

Frize.

Architrave.

ENTABLATURE.

Capital.

Shaft.

Base.

Cap.

PEDESTAL

Base.

Plinth.

23

IONICK.

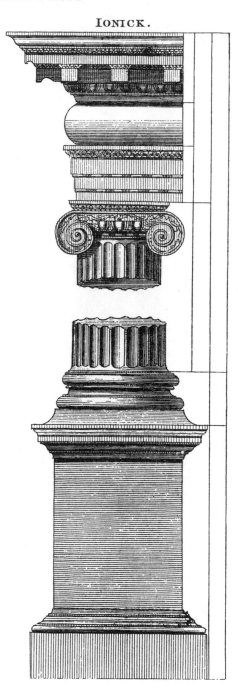

The Roman Ionic order. Less elegant
than the Greek prototype shown on
page 20. (From Plate 2 of Isaac
Ware's *A Complete Body of Architecture*.)
In his *Proportional Architecture*, William
Robinson described this order as
"decent, feminine and modest, and
is universally allow'd to be of an
elegant   Composition."   (Second
edition, 1736.)

breakdown of taste, following the debauching of standards by a neglect of elementary principles of design, and the complete subordination of structure to ornament. If we apply this convenient classification to the hundred and seventy years between 1660 and 1830, we might extend the Doric phase from the Restoration to the seventeen-thirties, the Ionic occupying the middle years of the eighteenth century, and the Corinthian coming at the end of the Georgian period, but with the threat of grossness temporarily modified by the Greek revival.

During that time the architectural environment of life was perfected, and from Wren to Soane, the English and Scottish architects and their patrons, and the builders and craftsmen who executed their designs, refreshed their knowledge of the orders by frequent reference to the examples afforded by the work of Vignola and Palladio, to the interpretations of such native masters as Inigo Jones, and by the occasional but highly detailed study of ruins in Italy and the old Roman provinces. Two noblemen of intellectual and artistic eminence financed and encouraged such researches: Henry Herbert, the ninth earl of Pembroke (1693–1751), who was known as "the architect earl," and Richard Boyle, third earl of Burlington (1695–1754). They discovered talent; in collaboration with their protégés, they designed buildings; and their influence spread what has been called Palladian architecture in England (which corresponds to the "Ionic phase" of Georgian design, if we accept Paul Reilly's classification). Palladianism was far more than a sedulous reverence for and imitation of the work of Andrea Palladio: it took account of the great contribution made by Inigo Jones to classical architecture, and preserved intact Vitruvian precepts, thus keeping alive the original inspiration of the Renaissance. There were critical differences of opinion among architects about the correct use of the orders and their ornamental details, but none regarding the principles of design. To the layman it seemed as simple and obvious as Gibbon made it appear when he wrote: "The practice of architecture is directed by a few general and even mechanical rules."[14] But the architect was conscious of an infinity of subtle variations in the interpretative powers of his contemporaries; and the polemical views of those who wrote about the subject disclose a lively intolerance of any departure from an exact representation of the great exemplars. For instance, Isaac Ware in the "Advertisement" to his translation of Palladio's *Four Books of Architecture*, published in 1737, makes some scathing comments on previous English translations. "In particular," he wrote, "two persons have published what they honour with the title of Palladio's works: the first, and in all respects the best of the two, was done in the year 1721 by Mr. Leoni; who has thought fit not only to vary from the scale of the originals, but also in many places to alter even the graceful proportions prescribed by this great master, by diminishing some of his measures, enlarging others, and putting in fanciful decorations of his own: and indeed his drawings are likewise very incorrect; which makes this performance, according to his

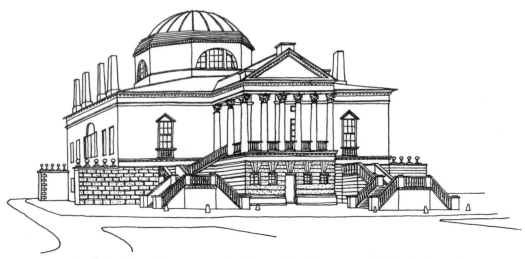

Lord Burlington's ornamental villa at Chiswick, a superficial imitation of
Palladio's Rotunda, built in 1725. (*Drawn by David Owen.*)

own account in the preface, seem rather to be itself an original, than an improvement on Palladio. The other work (published in the year 1735) is done with so
little understanding, and so much negligence, that it cannot but give great
offence to the judicious, and be of very bad consequence in misleading the
unskilful, into whose hands it may fall."[15]

Ware's Palladio was dedicated to the Earl of Burlington, and as Giacomo
Leoni had enjoyed Burlington's patronage, Ware's strictures on his rendering
of *I quattro libri dell' architettura* may have caused that nobleman to raise his
particularly expressive eyebrows. (See plate 6.) Another contributor to the
Palladian movement—which succeeded the work of Wren, Hawksmoor, and
Vanbrugh—was Colen Campbell, the author of *Vitruvius Britannicus*, a folio
consisting of engravings of classical buildings in Britain, and issued in three
volumes, the first appearing in 1715. It was a tendentiously selective work,
which contained a great deal of spirited advertising for the designs of the author,
and some rather excessive adulation of his patron, Lord Burlington, whom he
describes as "not only a great Patron of all Arts, but the first Architect."

This exalted view of Lord Burlington's capacity as a designer was not universally shared. The ornamental villa he built on his estate at Chiswick, which
was a superficial imitation of Palladio's Rotunda, was, in Horace Walpole's
words, "a model of taste, though not without faults, some of which are
occasioned by too strict adherence to rules and symmetry. Such are too many
correspondent doors in spaces so contracted; chimneys between windows, and
which is worse windows between chimneys; and vestibules, however beautiful,
yet too little secured from the damps of this climate. The trusses that support the

ceiling of the corner drawing-room are beyond measure massive, and the ground apartment is rather a diminutive catacomb, than a library in a northern latitude. Yet these blemishes, and Lord Hervey's wit, who said *the house was too small to inhabit, and too large to hang to one's watch*, cannot depreciate the taste that reigns in the whole."

Walpole's mixture of praise and reproof appears in the section on architects of the reign of George II in his *Anecdotes of Painting in England*, and he gave additional point to his strictures on Chiswick House in a note when he described the building as "Another of the numerous instances of the absolute necessity of adapting every architectural design to the nature of the climate in which it is raised. Fitness for the uses to which a building is designed, must always be the principal source of architectural beauty. An umbrella, whether of wood or stone, is a poor protection from the cold; and a building, designed chiefly to afford shelter from the sun and rain, however beautiful in its place, would make but a miserable figure for a residence in a cold climate."

The house designed by Lord Burlington for General Wade in Great Burlington Street, which moved Colen Campbell to such rapturous praise of his gifts as an architect, was condemned by Walpole as "ill-contrived and inconvenient," but its façade was so beautiful that Lord Chesterfield had said: "As the general could not live in it to his ease, he had better take a house over against it and look at it."

But long before the Palladian movement began its delicate and elegant transformation of English architecture, the classical background had been established by Wren and his contemporaries. When Wren began his career, England was still in an age of confusion, almost of anarchy, in architectural design; but before he died at the age of ninety-one, the new architecture, which had been the seventeenth century equivalent of the twentieth century "modern movement" in design, was accepted and practised, the orders were understood, their rules were followed, niceties of detail were discussed, disputed and even quarrelled over; and such diversions, though occasionally acrimonious, stimulated interest in design, injected vitality into the work of designers, and gave to their ideas an irrepressible fecundity.

Thomas Sprat in his *History of the Royal Society*, which was originally published in 1667, could say that "the *Furniture* and *Magnificence* of *Houses*, is risen to a wonderful Beauty within our Memory . . ."[16]. That tribute was embedded in a long paragraph of almost puritanical regret that "Mens Labours in all *Ages*" had been given to the service of pleasure rather than profit. Sprat was a churchman with a critical mind and he was one of the founders of the Royal Society. When he wrote his History he was a prebendary of Lincoln; in 1676 he was chaplain to Charles II, and subsequently became Bishop of Rochester. He had abundant opportunities of observing extravagance and luxury; but in his complaint about the results there is an oddly unspiritual note—a suggestion that scientific enquiry rather than morality is being neglected, and that material benefits would accrue if people were earnest about improving their environment. "How many, and how extravagant, have been the *Ornaments* about *Coaches*?" he asked. "And how few *Inventions*, about new Frames for *Coaches*, or about *Carts* and *Ploughs*? What prodigious expense has been thrown away, about the Fashions of *Cloaths*? But how little endeavours have there been to invent new *Materials* for *Clothing*, or to perfect those we have?" Of the building craft he said that "few or none have thoroughly studied the well-ordering of *Timber*, the hardening of *Stone*, the improvement of *Mortar*, and the making of better *Bricks*."(17)

But several improvements in building technique had been made; and one of the most important was the standardising of the size of bricks, for the size which is still in use, 9 by 4½ by 3 inches, had been adopted over forty years before Sprat's comments. There was also marked progress in the manufacture and use of window glass. Sash windows had been introduced, probably from Holland,

Cleveland House, St. James's, as it appeared in 1795, when it was included by J. T. Smith in his *Antiquities of London*. It was built about 1630 by Thomas Howard, first Earl of Berkshire, and called Berkshire House, and in 1668 Charles II gave it to Barbara Villiers who called it Cleveland House when she was created Duchess of Cleveland in 1670. The Duke of Bridgewater bought it in 1730 and changed its name to Bridgewater House, though J. T. Smith when he drew it, still retained the old name. Like most houses partly re-built and re-decorated after the Restoration, it showed the new orderliness that well-arranged windows with well-proportioned glazing bars could confer upon a façade. The house was completely re-built in the mid nineteenth century, to the designs of Sir Charles Barry.

Maids of Honour Row, Richmond. These early eighteenth century houses,
built to accommodate the maids of honour when Richmond Palace was a
Royal residence, are shown in their relation to the Palace and the Green on
Plate 13. (*Drawn by A. S. Cook.*)

and they had almost as great an effect upon the character and proportion of
houses as the use of the classic orders. Balanced sliding sash windows were first
used in England in 1685, in the windows of the Banqueting House, Whitehall,
with panes 13 inches by 10 inches, and glazing bars of wood, with continuous
rectangular sinkings (called rebates or rabbits) cut along the edges to receive
the panes, which were fixed with putty. Before the sash window was introduced
glazing bars of lead or iron enclosed small square, rectangular or diamond-
shaped panes, the glazing bars being framed by an iron casement, either fixed
or hinged to open, which was surrounded by stone members, vertical mullions
and horizontal transomes, so that those small-paned windows were barred and
stiffened with stonework. Inigo Jones improved the whole art of fenestration by
using a tall, rectangular window opening, centrally divided by a single mullion,
that was crossed by a transome at about three-quarters of the height of the
opening. With smaller windows a single dividing mullion would be used,
without a stone transome, but with two horizontal divisions, like the windows
in the College of Matrons, built at Salisbury in 1682, and shown on page 33.
(The small panes have since been removed from the windows of this building.)
The effect created by these well-proportioned windows was orderly without

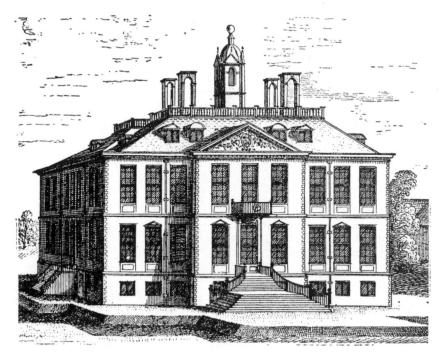

Melton Constable in Norfolk, built in 1687 and attributed to Sir Christopher Wren. This is taken from one of the views by Samuel and Nathaniel
Buck published in 1741. It is a robust design, obviously a home and a very
comfortable one, and a forerunner of the ample and generous buildings of
the eighteenth century, though lacking the refinements that appeared after
the third Earl of Burlington had revived and stimulated interest in Palladio.

being monotonous; they regulated the horizontal and vertical elements in the
façade, and when sliding sashes were used, they altered the whole aspect of a
building because they brought the reflecting surface of the glass panes almost
into the same plane as the walls that surrounded the windows. The result
was that windows smiled; they were no longer set back by the thickness of
the stone mullions that had framed the casements; they caught the sunlight,
and the panes sparkled between their broad, white-painted wooden glazing
bars.

The early double-sash windows were based on the proportion of the double
square: each sash was vertically divided by three glazing bars and horizontally
by two, framing twelve panes, an arrangement that persisted until the early
years of the eighteenth century, when larger panes and fewer glazing bars
were used in sashes. The double square is used for the sashes in Cleveland
House, which is shown on page 28, as it appeared at the end of the eighteenth

century; the original glazing had probably been replaced by sashes with six panes at the beginning of the century. The double square did not invariably determine the proportions of sashes, and the façade of Maids of Honour Row, at Richmond, Surrey, illustrated on page 29, is an example of variation in fenestration, which may be fortuitous. In the tall windows of the ground and first floors, four panes only are used to each sash, but the slenderness of the glazing bars suggest that these may be much later than the windows of the second floor. The storeys are marked horizontally by white string courses, and the top storey has a series of recessed brick panels which continue the lines of the windows above the cornice, so there is no abrupt termination of the vertical elements in the elevation. This row of four houses was built in 1724 to the order of the Prince of Wales (afterwards George II) to accommodate the Princess's Maids of Honour, after he had bought Ormonde Lodge at Richmond.

When the iniquitous window tax was imposed in 1697, it affected all houses with more than six windows and worth over £5 a year; but although it limited the number of windows used, the tax did not affect their proportions or alter their design. The importance of the window as an element in a façade was attested by the use of depressions in the brickwork of new houses, complete with sills and stone architraves if the house was elaborate, so that the harmony of the exterior was preserved, and a place left for a window to be pierced, if the owner should at any time feel inclined to meet the additional tax, or the tax was abolished. (It was not abolished until 1851.)

The increased use of the sliding sash coincided with great improvements in the manufacture of glass, for many highly skilled Huguenot glass-makers settled in England after the Revocation of the Edict of Nantes in 1685, by which act Louis XIV crippled the work of fostering and developing the industrial arts of France inaugurated by his great minister, Jean Baptiste Colbert, and England gained, as she has always gained, by giving both asylum and opportunities to the refugees. The *London Gazette* on June 4th, 1691, carried an advertisement that showed the mounting confidence of English glass-makers, and their consciousness of possessing an excellent product. "There is now made at the Bear-garden Glass-house on the Bank-side, Crown Window Glass, much exceeding French Glass in all its Qualifications, which may be squared into all sizes for Sashes for Windows and other uses and may be had (at Robert Dale's at St. Margaret's Hill in Southwark and) at most Glasiers in London. . . ."[18]

The design of the sash window during the Georgian period reflects phases of taste that were expressed in less formalised ways by furnishing and interior decoration; and there is a correspondence between the progressive refinement of the glazing bar and the increasing fragility of the framework of chairs and tables during the latter part of the eighteenth century. "The thick, flat sections of the late seventeenth century, with the external surface of the glass almost level with the woodwork that framed the small, rectangular panes—exemplified

Abingdon Market House, or "County Hall," designed by Sir Christopher Wren and built in 1678–81. From *Wren the Incomparable*, by Martin S. Briggs. (Reproduced by permission of the author and the publishers, George Allen and Unwin Ltd.)

by the windows of the east and south fronts of Wren's Hampton Court Palace— were ponderous compared with the attenuated glazing bars used in the spacious windows of houses designed by Soane or Nash. Wren was limited by the material available; his work was done at the beginning of a period of evolution in window design, which was to attain an elegant perfection in that gracious phase of domestic architecture which distinguished the opening decades of the nineteenth century. The window tax was increased six times between 1747 and 1808, and although it hardly affected the nobility and gentry, who as educated patrons of architecture set the fashions which ultimately permeated society, the size of windows certainly increased during the eighteenth century. The tax was levied upon the number of windows: not upon any assessment of their area. Windows on ground-floor rooms became taller, rising from skirting level and terminating just below the cornice line; and if they rose from dado height they were still carried up as high as possible, so that the horizontal member of the window architrave adjoined the lowest member of the cornice. This deliber- ate attempt to admit light as near the ceiling as possible in ground-floor rooms suggests that Georgian architects were anxious to make the most of available daylight; but they often defeated their object when they designed the interior decoration of those spacious rooms, for they restricted the admission

The College of Matrons, Salisbury, built about 1682 and attributed to Sir Christopher Wren. From *Wren the Incomparable*, by Martin S. Briggs. (Reproduced by permission of the author and the publishers, George Allen and Unwin, Ltd.)

of daylight with elaborate curtains, and stiff, heavy pelmets, which often concealed the upper part of the window, reducing its height, while the curtains narrowed its width. In designing windows on the ground floor the architect had to take account of three needs: the admission of daylight, the provision of protecting shutters, and the hanging of curtains. The shutters were generally accommodated in the window reveals; the curtains were either superimposed on or framed by the window architraves; and the minimum of interruption of the prospect without was guaranteed by the thinness of the glazing bars and the clarity of the glass. Bay windows again became popular in the middle years of the eighteenth century; curved or semi-hexagonal, they rose through two or three storeys, sometimes preserving the double square proportions of the sashes but often having a large square or rectangular central window, flanked by narrow lights which might be divided vertically by one glazing bar only, and horizontally by the same number as the central sashes. The Georgian architects had devised an infinitude of gracious variations upon the double hung sash, sometimes grouping the sashes; occasionally crowning the central window with an arched head, and using the delicate glazing bars of the sashes to reflect the disposition of the horizontal and vertical elements in their façades."[19]

Houses like Melton Constable Hall in Norfolk, which is sometimes attributed to Wren, and Abingdon Market House, for which he was certainly responsible, show how graciously a long period of inventive and elegant development in window design began. Celia Fiennes, who saw the latter building in 1694, described it as the finest market house in England. It was, she said, "all of free stone and very lofty, even the Isles or Walk below is a lofty arch on severall pillars of square stone and four square pillars, over it are large Roomes with handsome Windows, above which is some Roomes with windows a little like the Theatre att Oxford, only this is a square building and that round, it makes a very fine appearance."[20] She was referring to the Sheldonian Theatre at Oxford, which Wren designed after the Theatre of Marcellus in Rome.

The placing of windows in a façade when the columns or pilasters of some order were used could create an effect of disunity: the orders were so often introduced merely to supply an air of magnificence, though it could be said of most architects of the period that they appreciated the wisdom of Pope's lines:

> "Something there is more needful than expense,
> And something previous ev'n to taste—'tis sense:
> Good sense, which only is the gift of Heaven,
> And, though no science, fairly worth the seven. . . ."

Good sense usually prevailed in architectural design, and to accommodate the requirements of a classical elevation various surrounds for windows were suggested in the pattern books which circulated among architects and builders; but such surrounds were not always happily united with other features, particularly when some grandiose portico was used whose columns, ascending through two or more storeys, upheld an entablature and a pediment. Such disunity is apparent in Colen Campbell's design for Wanstead House in Essex, of which some aspects are shown on the opposite page; but this slightly troubled, overcrowded effect occurs only where the windows with their heavy architraves and pediments become competitive with the six Corinthian columns of the portico. The rest of Campbell's façade is admirably balanced.

It was far easier to associate the orders with the fenestration when the columns were not detached from the wall, or when pilasters were used, which is demonstrated by the illustration on page 36 of part of the buildings on the south side of Queen's Square, Bath, designed by John Wood the elder, and by those on pages 37 and 38, showing elevations of two small houses at Bath, Titanbarrow Logia, and Belcomb Brook Villa, reproduced from Wood's book, *An Essay Towards a Description of Bath*. The author describes the westward elevation of Titanbarrow Logia in these words: "The principal Front of this Example of Beauty faces the North West, and is composed of the *Corinthian* Order, crowned with a Balustrade: The central Part of the Front makes a Tetrastyle of almost whole columns; and while the Spaces between the Capitals

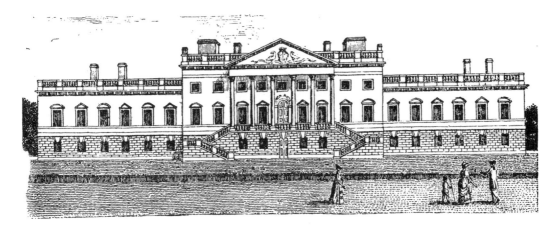

Above, a view of Wanstead House, Essex, from a contemporary print. Designed by Colen Campbell.

To the left is a portion of the west front, reproduced from Volume 3, Plate 40, of Colen Campbell's *Vitruvius Britannicus* (1721). A reproduction of a painting by Hogarth, showing an assembly at Wanstead House, appears on plate 25.

Part of the elevation of the buildings occupying the south side of Queen's Square in Bath, designed by John Wood in 1728. This is reproduced from the second volume of Wood's own book, entitled *An Essay Towards a Description of Bath.*

are filled with Festoons, the Windows are dressed so as to become rich Taber-nacles; and all the Mouldings and Sofits in the whole Front, proper to be carved, are to be fully enriched, that nothing may be wanting to decorate the Order, which, as it represents Nature in all her Bloom, requires the greatest Profusion of Ornament to embellish it that can be put together with Propriety and Elegance."[21] The term *tabernacle* was often used to describe an ornamental frame, surrounding a niche or recess, and designs for "tabernacle frames" were supplied by cabinet-makers: Chippendale illustrated examples in the third edition of his *Director* (1762), and Ince and Mayhew, in *The Universal System of Household Furniture* (1760), called them "architectural Frames." It was originally an architectural term describing the elaborate tracery used on canopied niches in mediaeval churches; and Wood's use of it indicates the importance architects attached to windows as decorative features in their own right, so to speak. Isaac Ware devoted eight chapters of his *Complete Body of Architecture* to windows, and gave minute directions for designing them to accord with the characteristics of the various orders.

Many of the smaller houses of the Georgian period were far more agreeably English in appearance than the impressive palaces built by architects like

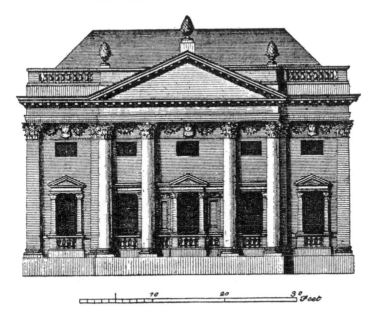

The ELEVATION, to the Weftward,

of Titanbarrow Logia, a fmall Houfe

begun to be erected in the Year 1748 by Southwell Pigott Efq;

againft the North Weft Corner of the Kings Down,

one of the Hills of Bath.

From John Wood's *Description of Bath*.

Vanbrugh, or the highly conscientious classical façades designed by Colen Campbell. With well-proportioned windows, and the judicious use of classical details for door and window architraves and cornices, architects and builders could create an effect of quiet and satisfying beauty. In the streets of many small English towns and villages, the surviving eighteenth century houses show how well the rules for good proportion had been learnt and applied. For instance, Richmond, in Surrey, still has many examples of simple, well-favoured houses, not only on the famous Green, but in such secluded and almost hidden streets like Ormond Road. (See illustrations on pages 42 and 43, also plates 12 and 13.)

William Hogarth could say, in his *Analysis of Beauty*, that "tho' the moderns have not made many additions to the art of building, with respect to mere

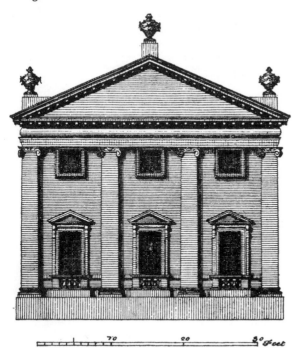

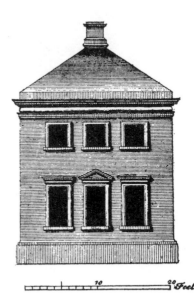

The ELEVATION, to the Southward, of Belcomb Brook Villa, a small House built by Mr. Francis Yerbury in the Year 1734, at the Foot of the South End of the Kings Down, one of the Hills of Bath.

The ELEVATION, to the Westward, of Lilliput Castle, a small House built by Mr. Jerry Peirce in the Year 1738, against the North End of Mons Badonca, one of the Hills of Bath.

The significance of windows in a façade is demonstrated by these two illustrations from plates in John Wood's *Description of Bath*. Of the south, or "chief front" of Belcomb Brook Villa he wrote: "This Front is adorned with Pilasters of the *Ionik* Order, forming the best Tetrastyle Frontispiece, in square Pillars of that Order, that hath been yet executed in or about *Bath*: The Windows of the principal Story are dressed so as to become compleat Tabernacles, while those of the half Story are adorned with single Architraves; and the Mouldings in the whole Front, proper to be carved, are all enriched in the best Manner the Workmen were then Masters of." Of the west front of Lilliput Castle he said: "The Windows . . . are dressed with Architraves; and those of the principal Story are crowned with Freezes and Cornices, the central Window having the addition of a Pediment to distinguish it . . ." Compare these with the designs for windows from Isaac Ware's *A Complete Body of Architecture*, on the opposite page.

Designs for windows from Isaac Ware's *A Complete Body of Architecture.*
Of these he wrote: "If the plain decorations of architrave, freeze and cornice,
the addition of the pediment, or the ornaments of sculpture, do not give
satisfaction, let no false, foolish and fantastic decorations be added, but
at once admit an order." Variations on these designs appear in Richard
Gillow's Customs House at Lancaster, on the next page.

The Customs House at St. George's Quay, Lancaster, built in 1764 from
the designs of Richard Gillow. The four Ionic columns are formed from
single stones, each being 15 ft. high. The architect was a son of Robert
Gillow, the founder of the Lancaster firm of furniture-makers. He had
obviously found satisfaction in "the plain decorations of architrave, freeze
and cornice," and "the addition of the pediment. . . ." and had added
"no false, foolish and fantastic decorations," being content with the Ionic
order, which he used with great delicacy. The refinement of the angular
capitals probably owed something to the work of the brothers Adam.
(*Drawn by Marcelle Barton.*)

beauty or ornament, yet it must be confess'd, they have carried simplicity,
convenience, and neatness of workmanship, to a very great degree of perfection,
particularly in England; where plain good sense hath preferr'd these more
necessary parts of beauty, which everybody can understand, to that richness of
taste which is so much to be seen in other countries, and so often substituted
in their room."[22] In laying out an estate and the spacious avenues which led,
like splendid processional ways, from the various gates to the great house that
was the core of the whole design, the Georgian architect could and generally

A Venetian window, with a semi-circular head, a balcony and coupled columns. This is from Isaac Ware's *A Complete Body of Architecture*, and he refers to the Venetian type of window as "a kind calculated for shew, and very pompous in their nature; and, when executed with judgment, of extreme elegance."

An interior view of a window of this type appears in Hogarth's print "The Lady's Last Stake," reproduced on plate 28. These Venetian windows, according to Ware, "take their proportions from the middle aperture, whose height should be always twice and one half its breadth. Being divided into three parts, sometimes one of those three parts is found convenient for the side openings; but where a considerable body of light is wanting, two must be given to the breadths of the side apertures."

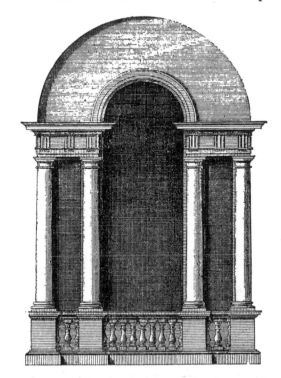

did follow the moderate counsels of Pope, and, with his client, rejoice in the results.

> "Still follow sense, of every art the soul,
> Parts answering parts shall slide into a whole,
> Spontaneous beauties all around advance,
> Start ev'n from difficulty, strike from chance;
> Nature shall join you; Time shall make it grow
> A work to wonder at—perhaps a Stowe."

Sir John Vanbrugh was, perhaps the exception. He was an amateur, like Wren, and his career had something of the flamboyance that occasionally appeared in his buildings. In the diversity of his talents he was as accomplished as Wren, but very different in character, for he was temperamentally adventurous and almost boisterously inventive. The impact of such a vivid personality on contemporary society shows how ready that society was to give abundant opportunities to the uncommon man, who had no need to hide his brilliance lest he gave offence to some jealous blockhead.

Vanbrugh was born in 1664, probably in London, though it is known that he spent much of his early life in Chester. He was of Flemish descent. "Like Inigo

Houses in Ormond Road, Richmond, Surrey. Formerly known as Ormond Row, this terrace of early eighteenth century houses still survives. (*Drawn by A. S. Cook.*)

Jones, he was concerned with the theatre, although only incidentally as a designer, for he was a dramatist whose plays were remarkable for their unbounded exuberance. He selected types of people that he disliked, caricatured them until their human likeness almost departed, and sent them struggling on to the stage to ridicule, somewhat in the manner of a Punch-and-Judy show, such peculiarities as foppishness, fortune-hunting, adultery, and drunkenness. In *The Relapse, or Virtue in Danger*, and *The Provoked Wife*, he preached sermons upon contemporary vices and stupidities, and, like some clergymen who discovered during the first world war that such words as 'bloody' opened the ears (though not the understanding) of many obtuse congregations, he spoke in contemporary terms; but, unlike the modern priests, he spoke with robust

Houses at the south-west corner of Richmond Green. These are shown in the print of Richmond in the early eighteenth century reproduced on plate 13. (*Drawn by A. S. Cook.*)

and ample humour, and never allowed his audience to suspect that he was preaching at all. Possibly he was unconscious of it himself; he wanted to hit silly and evil things, and the fact that he did the hitting in an atmosphere of lascivious harlequinade, and smote lechery and intemperance with a string of sausages, made the practitioners of those follies appear ridiculous rather than unrighteous.

"Vanbrugh was born to take liberties with all the arts that engaged his mind.

After finishing his education in France, he began his career as an ensign in the army. On another visit to France in 1690, he was arrested on a charge of espionage at Calais, and, after being imprisoned at Vincennes, was transferred, by a *lettre de cachet*, to the Bastille. He was released in November, 1692. He spent these terms of imprisonment in drafting *The Provoked Wife*.

"*The Relapse* was the first of his plays to be staged. It was produced at Drury Lane on Boxing Day, 1696, and its diverting unconventionality entertained London as much as it outraged the ornate piety of Jeremy Collier, who attacked it in his *Short View of the Immorality and Profaneness of the English Stage*. It has been conjectured that Collier's attack and the prejudices it fomented against his plays turned Vanbrugh's interest from the theatre towards architecture. In 1702 he had been appointed Comptroller of the Royal Works, under Wren. In the following year he wrote to his friend, Jacob Tonson, the bookseller, for a copy of Palladio. The witty playwright, the man of fashion, now nearly forty, had decided to study the rules of a new profession. Not that rules were ever allowed to curb the opulent boldness of his imagination. He built with the same disregard for conventional trimming and polishing that characterised his plays. Unencumbered by excessive technical knowledge, he jotted down his fine conceptions of country houses, and they grew into masterpieces of radiant stateliness. Without effort, without profound scholarship, but with the eye of an artist, he arranged his stone masses so that from every point of approach some fresh beauty of associated forms was disclosed.

"In Castle Howard, which he built for the Earl of Carlisle, the power and freedom of his imagination are fully revealed. The majestic stabilities of that mansion have been called ponderous; but in the garden elevation, where the alleged ponderousness should surely be apparent, the massive effect is relieved by the tall arched windows, while the fluted Corinthian pilasters are disposed to secure a most harmonious adjustment of horizontal and vertical lines; and everywhere upon the face of the building shadows are trapped so that the sun for ever underlines and daylight always discloses the perfections of grouping which illustrate Vanbrugh's genius for composition. Blenheim Palace and Castle Howard are the works of a man who invented beautiful shapes and made them accord so exactly with their surroundings that it seems as though he had designed a whole tract of country as well. He was like a painter composing in three dimensions. Something about all his work suggests that he stood outside architecture; that, intent upon personal expression, he used the classic orders as media through which coherent form was given to all manner of glorious dreams of beauty. Castle Howard and Blenheim, and such smaller houses as Seaton Delaval, enabled him to develop his dreaming with a grandeur of manner that was not always appreciated by his contemporaries or by the critics and amateurs of succeeding generations."[23]

Vanbrugh was an emphatic nationalist in designing buildings in the grand robust manner; perhaps he was the last. "In architecture he spoke Latin, but

The central part of the North front of Seaton Delaval, Northumberland,
designed by Sir John Vanbrugh. This is in Vanbrugh's grand manner.
(From *Vitruvius Britannicus*, Vol. III.)

continued to think in English, while some of his contemporaries and many of his successors imagined that by speaking Latin they were absolved from the necessity of thinking at all."[24]

Pope had feared that the worst would happen when Lord Burlington, who had sponsored various works on the designs of Palladio, published in 1730 his own book of fine engravings made from Palladio's drawings. In one of his moral essays, which he addressed to the noble author, he wrote those much quoted lines:

> "You show us Rome was glorious, not profuse,
> And pompous buildings once were things of use.
> Yet shall, my lord, your just, your noble rules
> Fill half the land with imitating fools;
> Who random drawings from your sheets shall take,
> And of one beauty many blunders make,
> Load some vain church with old theatric state,
> Turn arcs of triumph to a garden gate. . . ."

Although the study of antique examples was made easy not only for "imitating fools" but for young architects, who had not yet found a patron, there was a widespread belief in the virtue of studying Roman remains on the spot. One of the minor eighteenth century poets, John Dyer (1700?–1758), included some advice of this kind in his over-luscious poem, *The Ruins of Rome*, when praising the Pantheon.

> "Before its ample orb, projected stands
> The many-pillared portal; noblest work
> Of human skill: here, curious architect,
> If thou assay'st, ambitious, to surpass
> Palladius, Angelus, or British Jones,
> On these fair walls extend the certain scale,
> And turn the instructive compass: careful mark
> How far in hidden art the noble plain
> Extends, and where the lovely forms commence
> Of flowing sculpture: nor neglect to note
> How range the taper columns, and what weight
> Their leafy brows sustain. . . ."

Periodically, the interest in classical architecture was refreshed by the issue of such monumental guide books as Isaac Ware's *A Complete Body of Architecture*, which went into several editions; and at the beginning of the second half of the eighteenth century, the excavation of the buried Roman cities of Pompeii and Herculaneum gave fresh impetus to the study of classical remains. For example, Robert Adam lived in Italy from 1754 to 1757, where he made not

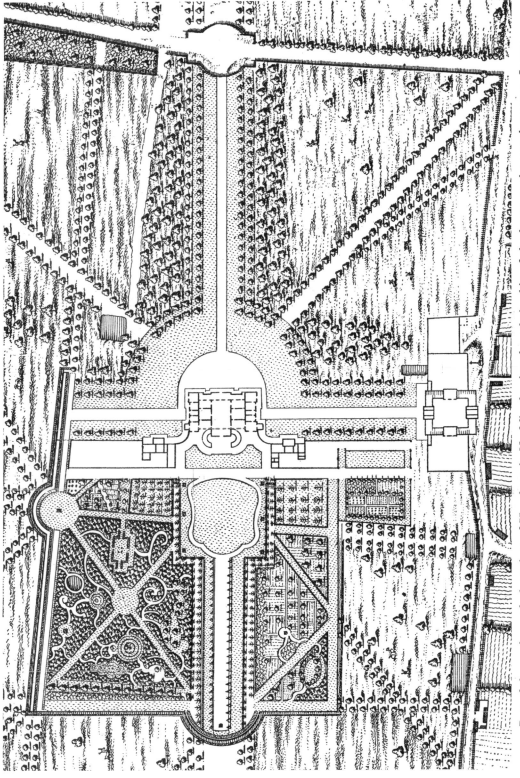

Part of the garden and plantations of Houghton in Norfolk, showing the relationship of the house to the grand avenues. It was designed for Sir Robert Walpole by Colen Campbell. (From *Vitruvius Britannicus*, Vol. III.)

Part of the section of Houghton, designed by Colen Campbell. See opposite page for the remaining elevations. The importance accorded to the chimney-piece is apparent, when its proportions are compared with those of the doors that flank it. (From *Vitruvius Britannicus*, Vol. III.)

Two sides of the interior of the great hall at Houghton. The great hall is a cube of forty feet. (From *Vitruvius Britannicus*, Vol. III.) The orders of architecture determined the proportions of interiors, and their decorative character; but they never imposed rigidity—they were flexible, in the hands of Georgian architects.

only an intensive study of Roman monumental planning, but crossed the
Adriatic to Spalato in the old Roman Province of Illyricum, in order to make
a detailed record of Diocletian's palace. He was accompanied by two draughtsmen whom he had engaged in Rome, and was able to make drawings on
the spot, thus acquiring an invaluable body of reference that enabled him,
when he began his practice as an architect in London, to bring not only great
authority to the use of Roman forms and ornamentation, but to draw from an
apparently inexhaustible treasury of notes the substance of a new and delicate
style of architecture and interior decoration.

While Robert and James Adam revivified "the good Roman manner,"
other influences on taste were arising. In 1757, Sir William Chambers published
his treatise on *Designs of Chinese Buildings, Furniture, Dresses, Machines and Utensils*,
that at least gave disciplined direction to the Chinese taste which was then
passing through one of its anarchial phases; but much more important, because
it inspired a fresh revival in architectural design, was the publication in 1762
of the first volume of *The Antiquities of Athens*, measured and delineated by
James Stuart, F.R.S., F.S.A., and Nicholas Revett, who described themselves
as painters and architects.[25] Four volumes were published in all and the
work was destined to have a great and far-reaching effect upon taste, and was
the real starting-point of the Greek Revival which occurred in the seventeen-
nineties and continued throughout the first three decades of the nineteenth
century. John, Robert and James Adam are listed among the subscribers to
The Antiquities of Athens, and an indirect tribute to the brothers Adam was paid
in the opening paragraph of the Preface to that work. "The ruined Edifices of
Rome have for many years engaged the attention of those, who apply themselves to the study of Architecture; and have generally been considered, as the
Models and Standard of regular and ornamental Building. Many representations of them drawn and engraved by skilful Artists have been published, by
which means the Study of the Art has been every where greatly facilitated, and
the general practice of it improved and promoted. Insomuch that what is now
esteemed the most elegant manner of decorating Buildings, was originally
formed, and has been since established on Examples, which the Antiquities of
Rome have furnished."

But, as Robert Morris had pointed out in 1728, the Greek orders were the
great progenitors, and James Stuart and Nicholas Revett reaffirmed this when
they said "that as Greece was the great Mistress of the Arts, and Rome, in this
respect, no more than her disciple, it may be presumed, all the most admired
Buildings which adorned that imperial City, were but imitations of Grecian
Originals."

The authors embarked for Greece from Italy in 1751, and spent in all five
years in what they described as "this laborious and expensive expedition,"
and in that time they made measured drawings of a great number of ruins,
and the beautifully engraved plates of their four volumes are evidence of their

Two sides of an interior from Isaac Ware's *A Complete Body of Architecture*, showing the dependence upon the orders of architecture for the proportions of doors and windows and their architraves, of skirting, dado and cornice, and of the detail of the chimney-piece.

Part of a loggia, showing the use of coupled Ionic columns. (From Isaac Ware's *A Complete Body of Architecture*.)

immense and continuous diligence. (See plates 2, 3, and 4.) It was perhaps inevitable that a work so thoroughly and superbly executed should stimulate widespread interest in Greek antiquities; and as it provided the most exhaustive directions concerning the proportions, and minute details of Greek architecture and sculpture, it was a temptation to architects to create a new rendering of classical architecture. Few of them resisted the temptation, and the Greek Revival, which was partly an intellectual movement expressed in terms of design, began to affect the form of nearly everything used by the fashionable world at the opening of the nineteenth century. It was the last flicker of inspiration derived from the respectful study and understanding of the classic orders.

By the fourth decade of the nineteenth century the authority of the architect as a master-designer had seriously diminished, and the source from which he had drawn such infallible guidance was becoming discredited. The chaos in architecture and the industrial arts that followed the abandonment of the classical tradition of design is familiar to us all: we are still living with it, and half-way through the twentieth century we are again in an age of architectural fumbling, comparable with the sixteenth and early seventeenth centuries. Then, architectural design was bedevilled by copy-books from the Continent and half-digested continental fashions: during the nineteen-twenties and thirties a continuous stream of photographs of continental examples of the modern movement in design, the bubbling epigrams of M. Le Corbusier, and the sober influence of the Bauhaus under the direction of Dr. Walter Gropius, helped to create a comparable situation. Three centuries ago the genius of Inigo Jones resolved our manifold confusions, and the golden age of design began a few years after his death. A new Golden Age may be on the way: its flowering may well be deferred until the twenty-first century; meanwhile it is instructive to see how a great society once created so much beauty and impressed it on English civilisation by the understanding and practice of a great system of design.

In the grounds of every gentleman's house, there would be elegant reminders of the debt to classical architecture and the great system of design it represented. (*From a drawing by Marcelle Barton.*)

CHAPTER III

THE GEORGIAN SCENE

BEFORE making a short tour of the Georgian scene, we should be sure how far our current prejudices and preferences are going to accompany us : are we going to step into our coach and six with hedonistic abandon, and enjoy everything we see, and even become uncritically sentimental about "the good old times," or are we going to put on dark glasses so that all the gilded decoration is dulled and the clothes which made men and women look like living jewels become as subdued and unadventurous as our own? However cautiously we observe the scene, we shall learn from the architecture and furniture and all other things produced by the industrial arts, that nearly everybody in the eighteenth century looked forward to a continuation and an agreeable expansion of gracious fashions, and designers worked with unwavering confidence in the established principles of design until that confidence was shaken at the very end of the period. If we are deliberately selective in our tour, we shall see only the best and perhaps the most extravagant examples of buildings and their contents, and choose our passage through the streets of various cities and villages with such care that we shall see only what we hoped and expected to see. It is difficult, and perhaps impossible, ever to take an objective view of any former period, even though we see it in perspective and may know more about what was happening and what influences, religious, economic and artistic, were being exerted or generated, than the people who were then living.

So many present-day writers and critics when they look at the past see and describe only what they think ought to be there ; their views may be distorted by their political affiliations ; and they may present the Georgian Age to us as a time of roaring dipsomania, modified though not redeemed by variously ridiculous affectations of speech and gesture which were inseparable from fashionable manners. Hogarth with his quick-witted hands and eyes and angry regard of folly would supply chapter and verse to support this view, and his savagery could be supplemented by Rowlandson's grossness. Some modern critics impatiently compare the serenities of the Georgian period with the experimental standards of their own, so that the ordered harmonies of classical architecture seem to them as wicked as, a hundred years ago, they seemed to Ruskin. Imbued with the insurgent emotionalism of the Gothic Revival,

John Ruskin could see nothing in Vitruvian rules but the evil, pagan repression of free expression and invention in design. Today innumerable little Ruskins find in abstract shapes and the current anarchy of form the essence of artistic salvation, as the great Ruskin found a comparable essence in Gothic shapes and ornamentation. Creative minds often appear to have powers of prevision, and the chaotic and tortured fashions in art and literature that darken and perplex our time, began to foreshadow, even before 1914, the chaotic and tortured condition of mid-twentieth century civilisation. Those movements were accelerated and strengthened by the First World War. But, as we concluded in the last chapter, we may now be on the threshold of a new Golden Age of design, and in an attempt to be objective about our own day and age—which is even more difficult than trying to be objective about the eighteenth century —we should realise that abstract shapes and paintings often resemble pieces of vivid, memorable prose, masquerading as complete in themselves, though they are really torn from the context of a large and ambitious work. That work is no less than the moral and visual reconstruction of society, in which perhaps the conscience will give way to the sub-conscious, and idealism be replaced by ideology. At the moment the modern movement in art and architecture is forcible, though hardly civilised; it is not imitating or reviving any previous art forms; it is turbulently original and has the savage veracity of purpose that distinguished the barbarian art of the Dark Ages after the fifth century, when the classical conventions of the Roman Empire were abandoned, and the great mediaeval civilisation had not yet arisen. Meanwhile the work of redesigning our partly reconstituted society in terms of architecture is only beginning; our new towns are tentative experiments, seeking to express the reach-me-down materialistic creeds that three generations of Marx-sodden economists and reformers have invested with the spurious majesty of social justice; and if this chapter was being written the other way round and a visitor from the Georgian period was touring modern England, he might doubt whether great architecture could be inspired by the Marxian slogan: "From each according to his ability, to each according to his needs." But it is time we left the century of the common man, and looked at England when it had reached the peak of its civilisation. The coach waits, for we should assume that we are going to travel in the greatest comfort, and not on foot like Joseph Andrews or Roderick Random.

First of all, let us drive up to one of those great country houses, like Chatsworth in Derbyshire, which still stands, and was an early example of those classical residences that architects were so well equipped to provide for their noble patrons. Designed by William Talman (1650–1719), and built during the sixteen-eighties, the lavish magnificence of Chatsworth House became a pattern for many of the minor palaces that graced the countryside. Vanbrugh's vast houses, which have already been briefly described, could create an even greater impression of magnificence; indeed Blenheim Palace brought

View of Chatfworth-Houfe, in the County of Derby

The Seat of his Grace the Duke of Devonshire.

Mr. Pope into action. It was, he felt, too stupendous to be wholly sensible, and as usual he said so.

> "See, sir, here's the grand approach;
> This way is for his grace's coach:
> There lies the bridge, and here's the clock,
> Observe the lion and the cock,
> The spacious court, the colonnade,
> And mark how wide the hall is made!
> The chimneys are so well design'd,
> They never smoke in any wind.
> This gallery's contrived for walking,
> The windows to retire and talk in;
> The council chamber for debate,
> And all the rest are rooms of state.
> Thanks, sir, cried I, 'tis very fine,
> But where d'ye sleep, or where d'ye dine?
> I find, by all you have been telling,
> That 'tis a house, but not a dwelling."

Addison had deplored the placing of a carved stone "figure of a monstrous lion tearing to pieces a little cock" over two of the portals of Blenheim Palace. In the *Spectator* (May 8th, 1711) he had said: "For the better understanding of which device, I must acquaint my English reader that a cock has the misfortune to be called in Latin by the same word that signifies a Frenchman, as a lion is the emblem of the English nation. Such a device in so noble a pile of building looks like a pun in an heroic poem, and I am very sorry the truly ingenious architect would suffer the statuary to blemish his excellent plan with so poor a conceit: but I hope what I have said will gain quarter for the cock, and deliver him out of the lion's paw."

Everybody was critically aware of the architectural character of everything that was built, and all the ornamental details that embellished a design were scrutinised, commented on, condemned or approved.

In this climate of well-educated opinion no vulgarities of form could survive; they were seldom attempted; and even the country-made furniture that ultimately followed the fashions of the town avoided any vulgarisation of those fashions, which were simplified, and occasionally improved, when, for their rural translation, the woods of the countryside were used. All the exterior details of houses, door handles, knockers, lamps, railings and gates, were equally well mannered. Whether you drove up to a mansion like Chatsworth, to an ornate palace by Vanbrugh, or a quiet and stately house like Sudbrooke Lodge at Petersham, near Richmond, in Surrey (which James Gibbs built for the Duke of Argyll, 1726–28), you were impressed not only by the perfection of the appointments, the refinement and appropriate placing of ornamental

Sudbrooke Lodge, at Petersham, near Richmond, built by James Gibbs for
the second Duke of Argyll, 1726–28. (*Drawn by David Owen.*)

details, but by the admirable proportions of the house itself. Two lines from
one of Lady Winchilsea's poems are generally applicable to the Georgian
home, for nothing

> "But graceful symmetry without is seen,
> And use with beauty are improv'd within."

No matter what rank or station in society your host enjoyed, you were always
conscious of approaching and entering a home when you accepted hospitality.
Although the magnificence might be almost overpowering, it was never
flashy. Pope's gibe that Blenheim was "a house but not a dwelling" was
directed not at the scale or elaboration of the architecture, but at the difficulty
of feeling at home in a place that seemed pre-eminently intended for display
and not for the well-ordered, comfortable life sought by all ranks. Even
Vanbrugh could impart to some of his smaller buildings the subtle air of welcome
that is inseparable from the English idea of home. A royal palace like Hampton

Gatekeeper's lodge, at the Richmond Hill Gate of Richmond Park, Surrey,
designed by Lancelot "Capability" Brown, for George III. The enclosed
porch is a later addition. These little structures often reproduced in miniature
the architectural characteristics of the great country house whose gates they
guarded. (*Drawn by A. S. Cook.*)

Court is very obviously a home; and this home-like air is apparent both in
the remains of the original Tudor building and in Wren's additions. It was
an atmosphere common to every type of dwelling, whether it was the country
seat of a nobleman, a small manor-house inhabited by a hard-riding, hard-
drinking squire, a farmhouse, or a town house, modest or modish.

Great estates were surrounded by high walls, and usually walls gave seclusion
to the grounds of country houses, large or small. Often this consistent regard
for privacy confined the approaches of a village to narrow, darkened lanes;
and when, in order to open up some attractive prospect or to create a vista
when an avenue was planted, walls were lowered or replaced by decorative
wrought-iron railings, the humbler inhabitants of the countryside could, at a
distance, see a little more of the life and pleasures of the great, which encouraged
respectful emulation rather than envy. It was an ordered and beautiful countryside, cleaner and brighter than the rural areas that survive today, unpolluted
by the drifting grime from industrial regions that has, for over a hundred years,
dimmed the clarity of English skies and soiled their clouds. Brightly coloured
clothes could easily preserve their fresh hues in such pellucid air; there was,
perhaps, less need to wash clothes and bodies; though so far as homes were
concerned we have the testimony of that observant Frenchman, François
de la Rochefoucauld (1765–1848), who visited England in 1784, and recorded
that the cleanliness that pervaded everything was a source of perpetual satisfaction. "Houses are constantly washed inside and out," he said; "generally
on Saturdays. People take the greatest possible pains to maintain the standard

of cleanliness: you come upon mats and carpets everywhere; there is always a strip of drugget on the stairs, and not a speck of dust anywhere." He qualified his approval by adding: "At first I was quite astonished at all this and did all that I could to make sure whether this cleanliness was natural to the English and so pervaded all their activities, or whether it was a superficial refinement. I was led to see quite clearly that it was only external: everything that you are supposed to see partakes of this most desirable quality, but the English contrive to neglect it in what you are not supposed to see."[26]

What you were supposed to see when you visited your friends could only gratify the sense of sight. From the moment the great gates had been opened to admit your coach, and you had passed the pair of neat lodges of brick or stone, whose classical details often reflected in miniature the design of the great

Elegant little classic temples like this would often close a vista, or be placed where three or four rides met in a park. (*From a drawing by Marcelle Barton.*)

Examples of termini or terms, from Isaac Ware's *A Complete Body of Architecture*. These terms, according to Ware, were frequent ornaments in gardens, and "some place them also in decorated rooms, to support vases, or other elegant works. . . ." Termini supported the roof of the Rotunda at Ranelagh Gardens. (See illustration on page 194, and plate 9.)

house beyond, you were aware only of ordered beauty, of formal harmonies which suggested that nature had obligingly collaborated with a landscape architect, and that the trees themselves were acquainted with some arboreal equivalent of the classic orders, for their proportions were noble. But then John Evelyn's *Sylva* was a best seller and there were other works that gave detailed directions for the planting of groves and glades and such devices as "the *Circle* with a *Star* of *Walks* radiating from it" which Evelyn considered "exceeding pleasant." He had written: "for all these varieties of Walks, Glades and Lawns, the stately Elm, spreading Oak, beautiful Lime, umbragious Platan, Beech, Walnut, Chestnut, Pines and Firs where they will grow, not omitting the Black-Cherry, are proper to be planted, kept, and govern'd skilfully. . . ."[27] Your host had almost certainly studied *Sylva*, and his solicitude for posterity might become apparent in the drive, which he had planted with young trees, so that in fifty or sixty years' time a majestic avenue would provide dignity and shade. On the way to the house you might pass a round point or circle, where a "star" of three or four rides or walks met; and at the end of each a group of statuary, a summer house or an arbour, could be descried. (As the eighteenth century grew older, a mock ruin or an urn upon a pedestal would often appear at the end of a vista.)

François de la Rochefoucauld had remarked that the characteristic quality of English parks was their vast size and their fine turf. He said: "above this stretch of grass, which follows the slope of the hills, are large trees, distributed in groups and grouped in relation to the view, so that a picturesque clock-tower or a pleasant village is clearly seen and anything that may be displeasing to the eye in an unattractive countryside is concealed. A bridge or a little pavilion or temple may be built at a point where a good view may be obtained: when the slopes of the hills are not gentle enough they are joined together to suit the owner's caprice—in fact a whole mountain may be removed. Above all, no pains are spared to bring together the streams and waters and to make them into a single river which is provided with such a natural course as to give the impression that it has always been there; similarly it is contrived to produce islands and pleasant scenery—nothing, in fact, is overlooked. In a well-kept garden, there is sometimes not a single weed in the whole extent of it, which is enormous. Such is the English conception of a park."[28]

Although the great parks might be walled, their owners liked to preserve their partnership with the countryside, and to incorporate with their own carefully devised prospects the "hamlets brown, and dim-discover'd spires" of which William Collins wrote in his *Ode to Evening*, for the pastoral theme in verse, in painting, or landscape gardening, had a perennial appeal to English taste. Even the country surrounding great cities was preserved until the very end of the Georgian Age by the socially pervasive desire for rural amenities to which all classes responded. Another foreign visitor, Louis Simond, a French American who made a tour through Britain in 1810 and 1811, describes his delighted astonishment at the aspect of Surrey. "We have made our first sortie out of London," he wrote, "to see what the spring was out of its smoke and dust, 30 miles off, in the county of Surrey. The surface of the country is gently waving, covered with pasturage of the finest green, with numerous flocks of sheep, and herds of cattle; here and there groves of forest trees—but little arable land, few inclosures, and great heathy commons. All this is very beautiful, and pleases me extremely; but surprises me equally. So near this Colossus of a town, with its 800,000 mouths to feed, I should have expected to see everywhere fields of corn for men, and of clover and sainfoin for animals; everywhere the plough,—no trees but fruit-trees,—no pastures, and, above all, no heath. We do not lose certainly by the exchange; but I do not understand how the proprietors of this valuable land calculate. I should suppose that all this beautiful country belongs to people of fortune, who think more of its beauty than its produce, and the conjecture is very much strengthened, by the appearance of multitudes of good-looking houses, half-mansions, half-cottage, but evidently inhabited by persons of taste and opulence."[29]

Few lands were as well cultivated as England, but travelling through its rich and lovely countryside was beset with difficulties, of which the chief was the execrable condition of the roads. The turnpike system had encouraged, in a piecemeal fashion, the making of good main roads, which in the latter part of the eighteenth century had made possible the development of the great coaching system; but once off the routes used by the mail coaches the road surfaces degenerated into mere tracks, often impassable in winter, and seamed with iron-hard ruts in summer. Landlords and tenants alike were often shut up during the winter months in self-contained groups on the great estates and the nearby villages. Such seclusion, enforced by the weather, became complete isolation, unless it could be relieved by some waterway. Although roads were ill cared for, particularly in the early part of the eighteenth century, rivers and streams were in constant use. The Thames was then a real highway, its banks diversified with villas and gardens, its surface bright with traffic which exhibited a continuous spectacle of work and pleasure. Mr. Pope, whose frequent strictures on other people's houses and admonitions about design have been quoted, had a delightful villa at Twickenham from which he could regard the Thames flowing past the foot of his garden. To go by water from the upper reaches of the Thames to London was an unforgettable experience. Sir Richard Steele (1672–1729) described how one night he lay at Richmond "and being restless, not out of dissatisfaction, but a certain busy inclination one sometimes has, I arose at four in the morning, and took boat for London, with a resolution to rove by boat and coach for the next four and twenty hours, till the many different objects I must needs meet with should tire my imagination, and give me an inclination to a repose more profound than I was at that time capable of. The hours of the day and night are taken up in the cities of London and Westminster by people as different from each other as

The riverside scene. The Thames was not only a highway but agreeably diversified with the villas and gardens of the nobility and gentry. Alexander Pope's house at Twickenham is shown in this reproduction of a contemporary engraving.

The riverside scene. Above and on the opposite page is a stretch of the river at Twickenham, east of Eel Pie Island. Lady Mary Wortley Montagu, writing to her sister the Countess of Mar in the mid seventeen-twenties, said that Twickenham "has become so fashionable, and the neighbourhood so much enlarged, 'tis more like Tunbridge or the Bath than a country retreat."

Horace Walpole, describing the view from Strawberry Hill, said, "to the left you see the town and church of Twickenham, encircling a turn of the river, that looks exactly like a seaport in miniature." (Letter to Sir Horace Mann, June 12th, 1753.) Twickenham Church is shown above, and it has not altered very much since this engraving was made over two centuries ago. (See page 65 for Pope's villa, a little farther west of the view on these two pages.)

View of Richmond in Surrey, from the river. This was engraved for
The Modern Universal British Traveller that was published in 1779.

Continuation of the view of Richmond, showing the bridge, designed by
James Paine, which was opened in 1777.

those who are born in different centuries. Men of six o'clock give way to those of nine, they of nine to the generation of twelve and they of twelve disappear, and make room for the fashionable world, who have made two o'clock the noon of the day.

"When we first put off from shore, we soon fell in with a fleet of gardeners bound for the several market-ports of London; and it was the most pleasing scene imaginable to see the cheerfulness with which those industrious people plied their way to a certain sale of their goods. The banks on each side are as well peopled, and beautified with as agreeable plantations, as any spot on the earth; but the Thames itself, loaded with the product of each shore, added very much to the landscape. It was very easy to observe by their sailing, and the countenances of the ruddy virgins who were supercargoes, the parts of the town to which they were bound. There was an air in the purveyors for Covent Garden, who frequently converse with morning rakes, very unlike the seemly sobriety of those bound for Stocks Market.

"Nothing remarkable happened in our voyage; but I landed with ten sail of apricot boats at Strand Bridge, after having put in at Nine Elms, and taken in melons, consigned by Mr. Cuffe of that place, to Sarah Sewell & Company, at their stall in Covent Garden."

Although that account was published in the *Spectator* in August, 1712, the riverside scene remained largely unchanged during the next seventy years. If Steele had started downstream from Mr. Pope's villa, he would have observed the same agreeable grouping of houses about Twickenham that was portrayed in one of the plates of that copiously illustrated work, *The Modern Universal British Traveller*, which was published in 1779. (See pages 66 and 67.) But he began his voyage at Richmond, and there he would have seen rather more changes, for in 1777 an elegant stone bridge designed by James Paine was opened and Asgill House had been built for Sir Charles Asgill, the banker, by Sir Robert Taylor (1714–1788). Most of the new buildings were adornments to the river, for in those upper reaches of the Thames anything new that was built was generally an improvement, such as the little boathouse, with its delicate Ionic columns, designed by James Wyatt (1747–1813) for the Duke of Northumberland in the grounds of Syon House, just opposite Richmond Gardens, as Kew Gardens were then named. At Isleworth there was evidence of industry, and Brentford, according to Louis Simond who described it in 1810, was "a sort of large trading village, or suburb of London,—black, dirty, and noisy."[30]

When you reached Wandsworth and Battersea the scenery began to suffer, for various industrial buildings had, by the end of the eighteenth century, elbowed their way into unneighbourly association with villas and market gardens. (See plate 14.)

Battersea was noted for its market gardens, especially for its asparagus, and in Battersea fields the famous Red House was situated, almost opposite

A print of the same scene as that shown on page 69, but made when Richmond Bridge was in course of construction. Quite obviously, the engraving for *The Modern Universal British Traveller* was faithfully copied from this engraving, but the Bridge was put in and some of the buildings on the Surrey side were altered.

71

The Duke of Northumberland's boathouse on the Thames near Syon House. This elegant little structure with its delicate Ionic columns, has been wrongly attributed to Robert Adam; but it was designed by James Wyatt who worked in the same delicate, graceful style as the brothers Adam. (From a drawing by J. D. Harding, engraved by W. B. Cooke, and included in Barbara Hofland's *Richmond and its Surrounding Scenery*, London, 1832.)

Ranelagh, which was kept by an old couple named Burt, whose ash blonde daughter, Sally, was one of the many loves of the engagingly frank William Hickey. One of the clubs to which Hickey belonged met regularly twice a week at the Red House, and after the party was over Hickey "generally remained to pass an agreeable hour or two with my fair Sally, and fair she literally was, her hair being the lightest in colour I ever saw. She was generally distinguished by the wits of the Thames, with the name of 'Silver Tail.' "[31] Hickey records how at the Red House he became acquainted with Mr. Symonds, "as worthy and truly honest a man as ever lived." This gentleman, who was a Liveryman of London, had inherited from his father a wholesale stationery business, and he became a good influence in the life of that accomplished young rake Hickey. Shortly after they met, Symonds inherited an estate of upwards of two thousand pounds a year, "in consequence of which he took the name of Smith." Hickey describes his "noble house upon the border of the river, a little above the town of Battersea, where he lived in the true style of old English hospitality in the midst of a happy family consisting of a wife, one son, and one daughter, entertaining his numerous friends with a warmth and cordiality that never was exceeded, seldom equalled."(32) That was written about the year 1767, and a view of that part of the Thames, including Mr. Smith's house, was engraved by J. Boydell in 1752. It is conceivable that Hickey mistook the date when Mr. Smith had changed his name from Symonds, for in 1752 Hickey was only three years old. In this view, reproduced on plate 14, the invasion of industry is already apparent; smoke ascends from some manufactory upstream towards Wandsworth; but the river and its traffic were much the same as they were on that early morning in August 1712, when Steele went down from Richmond to Strand Bridge, which was at the foot of Strand Lane. We may explore the eighteenth century scene a little further in Sir Richard's company, and see what happened when he landed, and how he carried out his resolve to spend the rest of his day roving.

He arrived at Strand Bridge at six o'clock, "when the hackney-coachmen of the foregoing night took leave of each other at the Dark House, to go to bed before the day was too far spent. Chimney-sweepers passed by us as we made up to the market, and some raillery happened between one of the fruit-wenches and those black men, about the devil and Eve, with allusion to their several professions. I could not believe any place more entertaining than Covent Garden, where I strolled from one fruit-shop to another, with crowds of agreeable young women around me, who were purchasing fruit for their respective families. It was almost eight of the clock before I could leave that variety of objects."

Then for a time he rode in a coach, until "the day of people of fashion 'began to break' and carts and hacks were mingled with equipages of show and vanity; when I resolved to walk it out of cheapness; but my unhappy curiosity is such, that I find it always my interest to take coach, for some odd adventure among beggars, ballad-singers, or the like, detains and throws me into expense. It happened so immediately; for at the corner of Warwick Street, as I was listening to a new ballad, a ragged rascal, a beggar who knew me, came up to me, and began to turn the eyes of the good company upon me, by telling me he was extreme poor, and should die in the streets for want of drink, except I immediately would have the charity to give him sixpence to go into the next alehouse and save his life. He urged, with a melancholy face, that all his family had died of thirst. All the mob have humour, and two or three began to take the jest; by which Mr. Sturdy carried his point, and let me sneak off to a coach. As I drove along, it was a pleasing reflection to see the world so prettily chequered since I left Richmond, and the scene still filling with children of a new hour. This satisfaction increased as I moved towards the city; and

View of Isleworth from Richmond Gardens. Engraved for *The Modern Universal British Traveller* in 1779.

Continuation of view of Isleworth, showing the church.

The classical regularity and elegance of shop fronts were not confined to
the fashionable shopping quarters of a city: even a village shop could reflect
the architectural conventions of the period, and display an individual
character that was often a tribute to the imaginative powers of some
anonymous country joiner. Here is a shop in the village of Woburn, Bedfordshire: compare this with the example from the same place, on the opposite
page. Both shop fronts illustrate a masterly grasp of the classical idiom, and
an understanding of the decorative possibilities of glazing. (*Drawn by
Marcelle Barton.*)

gay signs, well-disposed streets, magnificent public structures, and wealthy
shops, adorned with contented faces, made the joy still rising till we came
into the centre of the City, and centre of the world of trade, the Exchange of
London. As other men in the crowds about me were pleased with their hopes
and bargains, I found my account in observing them, in attention to their
several interests. I, indeed, looked upon myself as the richest man that walked
the Exchange that day; for my benevolence made me share the gains of every
bargain that was made. It was not the least of the satisfactions in my survey,
to go upstairs, and pass the shops of agreeable females; to observe so many pretty
hands busy in the foldings of ribands, and the utmost eagerness of agreeable
faces in the sale of patches, pins, and wires, on each side the counters, was an
amusement in which I should longer have indulged myself, had not the dear
creatures called to me to ask what I wanted, when I could not answer only
'To look at you.' "

The Black Horse Inn, and the shops adjoining, in Bedford Street, Woburn, Bedfordshire. (*Drawn by Marcelle Barton.*)

Of the London shops, that later observer, François de la Rochefoucauld, had nothing but praise, and he noted that they were built with their windows projecting forwards slightly, so that they could be seen from three sides. Shop windows followed a regular pattern, and the shop front was often designed to accord with one or other of the classic orders. The use of small, rectangular panes gave those windows a relationship to the sashes used in houses, and also gave them much the same friendly air; but the panes and their glazing bars imposed limitations on the display of merchandise. For example, the fashionable cabinet-makers and chair-makers preferred to show small-scale models of their

A shop front with the doorway flanked by Roman Doric columns. This early nineteenth century example shows the increasing size of shop windows, although they were still limited by the dimensions of the panes. (From *The New Practical Builder and Workman's Companion*, by Peter Nicholson, 1823.)

designs, for miniatures of cabinets, wardrobes, bookcases, chests of drawers, chairs and settees, beautifully made with great attention to detail and finish, looked far more attractive through those many-paned shop windows than the real articles: it was not until plate glass was made in large sizes during the nineteenth century that the use of such three-dimensional advertisements was discontinued.

Although the principles of architectural composition with the classic orders were everywhere respected and employed, there was little horizontal uniformity about groups of buildings, even in the streets of a great city like London. It is true that the almost universal use of the sash window gave a semblance of unity to many London streets, even when their horizontal irregularity was exaggerated by structures in a state of partial collapse, like Mrs. Salmon's famous Waxwork in Fleet Street: but this approach to unity was fortuitous, not contrived. It is understandable that the buildings fringing the banks of a river would be individually conceived, and that the disrupted skyline of Thames-side villages or little inland ports like Wisbech in the Isle of Ely,

Two early nineteenth century designs for shop fronts. The Greek Doric example at the top of the page shows the influence of the Greek revival. Below, the Ionic order is used with fluted columns. (Reproduced from *The New Practical Builder and Workman's Companion,* by Peter Nicholson, published in 1823.) (See opposite page.)

should disclose the architectural indecisions of local development, spread over two or three generations; but where an opportunity occurred for rebuilding or replanning a capital city after such a disaster as the fire of 1666 it is an astonishing tribute to the obtuse individualism of the English character that it was not so much ignored as deliberately rejected. Only when some scheme of development was designed by capable architects was it possible for a city, like Bath, for example, to acquire a consistent architectural character. Bath achieved coherent civic design on a large scale, and Smollett's jibes in *Humphry Clinker* were at least qualified by his respect for "the ingenuity and knowledge in the architect. . . ." The work of the Woods, father and son, made Bath the outstanding model of architectural good manners. London's architectural good manners were confined to a few spacious squares and crescents, and such isolated pieces of town-planning as the Adelphi, Portland Place, and, at the close of the period, Regent Street. The capital was a patchwork; but despite the irregularity of its buildings, the city that Steele and Addison knew and lived in and wrote about, had an orderly air. This is apparent from Kip's bird's-eye view of London, made in 1710, of which the western part is reproduced on plate 11. But although the cities displayed innumerable architectural felicities, and London in particular was thronged with noble buildings and magnificent churches by such architects as Wren, Hawksmoor, and Gibbs, the Georgian scene was at its bland and beautiful best in the countryside, which was laid out and very largely supervised by the great landowners. Richmond, and its vicinity, again afford an example of the harmonious composition of that scene. A prospect of that little town, engraved about 1726, occupies plates 12 and 13. Over eighty years later, that prospect was much the same, and of Richmond Hill and the view from it, Louis Simond could write that although the Hill itself could not pretend to much sublimity, it had a style of ornamental beauty "mild, riant, and pleasing." He continued his description and in the course of it gave the principal reason for the sense of design that characterised the Georgian landscape. "It is not a forest, for there is nothing rude and neglected; not a garden, for there is no art; not a country, for cultivation and business are nowhere going on;—the simplicity and unity of plan and means, trees and grass, and vast extent, give it an appearance of nature,—but nature was never seen so select and chaste, and unmixed with offensive objects. It is at least rich, elegant, and high-born nature, and something at any rate, unique of its kind. Most of this magical effect is owing to the following circumstances: Some rich proprietors happen to occupy all the fore-ground of the picture in the plain below,—Lord Dysart, Mr. Cambridge, etc.—They have spread their lawns, planted their groves, and levelled their enclosures. Further on are the royal grounds. All the rest of the country is sufficiently planted to give it, when seen fore-shortened in the remote view, a very woody appearance, and make it an uninterrupted and boundless continuation of the near scene. The blue haze of distance finishes the front

Mrs. Salmon's Waxworks in Fleet Street, which Boswell visited on July 4th, 1763, and commented, "It is excellent in its kind, and amused me very well for a quarter of an hour." (Boswell's *London Journal*.) This is how it looked in 1793, when it was drawn by Nathaniel Smith, and included in *The Antiquities of London*, by John Thomas Smith. Georgian London was full of conglomerations of untidy buildings, though the almost universal use of the sash window gave a semblance of unity to the streets, even when they were disrupted by a structure such as this, in a state of partial collapse.

View from the North Brink at Wisbech, from a drawing by Algernon Peckover made in 1827. (From *An Historical Account of the Ancient Town and Borough of Wisbech*, by William Watson, 1827.)

view. The fine old forest trees of the park of Richmond hanging on the left side of the hill, and on the right other trees, and good-looking houses, form the screens or frame of the picture."(33)

The taste and judgment of the landed proprietors were everywhere impressed upon the face of the country, and landscape gardening was a recognised branch of architecture and practised as such. Unfortunately, as the country grew richer, and more people were able to indulge their desires for country surroundings and views, the landscape began to suffer. Louis Simond, after the description just quoted, added the comment: "It is however a pity that so many people should have had the same taste as to the beauty of this view, and that it should be only eight or ten miles from London. Houses have accumulated along the top of Richmond Hill, forming a street, or rather a row, looking over the beautiful terrace, and inhabited by substantial citizens; —a class of people more respectable for their good conduct, than remarkable for their taste."(34)

Already, in its first decade, the character of the nineteenth century was foreshadowed, for it was to be crowded with characters in every walk of life who were "more respectable for their good conduct, than remarkable for their taste." Good manners which were expressed not only in personal behaviour, but in everything that was made, built and used, appear to have been incompatible with the sort of good conduct that became just another dull facet of respectability. The Georgians were not respectable in the Victorian sense; they were civilised, and lived at a time when no educated persons feared the erection of a new building; the design might not be wholly to their taste, but it would not offend them. Towards the end of the eighteenth century the nobility and gentry averted their eyes from certain ugly features that were creeping into the landscape: they chose to ignore the encroachment of industry and to allow reach after reach of beautiful streams like the Thames gradually to become defiled. The intermingling of commerce and industry with residential areas seemed to come about so naturally, and Marryat in *Jacob Faithful* describes how the good kind employer, Mr. Drummond, had his house, his office, his warehouse and his wharf in close proximity on the riverside, a little above Putney. Mr. Drummond did not belong to the nobility or gentry, which makes his insensitive acceptance of his industrial environment easier to understand, especially as he made his money from the river and its traffic.

There were two influences, one unrecognised and the other recognised, that began the debilitation of the Georgian scene: the first was industrial development and the second arose from a fashion for ruins. No tenderness was normally displayed towards old buildings; if they were in the way then they were demolished. The idea of preserving ancient and picturesque buildings is comparatively recent. For example, the purchase and restoration by the Royal Society of Arts of the old village of West Wycombe in Buckinghamshire as part of a campaign for preserving the ancient cottages of England, would have astonished the original founders of that Society. West Wycombe was acquired by the Society in 1929, and "is an excellent example of an ancient English rural community, including about fifty dwellings dating from Tudor to Georgian times, and two inns. . . ."[35]

The Society was founded in 1754 for the encouragement of the arts, manufactures, and commerce of the country; and at that time, our environment did not seem so precious. We were not then reaping the crop of sentiment raised by over a century of ruin-worship. The second, and conscious, disruptive influence which was to destroy the Georgian scene was this sentimental admiration and preservation of ruins, which was carried to the point of imitation ruins being built to embellish parks and gardens. But apart from this sentimentalising over Gothic remains, to which Horace Walpole gave the most continuous literary expression, no one ever shed a tear when an old building was replaced by a new one. Then, everyone could be confident that the new structure would be built according to the prevailing good taste; but today we know that when an old thing is pulled down it is all too often replaced by something that, if not offensively ugly, is undistinguished or aggressively disrupting. Consequently we have allowed a nostalgic attachment to the past to vitiate our judgment, and to make age rather than excellence the criterion for preserving an old building. We indulge this attachment to the extent of organising protests, almost automatically, whenever the Ministry of Health, or some local authority, condemns almost any old cottage as unfit for human habitation, for everybody—with the possible exception of the people who live in it—is shocked by the projected destruction of some old though not always worthy relic. Tenderness for the past began as an exclusive fashion in the middle years of the eighteenth century; and from those small, modish beginnings a taste for Gothic forms led ultimately to the oppressive earnestness of the Gothic revival in the following century. But usually the waves of taste that washed over Georgian society were controlled and kept tidy by architects and craftsmen; and the nature of those waves of taste, their recurrence and effect, are the subject of the next chapter. But let us first conclude this brief glance at the Georgian scene by hearing from a contemporary source what sort of background visitors expected when they went, say, to a city like Bath; what standards of furnishing and interior architecture were provided by the houses in that city of beautiful manners.

John Wood the elder (1704–1754) wrote *An Essay towards a Description of Bath* which was issued in 1749 in two volumes. In the preface to the second volume he described in detail the improvements in furnishing that had occurred since the development and rebuilding of the city. "The short period of one and Twenty years," he wrote, "has produced such great Alterations in the publick Accommodations of *Bath*, that it would appear next to Romantick to relate them, were they not well known to Thousands of living Witnesses." His account certainly discloses a remarkable transformation, and packs into five paragraphs a great store of facts about the character and quality of the things people used.

"About the Year 1727," he proceeded, "the Boards of the Dining Rooms and most other Floors were made of a Brown Colour with Soot and small Beer to hide the Dirt, as well as their own Imperfections; and if the Walls of any of the Rooms were covered with Wainscot, it was with such as was mean and never Painted: The Chimney-Pieces, Hearths and Slabbs were all of Free Stone, and these were daily cleaned with a particular White-wash, which, by paying Tribute to every thing that touched it, soon rendered the brown Floors like the Stary Firmament: The Doors were slight and thin, and the best Locks had only Iron Coverings Varnished: With Cane or Rush-bottomed Chairs the principal Rooms were Furnished, and each Chair seldom exceeded three half Crowns in Value; nor were the Tables, or Chests of Drawers, better in their Kind, the chief having been made of Oak: The Looking Glasses were small, mean, and few in Number; and the Chimney Furniture consisted of a slight Iron Fender, with Tongs, Poker and Shovel all of no more than three or four Shillings Value.

"With *Kiddermister* Stuff, or at best with Cheyne, the Woollen Furniture of the principal Rooms was made; and such as was of Linnen consisted either of Corded Dimaty, or coarse Fustian; the Matrons of the City, their Daughters and their Maids Flowering the latter with Worsted, during the Intervals between the Seasons, to give the Beds a gaudy Look.

"The Weekly Price of Lodgings thus Furnished, was ten Shillings a Room during the Seasons; and, at the same time, Garrets for Servants yielded five Shillings a Piece; but out of Season these Prices were reduced one half, and the best Rooms were Lett for five Shillings a Week, each Room, the Garrets for two shillings and Six Pence.

"As the new Buildings advanced, Carpets were introduced to cover the Floors, though Laid with the finest clean Deals, or *Dutch* Oak Boards; the Rooms were all Wainscoted and Painted in a costly and handsome Manner; Marble Slabbs, and even Chimney Pieces, became common; the Doors in general were not only made thick and substantial, but they had the best Sort of Brass Locks put on them; Walnut Tree Chairs, some with Leather, and some with Damask or Worked Bottoms supplied the Place of such as were Seated with Cane or Rushes; the Oak Tables and Chests of Drawers were exchanged, the former for such as were made of Mahoggony, the latter for such as were made either with the same Wood, or with Wallnut Tree; handsome Glasses were added to the Dressing Tables, nor did the proper Chimneys or Peers of any of the Rooms long remain without well Framed Mirrours of no inconsiderable Size; and the Furniture for every chief Chimney was composed of a Brass Fender, with Tongs, Poker and Shovel agreeable to it.

"Beds, Window Curtains and other Chamber Furniture, as well Woollen as Linnen, were, from time to time, renewed with such as was more fit for Gentlemens Capital Seats, than Houses appropriated for common Lodgings; and the Linnen for the Table and Bed grew better and better till it became suitable even for People of the highest Rank."[36]

Fortunately for the civilisation of England, people of the highest rank were educated, could appraise every branch of design, and were satisfied only by the best. Their standards were respected, imitated, and agreeably diffused throughout that well-regulated society.

An engraving of a painting by Hogarth, satirising contemporary taste. It was intended to ridicule the costume, gestures and habits of fashionable society in the year 1742. For example, the monkey at the bottom of the engraving is studying a menu which reads as follows:

Pour Dinner. Cox combs. Ducks Tongues. Rabbits Ears. Fricasey of Snails. Grande 'ouets Beurre.

The large painting in the background shows the Medician Venus on a pedestal, wearing stays and high-heeled shoes, and holding in front of her an enormous hoop petticoat. On the fire screen is a painting that shows what happened to hooped petticoats when a fashionable lady rode in a sedan chair. (Compare this with the illustration of a sedan chair on page 324.)

CHAPTER IV

ORNAMENTAL CONVENTIONS AND WAVES OF TASTE

CLASSICAL architecture, as we have seen from the previous chapters, penetrated every department of life and art; its rules, once mastered, trained the eyes and guided the hands of every type of craftsman; and the architectural precedents of Greece and Rome were consistently respected and constantly in mind. The individual characteristics of the orders were frequently used to illustrate some point in morals or manners. Lord Chesterfield sharpened his criticism of his son's "awkward, ungraceful, ill-bred . . . vulgar air and manners" by unflattering comparisons between them and the impression created by the Tuscan order. "I dare say you know already enough of architecture, to know that the Tuscan is the strongest and most solid of all the orders," he wrote; "but, at the same time, it is the coarsest and clumsiest of them. Its solidity does extremely well for the foundation and base-floor of a great edifice; but, if the whole building be Tuscan, it will attract no eyes, it will stop no passengers, it will invite no interior examination; people will take it for granted, that the finishing and furnishing cannot be worth seeing, where the front is so unadorned and clumsy. But if upon the solid Tuscan foundation, the Doric, the Ionic, and the Corinthian orders rise gradually with all their beauty, proportions, and ornament, the fabric seizes the most incurious eye, and stops the most careless passenger, who solicits admission as a favour, nay, often purchases. Just so will it fare with your little fabric, which at present, I fear, has more of the Tuscan than of the Corinthian order. You must absolutely change the whole front, or nobody will knock at the door. The several parts, which must compose this new front, are elegant, easy, natural, superior, good-breeding; an engaging address; genteel motions; an insinuating softness in your looks, words, and actions; a spruce, lively air; fashionable dress; and all the glitter that a young fellow should have."(37)

Not only did the orders provide the architectural bones which the great designers of the period clothed with such sumptuously alluring flesh; but the character of each order was preserved, as Lord Aberdeen had remarked,

87

Proportional

ARCHITECTURE;

or, the

Five Orders,

regulated by

EQUAL PARTS:

After so concise a Method that renders it Useful to all Artists and Easy to every Capacity.

To which is added a practical and familiar Explanation of the Terms herein used.

London printed & sold by W. Dicey at y Printing Office in Bow Church Yard & C Corbett at Addison's head against S. Dunstan's Church Fleet Street 1736.

The title page of Robinson's *Proportional Architecture; or the Five Orders.* The upper part of the frontispiece is reproduced at the head of Chapter 2, on page 17. The introduction is reproduced on the opposite page.

INTRODUCTION

Finding by experience that y̆ generality of Workmen are perplex'd, in practifing according to y̆ Rules laid down in Books of ARCHITECTURE; it cannot be supposed y̆ Time and Thoughts are ill spent in endeavouring to bring them into a more regular and ufeful method.

In order therefore to remove thofe impediments which have obstructed the study of y̆ Noble Art, it is here attempted to render y̆ underftanding of the Five Orders more intelligible, and y̆ ufe of some other Rules more practicable, presuming that it will be equally necefsary to thofe who bear y̆ Purfe, as to thofe who perform the Work, many of whom for various reasons, cannot per- ∶*use thofe many Volumes that treat thereof.*

The Approbation & succefs which this small Tract has met with, having given occasion for another EDITION. I have now added a practical & familiar Explanation of y̆ Terms used in it, which, I am inclin'd to think, will be acceptable to y̆ Reader, as J have endeavour'd to make it ufeful.

Bow Lane   **W. Robinfon**

The introduction from Robinson's *Proportional Architecture*. The book con-sisted of 32 engraved plates, and the second edition (from which this intro-duction and the title page opposite are reproduced) included a practical explanation of terms, really a short dictionary of architecture.

"throughout the minutest details." The orders were invested with individual charms or defects, not only by cultivated noblemen like Lord Chesterfield, but by writers who addressed the humble and diligent audience of workmen. For example, the second edition of Robinson's *Proportional Architecture*, issued in 1736, contained a short dictionary of technical terms, in which the Ionic order is described as "decent, feminine and modest," the Tuscan as "rude, strong and plain"—a far less harsh description than Lord Chesterfield's— and the Doric as "very Noble on Account of its masculine Aspect and excellent Proportion."[38] Each order had its correct ornamental accessories, and directions for their appropriate distribution on mouldings and other features were available alike to the noble patron and the village carpenter. In this manner, the grounding which all designers had in the proportions of the classical orders permeated every branch of their work; the orders were the great, and indeed inescapable, source for all ornamental inspiration.

Even when forms unknown to classical antiquity were brought into some scheme of decoration, they followed a predetermined framework. The various waves of taste floated into the fashionable world a multiplicity of fanciful conceits—exotic, romantic, occasionally eccentric, sometimes slightly foolish, but *never* clumsy or ungraceful. Hogarth, in his *Analysis of Beauty*, said: "The mere ornaments of buildings, to be sure, at least might be allow'd a greater latitude than they are at present: as capitals, frizes, &c. in order to increase the beauty of variety. Nature, in shells and flowers, &c. affords an infinite choice of elegant hints for this purpose; as the original of the Corinthian capital was taken from nothing more, as is said, than some dock-leaves growing up against a basket. Even a capital composed of the aukward and confin'd forms of hats and periwigs ... in a skilful hand might be made to have some beauty."[39] Hogarth illustrated such a freakish capital in one of the explanatory drawings he made, contrasting various forms in his attempt to analyse beauty. (This appears at the head of this chapter, and on the lower part of the right hand side of plate 5.) His fantastic composition had a certain grace, although it was a deliberate caricature, and it does suggest, at a first quick glance, a new order. Hogarth substitutes the homely English dock leaf for the acanthus leaf in his reference to the legendary origin of the Corinthian capital, which Vitruvius describes in the fourth of his ten books on Architecture. It is a story that Vitruvius obviously liked, and it relates how a certain Callimachus, whom the Athenians called Catatechnos, invented this elegant capital after seeing the tomb of a young Corinthian girl, whose nurse had collected various small articles the dead girl had liked, and had put them in a basket on her tomb with a tile on top to preserve them. The basket had been placed by accident on the root of an acanthus plant, which grew up in the spring, and its leaves reaching the corners of the tile curled round below them and formed volutes. This basket, wreathed with delicate foliage, prompted Callimachus to invent the Corinthian capital.

As Hogarth said, nature afforded "an infinite choice of elegant hints," and indeed formalised naturalistic motifs furnished most of the ideas for ornamentation. His book was an earnest but by no means dull attempt to examine exactly what contributed to beauty in the shape of things made for use and adornment. Nowhere in the *Analysis of Beauty* does he dispute the authority of the orders of architecture; but he was much exercised about basic form, and he suggests emphatically that behind all accepted practices there lay a subtle and universal formula for design. Unfortunately he never seemed

OLD HOUSES, S.ᵗ JOHN STREET.
London.

There was a time lag in taste: it filtered downwards from the highest levels to the professional classes and the more prosperous artisans. In this print of a group of old houses in St. John's Street, West Smithfield, reproduced from the *Gentleman's Magazine*, October, 1814, the furniture shown outside the chair and cabinet-maker's shop is half a century earlier in design than the date of the print. The three chairs with their plain back splats, would be in use during the seventeen-forties and fifties: the bureau would be about the same period.

able to explain what it really was, though his dissertations on composition
with waving lines and serpentine lines are interesting. Of the latter he admitted
"the very great difficulty there is in describing this line, either in words or
by the pencil...."[40] But with the waving line he was more confidently
expository. "How inelegant would the shapes of all our moveables be without
it? How very plain and unornamental the mouldings of cornices, and chimney-
pieces, without the variety introduced by the *ogee* member, which is entirely
composed of waving-lines." (See plate 5.) All sorts of waving lines were
ornamental when properly applied, he said, "yet, strictly speaking, there is
but one precise line, properly to be called the line of *beauty*...."[41] This
"line of beauty" was elusive and could not be expressed as a formula; but
his analysis provoked a long, and occasionally bitter, controversy that continued
to rage many years after his death. It has been said, rather unkindly, that if

The Greek anthemion or honeysuckle ornament: this form of decoration
became popular during the Greek Revival. (See pages 94 and 115.)

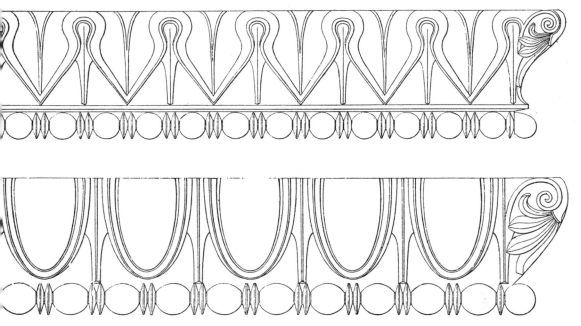

Examples of enrichment from the capitals of a Greek temple: the lower one
is the egg and tongue pattern, with beads below.

Hogarth had not been a painter of indisputable genius, nobody would have
paid the slightest attention to his *Analysis*. But there was far more sound sense
in his pages than most writers could command when they wrote about abstract
principles of design, and were not guiding their thoughts and statements by
an exclusive regard for the orders.

The work of Hogarth has been used extensively for the illustrations of this
book and the examples reproduced in the text and on various plates show how
conscientious he was about the backgrounds that appeared in his paintings
and drawings. Incidentally, he is listed among the subscribers to Isaac Ware's
translation of Palladio. His taste was always classically correct, but though
impeccable, it seems to have become arrested somewhere about 1730, if we
may judge by the furniture he almost invariably depicted. Many of the pieces
in his paintings were drawn from William Kent's designs, such as those that
appear in the Assembly at Wanstead House (reproduced on plate 25), but
he was also devoted to the form of chair known as "bended back," with sturdy
cabriole legs. He showed himself seated in such a chair in his self-portrait.
It was a type that was in vogue during the seventeen-twenties, and he used
it so often that in late Victorian times it was described, with romantic
inaccuracy, as a "Hogarth chair."

H

An example of the Greek anthemion ornament used on a mirror frame is shown to the
right. (Reproduced from Thomas Hope's
Household Furniture and Interior Decoration,
1807.) See page 92.

Guilloche ornament, based
on interlacing circles. Of
Greek origin, it was used to
enrich either a moulded or
a plain surface.

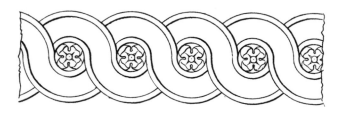

A simplified form of guilloche. A Roman version of
the Greek original.

The incidental decorative trimmings that occur in many of Hogarth's
paintings certainly emphasise the apparently inexhaustible treasury of devices
provided not only by the ornamentation proper to the classic orders, but, as
Hogarth himself pointed out, by nature. Perhaps the most ubiquitous natural
form ever adopted for ornamental purposes is the acanthus. The leaf of that
plant symmetrically disposed on capitals and mouldings, spread, like the
orders, over the whole of the Graeco-Roman world. In the hands of eighteenth
century designers and craftsmen it acquired an exquisite delicacy.

The use of forms based on plants and flowers and the limbs of animals is
probably as old as civilisation. The Greeks and the Romans conventionalised
those forms, gave them recognisable proportions, and the English chair-makers
and cabinet-makers and decorators and carvers of the eighteenth century,
released them from the rigidity which, certainly in Rome, had often made
them stiff, unyielding and oppressively dignified. The paws and hooves of

Fluting which consists of shallow, concave grooves used in a parallel series.

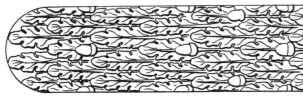

A Greek fret.

A torus moulding, enriched with oak leaves and acorns.

animals were used on furniture long before the Graeco-Roman civilisation; they may be seen on chairs and stools in Egyptian sculpture of the Fifth Dynasty, as far back as 2500 B.C. But in European countries, particularly in France and England during the eighteenth century, the most astonishing and consistent liberties were taken with all those inherited forms, and in France, the heady fantasies of the Rococo style eroded and at last destroyed the structural bones of furniture.

In England ornament never became a dominating or tyrannical influence, and although there was no restriction on its use between the Restoration and the eighteen-thirties, its employment and character reflected not merely the fashion of the moment, but an innate sense of fitness on the part of designers and craftsmen. Dr. Johnson once observed that "It is justly considered as the greatest excellency in art, to imitate nature; but it requires judgement to distinguish those parts of nature which are most proper for imitation." On another occasion he said: "The adoption of a noble sentiment, or the insertion of a borrowed ornament, may sometimes display so much judgment, as will almost compensate for invention; and an inferior genius may, without any imputation of servility, pursue the path of the antients, provided he declines to tread in their footsteps."

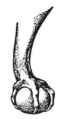

Claw - and - ball foot: early eighteenth century.

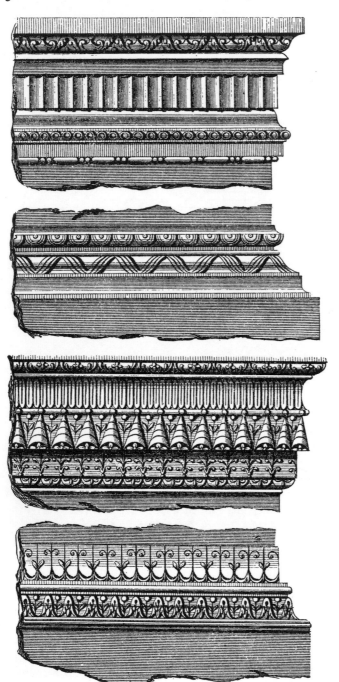

Enriched mouldings for an impost, which is a member immediately below the springing line above which an arch rests. This is suggested as suitable for a drawing-room. (From Plate LV of *The Builder's Magazine, or Monthly Companion*, London, 1774.) The designs shown below, from plate LV of the same work, are suggested for a parlour.

These detailed examples of correct ornamentation left the builder in no doubt about the appropriate enrichment for the different apartments of a house: he had no excuse if he did the wrong thing, for his customers were at least as well informed as he was, and were able to argue with the support of accurate knowledge of the orders.

Two designs for entablatures, suggesting methods of decoration for the frieze and the enrichment of the mouldings, from Plate XXII of *The Builder's Magazine, or Monthly Companion* (London, 1774). The upper illustration is suggested as suitable for a drawing-room or dining-room, the lower for a lady's dressing-room, "the frieze of which must be painted Ornaments."

English designers exhibited a consistent capacity for selecting appropriate natural forms for ornamental uses. Periodically some particular motif would become popular, such as the claw-and-ball or talon-and-ball foot on chair and table legs. This device, of Chinese origin, was first introduced into England in the late sixteenth century, though it was known and used much earlier on furniture. (In a contemporary oil painting of King Edward VI, a chair with a carved frame is shown with claw-and-ball feet.) It was reintroduced in the reign of Charles II, then fell into disuse, reappearing late in the second decade of the eighteenth century, and remaining in fashion until the seventeen-sixties. Sometimes the use of a particular form of design would be identified by name with a period: for instance "the Cabriole Period" is a term used by some

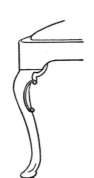
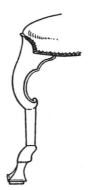
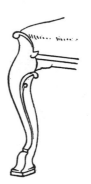

Five variations of cabriole leg. 1 and 2 are simple types, ending in a flat toe;
3 and 4 are more elaborate, with broken curves, and are hipped, that is
the legs continue up to the level of the seat, and the feet are formalised
hooves. All four are from the opening decades of the eighteenth century:
5 is a later and sturdier type, with talon-and-ball foot, and a carved knee
(the ornament would probably be a lion's mask). See pages 95 and 208.

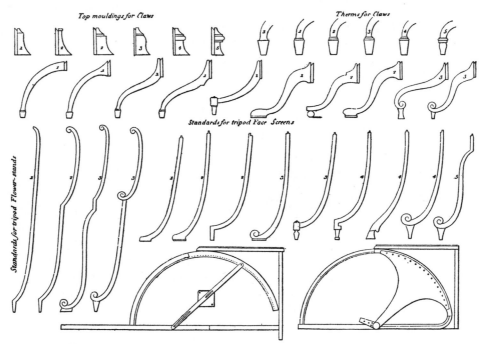

A plate of details from *The Prices of Cabinet Work,* 1797 edition, showing
various types of top mouldings and therms for claws, standards for tripods,
for screens and for flower stands. Detailed guides were available for every
type of furniture-maker, whether he was in a large or a small way of business.
Details of quadrants are given at the bottom right-hand side of the plate.

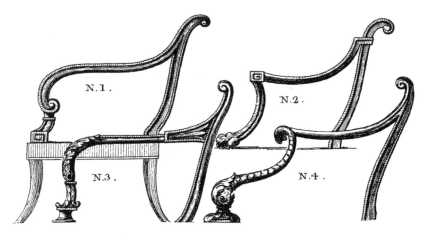

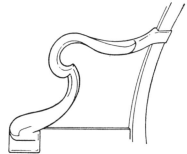

The refinements of line achieved in the late eighteenth and early nineteenth centuries are shown by these designs for arms for chairs, by Thomas Sheraton. They are from the lower part of Plate 2 of *The Cabinet Dictionary* (1803), and Sheraton refers to the four designs as follows: "Nos. 1, 2 and 4, whether made of beech or mahogany, should have the toe carved. No. 3 may have ornament painted, with carving."

Compare these slender curves with the more robust and far heavier scroll-over arm shown to the right, that was fashionable among chair-makers of the eighteenth century. (See elbow chair on page 207.)

modern writers to describe the furniture made between the last decade of the seventeenth and the middle of the eighteenth centuries. During those sixty years the cabriole, or bandy, leg was used extensively on chairs, stools, tables and cabinet stands. These legs were formed by two well-defined curves, with the upper part, the shoulder or knee, convex, and the lower part above the shaped foot, concave. The form was derived from the conventionalised representations of animals' legs in Greek and Roman furniture, and its adoption demonstrated the English furniture-makers' ability to "pursue the path of the antients" while declining "to tread in their footsteps."

The use of lions' masks on the knees of cabriole legs and on the arms and cresting of chairs during the seventeen-twenties has suggested the terms "Lion Mahogany" or "Lion Period" for denoting that particular phase of early Georgian taste. They are modern terms, dating from 1909, when they were

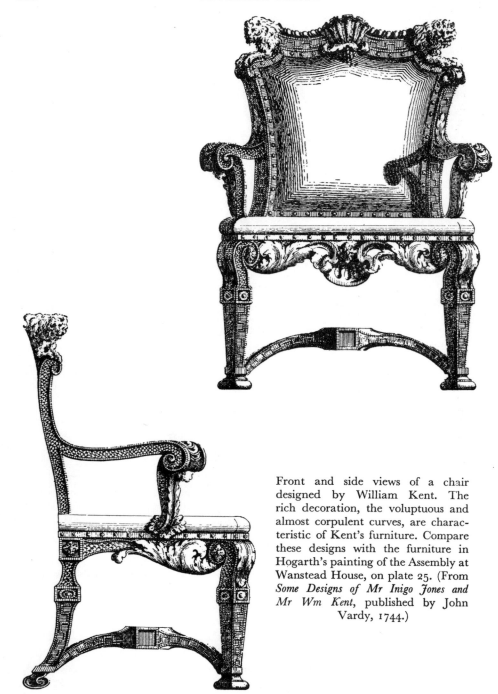

Front and side views of a chair
designed by William Kent. The
rich decoration, the voluptuous and
almost corpulent curves, are characteristic of Kent's furniture. Compare
these designs with the furniture in
Hogarth's painting of the Assembly at
Wanstead House, on plate 25. (From
*Some Designs of Mr Inigo Jones and
Mr Wm Kent*, published by John
Vardy, 1744.)

first used in one of a series of articles by Haldane Macfall.[42] The lions' mask motif often enriched the furniture designed by William Kent (see illustration on page 100); but it was only one of many transiently modish forms. It was revived and used by Sheraton and his contemporaries seventy years later. The natural form that was consistently used throughout the whole Georgian period was the acanthus leaf. There was an infinitude of ornamental devices: trophies, swags, ribbons, festoons, cornucopia, human and animal masks, the implements of trade, of gardening, of the artist and the architect, shields, swords, spears, helmets, musical instruments, and the fabulous monsters of Greek and Roman mythology, satyrs, centaurs, and the griffin, chimera and sphinx.

Of the various forms of exotic taste, the Chinese and the Rococo were the most copiously fantastic; and towards the end of the Georgian age an intermittent regard for Indian designs encouraged a few ornamental excesses; but generally, both Chinese and Indian decorative motifs were suitably modified and accommodated within the classical framework of design. Their occasional extravagances seldom disturbed the good proportions of houses and their contents: it was only when the effervescent fancies of the Rococo style came to England that classical regularity and admirably balanced architectural features became slightly deranged. But those periodic waves of taste, washing over the fashionable world, had only a superficial effect: when they receded, the established background with its familiar, classical proportions remained unaltered.

The Rococo style had developed in France during the early part of the Louis XV period, and it was originally inspired by the work of Pierre le Pautre, a designer and engraver, who was the eldest child of Jean le Pautre (1618–82), also a designer and engraver, who had worked in the Baroque style. The word "Rococo" is derived from *rocaille*, which means "rock-work," a term that was first used to describe the artificial grottoes and fountains in the gardens of Versailles. The characteristic forms of the style included foliage, slender and complicated exaggerations of the acanthus leaf, shells, scrolls and trophies. The swags and festoons, wreaths and ribbons were elegantly attenuated; and when the style reached England in the middle years of the eighteenth century, it was an excellent corrective to the rather heavy, almost Teutonic solidity of the early Georgian period, when the work of William Kent often gave excessive substance to furniture and interior decoration. The great cabinet-makers and chair-makers in the middle years of the eighteenth century were influenced by the Rococo style. As a transitory fashion it had a "loosening up" effect on English design; but did not bequeath any specific articles or habits or enrich English social life in the same way as the Chinese taste, which introduced a host of decorative forms and the habit of tea-drinking with all the apparatus required for honouring that function.

Horace Walpole, in the "Advertisement" to the fourth volume of his *Anecdotes of Painting in England*, makes a brief and penetrating estimate of the changes and advances in taste that had occurred since the reign of George I. He wrote this in 1780, when the final volume of the work was published; and despite his earlier criticisms of Lord Burlington's individual performances as an architect, gave a just assessment of his influence. "To architecture, taste and vigour were given by Lord Burlington and Kent," he said. "They have successors worthy of the tone they gave; if, as refinement generally verges to extreme contrarieties, Kent's ponderosity does not degenerate into filligrain." Five years earlier, in a letter to Sir Horace Mann (April 22nd, 1775), he was more explicit when he remarked that "as Vanbrugh dealt in quarries, and Kent in lumber, Adam, our most admired, is all gingerbread, filigraine, and fan-painting." He considered that the Pantheon in Oxford Street, "uniting grandeur and lightness, simplicity and ornament, seems to have marked the medium, where Taste must stop." In 1770, James Wyatt had won the competition for rebuilding the Pantheon, which brought him fame as an architect. The interior decoration of that building owed much to the influence of Adam, and it provided a magnificent setting for masquerades and routs. (See plate 10.) "The architect who shall endeavour to refine on Mr. Wyat," Walpole continued, "will perhaps give a date to the age of embroidery. Virgil, Longinus, and Vitruvius afford no rules, no examples of scattering finery. This delicate redundance of ornament growing into our architecture might perhaps be checked, if our artists would study the sublime dreams of Piranesi, who seems to have conceived visions of Rome beyond what it boasted even in the meridian of its splendour. Savage as Salvator Rosa, fierce as Michael Angelo, and exuberant as Rubens, he has imagined scenes that would startle geometry, and exhaust the Indies to realize. He piles palaces on bridges, and temples on palaces, and scales Heaven with mountains of edifices. Yet what taste in his boldness! what grandeur in his wildness! what labour and thought both in his rashness and details! Architecture, indeed, has in a manner two sexes; its masculine dignity can only exert its muscles in public works and at public expense; its softer beauties come better within the compass of private residence and enjoyment."

Walpole's praise of Wyatt's Pantheon, for "uniting grandeur and lightness, simplicity and ornament," enumerated the qualities and assimilative powers men of taste expected from a designer. They also expected him to honour the Vitruvian precepts that "architecture depends on fitness" and "utility arises from a judicious distribution of the parts, so that their purpose be duly answered, and that each have its proper situation."[43] The importance of simplicity, fitness and utility was constantly reiterated by writers and critics of architecture and the arts in the Georgian Age. During the second and third decades of our own century, the phrase "fitness for purpose" was popularised by the Design and Industries Association, a body formed in 1915, whose educational propaganda in time exerted a marked influence upon industrial design. The insidious potency of those three words was slightly diluted by the qualification,

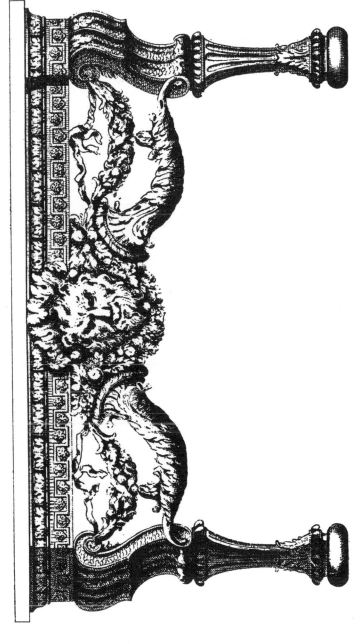

A side table, supporting a marble slab, designed by William Kent, a little overloaded with carved decoration, which would almost certainly be gilded, and having affinities with the furniture shown in Hogarth's painting of the Assembly at Wanstead House, reproduced on plate 25. (From *Some Designs of Mr Inigo Jones and Mr Wm Kent*, published by John Vardy, 1744.)

"pleasantness in use." The idea embedded in this trite phrase had been current for centuries, though in periods of great accomplishment in the arts it was seldom expressed in words, as fitness for purpose was taken for granted. Only when some capricious fashion invited reproof was the sanctity of fitness sharply recalled. Walpole's rather waspish reminder of its basic significance in his note about Lord Burlington's villa at Chiswick has already been quoted (page 26), and much earlier in the eighteenth century, Anthony Ashley Cooper, the third Earl of Shaftesbury, had discoursed with tedious preciseness on the dependence of beauty upon a just appreciation of simplicity and unity in design. His *Characteristicks of Men, Manners, Opinions, Times*, appeared anonymously in 1711, and the three volumes are pervaded by a niggling rationalism—a pallid anticipation of the robust agnosticism of Thomas Henry Huxley and Robert Green Ingersoll that startled England and America two centuries later. Subsequent editions of this work include a treatise entitled *A Notion of the Historical Draught or Tablature of the Judgement of Hercules*, and a letter concerning *Design*. In these later editions Shaftesbury's authorship was acknowledged, and an engraved portrait of him, attired in a Roman toga, appears as a frontispiece. The use of classical costume, even in conjunction with a curled and flowing wig, was not deemed incongruous in an age that was steeped in the literature of Greece and Rome; it was an accepted convention which blended agreeably with the architectural background, and did not introduce what Shaftesbury called a "false relish" to a painting or a piece of sculpture. (See opposite page.)

In his letter on *Design*, Shaftesbury describes the brisk watchfulness of patrons and critics and the public for any overt exhibition of profusion or distortion in taste. "The ordinary Man may build his Cottage, or the plain Gentle-man his Country-house according as he fancys," he wrote; "but when a great Man builds, he will find little Quarter from the Publick, if instead of a beautiful Pile, he raises, at a vast experice, such a false and counterfeit Piece of Magnificence, as can be justly arraign'd for its Deformity by so many knowing Men in Art, and by the whole *People*, who, in such a Conjuncture, readily follow their Opinion."[44] In his *Miscellaneous Reflections*, he had concluded that "*Beauty* and *Truth* are plainly join'd with the Notion of *Utility* and *Convenience*, even in the Apprehension of every ingenious Artist, the *Architect*, the *Statuary*, or the *Painter*."[45] In the treatise on *The Judgement of Hercules* he contended that reason, history and experience proved "that nothing is more fatal, either to Painting, Architecture, or the other Arts, than . . . *false Relish*, which is govern'd rather by what immediately strikes the Sense, than by what consequentially and by reflection pleases the Mind, and satisfies the Thought and Reason. So that whilst we look on *Painting* with the same eye, as we view commonly the rich Stuffs, and colour'd Silks worn by our Ladys, and admir'd in Dress, Equipage, or Furniture, we must of necessity be effeminate in our Taste, and utterly set wrong as to all Judgment and Knowledg in the kind.

The Right Honorable Anthony Ashley
Cooper Earl of Shaftesbury, Baron Ashley of
Winbourn S.t Giles, & Lord Cooper of Pawlett.
J. Closterman Pinx.   Sim: Gribelin Sculp.

From the frontispiece of Vol. I, *Characteristicks of Men, Manners, Opinions, Times*, by Anthony, Earl of Shaftesbury. (6th edition, 1737.)

A design for a girandole, from Chippendale's *Director* (3rd edition).

A girandole, with a representation of antique ruins as the principal motif. In this example of English Rococo, the influence of Piranesi is obvious: compare this design with the view of Roman ruins on the upper part of plate 2. An even more intricate example of a girandole, incorporating a clock, is shown to the right of the chimney-piece in Hogarth's painting, "Shortly After Marriage." (Plate 27.) From Chippendale's *Director* (3rd edition).

A frame for a marble slab, reproduced on a slightly reduced scale from plate CLXXVI of Chippendale's *Director* (third edition, 1762.) It is described as being "supported by two piping Fauns, leaning against two Vines, inter-mixed with Foliage, &c. It will have a grand appearance, if executed with Judgment, and neatly gilt." This has greater delicacy than the design by William Kent on page 103; the ornamentation is deftly handled, and the mask at the centre does not glower with the almost ferocious intentness of the earlier example. The refining influence of the Rococo style lightened the whole conception of the decoration of furniture and interiors in the middle years of the eighteenth century. (See pages 106, 107 and 110.)

For of this *imitative Art* we may justly say: 'That tho It borrows help indeed from Colours, and uses them, as means, to execute its Designs; It has nothing, however, more wide of its real Aim, or more remote from its Intention, than to make a shew of Colours, or from their mixture, to raise a *separate* and *flattering* Pleasure to the Sense.' "(46)

Architects and craftsmen were never allowed to forget for one moment that their work would be scrutinised by "knowing Men in Art," or that those men moulded and controlled public opinion. Cabinet-makers and carvers and upholsterers might be wooed by the enchanting convolutions of the Rococo style, but they would never tolerate the "discord and disproportion" that Walpole had condemned as characteristic of French taste. (Chapter I, page 15.) Even when master-craftsmen of the calibre of Thomas Chippendale were tempted to overload their published designs with intricate embellishments, such extravagances were generally confined to the plates in their books, which were really trade catalogues, and in the work they executed they preserved, as Dr. Johnson said in another connection: "a bottom of good sense." Indeed, such tradesmen assumed the right to reprove extravagance and to suggest, as the humble and obedient servants of their customers, that although they hoped to be favoured with a continuance of their esteemed commands, they trusted that they should never be asked to overstep the bounds of genteel restraint. Ince and Mayhew, for example, had concluded the preface to *The Universal System of Household Furniture*, which was issued about 1762, by admonishing their prospective patrons in these words: "In Furnishing all should be with Propriety—Elegance should always be joined with a peculiar Neatness through the whole House, or otherwise an immense Expense may be thrown away to no Purpose, either in Use or Appearance; and with the same Regard any Gentleman may furnish as neat at a small Expense, as he can elegant and superb at a great one."[47]

Of all the foreign fashions which were assimilated by English architects and craftsmen, that known as the "Chinese taste" was the most persistent. In France it became inextricably associated with the Rococo style; and as the influence of that style spread in mid eighteenth century England, it revived interest in Chinese ornament and decoration. There were successive waves of the "Chinese taste," and the first, a very gentle one, reached England during the seventeenth century, and instilled a desire for collecting painted silks and embroideries, porcelain, lacquered cabinets and screens. These precious and exquisite things were imported, and they helped to create a delightful illusion about Chinese civilisation that persisted in Western Europe for several generations. The refinement of a people that had invented the habit of tea-drinking seemed beyond dispute; and apparently the Chinese, guided and inspired by the teachings of a remarkable philosopher, had attained a political stability and a social order that surpassed anything achieved by Europeans. The first translation of Confucius appeared in 1687, and as Reichwein has pointed out: "Here we have, struck together for the first time, the three notes which in the learned world of the eighteenth century were never heard apart: China—Confucius—political morality."[48]

Since the middle years of the seventeenth century people had been reading about the Far East as well as collecting the productions of Oriental artists and craftsmen. Pepys recorded the purchase of a work on China from his bookseller, Martin, "a most excellent book with rare cuts. . . ." (*Diary*, January 14th, 1667–68.) John Evelyn in a letter to Mr. Vander Douse, dated September 13th, 1662, enumerated the books that were available on China and the East Indies; for he had been translating that Dutch gentleman's "Relation of China," and permitted himself to suggest that "In the mean time, it would be consider'd, whether this whole piece will be to the purpose, there having been of late so many accurate descriptions of those countries in particular, as what Father Alvarez Semedo has published in Italian; Vincent Le Blanc in French; and Mandelslo in high Dutch; not omitting the Adventures and Travels of Pinto in Spanish; all of them now speaking the English language."

The recurrent popularity of Chinese decorative motifs promoted an interest in irregular composition, that developed into a form of taste known as *sharawadgi*, which has been aptly defined by a modern critic, Mr. Hubert de Cronin Hastings, as "the art of not doing regularly." The word sharawadgi, or shara-waggi as it is sometimes spelt, was first used by Sir William Temple in his *Essay on Gardening*, written about 1685, in which he discussed the comparative charms of regularity and irregularity in the laying out and planting of gardens, with some guarded praise for the contrivement of asymmetrical effects by the Chinese. He was cautious rather than sceptical, for in gardens he admitted that, apart from the beauty achieved through regularity, "there may be other forms wholly irregular that may, for aught I know, have more beauty than any of the others; but they must owe it to some extraordinary dispositions of nature in the seat, or some great race of fancy or judgment in the contrivance, which may reduce many disagreeing parts into some figure, which shall yet, upon the whole, be very agreeable. Something of this I have seen in some places, but heard more of it from the others who have lived much among the Chineses; a people, whose way of thinking seems to lie as wide of ours in Europe, as their country does. Among us, the beauty of building and planting is placed chiefly in some certain proportions, symmetries, or uniformities; our walks and our trees ranged so as to answer one another, and at exact distances. The Chineses scorn this way of

A console table, described as a frame for a marble slab, reproduced from plate CLXXV of Chippendale's *Director* (third edition, 1762). Like the girandole on page 107, this example of asymmetric design shows how English carvers and furniture-makers adopted the gaiety and freedoms of the Rococo style without allowing the basic form of their work to be obliterated by an intemperate use of ornament. Compare the example above with the simpler, but far less assured design on the opposite page.

F. Hayman inv.t et delin.   S. F. Ravenet Sculp.

The frontispiece from *Fables for the Female Sex* (London, 1744), a book of
verses, with rather indifferent plates, which illustrated examples of contemporary interior decoration and furnishing. The console table supported
by dolphins, and the ornate mirror frame show how by the middle of the
eighteenth century, ornamental motifs were being handled with lightness
and freedom. (See console table on opposite page)

Rococo and Chinese whims might enjoy a transitory popularity, but the
allegiance to classical prototypes for ornament remained unshaken. Above
and opposite, for example, are designs for vases from Plate XV of *The Builder's
Magazine, or Monthly Companion* (London, 1774). It was suggested that these
would be suitable "for chimney pieces, dressing tables, etc."

planting, and say, a boy, that can tell an hundred, may plant walks of trees in
straight lines, and over-against one another, and to what length and extent he
pleases. But their greatest reach of imagination is employed in contriving
figures, where the beauty shall be great, and strike the eye, but without any
order or disposition of parts that shall be commonly or easily observed: and,
though we have hardly any notion of this sort of beauty, yet they have a particular word to express it, and, where they find it hit their eye at first sight, they
say the *sharawadgi* is fine or is admirable, or any such expression of esteem. And
whoever observes the work upon the best India gowns, or the painting upon their
best screens or purcellans, will find their beauty is all of this kind (that is) without order. But I should hardly advise any of these attempts in the figure of

See description on opposite page.

gardens among us; they are adventures of too hard atchievement for any common hands; and, though there may be more honour if they succeed well, yet there is more dishonour if they fail, and it is twenty to one they will; whereas, in regular figures, it is hard to make any great and remarkable faults."

Horace Walpole attributed the founding of the sharawadgi taste to his friend, the Hon. Richard Bateman. Nearly a hundred years after the word appeared in Temple's essay, Walpole, writing from Strawberry Hill to the Earl of Strafford, was congratulating himself on having made a macaroni named Storer a fresh convert to the Gothic taste. "I am as proud of such a disciple," he said, "as of having converted Dicky Bateman from a Chinese to a Goth. Though he was the founder of the Sharawadgi taste in England, I preached so effectually that his every pagoda took the veil." (June 13th, 1781.) Captivated by Gothic and Chinese forms, the fashionable world of the mid eighteenth century was

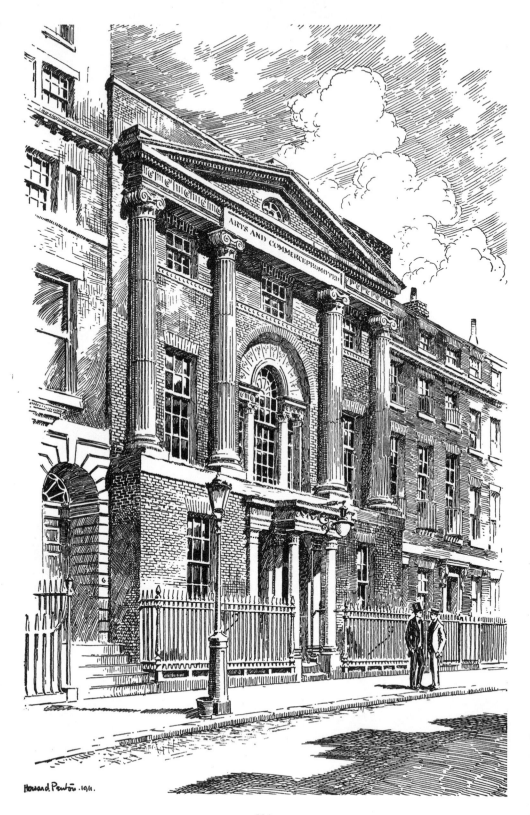

ARTS AND COMMERCE PROMOTED

A house in the Adelphi, London, designed by Robert Adam, *circa* 1770. The Greek anthemion ornament has been used as the motif for the pilasters and the first floor balcony railing. (See page 92.) (*Drawn by David Owen.*)

The premises of the Royal Society of Arts in John Adam Street, Adelphi, London, are shown on the opposite page. Designed by Robert Adam, and occupied by the Society since 1774. (From a drawing made in 1911 by Howard Penton, reproduced by permission of the Royal Society of Arts.)

occasionally accommodated with queer but indubitably decorative mixtures of both; and the sharawadgi taste was reanimated in the seventeen-nineties by the deliberate pursuit of the picturesque. During the late seventeenth and early eighteenth centuries sharawadgi was almost exclusively identified with the Chinese taste.

Until the seventeen-forties the contacts between European nations and China were severely circumscribed; and it was to the interest of the merchants in charge of the trading stations that had been established in Canton by the Dutch and the Portuguese, to prevent their customers at home from discovering that the Chinese regarded the Western world as wholly uncivilised, and habitually referred to Europeans as the "Red Barbarians." It was only after Richard Walter published his account of Lord Anson's voyage round the world in the years 1740–44 that China was revealed as an ancient tyranny, isolated from the rest of the world by a hitherto unsuspected depth of prejudice and ignorance. It was far from being a celestial Utopia, and anything but "a well-governed affectionate family, where the only contests were, who should exert the most humanity and social virtue."(49)

Richard Walter was Chaplain to H.M.S. *Centurion*; he had access to Lord

Hanging shelves for books
or china, from plate
CXXXVIII of Chippen-
dale's *Director* (3rd
edition, 1762.)

Anson's papers, from which he compiled his account, but he also wrote from
personal observation, and his views came as a shock to many people who had
idealised the Chinese, for they learned that "their Magistrates are corrupt, their
people thievish, and their tribunals venal, and abounding with artifice."(50)
They learned too that the capacity of Chinese craftsmen was limited and that the
Japanese had superior abilities, for on the arts and crafts of China he made the
following comments: "That the Chinese are a very industrious people, is
sufficiently evinced, from the great number of curious manufactures which are
established amongst them, and which are eagerly sought for by the most
distant nations; but though skill in the handicraft art seems to be the most
valuable qualification of this people, yet their talents therein are but of a second
rate kind, for they are much outdone by the *Japanese*, in those manufactures,

A china case, or china cabinet, from plate CXXXIV of Chippendale's *Director* (3rd edition, 1762). "Between the middle Feet is a small Canopy, for a Chinese Figure, or any other Ornament."

Small country clock-
makers in common with
other rural craftsmen,
followed the prevailing
Chinese taste. The brass
face of this clock, by John
Godden of Wingham, in
Kent, exhibits an admi-
rably engraved piece of
Sharawagdi. (See pages
110 and 113, and plate
42.)

which are common to both countries; and they are in numerous instances
incapable of rivalling the mechanic dexterity of the *Europeans*. Indeed, their
principal excellency seems to be imitation; and they accordingly labour under
that poverty of genius which constantly attends all servile imitators. This is
most conspicuous in works which require great truth and accuracy; as in
clocks, watches, fire-arms, etc., for in all these, though they can copy the
different parts, and can form some resemblance of the whole, yet they never
could arrive at such a justness in their fabric as it was necessary to produce the
desired effect. If we pass from those employed in manufactures to artists of a
superior class, as painters, statuaries, etc., in these matters they seem to be still
more defective; their painters, though very numerous and in great esteem,
rarely succeeding in the drawing or colouring of human figures, or in the grouping of large compositions; and though in flowers and birds their performances

are much more admired, yet even in these, some part of the merit is rather to be imputed to the native brightness and excellency of the colours, than to the skill of the painter; since it is very unusual to see the light and shade justly and naturally handled, or to find that ease and grace in the drawing which are to be met with in the works of *European* artists. In short, there is a stiffness and minuteness in most of the *Chinese* productions, which are extremely displeasing: And it may perhaps be truly asserted, that these defects in their arts are entirely owing to the peculiar turn of the people, amongst whom nothing great or spirited is to be met with."[51]

Walter's book was published in 1748; it was very popular, and was frequently

A design for the case of a table clock in the Chinese manner. From Chippendale's *Director* (3rd edition).

The Pagoda at Kew Gardens, Surrey. This was one of several ornamental buildings designed by Sir William Chambers and built between 1757 and 1762, when he planned the gardens for the Dowager Princess of Wales. It was a sober and well-proportioned example of the Chinese taste in architecture, free from the fantastic ornamentation that often overloaded and disfigured such decorative structures. Horace Walpole, writing to the Earl of Strafford from Strawberry Hill on July 5th, 1761, recorded the progress of its building. "We begin to perceive the tower of Kew from Montpellier Row," he wrote: "in a fortnight you will see it in Yorkshire." Montpellier Row was in Twickenham, and only a few hamlets and great houses with their surrounding parks lay between Twickenham and the Royal Gardens at Kew.
(*Drawn by David Owen.*)

reprinted, reaching its fifteenth edition by 1780. But although his blunt remarks destroyed a good many illusions about China, interest in Chinese ornament and works of art and in all the conceptions of "Chinese taste" did not diminish, if anything it was expanded, for in March, 1753, William Whitehead, writing in *The World*, could say that "According to the present prevailing whim, every thing is Chinese, or in the Chinese taste; or as it is sometimes more modestly expressed, *partly after the Chinese manner*. Chairs, tables, chimney-pieces, frames for looking-glasses, and even our most vulgar utensils, are all reduced to this new-fangled standard; and without-doors so universally has it spread, that every gate to a cow-yard is in T's and Z's, and every hovel for the cows has bells hanging at the corners."[52] Whitehead added some facetious qualifications to his account of the character and popularity of Chinese ornamental ideas, as interpreted in England, which also recorded the spreading influence of French fashions at the beginning of the second half of the century. "Many good patriots," he wrote, "have been greatly alarmed at the spreading of the French language and the French fashions so universally over Europe; and have apprehended, perhaps too justly, that their modes of religion and government might insinuate themselves in their turns. If any pious Englishman should have the same fears with regard to the Chinese customs and manners, I have the satisfaction to inform him, that nothing of that kind can reasonably be dreaded. We may rest secure that our firm faith will never be staggered by the tenets of Fohi, nor our practice vitiated by the morals of Confucius: at least we may be certain that the present innovations are by no means adequate to such an effect: for on a moderate computation, not one in a thousand of all the stiles, grates, rails, pales, chairs, temples, chimney-pieces, &c. &c. &c. which are called Chinese, has the least resemblance to any thing that China ever saw: nor would an English church be a less uncommon sight to a travelling mandarin, than an English pagoda. I think it necessary to say thus much, in order to quiet the scruples of conscientious persons, who will doubtless be more at ease when they consider that our Chinese ornaments are not only of our own manufacture, like our French silks and our French wines, but, what has seldom been attributed to the English, of our own invention."[53]

Fresh enthusiasm was generated for Chinese design by the treatise which Sir William Chambers published in 1757, on *Designs of Chinese Buildings, Furniture, Dresses, Machines, and Utensils*; which was written and illustrated from first-hand information, for Chambers had travelled extensively in the East, had visited Canton, and had made sketches of actual Chinese buildings and costumes. Thomas Chippendale's plates in *The Gentleman and Cabinet Maker's Director* (1754) included many designs for Chinese chairs and other articles of furniture; but Chippendale gave equal prominence to Gothic designs, for although Whitehead had suggested that Gothic was outmoded, he had admitted that its influence persisted and that its attractions were still potent, for "there is something, they say, in it congenial to our old Gothic constitution . . ."[54] This followed his observation that "a few years ago everything was Gothic; our houses, our beds, our book-cases, and our couches, were all copied from some parts or other of our old cathedrals."[55] Professor Isaacs has identified three phases in the growth and development of the Gothic taste in the eighteenth century: Baroque, Rococo, and Romantic.[56]

Strawberry Hill, Twickenham, the seat of Mr. Horace Walpole. (From a contemporary print.)

Horace Walpole is often regarded as a pioneer of the Gothic taste, but he represents the second, the Rococo phase: several years before he acquired Strawberry Hill in 1747, the fashion for studying, illustrating, and imitating Gothic ruins had become popular, and Batty Langley (1696–1751) had endeavoured to regularise the use of Gothic forms by inventing five orders. This attempt "to adapt Gothic architecture to Roman measures" was scornfully condemned by Horace Walpole, who, describing Langley as a "barbarous architect" in his *Anecdotes of Painting in England*, said: "All that his books achieve, has been to teach carpenters to massacre that venerable species, and to give occasion to those who know nothing of the matter, and who mistake his clumsy efforts for real imitations, to censure the productions of our ancestors, whose bold and beautiful fabrics Sir Christopher Wren viewed and reviewed with astonishment, and never mentioned without esteem." When those "bold and beautiful fabrics" were in ruins, they had an irresistibly romantic charm, especially when the remains of some great monastic establishment were mournfully portrayed. The taste for ruins was fostered by artists and engravers, and in the late seventeen-twenties Samuel and Nathaniel Buck began to publish a series of engravings of abbeys and ruined churches and castles, which sold by the thousand, and remained in popular demand for many years. (See plate 4.)

Strawberry Hill as it is today (1953): the towers are Victorian additions.
(*Drawn by Marcelle Barton from a photograph by Paul Rathbone.*)

Ruins were considered essential for the creation of picturesque effects. This was emphasised by Sir Uvedale Price in his famous essay *On the Picturesque*, which he wrote in 1795. "A temple or palace of Grecian architecture in its perfect entire state," he said, "and with its surface and colour smooth and even, either in painting or reality, is beautiful; in ruin it is picturesque. Observe the process by which Time, the great author of such changes, converts a beautiful object into a picturesque one: First, by means of weather stains, partial incrustations, mosses, &c., it at the same time takes off from the uniformity of the surface, and of the colour; that is, gives a degree of roughness, and variety of tint. Next, the various accidents of weather loosen the stones themselves; they tumble in irregular masses upon what was perhaps smooth turf or pavement, or nicely-trimmed walks and shrubberies—now mixed and overgrown with wild plants and creepers, that crawl over, and shoot among the fallen ruins. Sedums, wall-flowers, and other vegetables that bear drought, find nourishment in the decayed cement from which the stones have been detached; birds convey their food into the chinks, and yew, elder, and other berried plants project from the sides; while the ivy mantles over other parts, and crowns the top. The even, regular lines of the doors and windows are broken, and through their ivy-fringed openings is displayed, in a more broken and picturesque manner, that striking image in Virgil,

> " 'Apparent domus intus, et atria longa patescunt;
> Apparent Priami et veterum penetralia regum.' "

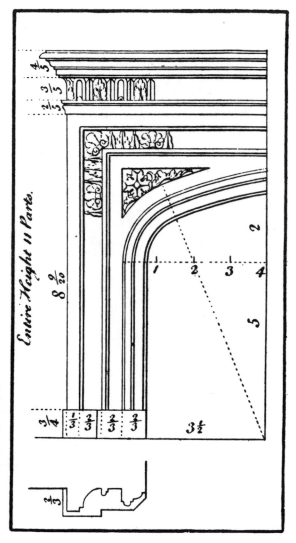

An example of a Gothic chimney-piece, from plate 179 of *The Builder's Director or Bench-Mate*, by Batty Langley (1751). This design might easily be taken for something produced a hundred years later, after England had been smitten by the Gothic Revival.

From the unique properties of ruins, almost any ruins, Sir Uvedale Price argued that irregularity of line and the unsymmetrical grouping of features were desirable if the richly variegated beauties of the picturesque were sought. This was a re-statement of the case for the sharawadgi taste, and by advocating the charm of irregularity for its own sake Price was helping to change, as the Rococo style had already tended to change, the belief, firmly held since the revival of classical architecture in Europe, that beauty and symmetry were identical. He was fully alive to the contribution Gothic architecture could make

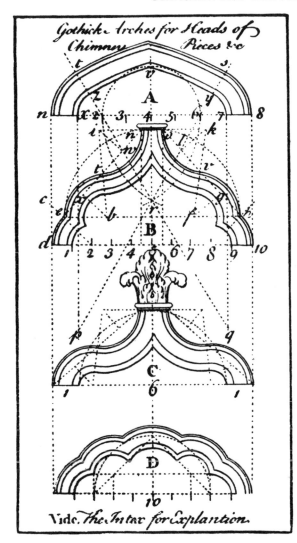

Gothick Arches for Heads of Chimney Pieces &c

Vide. The Index for Explantion.

Directions for accommodating every phase of fashionable taste, and guides for town and country workmen, so that they could execute designs while preserving good proportions, were supplied by many pattern books. Here are directions for Gothic arches for the heads of chimney-pieces, set forth on plate 168, by Batty Langley, in *The Builder's Director or Bench-Mate*, (1751).

to the attainment of irregularity, for it was, he wrote, "generally considered as more picturesque, though less beautiful, than Grecian; and upon the same principle that a ruin is more so than a new edifice. The first thing that strikes the eye in approaching any building, is the general outline, and the effect of the opening. In Grecian buildings, the general lines of the roof are straight; and even when varied and adorned by a dome or a pediment, the whole has a character of symmetry and regularity. But symmetry, which in works of art particularly accords with the beautiful, is in the same degree adverse to the picturesque; and among the various causes of the superior picturesqueness of

An orderly and very gentlemanly piece of Gothic, described as a design for a temple. (From Plate XVI of *The Builder's Magazine, or Monthly Companion*, London, 1774.)

ruins, compared with entire buildings, the destruction of symmetry is by no means the least powerful.

"In Gothic buildings, the outline of the summit presents such a variety of forms, of turrets and pinnacles, some open, some fretted and variously enriched, that even where there is an exact correspondence of parts, it is often disguised by an appearance of splendid confusion and irregularity. There is a line in Dryden's Palamon and Arcite, which might be interpreted according to this idea, though I do not suppose he intended to convey any such meaning—

" 'And all *appear'd* irregularly great.'

"In the doors and windows of Gothic churches, the pointed arch has as much variety as any regular figure can well have; the eye, too, is less strongly conducted than by the parallel lines in the Grecian style, from the top of one aperture to that of another; and every person must be struck with the extreme richness and intricacy of some of the principal windows of our cathedrals and ruined abbeys. In these last is displayed the triumph of the picturesque; and their charms to a painter's eye are often so great, as to rival those which arise from the chaste ornaments, and the noble and elegant simplicity of Grecian architecture."

The tenderness for Gothic ruins, genuine or artificial, persisted; and an inclination to reassess the virtues of the Gothic style became apparent in the last quarter of the eighteenth century. It was felt to be something more than a delightful fashion. A few churchmen were beginning to think of the spiritual significance of Gothic, and their thoughts were leading them to doubt the suitability of classical architecture as a background for Christian worship. Already the denunciations of Pugin and Ruskin were foreshadowed. But such criticism was tentative and always urbane in tone. For example, William Woty, in his poem on Church-Langton, could gently condemn St. Paul's when he was praising the Gothic glories of Langton in these lines:—

> "On yon proud eminence where LANGTON stands,
> That yields a prospect of the richest lands,
> There shall the grand collegiate CHURCH arise,
> A welcome, free-will off'ring to the skies.
> *Gothic* the Stile, and tending to excite
> Free-thinkers to a sense of what is right,
> With length'ning ayles, and windows that impart
> A gloomy steady light to chear the heart,
> Such as affects the soul, and which I see
> With joy, celestial *Westminster*! in thee.
> Not like Saint PAUL's, beneath whose ample dome,
> No thought arises of the life to come.
> For, tho' superb, not solemn is the place,
> The mind but wanders o'er the distant space,
> Where 'stead of thinking on the GOD, most men
> Forget his presence to remember *Wren*."(57)

These views about the religious aspects of the Gothic style were unlikely to appeal to amoral noblemen and gentlemen, who might be disquieted by the lack of religion among the lower orders, but were not prepared to allow a charming fashion to become debilitated by earnestness. That quality was deplorably uncivilised; it was associated with the more unpleasantly repressive forms of Christianity, and although the English governing classes were probably aware of the debt they owed to John Wesley and his Methodism for making the lower orders religious rather than revolutionary, they would never have dreamt of deserting the easy-going Church of England. The Methodist and other Non-

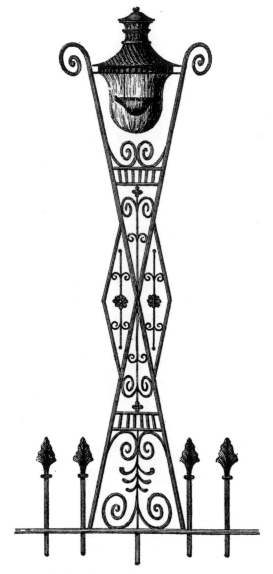

Design for a lamp standard, rising
from railings. (From Plate LXIII of
*The Builder's Magazine, or Monthly
Companion*, London, 1774.)

conformist sects had much to recommend them; but the quite alarming self-righteousness of their members began to remind people of the grim and godly Puritans of the Commonwealth. Sydney Smith, most unclerical of Churchmen, castigated them unmercifully, and in particular objected to "the dreadful pillage of the earnings of the poor" by the forerunners of Mr. Stiggins.

Of course there were many sincerely religious people, but they accepted the order and beauty and gay life of their time; though at the close of the century

Two designs of Iron-work for Door-cases or Frontispieces. (From Plate XLIII of *The Builder's Magazine, or Monthly Companion*, London, 1774.)

some of them, like that prim blue-stocking, Fanny Burney, seemed incredibly innocent. For example, she never suspected that the French refugees from the Revolution who lived so gracefully in their little colony at Juniper Hall near Dorking, were also living in sin. Not that those engaging aristocrats concealed their *affaires*; they were quite open about their lovers and mistresses, but Miss Burney saw nothing wrong. She saw very little wrong with English society either, if her novel *Evelina* really reflects her powers of observation. In that book,

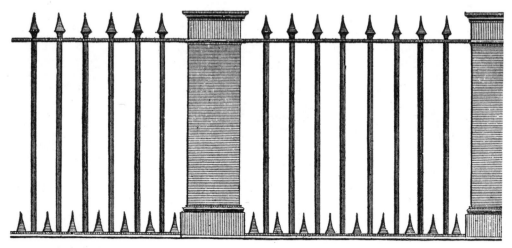

A design for a plain type of iron fencing, from *A Complete Body of Architecture*, by Isaac Ware. By the mid eighteenth century, architects were beginning to realise the possibilities of cast iron.

without any detailed description of the environment, she manages to suggest that life at the higher levels was lived against the most gracious background, and that human contacts were smoothed and elevated by exquisite manners which apparently took the place of passions and appetites. That background was still classical in form and detail and decoration. The Gothic taste had, so far, disturbed nothing but the minds of collectors and the ideas of a few architects and tradesmen.

The collection of Gothic fragments did not diminish the ardour of those who preferred to acquire examples of the work of classical antiquity. Sad and moving stories of the ruins of Greek buildings, their neglect and casual destruction by the barbarous Turks, were constantly recorded. Dr. Richard Chandler, whose travels in Asia Minor and Greece from 1764 to 1766 were sponsored by the Society of Dilettanti, gave the most lugubrious account of the state of the temples of Athens. "It is not easy to conceive a more striking object than the parthenon," he wrote, "though now a mere ruin." And he mentioned, with satisfaction, that "we purchased two fine fragments of the frieze, which we found inserted over door-ways in the town; and were presented with a beautiful trunk, which had fallen from the metopes, and lay neglected in the garden of a Turk." [58] (See plate 3.)

When the Society of Dilettanti resolved "that a person or persons, properly qualified, be sent with sufficient appointments to some parts of the East, in order to collect informations, and to make observations, relative to the ancient state of those countries, and to such monuments of antiquity as are still

Two examples of decorative iron fencing from *A Complete Body of Architecture*, by Isaac Ware.

remaining. . . ." it was following up the work of Stuart and Revett, whose work on *The Antiquities of Athens* had begun to appear in 1762, and, as we observed in Chapter II, had inspired the Greek Revival. (See Appendix 4.) The Society voted a sum "not exceeding two thousand pounds" for financing Dr. Chandler's expedition, and he was accompanied by Mr. Revett and Mr. Pars whose task was to "procure the exactest plans and measures possible of the buildings you shall find, making accurate drawings of the bas-reliefs and ornaments, and taking such views as you shall judge proper; copying all the inscriptions you shall meet with, and remarking every circumstance, which can contribute towards giving the best idea of the ancient and present state of those places."[59] So another treasury of ruins became available, rivalling the "sublime dreams" of Piranesi, and, by showing the Turk as a ruthless despoiler, generating an active sympathy with the enslaved Greeks. The habit of associating anything Turkish with Greek ruins even spread to the design of labels used by apothecaries for Turkey Rhubarb. (See plate 3.)

Thomas Warton's lament over the ruins of Persepolis has often been quoted, and his verses reveal that the romantic yearnings and regrets inspired by the architectural wreckage of antiquity were comparable to those lavished on Gothic remains.

> "Here, like a blasted oak, ascends the clouds;
> Here Parian domes their vaulted halls disclose
> Horrid with thorn, where lurks th'unpitying thief,
> Whence flits the twilight-loving bat at eve,
> And the deaf adder wreathes her spotted train,
> The dwellings once of elegance and art.
> Here temples rise, amid whose hallow'd bounds
> Spires the black pine, while thro' the naked street,
> Once haunt of tradeful merchants, springs the grass:
> Here columns heap'd on prostrate columns, torn
> From their firm base, increase the mould'ring mass.
> Far as the sight can pierce, appear the spoils
> Of sunk magnificence! a blended scene
> Of moles, fanes, arches, domes, and palaces,
> Where, with his brother Horror, Ruin sits."[60]

Ruins were a potent source of inspiration, not only to poets. It was at Rome, on the 15th of October 1764, as Edward Gibbon "sat musing amidst the ruins of the Capitol, while the bare-footed friars were singing vespers in the temple of Jupiter (now the church of the Zoccolants, or Franciscan friars), that the idea of writing the Decline and Fall of the city first started to his mind."[61] The contemplation of ruins as far afield as Persepolis, and the increasing numbers of educated gentlemen who were prepared to endure the fatigues and face the difficulties and dangers of journeys to Eastern Europe, Asia Minor, Persia and

When new materials were introduced, they were used with confident ability by architects, as another means of expressing the infinite versatility of the system of classical design. In the mid eighteenth century, cast iron was as new and stimulating a material as concrete was two hundred years later; and it was properly regarded as a new material, full of possibilities, though later it was degraded to the level of a substitute, and used to imitate stone. When Thomas Farnolls Pritchard, an architect and builder of Shrewsbury, designed the first cast iron bridge that spanned the Severn between Madeley and Broseley, in Shropshire, he used the material to create a light and elegant structure that had an obvious affinity with the classical tradition. The bridge was constructed by Abraham Darby, the ironfounder of Coalbrookdale, and erected in 1777–79. (*Drawn from a steel engraving made in 1782, in possession of the Coalbrookdale Company.*)

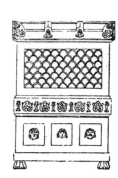

Examples of the use of Greek motifs, by
Thomas Hope. The chairs on the left have
swept, or sabre, legs. (From *Household Furniture and Interior Decoration*, 1807.)

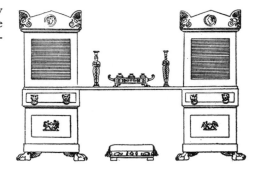

Egypt, evoked fresh enthusiasms for antique design in architecture and ornament.
Hitherto the itinerary of such travellers had been limited by their devotion
to some particular and well-known period of history. As the late Stanley
Casson has pointed out, with the characteristic contempt of a twentieth century
intellectual for the diversions of the rich in the Georgian Age and the bland
assurance of their taste: "The wealthy collectors took no interest except in
the remains of known peoples like the Greeks and Romans. They confined
themselves, as is the manner of the rich, to periods and peoples whose existence
was certified by competent and accepted historians, and whose repute as
civilised people was above reproach. Their choice of objects collected was
strictly regulated by the traditional taste established by the scholars of the
Italian Renaissance. For the wealthy are always slightly afraid of investigating
any period or people which had no properly authenticated pedigree. They
have their social and personal reputation to consider. One consequence of
this strict adherence to traditional taste on the part of the seventeenth and
eighteenth century collectors was that the type of works of art they collected
was strictly limited. They chose only what conformed to the known canons
of 'The Antique' and those known canons were based upon the judgments of
Pliny and the Italian scholars who followed him."[62]

Perhaps the successive waves of Chinese and Gothic taste had, by the end of the eighteenth century, disturbed the exclusive devotion to Greek and Roman remains of which Casson complains. The very word antique comprised far more than it did in the seventeen-fifties, when Isaac Ware defined it as "a term at large expressing any thing antient, but appropriated to signify a building, part of a building, or other work, that has been executed by Greeks or Romans, when the arts were in their greatest purity and perfection among those people." The "antique manner" was "a phrase used to express any modern building, or part of a building, which is executed according to the strict rules and good taste of the antients."[63] When wealthy travellers returned from journeys that had taken them far beyond the confines of the old Roman Empire, they brought back so many souvenirs and records of ornament and decoration that the meaning of "antique" had to be enlarged to accommodate such artistic imports.

Of all those perambulating collectors, probably the most influential was Thomas Hope (1770–1831); "Anastasius" Hope, as he was nicknamed after his novel, *Anastasius, or the Memoirs of a Modern Greek, written at the close of the 18th century.* This work was published anonymously in 1819, it caused an immense sensation, and was at first attributed to Lord Byron, which must have infuriated the poet, who had contemptuously labelled Hope as a "House-furnisher." Hope's travels had provided him with the materials not only for his novel, but for a folio volume of drawings which he published in 1807 under the title of *Household Furniture and Interior Decoration.* The thoroughness of Hope's studies is revealed in a condensed account of his travels, that was included in the preface to *An Historical Essay on Architecture,* posthumously published in 1835. His words disclose far more than his personal preferences; they show how the love of architecture imposed the duty of studying it abroad, and accepting without question its principles for the guidance of taste at home.

"Architecture," he wrote, "as it is one of the noblest, is likewise one of the most arduous and difficult, among the fine arts. No man can be entitled to the appellation of a proficient in its higher branches, who has not seen much and thought more.

A side view of a chair with sabre legs rather exaggerated, and a scroll back. (From Thomas Hope's *Household Furniture and Interior Decoration,* 1807.)

A drawing-room by Thomas Hope. This room was designed for the reception of four large pictures representing Oriental buildings. For this reason, some of the ornamental details of the decoration and the general arrangement of the room had a Saracenic flavour. (Reproduced from *Household Furniture and Decoration, executed from designs by Thomas Hope*, 1807.)

"That taste, that knowledge, which, in minds the most happily disposed for the arts, are never the result of sudden inspiration, but must be acquired by long study and mature reflection, I dare venture to assert, that I have done more to obtain, than almost any other person of my own age living. From an infant, architecture was always my favourite amusement. I scarcely was able to hold a pencil, when, instead of flowers, landscapes, and all those other familiar objects of which the imitation chiefly delights the generality of such children as show a turn for design, I already began dealing in those straight lines which seem so little attractive to the greatest number, even of good draughtsmen of a more advanced age. No sooner did I become master of my own actions, which unfortunately happened at the early age of eighteen, than, disdaining any longer to ride my favourite hobby only in the confinement of a closet, I hastened in quest of food for it, to almost all the different countries where any could be expected.

An interior from Thomas Hope's *Household Furniture and Interior Decoration* (1807), showing his use of Egyptian motifs.

"Egyptian architecture I went to investigate on the banks of the Nile—Grecian, on the shores of Ionia, Sicily, and the Peloponnesus. Four different times I visited Italy, to render familiar to me all the shades of the infinitely varied styles of building peculiar to that interesting country, from the most rude attempts of the Etruscan, to the last degraded ones of the Lombards. Moorish edifices I examined on the coast of Africa, and among the ruins of Grenada, of Seville, and Cordova. The principle of the Tartar and Persian construction I studied in Turkey and in Syria. Finally, of the youngest branch of the art, that erroneously called Gothic, I investigated the most approved specimens throughout England, and most of the provinces of France, Germany, Spain, and Portugal.

"During eight years that this research lasted, I willingly encountered, to perfect myself in an art which I studied from mere inclination, and from which I expected nothing beyond the pleasure of understanding it, fatigues, hardships, and even dangers, which would have disheartened most of those who follow it as a lucrative profession, and who build on it their hopes of subsistence and fortune. Soon after my roving life ceased, I determined to add practice to theory. I must, in justice to myself, add, that had I more extensive means, and a better opportunity, I feel myself capable of designs far beyond the few and trifling specimens I have hitherto been able to exhibit."[64]

Hope's closing sentence suggests that his means were restricted; but he was a rich man, the eldest son of a wealthy merchant of Scottish descent, whose family had lived in Amsterdam for several generations. He came to England in 1795, when the French occupation of Holland compelled him and his family to leave that country, settled in London, and bought a house in Duchess Street, Portland Place, which had been built for General Clark by Robert Adam. Here he accommodated his large collection of antique vases and sculpture, and presently added a gallery in the Greek Revival style for the Flemish and Dutch pictures, owned by his brother, Henry Philip Hope. He made innumerable experiments in furnishing, and when his *Household Furniture and Interior Decoration* appeared, it expanded the already growing taste for the neo-Greek style, and encouraged the use of Egyptian decorative motifs. His preoccupation with furniture design had already established his reputation several years before he surprised everybody by writing *Anastasius*, which was not only an unusual romance, but was as Sydney Smith observed, "a novel which all clever people of a certain age should read, because it is full of marvellously fine things." He also said, as a tribute to what was normally expected from the author, "Is this Mr. Thomas Hope?—Is this the man of chairs and tables?—the gentleman of the sphinxes—the Oedipus of coalboxes—he who meditated on muffineers and planned pokers?—Where has he hidden all this eloquence and poetry up to this hour?"

Hope's influence on contemporary furnishing was perceptible; the "gentleman of the sphinxes" diffused a taste for Egyptian ornament that occasionally enriched the furniture of the Regency period. Such decorative motifs were never used with the lavishness that often overwhelmed French Empire furniture; nor was there any affinity between French and English design during the opening decades of the nineteenth century. The term "English Empire" implies that the Regency style owed its inspiration to France; but it is a misleading modern term, for, apart from the brief peace of Amiens, England and France were at war from 1793 to 1815, and the influence of French taste and fashion was progressively diminished, until it was negligible. The Regency style was derived from the Grecian and neo-Greek revivals, which owed their inception partly to the records of Stuart and Revett (see page 50), and their exquisite development to the brothers Adam and their contemporaries and their immediate successors.

Four years before Hope's book on furniture was issued, Thomas Sheraton had published *The Cabinet Dictionary* (1803), which included many engravings that had appeared in his principal work, *The Cabinet Maker's and Upholsterer's Drawing Book*, which was originally issued in four parts between 1791 and 1794.

In *The Cabinet Dictionary* Sheraton gave explicit directions for the guidance of parvenus. They are included in the opening paragraph of the entry "Furnish" where he said "particular regard is to be paid to the quality of those who order a house to be furnished, when such order is left to the judgement of the upholsterers; and when any gentleman is so vain and ambitious as to order the furnishing of his house in a style superior to his fortune and rank, it will be prudent in an upholsterer, by some gentle hints, to direct his choice to a more moderate plan."[65] This echoed the advice given by Ince and Mayhew over forty years earlier; and in the early nineteenth century such advice was badly needed. Even in Sheraton's plates a suspicion of grossness was apparent. When George Smith, upholder and cabinet-maker to the Prince of Wales, published the first of his books, *A Collection of Designs for Household Furniture and Interior Decoration* (1808), a marked deterioration in design was exhibited in many of the plates. The transition from the informed taste of the Georgian Age to the Victorian preoccupation with the mechanics of comfort was already beginning, and in furniture particularly there was a growing tendency to choose articles that were solid, and sometimes positively corpulent, in form. Why this transition occurred has never been convincingly explained; although many theories have been advanced to account for the change from good proportions to bad, from Georgian grace to clumsy Victorian comfort. That the modes of the Court were not without influence upon the form of furniture is acknowledged, though it is perhaps frivolous to suggest that the collapse of good design began when the Prince Regent discarded his corsets, a concession to comfort that was indelicately recorded by Creevey, who wrote, "Prinny has let loose his belly, which now reaches his knees; otherwise he is said to be well." This royal rejection of any further pretensions to elegance certainly coincided with a growing tendency to grossness in the form of furniture.

One of the chief causes of the unwieldy aspect of furniture produced after the mid eighteen-twenties, was the inability of makers to keep under proper control their wish to suggest an air of richness and luxury in terms of ornamentation. Throughout the previous century, and during the Regency period, elegance was happily allied with luxury through a discerning choice of materials and an instinctive knowledge of how to begin and, still more important, where to stop with ornamentation.

Thomas Sheraton (1751–1806) was perhaps the unconscious progenitor of Victorian furniture. Although he was trained as a cabinet-maker, it seems unlikely that he ever had a workshop of his own; and his trade card, issued from his address at 106 Wardour Street, Soho, bore this statement: "Teaches Perspective, Architecture and Ornaments, makes Designs for Cabinet-makers, and sells all kinds of Drawing Books, etc." (Sheraton Street, between Wardour Street and Great Chapel Street, Soho, has been named after him.) He subsequently moved to 8 Broad Street, Golden Square, and it was there that young Adam Black, the founder of the publishing house of A. & C. Black, lodged with him when he left Edinburgh and came to London, to seek and make a fortune, like many other Scots. Sheraton was then living in extreme poverty. In the diary which he addressed to his parents, Adam Black described him as "a man of talents, and, I believe, of genuine piety. He understands the cabinet-business—I believe was bred to it; he has been, and perhaps at present is, a preacher; he is a scholar, writes well; draws, in my opinion, masterly; is an author, bookseller, stationer, and teacher. We may be ready to ask how comes it to pass that a man with such abilities and resources is in such a state? I believe his abilities and resources are his ruin, in this respect, for by attempting to do everything he does nothing."(66)

Sheraton's versatility was his undoing, and it led him into some ill-conceived extravagances in design. The gross lineaments of a coarser age are occasionally foreshadowed in the plates of *The Cabinet Dictionary*.

The Regency period gave a respite to good design; for a while designers retained complete control of form, materials and ornament, and when occasionally they ventured to make ornate experiments, of the heady and exuberant kind that may be seen in the Royal Pavilion at Brighton, they never committed the sins against good proportion that became commonplace before the death of George IV. In the design of chairs alone, the use of the turned and tapering leg and the sabre or swept leg, produced some elegant models in the opening decades of the nineteenth century; but the turning became bloated, and by the eighteen-twenties the balanced relationship between the turned front legs of a chair and the swept back legs was often disrupted; they became conflicting elements, arbitrarily associated, like two quarrelsome actors cast for the front and hind legs of a pantomime horse. By the eighteen-thirties there was more often than not a complete lack of harmony between the front and back legs of chairs, and the arms of elbow chairs would be attached almost as an afterthought, without consideration for the general proportions of the chair. Sheraton had given explicit directions for the form and embellishment of arms for chairs on plate 2 of *The Cabinet Dictionary*, with particular attention to the carving appropriate for the toe, or junction of the arm with the seat frame. (See page 99.) Only thirty years elapsed between the publication of Sheraton's *Cabinet Dictionary* in 1803 and John Claudius Loudon's *Encyclopaedia of Cottage, Farm and Villa Architecture and Furniture* in 1833, but the contrast between what was acceptable to Sheraton and what Loudon was prepared to praise is marked by the illustrations they used and the descriptions they published. Sheraton writes and draws always as a designer with a background of practical experience at the bench—Loudon as a connoisseur of styles.

In 1826 two books appeared which showed how the urbanities of the long Georgian period had almost disappeared: one was George Smith's *The Cabinet Maker and Upholsterer's Guide*, in which he amply fulfilled the boorish promise

Two armchairs designed by Thomas Sheraton, from plate 3 of *The Cabinet Dictionary* (1803). Of these, Sheraton said, "No. 1 . . . I think will look best for a parlour carved in mahogany. No. 2 has a stuffed top rail, also the square pannel in the back. This chair would look well in mahogany, with a brass bead round the stuffing to hide the tacks, etc. and which produces a lively effect." Sheraton here uses lions' masks in No. 2 at the junction of the front legs and the seat frame: a much less happier use of the motif than William Kent's, who used them on the top rail of an armchair. (See pages 99 and 100.)

of his earlier work, the other was *The Practical Cabinet-Maker, Upholsterer and Complete Decorator*, by Peter and Michael Angelo Nicholson. The furniture and interior decoration of this period between the end of the Regency and the accession of William IV showed that designers were still able to preserve a few affinities with the Georgian Age; but those two books, which anticipated so many forms that have since been regarded as typical of Victorian taste, illustrate the fumbling uncertainty·of furniture-makers about where and how their works should be embellished. Already the insurgent emotionalism of the Gothic revival was beginning to destroy respect for the classical conventions of design, and to justify slovenliness in the name of freedom.

Georgian grace became a memory; after the eighteen-thirties the serenity and ordered harmonies of the civilisation it reflected were forgotten; and educated taste was an early casualty in the battle of the styles. Ruskin unconsciously wrote its epitaph in *The Stones of Venice* when he said: "Whatever has any connection with the five orders; whatever is Doric or Ionic or Corinthian or Composite, or in any way Grecised or Romanised; whatever betrays the smallest respect for Vitruvian laws or conformity with Palladian work—that we are to endure no more."

Part Two

THE ACCOMPANIMENTS TO LIFE

W.ᵗ Hogarth. delin.　　　　　　　　　　　James Basire. Sculp.

The Farmer's Return.

David Garrick, who wrote *The Farmer's Return from London*, took the part himself, and the crude good cheer of the farmer's kitchen is apparent in Hogarth's rendering of it. Boswell recorded his appreciation of this piece in his *Journal* (November 22nd, 1762) and the *London Magazine* for April of that year said: "This Interlude, which has, for some time past, so agreeably entertained the town, at Drury-Lane theatre, is at length published, with a frontispiece, containing a sketch of the Farmer and his Family, of which it is a sufficient recommendation, to say that it comes from the hand of Hogarth, to whom the author has handsomely inscribed the piece itself, which, we are at the same time informed, was written merely with a view of serving Mrs Pritchard at her benefit."

CHAPTER I

"FILL EVERY GLASS"

COARSE delight in quantity was far more common than a civilised appreciation of quality in wine and food during the early part of the eighteenth century. Matthew Green might have been describing a typical man of that time when he wrote:

> ". . . in whose gay red-lettered face
> We read good living more than grace. . . ."[67]

Good living meant vast meals and deep potations, which provoked an animal vigour in male conversation that was restrained only by the presence of ladies. This bawdy freedom of speech persisted throughout the Georgian Age and lasted well into the nineteenth century. Lord Melbourne, we know, was always delighted when the gentlemen were left alone after dinner to the enjoyment of their wine. "Now we can talk broad," he would say.[68] What happened after "the retiring of cultivated and virtuous women from table and elsewhere" was accurately described by Dr. James Fordyce in a discourse on *The Character and Conduct of the Female Sex*, and he was probably speaking from first-hand knowledge, for respect for the cloth was diminished by the sociable and sporting habits of many parsons. "Does the conversation become either livelier, or more refined?" he asked. "Or will you say, that your behaviour in general takes a better cast? You will scarcely say, that it is improved in politeness. But it is improved in freedom.—O yes; the cruel restraints of decency are removed: you are now at liberty to burst forth into clamour, oaths, obscenity, prophaneness, defamation of the sex, and—if you are so disposed, to get drunk into the bargain. Glorious privileges! Worthy, no doubt, to be highly prized by reasonable beings, by persons of education, and by gentlemen."[69]

Food and drink had a proper importance, which only occasionally became exaggerated, so that a critical writer could say "that the sumptuous side-board, to an ingenuous eye, has often more the air of an altar than a table."[70] But the sumptuous sideboard was always well designed; commodious and graceful in form, it was descended from the mediaeval serving table, and was dressed with plate and glass. (In his *Directions to Servants*, Swift gave this facetious advice to the butler: "When you dress up your Side-board, set the best Glasses as near the edge of the Table as you can. . .") Although there are records of sideboard

Two designs for sideboard tables from Plate LXI of Chippendale's *Director*,
third edition, 1762. (These are reduced in size from the plate.) On the plate,
Chippendale names them as sideboard tables: in his description, he calls
them "Side-boards"—obviously the terms were at that time interchangeable.
The design at the top has truss legs.

cupboards in the second half of the seventeenth century, the specialised type of
side table with drawers and cupboards does not appear to have been invented
until about a hundred years later.[71] Before that invention, which has been
attributed to Thomas Shearer, large side tables with marble or wooden tops
were used; and the former were often called frames for marble slabs. Chippendale uses that term in his *Director*. Side or sideboard tables, flanked by pedestals
which were surmounted by urns—those delicate classical shapes that adorned
so many balustrades and copings—were in use during the latter part of the
eighteenth century. Meanwhile cabinet-makers adopted and developed the
type originally illustrated by Shearer, and by the end of the Georgian period it
was made in a variety of forms, affording the most comprehensive accommoda-

tion, with cupboards and drawers for glass and cutlery and silver, and, in the larger types, a discreetly inconspicuous cupboard for a chamber pot. Nothing is known of Shearer, apart from the engraved plates in *The Cabinet-Makers' London Book of Prices*, printed in 1788 for the London Society of Cabinet Makers, which were re-issued under his name as *Designs for Household Furniture*; and the sideboards included in those volumes may have originated in the workshops of any of his contemporaries. The name of Hepplewhite is also closely associated with this article of furniture, and both sideboards and sideboard tables are shown in *The Cabinet Maker and Upholsterer's Guide*, which was published in 1788, by George Hepplewhite's widow, Alice, two years after his death. Such convenient, labour-saving designs did much to increase the speed and general tidiness of service in the dining-room.

Meals in a well-appointed household at the close of the century were very different from the carelessly served abundance that had so often astonished and disgusted foreign visitors in its opening years. That rather grumpy observer, Zacharias Conrad Von Uffenbach, who visited London in 1710, had some hard things to say about the way dinner was served in the Hall of the Middle Temple. "They dine here in as slovenly a fashion as they do in the colleges in Oxford," he wrote. "The table had just been laid, and on it were wooden platters and green earthenware pots, into which the bones are cast; there were no napkins and the table-cloth looked as if a sow had just had a litter on it. We had no desire to dine there, and we hastened to look at the Library."(72)

Everybody ate enormously, and nobody was ashamed of acknowledging and indulging in the pleasures of the table. Even the mid seventeenth century

Left: a small sideboard of a type made in the second half of the eighteenth century. Both sideboard and knife box are in mahogany. (*From a drawing by Marcelle Barton.*)

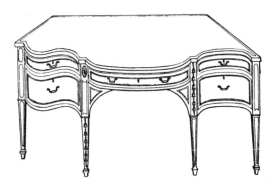

Right: a simplified drawing of a sideboard included in Shearer's book, *Designs for Household Furniture* (1788). This shows alternative treatments for the Marlboro' legs and the curves of the front.

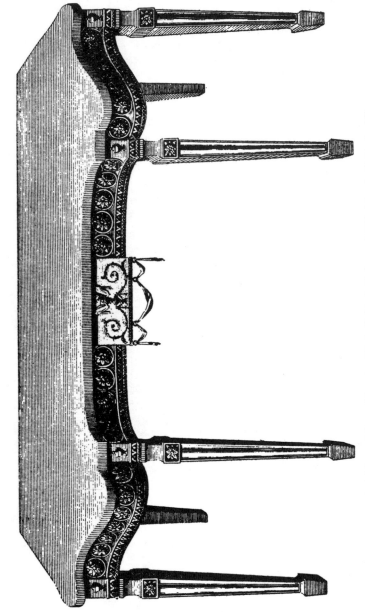

A sideboard from Hepplewhite's *Cabinet Maker and Upholsterer's Guide* (1788).

A serpentine-fronted sideboard included in *The Cabinet Maker and Upholsterer's Guide*, by A. Hepplewhite and Co. Although the *Guide* was published in 1788, some of the plates were issued earlier, and this sideboard which is reproduced from the second edition of 1789, bears this inscription: "London, Published by I. and J. Taylor, No. 56, High Holborn, July 2nd, 1787."

Puritans had relished good food and good drink too. The weight of their displeasure had fallen chiefly upon items of food that could be identified with Popish feasts. They had, for instance, forbidden mince pies at Christmas. Men and women in the eighteenth century, free from such inhibitions, never questioned the right to enjoy themselves, never addressed their energy to the task of repressing their own inclinations, or legislating for the direction of other people's pastimes. Chesterton's "great big black teetotaller" had not yet been "sent to us for a rod." The selection and preparation of meals was a branch of domestic art that was practised in the cottage, the manor, the great country house, and the fashionable town dwelling. Boswell tells us that Dr. Johnson "found great fault with a gentleman of our acquaintance for keeping a bad table. 'Sir, (said he), when a man is invited to dinner, he is disappointed if he does not get something good. I advised Mrs. Thrale, who has no card-parties at her house, to give sweet meats, and such good things in an evening, as are not commonly given, and she would find company enough come to her; for every body loves to have things which please the palate put in their way, without trouble or preparation.' "[73]

Good food in great abundance was always expected. An invitation to dinner or breakfast was a promise of rich satisfaction for hearty appetites, though after the middle years of the century the really large breakfast was already qualifying for the description of "old English." William Hickey, returning from the West Indies in 1776, breakfasted with Captain Dobbins, the master of the vessel that had brought him home, on steak with oyster sauce at the Hoop and Griffin Inn. He had sat down to tea and coffee, but could not resist the steak, "the slip slops going away untouched." To him, this was an "old English breakfast."[74]

Naturally, those who habitually ate and drank too much paid the penalty, and occasionally the newspapers and magazines published the deplorable results. We find in the *Norwich Mercury*, for Saturday, February 23rd, 1788, the following item:—

"Lewes, Feb. 18. A few days since as Mr. Tribe, Blacksmith, at Thakeham, a corpulent man, was stooping to take up something from the ground, his belly burst in such a manner, as to occasion his bowels partly to come out. A surgeon was immediately sent for, by whose attendance Mr. Tribe is in a fair way of recovery. He had for a long time past complained of a pain about the rim of his belly, and, as a relief, constantly wore a girdle."

Again, in the *European Magazine* for September, 1798, we learn of the death of "Mr. George Maddock, grocer, at Nottingham, aged 49 years, of extreme corpulency." In the same number of that magazine we hear how, on September 5th, "Mr. Oliver Bond died suddenly in Newgate. He had played at rackets the preceding day till he was much fatigued. At night he eat a hearty supper, drank freely, and was found dead next morning, supposed to have died in an apoplectic fit. Some suspicions were endeavoured to be excited in Dublin with respect

A sideboard table from *The Cabinet Dictionary*, "which exhibits a mirror with lights on each side, fixed to the brass rail. The lions heads are to be carved in mahogany, and the rings may be of brass. The general height of the sideboard is 3 feet, the width 2 feet 9 inches, the length from 5 feet to 10." Sheraton concluded his description of the design by observing that "The most fashionable sideboards at present are those without cellerets, or any kind of drawer, having massy ornamented legs, and moulded frames." This illustration is reduced in size from the original plate.

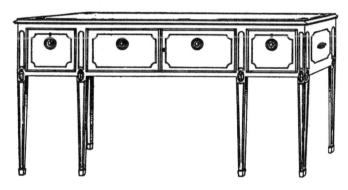

A Sheraton sideboard in mahogany, of a very simple type. It has been in the possession of Adam and Charles Black, the publishers, since the early nineteenth century, and there is a tradition that it may have been made by Sheraton for Adam Black, who lodged at Sheraton's house when he first came to London. (See page 140.) (*From a drawing by Marcelle Barton.*)

to the sudden death of Oliver Bond. It appears, from the evidence on the inquest, that he sat up nearly the whole of the night drinking punch, and slept only a short time in his clothes. He was found dead in the morning on the steps leading from his apartment to the courtyard. The following is the report from the surgeons:

" 'New Prison, Sept 6, 1798.

" 'On examining the body of Oliver Bond, who died this morning, between five and six o'clock, we certify, that no circumstance appears which would lead us to believe that his death was not a natural one.

" 'G. STEWART
" 'W. LAKE
" 'E. GEOGHEGAN' "

Perfectly natural in that hearty time; but what men they were who sat down to those drinking bouts and colossal meals, and if they or their children paid for their enjoyment in terms of gout and dropsy, it seldom occurred to them to complain. Charles James Fox, dropsical, enormous and consistently cheerful in his old age, plays cricket with his nephews, seated in a wheeled chair; Horace Walpole, racked with gout (though we can hardly suppose as a result of his own excesses), merely jests about his fingers being deformed and chalky; and there is a reverse side of the picture. Lord Hervey, whose strict diet of milk and vegetables, originally adopted under the advice of Dr. Cheyne to alleviate the violent pains that were probably caused by gallstones, earned the scorn of Pope, who, in his epistle to Dr. Arbuthnot, called him Sporus, a salacious reference to the young eunuch "married" by the Emperor Nero—an allusion that was as offensive as it was unjust. Pope expanded the insult in this couplet:

"Let Sporus tremble—What? that thing of silk,
Sporus, that mere white curd of ass's milk?"

Any age, judged only by its excesses or austerities, appears monstrous; and our view of eighteenth century social life tends to be coloured by the extremes of debauchery and misery that were so often portrayed by Hogarth, Rowlandson, and Gillray, and described by Fielding, Smollett and their contemporaries. Hogarth was reproving the sins of society, and the beastliness and grossness of the figures in "Gin Lane" and "Beer Street" were intended to be, and indeed have remained, unforgettable. Those two prints were issued in 1751, the year when Fielding attacked the widespread habit of gin drinking in his pamphlet, *An Inquiry into the causes of the late increase of robbers, &c., with some proposals for remedying the growing evil*. Gin was, he said, "responsible for a new kind of drunkenness, unknown to our ancestors," and was "the principal sustenance (if it may so be called) of more than 100,000 people in the metropolis . . ." The laws restricting its distillation and sale were largely ignored, and in London a roaring

Left: Glass for spirits, which holds a very small quantity of liquor. *Centre:* A tall goblet with a baluster stem. Glasses of this type would sometimes be anything from eight to ten inches in height. Early eighteenth century. *Right:* Goblet with a drawn stem. Mid eighteenth century.

black market flourished. In 1736 *The General Evening Post* had reported that "Notwithstanding the Diligence of the Magistracy in putting the late Act against the retailing of Spirituous Liquors in force, the People are so madly fond of it, that it was sold publickly on the Road at Horn-Fair, by People with Wheelbarrows, Baskets, &c." (October 21st.) The report added, optimistically, that "The benefit of the aforesaid Act begins to be felt already in the Suburbs and Out-parts of the Town, where some Bakers vend (at least) one third more of Bread than they did before the Commencement thereof. The people will have it, according to the Adage, in Meal or in Malt."

Feasting and jollity were still thoroughly understood, though in the middle years of the eighteenth century they lost much of their innocence as the disastrous habit of gin-drinking spread. When Fielding denounced it, the vice had turned thousands of men and women into irresponsible paupers, for the dismal dens and cellars where gin was sold dirt cheap invited customers to become "drunk for a penny, dead drunk for two-pence," and promised "clean straw for nothing." The unlicensed premises, the boozing kens, hush-cribs and whistling shops—innumerable slang terms arose and persisted—were reduced in number, but were never wholly eliminated, despite savage penalties. Gin addicts would sell their garments for the stuff, and part with everything they owned—it was well named "strip-me-naked." The habit was as dangerous and debilitating and as great a social evil as drug-taking. In the end the English people, helped by the law, decided that "beer was best," for it had always been the popular beverage, and was sometimes called the "British Burgundy."

The English love of festivity, apparent on every day except Sunday, found a sprightly outlet in drinking songs; and the praise of good drink and conviviality, like the joys of country life, always won applause in the theatre. Sometimes drinking songs would express a pagan abandon, such as those in *The Beggar's Opera*. The tradition of polite dalliance, dramatised with such jocund zest by the playwrights of the Restoration, was continued by Gay in the song that concludes the first scene of Act II.

> "Fill ev'ry glass, for wine inspires us,
>   And fires us
> With courage, love, and joy.
> Women and wine should life employ;
>   Is there aught else on earth desirous?"

Again, when Lucy Lockit is cajoling Polly Peachum, she puts a very persuasive case for judicious indulgence as she sings:

> "Come, sweet lass,
>   Let's banish sorrow
>   Till to-morrow:
> Come, sweet lass,
>   Let's take a chirping glass.
> Wine can clear
>   The vapours of despair
>   And make us light as air;
> Then drink and banish care."

It is true that these songs were sung by highwaymen, and by the daughter of a turnkey in Newgate, who was enticing a highwayman's sweetheart (or, as we should put it today, a gangster's moll); but they have an innocent freshness, and an appeal that has endured for over two centuries. Boswell said that *The Beggar's Opera* had in it "so much of real London life, so much brilliant wit, and such a variety of airs, which from early association of ideas, engage, soothe, and enliven the mind, that no performance which the theatre exhibits, delights me more."[75]

Artists might depict coarse scenes of gluttony, with bloated men and women gobbling and swilling down drink, but the background of such scenes usually revealed the most faultless taste. Nearly all drinking vessels were well shaped; those used by the countryman were usually of wood or pewter; and thick, corpulent glasses would be found in some inns, though the better class inn had glass as elegant as that to be found on the tables of the nobility and gentry. Bottles of leather, wood, stone and pewter were common in the countryside,

Left and centre: Wine glasses with baluster stems and domed bases. Such glasses were in use between the late seventeenth and the middle of the eighteenth century. *Right:* A mid eighteenth century rummer with a plain glass stem.

Left: A rummer of the type used in inns, capacious rather than elegant. *Right:* Wine glass of the type used in inns. Late eighteenth or early nineteenth century.

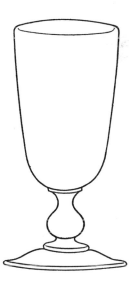

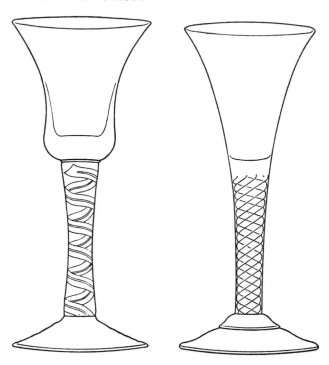

Wine glasses with white twist
stems. Second half of eighteenth century.

but glass bottles did not come into general use until the second half of the
seventeenth century. Cobbett in his *Cottage Economy* (1822) contemptuously
dismissed all fragile substances, such as crockery, asserting that "plates, dishes,
mugs, and things of that kind, should be of *pewter*, or even of wood." He added:
"As to *glass* of any sort, I do not know, what business it has in any man's house,
unless he be rich enough to live on his means. It pays a tax, in many cases, to the
amount of two-thirds of its cost." The big leathern vessels known as black-jacks
were used in the country until the end of the eighteenth century for small beer;
but the tankard, originally a wooden vessel which held a couple of gallons or
more, was the standard receptacle, and was of pewter, in quart, pint, and half-
pint sizes. There were, more rarely, silver tankards; and these were decorated,
in common with other silver articles, with the formalised acanthus leaves, and
other ornamentation derived from classic architecture.

English glass after the Restoration had, like English furniture, an almost
exotic decorative character, but during the last decade of the seventeenth
century, simpler forms were introduced, and in the design of table glass the
prevailing respect for good proportion, apparent in architecture, found continuous expression. For example, wine glasses with a stem consisting of a solid
baluster, echoed an architectural form; and the stems of these baluster wine
glasses were greatly varied, and occasionally included an air bubble. Ale glasses

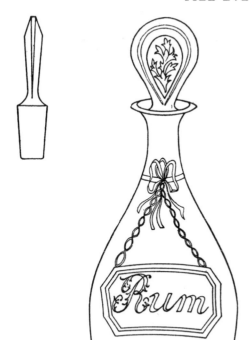

A late eighteenth century blue glass decanter, with the label and decoration in gold.
(*Drawn by Marcelle Barton from an example in the author's possession.*)

had much shorter stems, and thick bases, but were not squat or ill-proportioned. Later in the eighteenth century, table glass was slightly influenced by the Rococo style which was then being anglicised by architects and cabinet-makers; but, like English furniture, it never became too fragile in the interests of fashion. Cutlery and tableware exhibited a comparable elegance, and the potters, of whom perhaps Josiah Wedgwood was the greatest, established an alliance between art and industry that had richly productive results, until the beginning of the Victorian period.

The dining-room was, according to Sheraton, "one of the principal apartments of a house and ought always to be of a bold and an accommodating proportion." The development and character of the sideboard have already been described. In *The Cabinet Dictionary*, Sheraton gives the following directions for furnishing. "In noblemen's dining-rooms, when the windows are all on the side opposite to the fires, there may then be a recess at each end of the room, in which a sideboard may stand, with columns before it placed at the extremities, which produces a very august appearance, and renders the service considerably more

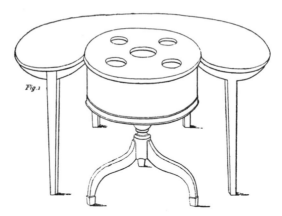

Fig. 1

A gentleman's social table, or, as it was sometimes called, a sociable table, which allowed two or three people to sit with their wine near a fire. It is kidney-shaped, with four legs, and a revolving cylindrical receptacle for wine bottles, supported on a pillar and claw stand, which fitted into the concave curve of the table. (From *The Prices of Cabinet Work*, 1797 edition.)

easy at dinner than when there is but one sideboard. The furniture of a dining-room ought to be bold, substantial, and magnificent, in proportion to its dimensions."

The table and the sideboard were the two most important pieces of furniture. François de la Rochefoucauld described dinner as one of the most wearisome of his English experiences, for it lasted from four to five hours, and he complained that "The first two are spent in eating, and you are compelled to exercise your stomach to the full in order to please your host."[76] When the cloth was removed, "the most beautiful table that it is possible to see" was disclosed. "It is most remarkable," he said, "that the English are so much given to the use of mahogany; not only are their tables generally made of it, but also their doors and seats and the handrails of their staircases."[77] All the dining tables he saw had "a brilliant polish like that of the finest glass."

By the early nineteenth century the form of the dining table had been perfected, for the legs no longer provided a problem for those seated round the board. As Sheraton described them in the *Cabinet Dictionary*, "The common useful dining tables are upon pillars and claws, generally four claws to each pillar, with brass casters."

Apart from the sideboard and the dining table there were many specialised pieces of furniture, such as the social or sociable table. This was a small, kidney-shaped table with four legs, and a revolving, cylindrical receptacle, for wine, that was supported on a pillar-and-claw stand, which fitted into a corresponding concave curve of the table. This allowed a small, comfortable and convivial party of three or four people to sit with their wine after dinner, near a fire. There was also the horseshoe dining table, which may have been designed originally by Thomas Shearer. This had flaps, allowing it to be extended to form a half circle. The guests sat on the outer curve, and were served from the inner, and when the table was not in use, the flaps were folded back on the top so that it then became segmental in shape. It had plain, tapering, or, as they were called, Marlboro' legs. Another type of small dining table had leaves at each end that could be pulled out to extend the top. This was known in the late eighteenth century as a universal dining table, though it was a refined edition of the draw-tables that had been in use since the middle years of the seventeenth century, and which were known sometimes as "drawing tables." Toddy table is a modern term, occasionally used to describe the small tables introduced in the mid eighteenth century, to hold a tray for the hot water, spirits, sugar, tumblers, ladle and other accessories for making toddy.

There were special tables for other meals. Chippendale illustrates small, four-legged tables with hinged flaps, so the top could be extended, and describes them as breakfast tables in the third edition of his *Director*. A Pembroke table with a drawer or drawers below the top, and flaps that could be extended on

A Pembroke table, sometimes called a Universal table. It was described by Sheraton as "a name given to a kind of breakfast table, from the name of the lady who first gave orders for one of them, and who probably gave the first idea of such a table to the workmen . . ." (Reproduced from *The Cabinet Maker's and Upholsterer's Drawing Book*, third edition, 1802.)

Two designs for breakfast tables, by
Thomas Chippendale: the one below
has a pierced, diagonal stretcher
and slightly tapering legs; the other
has a decorative apron of Chinese
fretwork, and legs of square section.
Both tables have hinged flaps, which
may be let down. In these simplified
drawings, made from plate LIII of the
Director (3rd edition, 1762), the tops
are shown fully extended. Chippendale described them as follows: "One
hath a Stretching-Rail, and the Feet
are canted and sunk in. The other
hath a Shelf, inclosed with Fretwork.
Sometimes they are inclosed with
Brass Wirework. In the Front is a
Recess for the Knees, &c."

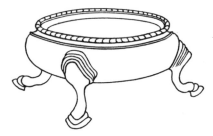

Variations of the cabriole leg were used by silver-smiths as well as cabinet-makers and chair-makers, as exemplified by this early Georgian salt cellar. (*Drawn by Marcelle Barton.*)

hinged brackets, was described by Sheraton as "a kind of breakfast table," and he suggested that it took its name from "the lady who first gave orders for one of them." Then there was the canterbury, a forerunner of the modern trolley table, that was, according to Sheraton, "a supper tray made to stand by a table at supper, with a circular end and three partitions crosswise to hold knives, forks and plates at each end, this made circular on purpose." The name canter-bury was also used for a stand to hold music.

Dining tables, small service tables, and sideboards, were supported on well-formed legs; the cabriole leg after the first half of the eighteenth century giving place to the tapering Marlboro' leg, which was replaced by the turned leg. There were innumerable versions and decorative variations of these basic forms of leg. There was also the claw table, a contemporary term for a tripod table with the supporting pillar resting on three claw feet. The derivation of some of the terms for legs does not always go back very far: for example, the bandy leg, or cabriole leg, which became fashionable at the end of the seventeenth century, was not then known as a cabriole leg: that term became current at the end of the Victorian period. The word cabriole was used for a type of chair introduced during the last decades of the eighteenth century, and an advertisement in the *Bristol Journal*, for a sale at St. James's, London, dated February 22nd, 1783, includes "Drawing room Cabriole Chairs." The trade term Marlboro', used by cabinet-makers for a tapering leg of square section, may have been invented and used as a compliment to George Spencer, the fourth Duke of Marlborough, to whom Ince and Mayhew dedicated *The Universal System of Household Furniture* (*circa* 1762); but that is purely conjectural. Whatever their shape and whatever they were called, the legs that supported tables and chairs in the dining-room had throughout the Georgian Age the admirable proportions and firmness that characterised nearly all forms of English furniture.

As the kitchen was often a long way from the dining-room, a haster was used for keeping plates warm. This was a tall cupboard, usually made of deal and lined with metal, with an open back that was placed against the fire, and the doors in the front shut. It stood about five feet high, was just over two feet in depth, and over three feet in width. A smaller and much simpler device that per-formed a comparable function was the cat, a six-legged stand, really a double tripod, with the legs or spokes radiating from a sphere, though other shapes

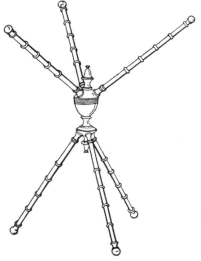

This small, six-legged brass stand for keeping plates warm by a fire, was called a "cat." The legs or spokes radiated from a central sphere; in this example from an urn. How ever the stand is placed it always rests upon three legs. Cats were sometimes made of mahogany, ebony, or other woods, and the term appears to date from the late eighteenth or early nineteenth century. (*Drawn by Marcelle Barton from a photograph of an example, formerly in the collection of the late Sir Albert Richardson, P.P.R.A.*)

sometimes formed the central feature into which the spokes were socketed: an urn is used in the example shown on this page. These stands were made in brass or various woods such as mahogany or ebony, and the fanciful name, which appears to have originated in the late eighteenth century, is suggested by the ability of the stand, however placed, always to land on its feet, like a cat. The cat was specifically designed for holding plates; the trivet, a much older appliance, could support kettles or larger vessels. The flat, pierced metal top of the trivet was fitted with a turned wooden handle; and it rested on three metal legs, which occasionally reproduced the cabriole form. The cat and the trivet were used in the parlour and the bedroom as well as the dining-room.

In an age when wine was thoroughly appreciated, one of the most significant articles was the cellaret, which was really a miniature cellar, lined with lead, and designed to contain a small store of wine. It was a free-standing piece of furniture, though the term was also used to describe the deep drawer of the fitted sideboard. Wine keeper, or *garde de vin* were alternative names. The term cellaret, according to Sheraton in *The Cabinet Dictionary*, "denotes a convenience for wine, or a wine cistern. A cellaret sideboard, denotes that it has a place at one end, in which to hold bottles of wine, and at the other sometimes a plain drawer for plate, and sometimes lined with lead, to wash glasses in." These cellaret drawers were made to hold nine bottles, or a dozen in very large sideboards. Wine cisterns or wine coolers were introduced during the seventeen-thirties, and were usually oval in shape, resting upon four legs or a solid moulded base; mahogany, richly embellished with carved ornamentation, was generally used, though massive examples in silver and marble have survived. Another term that Sheraton used for the wine cooler and the cellaret was sarcophagus, which, as he pointed out in *The Cabinet Dictionary*, "is, in some faint degree, an imitation of the figure of these ancient stone coffins, on which account only the term can with any colour of propriety be applied to such wine cisterns. They are adapted to stand under a sideboard, some of which have covers, and others without. . . ."

After dinner, when the ladies had withdrawn, and the glasses were darkly reflected in the mahogany, the bottles and decanters began their circuit—"a continuous circuit of the table," according to François de la Rochefoucauld, "for the host takes note that everyone is drinking in turn."[78] To facilitate this rapid passage of the wine, a round tray for use on the table, with baize on the underside, was introduced about the middle of the eighteenth century, which was called a coaster—the name is contemporary—so there was no delay when the host cried: "buzz the bottle." Coasters, also called sliders, were made of wood, though sometimes of silver or Sheffield plate. (See plate 34.) There were also cheese coasters, which were curved, shallow wooden trays, and beer coasters or beer wagons, which were trolleys wheeled along the floor, much heavier and larger than the wine coasters for use on the table. A similar type of wagon, with legs mounted on castors, and partitions on the top for bottles and decanters, was called a wine waiter.

Though not used in the dining-room, there were special types of furniture that were made to alleviate the sufferings of those who had spent too much of their time in that apartment. Of these the gouty or gout stool is the best known. It had an adjustable seat, and in Hepplewhite's *Guide*, where an example is illustrated, its comfort was delicately commended, as a device that "by being so easily raised or lowered at either hand, is particularly useful to the afflicted." Even when the afflicted received the medicines ordered by his physician—who

A gouty or gout stool, from plate 15 of Hepplewhite's *Cabinet Maker and Upholsterer's Guide* (1788).

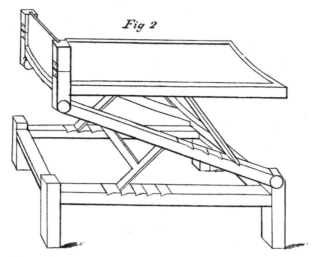

Fig 2

Another form of gouty or gout stool, which could very easily be raised or lowered, to increase the comfort or at least to diminish the pain of the sufferer. (From *The Prices of Cabinet Work*, 1797 edition.)

might be and often was an unqualified quack—the labels on the bottles and packets and boxes were as well designed as the furniture and glass and silver in the room where the trouble had originated.

The extent of the troubles that began in the dining-room may be judged from the advertisements for remedies and cures that appeared in contemporary newspapers. The following example is from *The Whitehall Evening-Post*; *or*, *London Intelligencer* for August 21st to 24th, 1756:—

"*The So-much Famed* HYPO DROPS

"WHICH in a few Days infallibly cure HYPOCHONDRIAK MELAN-CHOLY in Men, and the VAPOURS in WOMEN, so as never to return again be they ever so severe, or of many Years standing, and even after all other Remedies have proved ineffectual; and that by immediately striking at the very Root or true Cause, as well as remedying the Effects of those perplexing Maladies and all their Variety of Symptoms, by which they mimick by Turns, almost all the Diseases poor Mortals are afflicted with, and have their Rise from a depraved Appetite, vicious Ferments in the Stomach, and Indigestion of Food, whence proceed Crudities and flatulent or windy Disorders. . . ."

The distressing symptoms were then described with such a wealth of ana-tomical details that sufferers from "Giddiness, Dimness of Sight, Frights, groundless Fears, and the deepest Melancholy, with direful Views, and terrible Apprehensions" must have been comforted by the reflection that their troubles

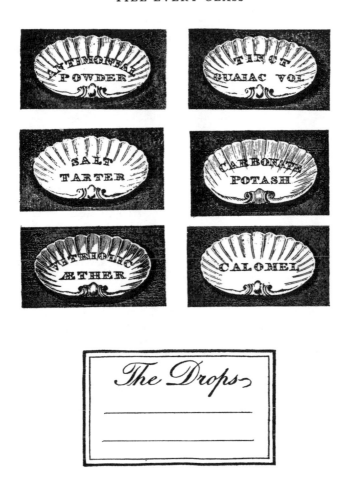

Remedies arrived with elegantly lettered directions and descriptions. Apothecaries' labels retained their Georgian standards of design during the first half of the nineteenth century. (See page 167 and plate 3.)

arose from a multiplicity of internal derangements and not from mere self-indulgence. Such complaints are obviously the components of a gargantuan hang-over, and their collective effect must have kept up the sales of "these so much famed and most pleasant Drops." They were alleged to be "chymically prepared from the most valuable Specificks in the Mineral, Vegetable and Animal Kingdoms, and exalted to the highest Perfection possible. . . ." No commercial modesty, indeed no modesty of any kind, qualified or diminished the sweeping claims made by the advertiser of Hypo Drops. "Promise—large promise—is the soul of an advertisement," wrote Dr. Johnson. No wonder, when newspapers were larded with announcements of the sort just quoted. (See appendices 9 and 10.) The advertisement for Hypo Drops, which is typical, suggests the real nature of the vapours, the complaint that afflicted so many Georgian ladies, for it was asserted that after quelling the symptoms and annihilating their cause, the drops would bring the stomach into right order, create a good appetite, rectify the digestion and by "occasioning a laudable Chyle, and of Course, good Blood, Plenty of calm, free, and chearful Spirits, a regular Circulation of all the Fluids and Strength of Nerves," remove "both the Cause and Effect of Melancholy and Vapours. . . ."

The drops were not, by modern standards, expensive; but we have no means of knowing the exact size of the bottle or the amount of the contents. Purchasers were assured that "whoever takes them for three Days only, will be sensible they are absolutely to be depended upon for an effectual and lasting Cure, and certain it is that no Medicine on Earth can equal them; be careful therefore to have the right Drops, which are now again to be had only of Mrs. Holt, at Mr. Tatsham's at the Cross-Keys and Star in Princes-street, facing the Mansion-House, London, at Three Shillings and Sixpence a Bottle, with printed Directions and Advice at large."

That staid philanthropist, Jonas Hanway (1712–1786), who regarded pleasure with suspicion and indulgence with horror, admitted that he had "heard it remarked, that the longest livers have generally had good appetites," though he diluted the admission by three questions. "But how many die early by INDULGING their appetite, in eating and drinking too much of improper kinds? How many hurt the faculties of the mind? In a word, how many live and die miserably, when, by the power of temperance and moderation, they might enjoy a continual feast in life, and death?"[79]

Temperance was still identified with civilised moderation in the mid eighteenth century, though in Bailey's *Universal Etymological English Dictionary*, temperance "with Divines" denoted "a Virtue that consists in Abstinence from sensual Pleasures, which renders the Body tame and governable, and so service-able to the Soul, and also chearful in the Exercise of Religion. . . ."[80] That definition foreshadowed the coming of the fanatical teetotaller, who was to appropriate that good word for his own narrow, puritanical use, so that it came in time to denote the dismal extreme of total abstinence. "To set the mind

A group of decorative labels used by apothecaries and confectioners: the influence of contemporary architectural design is apparent. (See also the labels on plate 3.)

above the appetites is the end of abstinence," wrote Dr. Johnson; "which one of the fathers observes to be, not a virtue, but the *ground-work of a virtue*. By forebearing to do what may innocently be done, we may add hourly new vigour to resolution, and secure the power of resistance when pleasure or interest shall lend their charms to guilt."

The Georgian moralists were certainly not responsible for debasing the word temperance: the Victorians were, and they consistently misused it.

In the collection of moral essays and reflections that was published by Steele early in the eighteenth century under the title of *The Ladies Library*, excessive drinking was described as a "beastly vice" and one that was "detestable in all, but prodigious in Women; who put a double Violence on their Nature, the one in the Intemperance, the other in the Immodesty: and tho' they may take the immediate Copy from Men, yet to the Praise of their Proficiency, they outdo their Exemplar, and draw nearer the Original: nothing humane being so much a Beast as a drunken Woman. . . . She who is first a Prostitute to Wine will soon be to Lust also; she has dismist her Guards, discarded all the Suggestions of Reason as well as Religion, and is at the Mercy of any, of every Assailant: And when we consider how much fuller the World is of *Ammons* than of *Josephs*, it will not be hard to guess the Fate of that Woman's Chastity, which has no other Bottom than that of Men's."[81]

Works on morality were popular, and *The Ladies Library* which first appeared in 1714 had reached its fifth edition by 1739. The more light-hearted *Fables for the Female Sex*, published in 1744, conveyed advice and reproof in rhyme and relied less upon the moral enormity of indulgence than upon the social disasters it begot. The fable of "The Owl, and the Nightingale" begins by condemning, as comparable vices, secret drinking and excessive reading; both considered improper, or at least unfashionable, in gentlewomen of breeding.

> "To know the mistress' humour right,
> See if her maids are clean, and tight;
> If Betty waits without her stays,
> She copies but her lady's ways.
> When miss comes in with boist'rous shout,
> And drops no curt'sy, going out,
> Depend upon't, mamma is one,
> Who reads, or drinks too much alone.
> If bottled beer her thirst asswage,
> She feels enthusiastic rage,
> And burns with ardour to inherit
> The gifts, and workings of the spirit.
> If learning crack her giddy brains,
> No remedy, but death, remains."[82]

There was every encouragement to over-indulgence. Side by side with advertisements for patent medicines were announcements extolling the cheapness and variety of innumerable liquors, some of doubtful origin and quality. In the issue of the *Whitehall Evening-Post* that carried the advertisement for Hypo Drops was another, printed for The Raisin Wine and Brandy Warehouse, in Catherine Street, in the Strand, which read as follows:—

"Brandy, at 4s. per Gallon, brought to such Perfection by a new Method of making, that it is difficult to be distinguished from Foreign. Two Gallons the least Quantity sold, sent to any Part of London, and taken again if not liked. Geneva, equal in Goodness to Holland's, at 3s. per Gallon."[83]

Even good liquor was cheap. One of the frequent advertisers in *The General Evening Post* was the London Punch-House. Here is a specimen from that newspaper during October 1736:—

"LONDON PUNCH-HOUSE,
"*LUDGATE-HILL.*

"PUNCH Continued to be made (*by* LICENCE, *Pursuant to* ACT OF PARLIA-MENT, *and in all just and exact Observance of the Laws*) to its utmost Perfection.

"*At the following* Prices *and* Proportions, *viz.* A Quart *of* ARRACK *made into* PUNCH for 1os. 8d. and so in Proportion, to half Half a Quartern for 4d.

"*A Quart of* RUM *or* BRANDY *made into* Punch for 8s. and so in Proportion, to half Half a Quartern for 3d.

"All which Brandies, Rum, and Arrack, are Double-Distill'd, and so strong, fine and full flavour'd, as to make so much Sherbert into PUNCH, that I sell it now no dearer than other People did before the Commencement of this Act.

"J. ASHLEY.

"At the CELLARS
"*Under the said* LONDON-PUNCH HOUSE,
"ARE TO BE SOLD,
"*By* BENJAMIN LEE, *and Comp.*

"A large Parcel of curious old Coniac Brandy, Jamaica Rum, and Batavia Arrack, deliver'd at the Cellar-Door.

"Brandy at 7s. 3d. Rum at 6s. 9d. Arrack at 11s. 6d. per Gallon, all choice, genuine, and good as ever were imported, WARRANTED entirely Neat.

"Buy and sell for Ready Money only."[84]

For those who did not wish to dine or sup at home, there were well-appointed inns, many houses of entertainment, and pleasure gardens like Vauxhall and Ranelagh. Nobody minded if some of the visitors to public places were tipsy. William Hickey describes how he attended a masquerade at the Opera House, dressed as a nun, when he was so drunk that he "reeled about, singing, talking sad nonsense, and jostling every person that came in my way, every now and then tumbling and unable to rise until assisted by the bystanders."[85]

Before going off to the masquerade, he had visited his aunt and cousins, and "made a number of complimentary flattering speeches to them, with which they seemed highly gratified, declaring that being tipsy made me vastly agreeable, a pretty broad insinuation that they did not consider me so when sober."[86] These amiable ladies were far from being shocked by his condition. It was his elder sister who provided the costume of the nun, in which he distinguished himself at the masquerade.

One of the Georgian equivalents of the night club was "the Folly" which had been popular long before the beginning of the Georgian period. It was a house-boat, built during the second half of the seventeenth century, that remained moored in the Thames opposite Somerset House, until it became too openly scandalous to be tolerated, even in that lax age. It was visited by Zacharias Conrad Von Uffenbach, in 1710, who described it as follows:—

"In the afternoon, the weather being fine, we took a boat and were rowed up the Thames to see 'London's diversion,' or, as it was written in gold letters on the ship itself: 'Royal diversion'; or, as it is commonly called in English and French, 'Folie.' But the 'Folie' is in reality a great ship, square, like a large and deep barge or ferryboat; it rides at anchor in the middle of the Thames and is used both as a tavern and bawdy-house. Above is a balcony, and, when the weather is fine, it is most agreeable to sit there and enjoy the charming prospect over London and watch the numerous ships that pass. But below inside the ship there is a series of small rooms, where one can sit enclosed by curtains. All manner of wine and beer can be drunk there, but it sells prodigious dear. They play an organ and violin, as in the gaming-houses in Amsterdam. Innumerable harlots are to be found here, and those who would resort to them can take them over into Cupid's garden (of which I shall speak further below) or to any other place."[87]

By Cupid's garden, Von Uffenbach obviously meant Cuper's Garden, on the south bank, opposite Somerset House, a resort that was closed in 1753. He described it in his usual disparaging way, but was wrong about the derivation of the name, for Cuper had been a gardener. "It is obvious," he wrote, "why it is called Cupid's Garden, since countless whores are to be found here and there are disgraceful goings-on. It is, moreover, a wretched garden, but with two fine alleys or walks and two bowling greens. Near it is a tavern, where men drink and find occasion for the devil's own work. From thence we drove to Lambeth to see Lambeth-wells or the medicinal spring there. Near it is a house where they dance on certain days, though it is frequented for the most part only by riff-raff. Judging by its taste, the spring contains alum and iron. From here we drove further along this side of the Thames to Foxhall, where there is a large garden of matchless elegance called the Spring Garden, because it is most agreeable in spring, when vast quantities of birds nest and sing there. It consists entirely of avenues and covered walks where people stroll up and down, and green huts, in which one can get a glass of wine, snuff and other things, although everything is very dear and bad. Generally vast crowds are to be seen here, especially females of doubtful morals, who are dressed as finely as ladies of quality, most of them having a gold watch hung round their neck."[88]

A fictitious and far less jaundiced account of a visit to the gardens at Foxhall —or Vauxhall as it was more generally known—is given by Addison in *The Spectator* for May 20th, 1712. Mr. Spectator went there with his old friend, that benevolent though mildly critical character, Sir Roger de Coverley. "We

This houseboat, which was anchored in the Thames opposite Old Somerset House, was known as the "Folly." It was an eighteenth century equivalent of a night club, but although it began by being fairly respectable, it gradually degenerated until it was little better than a brothel. This is from an engraving made about 1720 by John Kip after a painting by Knyff. The tall windows of the houseboat preserve the proportions of those used in contemporary houses, and classical balustrading was used on the upper deck. The "Folly" was moved to various parts of the Thames during the eighteenth century, but was finally closed down and abandoned after it became too outrageously disorderly.

were now arrived at Spring Garden," he wrote, "which is exquisitely pleasant at this time of the year. When I considered the fragrancy of the walks and bowers, with the choirs of birds that sung upon the trees, and the loose tribe of people that walked under their shades, I could not but look upon the place as a kind of Mahomedan paradise. Sir Roger told me it put him in mind of a little coppice by his house in the country, which his chaplain used to call an aviary of nightingales. 'You must understand,' says the knight, 'there is nothing in the world that pleases a man in love so much as your nightingale. Ah, Mr. Spectator! the many moonlight nights that I have walked by myself and thought on the widow by the music of the nightingale!' He here fetched a deep sigh, and was falling into a fit of musing, when a mask, who came behind him, gave him a gentle tap upon the shoulder, and asked him if he would drink a bottle of mead with her? But the knight being startled at so unexpected a familiarity, and displeased to be interrupted in his thoughts of the widow, told her she was a wanton baggage, and bade her go about her business. We concluded our walk with a glass of Burton ale and a slice of hung beef."

The quality of the company was varied; and, like Von Uffenbach, Sir Roger had something hard to say about it. "As we were going out of the garden, my old friend thinking himself obliged, as a member of the Quorum, to animadvert upon the morals of the place, told the mistress of the house, who sat at the bar, that he should be a better customer to her garden if there were more nightingales and fewer strumpets."

In an account of Vauxhall gardens, published in 1761, they are described as "a place of genteel entertainment, during the spring and summer seasons." The writer claimed that "They were the first of the kind perhaps in the world," and then gave some details of the way they were laid out and their various attractions. "In the midst of the garden is a superb orchestre containing a fine organ and a band of music with some of the best voices, and the seats or boxes are disposed to the best advantage with respect to hearing the music. In most of the boxes are pictures painted from the designs of Mr. Hayman, on subjects admirably adapted to the place. But there are in the grand pavilion four pictures of his own hand from the historical plays of Shakespear that are universally admired for the design, colouring and expression. The trees are scattered here with a pleasing confusion. At some distance are several noble vistas of very tall trees, where the spaces between each are filled up with neat hedges, and on the inside are planted flowers and sweet smelling shrubs. Some of these vistas terminate in a view of ruins, and others in a prospect of the adjacent country, and some are adorned with the painted representation of triumphal arches. There are here also several statues, and in particular a good one in marble by Mr. Roubiliac of the late Mr. Handell playing on a lyre in the character of Orpheus. As Ranelagh has its rotunda, so here also is a rotund and ball room, finely illuminated, in which is an orchestre with an organ, where if the evening proves rainy the company may be safely sheltered and entertained. When it grows dark the garden near the orchestre is illuminated, almost in an instant, with about 1500 glass lamps, which glitter among the trees, and render it exceeding light and brilliant. . . ."[89]

The account concluded with the statement that "Every thing is provided in these gardens in the most elegant manner for the company who chuse to sup." Certainly some of the most elegant and fashionable people often chose to sup there.

In a letter to George Montagu, dated June 23rd, 1750, Horace Walpole describes a midsummer night's party at Vauxhall, which brings to life so many people and events that you feel, as you read, that you were one of the party, or at least a privileged observer.

"I shall relate it to you," he wrote, "to show you the manners of the age, which are always as entertaining to a person fifty miles off as to one born an hundred and fifty years after the time." After two centuries his lively sentences restore vividly the atmosphere of his time; and as he had the same quality of confidence in his powers as a woman who knows she is attractive to men, he could never have been troubled by the slightest doubt that he would be read and enjoyed by posterity.

The letter continues: "I had a card from Lady Caroline Petersham to go

A part of Vauxhall Gardens, showing the orchestra. This is from the complete view of the gardens shown on plate 9, which is reproduced from a print published in 1751, by courtesy of the Trustees of the British Museum. On page 176 a supper party is in progress, at a table just in front of the orchestra. The regretful, indeed languishing look on some of the faces is appropriate enough, for the scene is taken from a contemporary engraving that appears at the head of a song entitled "The Adieu to the Spring-Gardens." The words, written in 1735 by Mr. Lockman, are regretfully sentimental: they were set to music by Mr. Boyce. (See page 177.)

with her to Vauxhall. I went accordingly to her house, and found her and the little Ashe, or the pollard Ashe, as they call her; they had just finished their last layer of red, and looked as handsome as crimson could make them. On the cabinet stood a pair of Dresden candlesticks, a present from the virgin hands of Sir John Bland: the branches of each formed a little bower over a cock and hen treading, yes, literally. We issued into the Mall to assemble our company, which was all the town, if we could get it; for just so many had been summoned, except Harry Vane, whom we met by *chance*. We mustered the Duke of Kingston whom Lady Caroline says she has been trying for these seven years; but alas! his beauty is at the fall of the leaf; Lord March, Mr. Whitehed, a pretty Miss Beauclerc, and a very foolish Miss Sparre. These two damsels were trusted by their mothers for the first time of their lives to the matronly conduct of Lady Caroline. As we sailed up the Mall with all our colours flying, Lord Petersham, with his nose and legs twisted to every point of crossness, strode by us on the outside, and repassed again on the return. At the end of the Mall she called to him; he would not answer: she gave a familiar spring, and, between laugh and confusion, ran up to him, 'My Lord, my lord! why you don't see us!' We advanced at a little distance, not a little awkward in expectation how all this would end, for my lord never stirred his hat, or took the least notice of anybody: she said, 'Do you go with us, or are you going anywhere else?'—'I don't go with you, I am going somewhere else'; and away he stalked, as sulky as a ghost that nobody will speak to first. We got into the best order we could, and marched to our barge, with a boat of French horns attending, and little Ashe singing. We paraded some time up the river, and at last debarked at Vauxhall. There, if we had so pleased, we might have had the vivacity of our party increased by a quarrel, for a Mrs Lloyd, who is supposed to be married to Lord Haddington, seeing the two girls following Lady Caroline and Miss Ashe, said aloud, 'Poor girls, I am sorry to see them in such bad company!' Miss Sparre, who desired nothing so much as the fun of seeing a duel—a thing which, though she is fifteen, she has never been so lucky to see—took due pains to make Lord March resent this; but he, who is very lively and agreeable, laughed her out of this charming frolic with a great deal of humour. Here we picked up Lord Granby, arrived very drunk from Jenny's Whim; where, instead of going to old Strafford's catacombs to make honourable love, he had dined with Lady Fitzroy, and left her and eight other women and four other men playing at Brag. He would fain have made over his honourable love upon any terms to poor Miss Beauclerc, who is very modest, and did not know at all what to do with his whispers or his hands. He then addressed himself to the Sparre, who was very well disposed to receive both; but the tide of champagne turned, he hiccupped at the reflection of his marriage, of which he is wondrous sick, and only proposed to the girl to shut themselves up and rail at the world for three weeks. If all the adventures don't conclude as you expect in the beginning of a paragraph, you must not wonder, for I am not making a history, but relating one strictly as it happened, and I think with full entertainment enough to content you. At last, we assembled in our booth, Lady Caroline in the front, with the vizor of her hat erect, and looking gloriously jolly and handsome. She had fetched my brother Orford from the next box, where he was enjoying himself with his *petite partie*, to help us mince chickens. We minced seven chickens into a china dish, which Lady Caroline stewed over a lamp with three pats of butter and a flagon of water, stirring, and rattling, and laughing, and we every minute expecting to have the dish fly about our ears. She had brought Betty, the fruit-girl, with hampers of strawberries and cherries from Rogers's, and made her wait upon us, and then made her sup by us at a little table. The conversation was no less lively than the whole transaction. There was a Mr. O'Brien arrived from Ireland, who would get the Duchess of Manchester from Mr. Hussey, if she were still at liberty. I took up the biggest hautboy in the dish, and said to Lady Caroline, 'Madam, Miss Ashe desires you would eat this O'Brien strawberry'; she replied immediately, 'I won't, you hussey!' You may imagine the laugh this reply occasioned. After the tempest was a little calmed, the Pollard said, 'Now, how anybody would spoil this story that was to repeat it, and say, I won't, you jade!' In short, the whole air of our party was sufficient, as you will easily imagine, to take up the whole attention of the garden; so much so, that from eleven o'clock till half an hour after one we had the whole concourse round our booth: at last, they came into the little gardens of each booth on the sides of ours, till Harry Vane took up a bumper, and drank their healths and was proceeding to treat them with still greater freedom. It was three o'clock before we got home."

There were no restaurants as we know them, with spotless table cloths, thick carpets on the floor, ornate schemes of interior decoration, and ornate dishes on the menu; but there were many good eating houses, like Dolly's Steak-house in Paternoster Row, which Boswell patronised. In his *London Journal* he described a beef-steak house as "a most excellent place to dine at. You come in there to a warm, comfortable, large room, where a number of people are sitting at table. You take whatever place you find empty; call for what you like, which you get well and cleverly dressed. You may either chat or not as you like. Nobody minds you, and you pay very reasonably. My dinner (beef, bread and beer and waiter) was only a shilling."[90] A very different type of eating house was described by Smollett in *Roderick Random*, which was visited by Roderick and Strap when they first took lodgings in London. "About dinner time, our landlord asked us how we proposed to live, to which we answered that we would be directed by him. 'Well then, (says he) there are two ways of eating in this town, for people of your condition; the one more creditable and expensive than the other: the first is, to dine at an eating house frequented by well dressed people only, and the other is called diving, practised by those who are either obliged or inclined to live frugally.' I gave him to understand,

A supper party at Vauxhall Gardens. (Reproduced by courtesy of the Trustees of the British Museum.) See opposite, also page 173.

One of the songs in praise of Vauxhall Gardens. The upper part of the broadsheet from which this is taken, is reproduced on the opposite page. (Reproduced by courtesy of the Trustees of the British Museum.)

177

that provided the last was not infamous, it would suit much better with our circumstances than the other. 'Infamous, (cried he) God forbid, there are many creditable people, and rich people, ay and fine people, that dive every day. I have seen many a pretty gentleman bedaubed all over with lace, dine in that manner, very comfortably for three pence half-penny, and go afterwards to the coffee-house, where he made a figure with the best lords in the land:— But your own eyes shall bear witness. I will go along with you today, and introduce you.' He accordingly carried us to a certain lane, where stopping he bid us observe him, and do as he did, and walking a few paces, dived into a cellar and disappeared in an instant. I followed his example, and descended very successfully, where I found myself in the middle of a cook's shop, almost suffocated with the steams of boiled beef, and surrounded by a company consisting chiefly of hackney coachmen, chair-men, dray-men, and a few footmen out of place, or on board wages; who sat eating shin of beef, tripe, cow heel, or sausages, at separate boards, covered with cloths, which turned my stomach."[91]

The comfortable tavern, whether in town or country, could usually provide private dining-rooms that were as well furnished and commodious as those in a private house. An advertisement in the *Whitehall Evening-Post*, for May 31st to June 3rd, 1760, carries the following advertisement:—

"THE GEORGE INN, the Post-Office, at Brough in Westmorland, in the great Road to Carlisle, lately kept by Thomas Lamb, is now enter'd upon by Joseph Wootton, from London; the House being neatly fitted up with clean Furniture, the Nobility, Gentry, Tradesmen, &c who shall please to honour the said Joseph Wootton with their Commands may depend on his utmost Endeavours to make their Entertainment in every Respect as agreeable to them as possible, and their Favours gratefully acknowledged, by
"Their most obedient humble Servant,

"JOSEPH WOOTTON.

"Neat Four-Wheel Post-Chaises with able Horses."[92]

That phrase "neatly fitted up with clean Furniture" meant, in the eighteenth century, that everything was not only neat and tidy and well made, but of good design: unpretentious, but shapely chairs and tables in the dining-rooms, made in the woods of the countryside, fashionable in form without ornamental frills; sound pewter vessels, and serviceable glass. The good innkeeper welcomed guests, and liked them to feel at home, but was often a stickler for social distinctions. Respect for the nobility and gentry and a desire for their patronage might easily degenerate into habitual obsequiousness, accompanied by snobbish discrimination. An example of the results, from the traveller's point of view, is given by the Hon. John Byng (who was later the fifth Viscount Torrington), during one of his tours to Wales and the West Country in 1784. After passing through the town of Chipping Norton he arrived at Chapel-House, formerly an inconsiderable inn, "but now, by the fashion of the Shrewsbury road; is become grand, and offensive; and is enlarging into a small town: what cou'd tempt me to stop where none but fine people and chaises & 4 resort, and where I was ill serv'd, and ill attended?"(93)

The phrasing of Joseph Wootton's announcement for the George Inn at Brough might be tinctured with servility; but it was the normal language of the Georgian tradesman, and when he said that those who honoured him with their commands "may depend on his utmost Endeavours to make their Entertainment in every Respect as agreeable to them as possible" he meant what he said, for "promise—large promise," was *not* the soul of this advertisement. It expressed a modest intention; and patrons could be sure that nothing within the house would offend the eye. Of that immunity they could be certain whenever and wherever they filled a glass or enjoyed a meal—at home, at a tavern, or in a booth in Vauxhall, and for the very good reason that every article used in the service of eating and drinking was, as Chippendale said about the plates in *The Gentleman and Cabinet Maker's Director*, "calculated to improve and refine the present Taste, and suited to the Fancy and Circumstances of Persons in all Degrees of Life."

A commode table from Chippendale's *Director* (3rd edition), which is
described as having "two doors, which represent drawers and a long drawer
above. The pilasters at the ends must be fixed to the doors and open with
them." The plan showing the serpentine front appears below. Although more
often used in the drawing-room, such pieces of furniture occasionally graced
the dining-room.

CHAPTER II

A DISH OF TEA

WITHIN a hundred years of its introduction to England in the mid seventeenth century, tea became a national beverage, enjoyed alike by the nobility and gentry and their imitators. Its popularity wrought some significant social changes; and its improving effect upon manners and habits was clearly a case of *serendipity*—a word invented by Horace Walpole to denote "accidental sagacity." He explained its fanciful origin in a letter to Sir Horace Mann, dated January 28th, 1754, pointing out that it was easier to understand "by the derivation than by the definition." He proceeded: "I once read a silly fairy tale called 'The Three Princes of Serendip': as their Highnesses travelled, they were always making discoveries by accident and sagacity, of things which they were not in quest of: for instance, one of them discovered that a mule blind of the right eye had travelled the same road lately, because the grass was eaten only on the left side, where it was worse than the right—now do you understand SERENDIPITY? One of the most remarkable instances of this *accidental sagacity* (for you must observe that *no* discovery of a thing you *are* looking for comes under this description) was of my Lord Shaftesbury, who, happening to dine at Lord Chancellor Clarendon's, found out the marriage of the Duke of York and Mrs. Hyde, by the respect with which her mother treated her at table."

It is most unlikely that English people were consciously looking for the changes and improvements in manners that arose from the custom of tea-drinking; nor was anybody abruptly or suddenly conscious that any changes had occurred, for they came about gradually, supplanting former habits, and in the course of two or three generations, altering the times of meals. When tea was first imported in the sixteen-fifties, it was sold by the pound at anything from £6 to £10; and though it did not stay at that level, for nearly half a century its price remained high. According to Jonas Hanway, who wrote his famous essay on tea in the middle of the following century, the price in 1666 was "no less than sixty shillings the pound," and he wrongly attributes its introduction in that year to Lord Arlington and Lord Ossory, "who brought it from Holland. . . ."(94) The expense was offset by the weakness of the beverage, for very little tea went into the pot: it was carefully measured out, and the tea caddy was kept under lock and key. In the early days of tea-drinking, the cost may have encouraged some people to excuse their indulgence in such a luxury by claiming that it had medicinal properties. On returning home one summer's day, Pepys found his wife "making of tea; a drink which Mr. Pelling, the Potticary, tells her is good for her cold and defluxions." (*Diary*, June 28th, 1667.) Seven years before that he recorded how he had tasted his first "cup of tee. . . ." (September 28th, 1660.)

Coffee and chocolate were introduced about the same time as tea, and all three drinks were sold in the coffee-houses that were established in every part of London in the second half of the seventeenth century. During that period the times of meals began to be changed to accommodate the new form of taste for these mild, exotic beverages. Until then dinner had been the principal meal, and was usually served about midday; but the custom of drinking tea, coffee and chocolate encouraged people to dine later, so dinner was advanced farther and farther into the afternoon, as a light breakfast with chocolate or coffee, taken about nine or ten o'clock in the morning, became increasingly fashionable. These gentle drinks created fresh social habits; and tea-drinking became an agreeable ceremony, conducted largely by women—an occasion for conversation when men and their views took second place. There were sporadic rebellions against the refined tyranny of the tea table; hearty sensualists like William Hickey might now and then dismiss tea and coffee as "slip slops," but, like other gentlemen, he usually partook of one or the other in the drawing-room. The hospitality Hickey enjoyed at the house of his wise and kind friend Mr. Smith of Battersea has been mentioned earlier, and he describes how "after a liberal quantity of the best port and madeira, which followed an excellent dinner" his host and his guests "adjourned to the billiard table, or Bowling Green, according to weather or the season of the year. From either of those amusements they went to the drawing-room, where tea and coffee being served, music filled up the space till ten, at which hour supper was served, and at eleven every body retired to their homes, or if his guests for the night, to their chambers, where every comfort awaited them."[95] As Hickey himself reflected, this sober and enjoyable evening was vastly different from those he usually spent, "in theatres, taverns, and brothels, amidst abandoned profligates of both sexes, and in every species of folly and intemperance. . . ."

It seems astonishing that tea-drinking could ever be reprobated as a harmful indulgence; but William Cobbett's savage attacks in his *Cottage Economy* were anticipated some sixty-six years earlier by an eccentric philanthropist, Jonas Hanway (1712–86), whose character combined, in about equal proportions, reforming zeal, practical common sense, and crankiness. Many of his ideas would have been dismissed by his contemporaries as "absolute crinkum-crankum," to use a phrase of the time; but he was a man of great moral integrity, though deficient in humour. It is a tribute to his common sense that he was the first man to use an umbrella in London, though such sagacity probably contributed to his reputation for variegated eccentricity. His essay on tea appeared as an addition to *A Journal of Eight Days Journey from Portsmouth to Kingston upon Thames*, and was issued in 1756. This essay took the form of a series of twenty-five letters "addressed to two ladies," and after reading them it is easy to understand why he lived and died unmarried. In the third letter, he briefly describes the growth of tea-drinking during the first half of the eighteenth century. In 1707 the price was still sixty shillings a pound, and at that time English society was not "so universally LUXURIOUS, nor so vigilant as we are now; at least this was not the pleasure in GENERAL vogue at that time; and if it had always remained sacred to LADIES of quality, it had been HAPPIER for us." What alarmed Hanway was the extension of tea-drinking to all classes; he attacked it with the same vigour and sincerity that inspired Fielding's attacks on gin. "The use of tea descended to the PLEBEIAN order amongst us, about the beginning of this century," he wrote; "but it was not before the year 1715, that we began to buy large quantities of GREEN TEA of the CHINESE, having been till then contented with BOHEA. In 1720, the consumption was so much augmented, that the FRENCH, who had hitherto brought home only raw-silk, porcelain, and silken manufactures from CHINA, began to import considerable quantities of tea into FRANCE; and by establishing the trade of running it into this island, have found their PROFIT in OUR FOLLY ever since. From 1717 to 1726, we imported annually about 700,000 pounds. The quantities run in upon us, however, must have been prodigious, for it was calculated in 1728, that 5,000,000 pounds were imported into EUROPE, of which we were much the greatest consumers. Our own importation increased, insomuch that from 1732 to 1742, I find 1,200,000 pounds annually imported into LONDON; and now the quantity is 3,000,000."[96]

Every letter addressed to those two ladies is freighted with sombre reflections. He begins the fifth on a particularly grave note. "Though habit reconciles US to the use of TEA, as it does TURKS to OPIUM, may we not with great propriety ask these simple questions? Is it not disturbing the operations of nature to drink when neither thirst nor heat provokes? Do we not often drink tea when we have already drank too great a quantity of water, or other diluting liquors? Would not COLD liquids sometimes relieve nature better than HOT? —The polite question is, 'have you drank your tea?' It is supposed that EVERY BODY drinks tea EVERY evening, and EVERY morning. Will the sons and daughters of this happy isle, this reputed abode of sense and liberty, for ever submit to the bondage of so tyrannical a custom? Must the young and old, and middle aged, the sickly and the strong, in warm weather and cold, in moist and dry, with one common consent, employ so many precious hours, and RISK their health in so LOW a gratification as DRINKING TEA? Must we be bred up from generation to generation to this unnecessary and absurd expence; and by creating a want which nature does not make, become unhappy, if it is not regularly supplied?"

Four designs for tea-chests, from Chippendale's *Director* (3rd edition).   Brass or silver is
specified for the ornament.

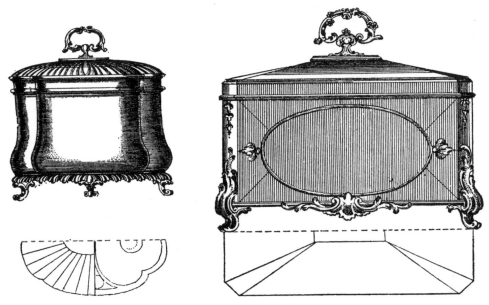

Two designs for tea-chests, from Chippendale's *Director* (3rd edition).   See opposite page.

This brings him to a conclusion that was calculated to alarm his readers. "I am not YOUNG," he wrote, "but methinks there is not quite so much beauty in this land as there was. Your very chamber maids have lost their bloom by SIPPING tea; even the agitations of the passions at CARDS are hardly so great enemies to beauty."[97]

The moral earnestness of the Victorian period is anticipated in Hanway's words and the habit of mind they reveal, particularly in his solicitude for the welfare of the young and the lower orders. "Who can behold without sorrow and indignation, young persons sipping tea and sugar, late in the evening, perhaps a short hour before their supper? What purpose is this tea to answer? As a NUTRIMENT? It is not a SOLID to NOURISH; it is not a LIQUID to quench thirst, for the sugar makes them thirsty. What is it? An idle custom; an absurd expence; tending to create fantastic desires, and bad habits, which must render us less happy, or more miserable, than we should otherwise be."[98]

In the eighth letter he admits that "if the choice tea of CHINA was drank only in small quantities, not hot, nor strong, and confined to the higher orders of the people, it could do no GREAT MISCHIEF. But it is the CURSE of this nation, that the laborer and mechanic will APE the LORD; and therefore I can discover no way of abolishing the use of tea, unless it be done by the irresistible force of EXAMPLE. It is an EPIDEMICAL disease; if any seeds of it remain, it will again engender an universal infection. There is a certain lane near RICHMOND, where BEGGARS are often seen in the summer drinking their tea. You may see it drank in cinder carts; and what is not less absurd, sold out in cups to hay-makers."(99)

He regarded the national popularity of tea with perplexity and dread. The results, he felt, must be disastrous. He honestly believed that "the vast consumption, and injurious effects of tea, seemed to threaten this nation equally with GIN."(100) Personal observation confirmed his theories and intensified his fears. "Look into all the cellars in LONDON," he said; "you will find men or women sipping their tea, in the morning or afternoon, and very often both morning AND afternoon: those will have TEA who have not BREAD. I once took a ramble in ENGLAND for some months, far into the country, attended only by a servant: when I was tired of riding, I walk'd, and often stroll'd, with as much decency as I could, into little huts, to see how the people lived. I still found the same GAME was playing; and MISERY itself had no power to banish TEA, which had frequently introduced that misery. What a wild infatuation! it took its rise from EXAMPLE; by EXAMPLE it is supported; and EXAMPLE only can abolish the use of it. The business depends entirely on the example of ladies of rank in this country. With what countenance can my LADY'S woman, or gentlewoman's chamber-maid, pretend to drink a liquor which her mistress no longer uses?"(101)

Hanway's attack on tea brought Dr. Johnson into action. His defence of "that elegant and popular beverage" showed, as Boswell said, "how very well a man of genius can write upon the slightest subject, when he writes, as the Italians say, *con amore*: I suppose no person ever enjoyed with more relish the infusion of that fragrant leaf than Johnson. The quantities which he drank of it at all hours were so great, that his nerves must have been uncommonly strong not to have been extremely relaxed by such an intemperate use of it. He assured me, that he never felt the least inconvenience from it. . . ." Hanway was furious, and wrote an angry answer to Johnson's review of his Essay. The Doctor "after a full and deliberate pause, made a reply to it; the only instance, I believe," said Boswell, "in the whole course of his life, when he condescended to oppose any thing that was written against him."(102)

Sir Frederic Eden said some harsh things about tea in his monumental history of the labouring classes in England, which was published in 1797 under the title of the *State of the Poor*. "In the South of England," he wrote, "the poorest labourers are habituated to the unvarying meal of dry bread and cheese from week's end to week's end: and in those families, whose finances do not allow them the indulgence of malt liquor, the deleterious produce of China constitutes their most usual and general beverage."(103)

After the doleful conclusions of Hanway, and the restrained condemnation of Eden, Cobbett's invective against tea seems almost hysterical, for that indignant Englishman could seldom resist writing as if he were shouting. He asserted that "tea drinking fills the public house, makes the frequenting of it habitual, corrupts boys as soon as they are able to move from home, and does little else for the girls to whom the gossip of the tea table is no bad preparatory school for the brothel. At the very least, it teaches them idleness. The everlasting dawdling about with the slops of the tea tackle gives them a relish for nothing that requires strength and activity."[104]

Of course, nobody in the age of reason and pleasure and good design took the slightest notice of such admonitions, and what Cobbett contemptuously described as "the tea tackle" had merely created an opportunity for adding a whole new range of graceful and decorative articles to the equipment of every type of home—even the cottage. Silversmiths, manufacturers of porcelain and pottery, and cabinet-makers exercised their inventiveness and trained imagination in the service of this popular social occasion. Tea-sets in silver, and the delicate productions of the porcelain works established at Chelsea, Bow, Worcester and Derby, reflected the infallible taste of the period and the elegance of tea-drinking. Tea-pots, jugs, bowls, cups, and the tea-kettle itself, exhibited by their form and ornamentation the operation of the universal system of design.

The tea-caddy is an example of the fecundity of invention that cabinet-makers could bestow upon articles, large or small. Originally the term *caddy* was used only to describe porcelain jars that were imported from China and used as receptacles for tea; but during the eighteenth century caddies were made from many different materials, including metals, such as silver and copper, and alloys, like pewter and brass. When a caddy was made wholly of metal it was frequently called a tea-canister. The form that was finally evolved was a casket or box, usually of some decorative wood like mahogany or rosewood, so by the middle of the century the term tea-caddy or tea-chest denoted a small chest that could be locked. This was often lined with metal and fitted with special receptacles for tea and sugar.

There were probably a few odd and fanciful variations of the tea-chest, such as that described in *The World*, for March 21st, 1754, in an imaginary account of a visit to Lord Finical, who was "remarkable for having a very elegant library." After a tedious examination of his lordship's literary taste and treasures, tea was ordered. "We now sat down at the table, and my lord, having ordered the tea-water, begged the favour of me to reach out my hand to the window-seat behind me, and give him one of the books, which lay flat one upon another, the backs and leaves alternately. I did so: and endeavouring to take the uppermost, I found that they all clung together. His lordship seeing my surprise, laughed very heartily, saying it was only a tea-chest, and that I was not the first by many whom he had played the same trick upon. On examining it, I found that the upper book opened as a lid, and the hinges and key-hole of the lock were concealed so artfully, as they might easily escape common observation. But it was with great concern that I beheld the backs of these seeming books lettered POPE'S WORKS. Poor Pope! with what indignation would he have swelled, had he lived to see but the mere phantom of his works

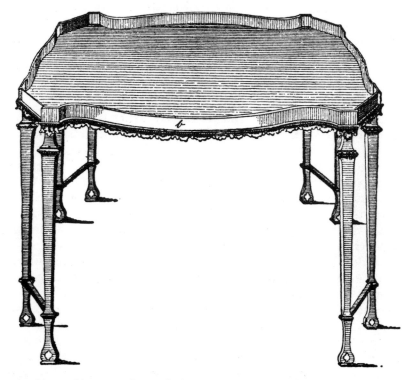

A china table, one of two designs shown on plate LI of Chippendale's
Director (3rd edition, 1762.) They were intended to hold "a Set of China,"
and could "be used as Tea-Tables."

become the vehicle of grocery! His lordship, observing my eyes fixed with attention on the lettering, gave me the reason of it: 'What could I do?' said he, 'the
credit of my library required the presence of the POET; but where to place
him was the difficulty; for my shelves were all full, long before the last publication
of him, and would have lost much of their beauty by any derangement. . . .' "(105)

This piece of fiction is as critical of the deplorable device for storing tea
as of the scholarly pretensions of the nobleman. To employ disguise in place
of design was alien to the taste of the Georgian Age, though it was characteristic
of the Victorian period.

Tea-chests afforded an immense choice of design. In the third edition of
his *Director* (1762), Chippendale illustrates nine examples, and specifies that
"the ornaments should be of brass or silver." Six of these designs are shown
on pages 184 and 185, and they should be compared with the extremely
simple, box-like case for the tea-caddy on plate 24, which reproduces a painting
of an English family at tea, dated about 1720. This case contained two caddies,

and in the picture one of them is being used to measure out tea. This painting includes the principal articles used in tea-drinking, and by that date a special type of tea-table had already been produced, with a top that was not unlike a shallow tea-tray. These tables were often made with a gallery, usually of fretwork surrounding the top, to prevent the cups and saucers from sliding off; they were sometimes called China Tables. Chippendale illustrates two on plate LI of the third edition of his *Director*, and one of them has eight legs, grouped in pairs. They were designed "for holding each a Set of China, and may be used as Tea-Tables." Chippendale added that "Those tables look very well, when rightly executed." The example in plate 24 has a rim, and delicately curved cabriole legs. Behind the maid, who is holding the kettle ready for pouring boiling water into the tea-pot, is a round-topped tripod table which is known as a tea-kettle stand; a contemporary term was "claw table," as it stood on three scrolled or carved claws. Such low mahogany tables usually stood under the tea-table when not in use. A variation of the tea-kettle stand, called an urn stand, was introduced in the mid eighteenth century, and these tables usually had a pull-out slide for holding the tea-pot. In *The Prices of Cabinet Work* (1797), three types of these stands are described—square, oval and serpentine, each with "a slider for the tea pot to stand on."

The word tea left its mark upon the nomenclature of furniture. For example, "tea chest top" was used as a trade term by cabinet-makers in the late eighteenth century for any hinged top with a rim on the underside. Tea was sometimes wrongly associated with an article, and an instance of this is the *teapoy* or *tepoy*, which was a small pillar table or stand with a tripod base. The term was

A tea-kettle stand, with a galleried top, from plate LV of Chippendale's *Director*. Alternative designs are shown for the legs and feet of the tripod.

derived from the Hindu word *tepai*, and not from any connection with tea. Teapoys are not mentioned before the early nineteenth century, when they are referred to and illustrated in George Smith's *Household Furniture* (1808). During the nineteenth century the tray top of the teapoy was replaced by a tea-caddy.

The tea-tray when it was first introduced resembled the top of a tea-table and had a gallery round it, often of fretwork. Tea-trays were sometimes described as "hand tea tables," but usually known as "tea boards." Sheraton defines trays as "boards with rims round them, on which to place glasses, plates, and tea equipage. Hence there are tea trays of various shapes and sizes. Dinner trays, butler's trays, knife trays, and comb trays."[106]

In the opening years of the eighteenth century japanned wood was generally used, and it was not until the middle of the century that ornamental mahogany trays became popular. Designs for tea-trays or voiders were included in the first edition of Chippendale's *Director* (1754), and in the *Universal System of Household Furniture* by Ince and Mayhew; they also appeared in Hepplewhite's *Guide*. The character of the trays illustrated in Hepplewhite's *Guide* justifies the description of "hand tea tables," for in shape and ornamentation they were exactly like the tops of tea-tables, and were inlaid with the delicate intricacies of floral and classical motifs, "the gingerbread, filigraine, and fan-painting," made fashionable by the brothers Adam. Mahogany and satinwood trays had inlays of rosewood, walnut, and such woods as holly, box and willow, which could be stained with various colours; the shape was usually oval, and brass handles were used.

The form of decoration known as japanning seemed most appropriate for tea-trays and tables, for it was an imitation of the Japanese lacquerwork that had been imported by merchant-adventurers during the second half of the seventeenth century. Lacquer- or lacker-work originated in China, where it was developed and practised with great skill. The process consisted of the coating of wooden or papier-mâché surfaces with the prepared sap of lacquer trees. In Japan the technique was imitated, and in time acquired distinctive characteristics. Japanning became a generic term for the process of coating wood or metal surfaces with various varnishes, which were subsequently dried and hardened by heat. A black background was usually employed, but when japanning was imitated in England backgrounds of various colours were used, and a special handicraft flourished during the eighteenth century at Pontypool in Monmouthshire, devoted to decorating with paint and varnish such articles as urns, boxes, candlesticks, and, in particular, tea-trays. This was known as Pontypool japanned ware, and the characteristic groundwork was scarlet, green, yellow, blue, black or white. The surface was heavily varnished to protect the paint, and the varied decoration, swags and garlands and landscapes, was carried out on tin. Thomas Allwood, a native of Northampton, invented the process in the reign of Charles II, and settled in Pontypool; within a

Three claw tables, showing alternative designs for the claws. Usually the tops of such tables were hinged, so that they could stand flat against a wall; and they were sometimes called snap tables, because the top snapped back into place. Snap and claw are contemporary terms. These designs are reproduced from the second edition of *Genteel Household Furniture in the Present Taste*, by the Society of Upholsterers, Cabinet-Makers, etc., which was probably published in 1765. This second edition is undated: the first appeared in 1760.

century Pontypool japanning had become an established handicraft, and abundantly justified Dr. Johnson's view that "the genius of the English nation is said to appear rather in *improvement* than *invention*."

Papier-mâché was another importation from the East, and was a material made from paper pulp, pressed and moulded into a variety of shapes, and having some of the characteristics of those chemically-produced substances that may be shaped by the application of heat and pressure, which we now call plastics. It was used for frames, and also for boxes and tea-trays, in the latter part of the eighteenth century, probably earlier, as there is a record in 1763 of Peter Babel, "Papier mâché frames and Ornaments maker, near James's Street in Long Acre."[107] The material was lacquered and varnished, embellished with painted decoration, and its extreme lightness, and the fact that unlike wood it was not liable to warp, made it an admirable substance for tea-trays.

Silver and other metals were used extensively; and copper, coated with a thin layer of silver, and known as Sheffield Plate, could give the outward impression of a lavish use of the more precious metal. This process was accidentally discovered in 1742 by a Sheffield workman named Thomas Bolsover, and was developed in that city. Thereafter not only trays, but a considerable number of other articles connected with the serving of tea, and for other purposes, were made of Sheffield Plate.

In addition to the specialised articles and pieces of furniture introduced by tea-drinking, the habit exerted a profound influence upon the furnishing and decoration of the drawing-room; and the frequent happy returns of the Chinese taste, which was always being resurrected for a fresh lease of popularity after being pontifically condemned and officially buried by its critics, were obviously encouraged by a social custom that was a constant reminder of Chinese civilisation. By the middle years of the eighteenth century the drawing-room was in a fair way to being a serious rival to the dining-room, and it became increasingly difficult for polite gentlemen to linger too long over their claret and port. It is true that when they did join the ladies, they might smell strongly of wine, and some might be a little the worse for liquor, but good manners compelled them to display respect for feminine society by adapting their deportment to the greater delicacy and elegance of the apartment where tea and coffee were served under the direction of their hostess. Even Hanway grudgingly admitted that tea-drinking had some virtue as a stimulus to conversation when he wrote: "You have abused the use of this drug in a double capacity; first, by suffering it to become so VULGAR an entertainment; and next, by playing at cards, instead of DISCOURSING over your CUPS, abolishing the PRIMITIVE establishment, and the only GOOD of TEA-DRINKING."[108]

Cards, like tea-drinking, had challenged the skill of furniture-makers, and the card-tables and gaming-tables of the eighteenth century were specially designed for the comfort of those who sat for many hours at play. (Some of the earlier types, with boldly formed cabriole legs, are shown in the Hogarth interiors on plates 27 and 28.) Such tables, and all drawing-room furniture, became increasingly refined in form during the second half of the century. The drawing-room and its contents indicated a change of atmosphere: chairs and other articles grew slimmer, their lines were progressively attenuated, and the burly, almost corpulent, chairs that appear in Hogarth's painting, "Shortly after Marriage" (plate 27), were replaced by the slender types with Marlboro' or turned legs that figure in Hepplewhite's *Guide* and in the furnishing schemes designed by the brothers Adam.

It was a formal age; ladies and gentlemen seriously studied their postures and gestures; and it was only after the dining-room door had closed on the ladies that men lounged about and sat back heavily in their chairs as bottle succeeded bottle, and conversation sank to the levels that Dr. James Fordyce had so eloquently deplored. The difference in manners permitted in the dining-room and expected in the drawing-room is demonstrated by the character of the chairs used in those apartments; and after the middle of the century dining-room chairs were subjected to the process of refinement that had conferred a notable elegance on drawing-room chairs. Such chairs, said Sheraton, "should always be the produce of studied elegance, though it is extremely difficult to attain to any thing really novel." He added this advice: "If those who expect the purest novelty in such compositions would but sit down and make a trial themselves, it would teach them better how to exercise candour when they see designs of this kind." When Sheraton wrote that in *The Cabinet Dictionary* (1803), the appetite for novelty for its own sake was already beginning to blunt appreciation for elegance in design.

Sheraton described the drawing-room as "The Chief apartment of a noble, or genteel house, to which it is usual for company to draw to after dinner, and in which formal visits are paid. In these rooms the most elegant furniture is requisite, as they are for the reception of persons of the highest rank. The proportion of a good drawing-room should be in length, at least, equal to the diagonal of the square of its width, and the height equal to its width." The furniture, he said, would include "sofas, chairs to match, a commode, pier tables, elegant fire-screens, large glasses, figures with lights in their hands, and bronzes with lights on the cap of the chimney piece, or on the pier tables and commodes, and sometimes a mirror with lights fixed at the end of the room, or the side, as may best suit for the reflection or perspective representation of the room, on the surface of the mirror."[109]

These carefully placed mirrors would reflect a company of people whose easy dignity and bearing owed much to the polite interchanges of the tea-table, for tea-drinking was a great formative influence on manners, and brought fresh subtleties and graces to the background of life in the Georgian period. It encouraged feminine ascendancy, and this was not confined to the drawing-room, for the taste for tea was catered for not only by the coffee-houses, but by the better class of tavern, and by such modish resorts as the pleasure gardens

Inside the Rotunda at Ranelagh Gardens. This is part of a general view of the interior, with the company at breakfast, which is shown on plate 9. An exterior view is given on the opposite page. (Reproduced from a print published in 1754, by courtesy of the Trustees of the British Museum.)

The exterior of the Rotunda at Ranelagh Gardens, reproduced from an engraving in
Volume V of *London and its Environs Described* (1766). See plate 9, also opposite page.

of Ranelagh. Those gardens were upstream from Vauxhall, on the Middlesex
bank of the Thames, and a little to the south-east of the Royal Hospital at
Chelsea.

Ranelagh was described as "one of those public places of pleasure which is not
to be equalled in Europe, and is the resort of people of the first quality. Though
its gardens are beautiful, it is more to be admired for the amphitheatre. This is a
circular building, the external diameter is 185 feet, round the whole is an arcade,
and over that a gallery with a balustrade (to admit the company into the upper
boxes) except where the entrances break the continuity. Over this are the windows . . . and it terminates with the roof. The internal diameter is 150 feet, and
the architecture of the inside corresponds with the outside, except that over every
column, between the windows, termini support the roof. In the middle of the
area, where the orchestra was at first designed, is a chimney having four faces.
This makes it warm and comfortable in bad weather. The orchestra fills up the
place of one of the entrances. The entertainment consists of a fine band of music
with an organ, accompanied by the best voices. The regale is tea and coffee."[110]

Horace Walpole preferred Vauxhall. He was present the night after Ranelagh
opened, and recorded the occasion in a letter to Horace Mann (May 26th,

1742). "Two nights ago Ranelagh Gardens were opened at Chelsea; the Prince, Princess, Duke, much nobility, and much mob besides, were there. There is a vast amphitheatre, finely gilt, painted, and illuminated, into which everybody that loves eating, drinking, staring, or crowding, is admitted for twelvepence. The building and disposition of the gardens cost sixteen thousand pounds. Twice a week there are to be ridottos, at guinea tickets, for which you are to have a supper and music. I was there last night, but did not find the joy of it. Vauxhall is a little better: for the garden is pleasanter, and one goes by water."

Some time before the amphitheatre was completed, there was a brisk business in breakfasts, and Horace Walpole had been there. "The building is not finished," he wrote, "but they get great sums by people going to see it and breakfasting in the house: there were yesterday no less than three hundred and eighty persons, at eighteen pence a-piece." (Letter to Horace Mann, April 22nd, 1742.) Contemporary engravings of the Rotunda reveal the classical concinnity of the interior, where the architect has refuted Lord Chesterfield's view that the Tuscan order was coarse and clumsy by using it with an unerring sense of style. (See plate 9.) Two years later Horace Walpole had changed his original preference, and in a letter to the Hon. Henry Seymour Conway he wrote: "every night constantly I go to Ranelagh; which has totally beat Vauxhall." (June 29th, 1744.)

Its effect upon Evelina, the discreet and modest heroine of Fanny Burney's novel, was marked. "Well, my dear Sir, we went to Ranelagh. It is a charming place, and the brilliancy of the lights on my first entrance, made me almost think I was in some enchanted castle, or fairy palace, for all looked like magic to me. The very first person I saw was Lord Orville. I felt so confused!... but he did not see me. After tea, Mrs. Mirvan being tired, Maria and I walked round the room alone."(111)

A little later, Evelina compared the Pantheon with the Rotunda at Ranelagh. "I was extremely struck with the beauty of the building, which greatly surpassed whatever I could have expected or imagined. Yet, it has more the appearance of a chapel than of a place of diversion; and, though I was quite charmed with the magnificence of the room, I felt I could not be as gay and thoughtless there as at Ranelagh, for there is something in it which rather inspired awe and solemnity than mirth and pleasure."(112)

There were many tea gardens in London. William Hickey mentions dining at "Smith's Tea Gardens," before finishing the night at Vauxhall.(113) There were others less ambitious, which were not "the resort of people of the first quality," and of these the Jew's-Harp House, Tavern and Tea Gardens, near Marylebone Fields, was very popular. In his volume of recollections, *A Book for a Rainy Day*, John Thomas Smith, whose best known work is his biography of Joseph Nollekens the sculptor, described the Jew's-Harp House. "It consisted of a large upper room, ascended by an outside staircase, for the accommodation of the company on ball nights; and in this room parties dined. At the south front of these premises was a large semicircular enclosure with boxes for tea and ale-drinkers, guarded by deal-board soldiers between every box, painted in proper colours. In the centre of this opening were tables and seats placed for the smokers. On the eastern side of the house there was a trap-ball ground; the western side served for a Tennis-hall; there were also public and private skittle-grounds."[114]

In the entry for 1771, Smith described the May revels of the milkmaids in London, and the prominence that was given to the tea-urn, presumably as a symbol of the prosperity of those engaged in the milk trade. "The gaiety of the Merry month of May was to me most delightful," he wrote; "my feet, though I knew nothing of the positions, kept pace with those of the blooming milk-maids, who danced round their garlands of massive plate, hired from the silversmiths to the amount of several hundreds of pounds, for the purpose of placing round an obelisk, covered with silk fixed upon a chairman's horse. The most showy flowers of the season were arranged so as to fill up the openings between the dishes, plates, butter-boats, cream-jugs, and tankards. This obelisk was carried by two chairmen in gold-laced hats, six or more handsome milkmaids in pink and blue gowns, drawn through the pocket-holes, for they had one on either side: yellow or scarlet petticoats, neatly quilted, high heeled shoes, mob-caps, with lappets of lace resting on their shoulders; nosegays in their bosoms, and flat Woffington hats, covered with ribands of every colour. But what crowned the whole of the display was, a magnificent silver tea-urn which surmounted the obelisk, the stands of which was profusely decorated with scarlet tulips. A smart, slender fellow of a fiddler, commonly wearing a sky-blue coat, with his hat profusely covered with ribands, attended; and the master of the group was accompanied by a constable to protect the plate from too close a pressure of the crowd, when the maids danced before the doors of his customers."[115]

All classes had taken to tea, and it was enjoyed equally in the drawing-room of the great town house, the modest parlour of the merchant, the farmhouse kitchen, and the inn. Nobody could credit Cobbett's preposterous statement that it was "a weaker kind of laudanum, which enlivens for the moment and deadens afterwards."[116] The articles that were used for making and serving tea show by their consistent excellence of design that the habit had made a great and permanent contribution to the arts and graces of Georgian life.

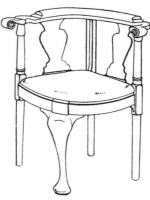

Above: A writing chair, with vase-shaped back splats and a single cabriole leg. (See plate 40.)
(*Drawn by Marcelle Barton.*)

Above: A reading chair, with an adjustable desk and arms for candles. Designed by Thomas Sheraton, and included in his *Cabinet Maker's and Upholsterer's Drawing Book* (1791–93) and *The Cabinet Dictionary* (1803).

Right: A conversation chair, from plate 29 of *The Cabinet Dictionary*. The design was deliberately intended to encourage an inelegant attitude, or, as Sheraton put it, an "idle position."

CHAPTER III

PRAY BE SEATED

FEW articles of furniture depict the manners and habits of people so well as seats. Chairs in particular make the most revealing disclosures about posture and carriage, and the relative esteem in which elegance and comfort are held in any period. The influence of costume is also apparent in chair design, and eighteenth century chair-makers always considered the correct appearance of elaborately clothed men and women when seated: they were as well informed about the manners and deportment of their patrons as they were about the proportions and ornamental details of classical architecture. Men with periwigs and women with tall head-dresses and voluminous skirts, could never for one moment be allowed to seem awkward or ridiculous or uncomfortable, when they conversed over a dish of tea in the drawing-room, sat down to cards, or listened to music.

The peculiarities of English rooms, with their unpredictable currents of cold air, were also considered; and it may not be over fanciful to suggest that the winged easy chair that appeared during the late seventeenth century, was designed partly to protect ladies and gentlemen from draughts, allowing them to be comfortable while providing a graceful framework for their beautifully dressed hair. The side pieces, the wings, or lugs as they were sometimes called, invited one to retire, as it were, into a sheltered place. The back was not vertical; it was slightly inclined. Such chairs were very rightly known as easy chairs, and as such they were described during and after the eighteenth century, though in Hepplewhite's *Guide*, the term "saddle cheek" is used in connection with such a chair, presumably because the cheeks or wings suggested the shape of a saddle. The high-backed, winged easy chair was made throughout the Georgian period, and though its form varied, its basic capacity for comfort was never diminished by any quirk of fashion; moreover, it allowed comfort to be enjoyed while dignity was preserved. For example, in the portrait of Pope by Jervas, reproduced on plate 6, the poet's contemplative attitude suggests that he was very comfortably settled in front of a fire; but he was not lounging, nor in a well-upholstered high-backed chair was there any temptation to sprawl without dignity. Upholstery is a term which includes the padding, stuffing, and covering of seats of all kinds; and the upholsterer, or upholder, as he was formerly called, also made mattresses and draperies for beds and windows. The practice of fixing padding to the seats of chairs originated in the fifteenth century, if not earlier; but it was not until the second half of the seventeenth century that upholstery was seriously developed in relation to the frame of the chair. Before that, chairs had occasionally been covered with material, but the comfort of the seat depended upon an independent cushion: by the beginning of the eighteenth century, seat, back and arm-rests or elbows were stuffed and padded. The winged chair that appears in Pope's portrait has open sides and the padded arms or elbows are a continuation of the wings, curving down and terminating in volutes. The shape of the back and the ample width of the seat were admirably adapted for the broad-skirted coats worn by men. (See opposite page.)

Ladies nearly always sat bolt upright; they were encouraged to do so by their training and their corsets; and their skirts demanded continuous study and careful management when they seated themselves, or arose from a seat. Occasionally both men and women failed in grace. In Hogarth's painting of the "Countess's

An easy chair, described as a saddle cheek chair, in plate 15 of Hepplewhite's *Cabinet Maker and Upholsterer's Guide* (1788).

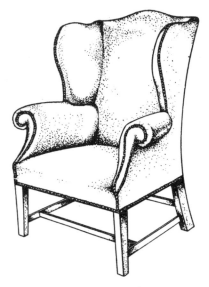 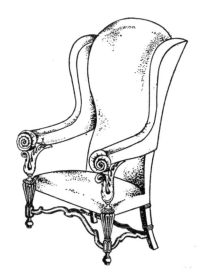

Left: A simple eighteenth century high-backed easy chair with wings. This type persisted throughout the eighteenth century, and should be compared with the example from Hepplewhite's *Guide* on the opposite page. The under-framing is of mahogany. *Right:* A high-backed winged chair with tapering fluted legs, and the arms supported by scrolls with a rising arched stretcher below. This is the chair in which Alexander Pope is seated in the portrait that is reproduced on plate 6. (*Drawn by Marcelle Barton.*)

Dressing Room," in *Marriage à la Mode* (plate 26), the gentleman to whom the Countess is devoting her earnest attention has so far forgotten himself as to put up both feet on the settee, an article that was not adapted for such treatment; and in the scene, "Shortly After Marriage" (plate 27), the dissipated couple lounging and stretching, are obviously battling with the onset of a hangover, which may account for their dejected and graceless postures. In another scene by Hogarth, "The Lady's Last Stake" (plate 28), the lady, despite the emotional tension of the moment when she is being tempted to lose her honour instead of her jewels, is too well trained and rigidly corseted to abandon a dignified attitude in her easy chair.

Chairs were designed to encourage and sustain an erect position; though it is not to be supposed that every well-mannered man or woman kept an arrow-straight back all day long; indeed there is plenty of evidence that they relaxed when not in company, and it is supplied by the day-beds, couches, sofas and settees, and such dual-purpose devices as the duchesse. Horace Walpole writing from an inn at Newmarket to Horace Mann, criticised the furnishing, but admitted that he would have thought it "a paradise" compared with Italian inns. "Now I am relapsed into all the dissatisfied repinement of a true English grumbling voluptuary," he said. "I could find it in my heart to write a *Craftsman* against the Government, because I am not so much at ease as on my own sofa. I could persuade myself that it is my Lord Carteret's fault that I am sitting in a common arm-chair, when I would be lolling in a *péché-mortel*." (October 3rd, 1743.) Even such a correctly elegant gentleman as Horace Walpole could loll, on the appropriate type of seat and in the seclusion of his private house. A *péché-mortel* was a couch, and Chippendale illustrates two alternative designs for them on plate XXXII of the third edition of his *Director* (1762), referring to the French name in his description, and saying that "They are sometimes made to take asunder in the Middle; one Part makes a large Easy-Chair, and the other a stool, and the Feet join in the Middle, which looks badly." (See pages 204 and 205.) In this occasional dual-purpose function, the *péché-mortel* resembled a duchesse, which was a long seat, formed by two tub-backed easy chairs with a stool between them, so that when the chairs were placed at either end of the stool it became a type of day-bed. Such composite chairs and stools were in use during and after the middle years of the eighteenth century, and were probably introduced much earlier. In the will of Celia Fiennes, dated November 6th, 1738, there is a reference to an easy chair on wheels, and two "square stools that have hooks and staples to hang on to the chair as a couch."[117] A duchesse is shown on one of the plates of Hepplewhite's *Guide*. (See opposite.) That the *péché-mortel* was a luxurious type of seat, Thomas Gray suggests in a letter to Edward Bedingfield (Cambridge, December 29th, 1756). "*Frere Thomas* is not so devoted to his books or orisons," he wrote, "as to forget the promise you have made him; & whenever any occasion calls you this way, his *other* Great-Chair holds open its arms to receive you, if not with all the grace, yet with as much good-will, as any Dutchesses quilted Péché-Mortel, or Sofa with a triple gold-fringe."[118] Twelve years later he refers to "Sofas & Péché-mortels" in a letter to the Rev. Norton Nicholls.[119]

Apart from the elbow chairs and side or single chairs which appeared in dining-rooms and drawing-rooms, there were specialised types, designed for reading and writing and conversation. Of these the reading chair was the most complex; for it had broad arms in the form of a yoke, and an adjustable reading desk fitted to the back, flanked by a pair of candle holders. (See page 198.) "The reader," said Sheraton, in *The Cabinet Dictionary*, "places himself with his back to the front of the chair and rests his arms on the top yoke." Such chairs were made from the early eighteenth century onwards, and have sometimes been wrongly described as cock-fighting chairs, on the strength of their appearance in one or two engravings of cock-fights; but that was not a contemporary description. The writing chair usually had a seat placed diagonally, so that one of the corners was in front if the seat was square, but often the seat was fan-shaped with a curved front. Such chairs date from the early decades of the eighteenth century, and were sometimes called corner or angle chairs, and they were extremely comfortable when drawn up at a desk or table. The conversation

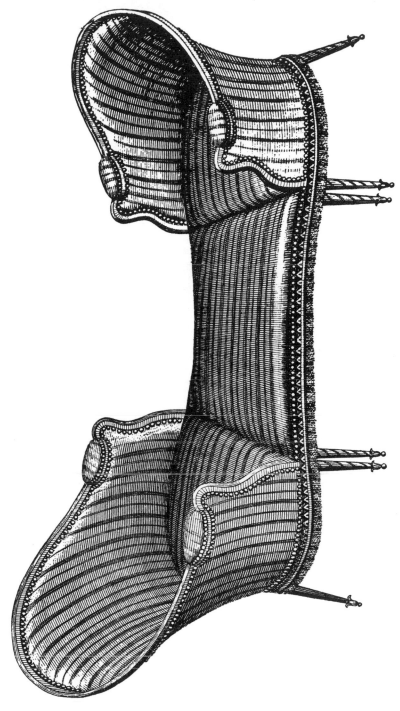

A duchesse consisted of two easy chairs and a stool between them, which could be used either as three separate pieces of furniture, or the chairs could be placed at either end of the stool, to form a bed. This example is from Hepplewhite's *Cabinet Maker and Upholsterer's Guide* (1788).

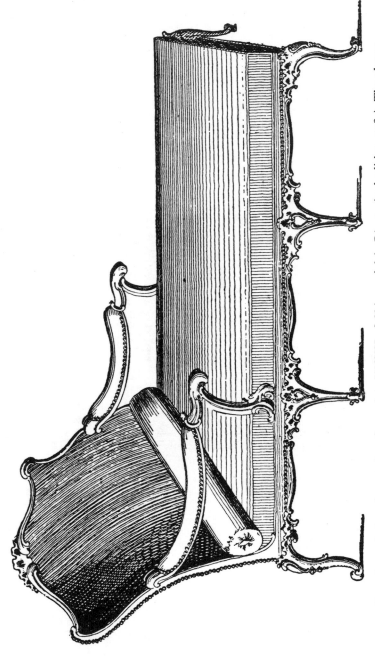

One of two designs for couches, from plate XXXII of Chippendale's *Director* (3rd edition, 1762). The alternative design is shown on the opposite page. Compare these examples with the duchesse from Hepplewhite's *Guide*, reproduced on page 203.

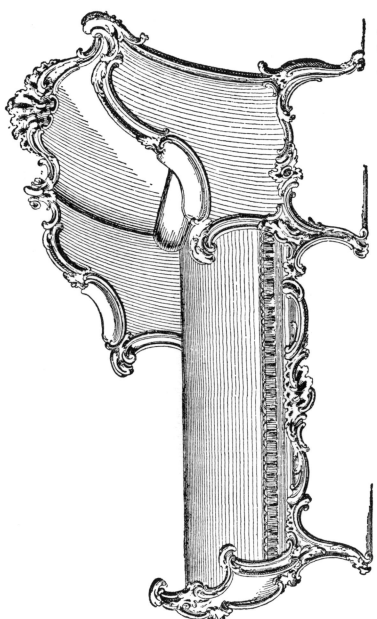

The two examples from Chippendale's *Director*, reproduced above and on the opposite page, were described as "Two designs of Couches, or what the French call *Péché Mortel*. They are sometimes made to take asunder in the Middle; one Part makes a large Easy-Chair, and the other a Stool, and the Feet join in the Middle, which looks badly. Therefore I would recommend their being made, as in these Designs, with a pretty thick Mattrass. The Dimensions are six Feet long in the Clear, and two Feet, six Inches to three Feet broad."

chair was a single chair with a padded top rail, so that a gentleman could sit facing the back, with his arms resting on the rail, the ample skirts of his coats overflowing and remaining uncrushed. Sheraton, permitting himself a comment in *The Cabinet Dictionary*, said that the design was "peculiarly adapted for this kind of idle position, as I venture to call it, which is by no means calculated to excite the best of conversation." The use of such conversation chairs may have indicated a slight decline in the standard of manners. It is difficult to imagine any of the conscientiously upright gentlemen who figure in the tea-table scene on plate 24, or in Hogarth's painting of the Assembly at Wanstead House on plate 25, sprawling across a conversation chair.

During the last couple of centuries chairs, and other articles of furniture, have acquired a variety of fanciful names; some, like the cock-fighting chair, derived from the assumption that they were expressly designed for a particular purpose; others, attributing the credit for their invention to an individual on the strength of a pictorial association, as exemplified by the Hogarth chair mentioned in an earlier chapter. (Page 93.) Comparatively few of such names are contemporary; some indeed are slightly ridiculous when their origin is traced; and of these the Darby and Joan chair has an engaging absurdity. The name has been given to a seat wide enough to hold up to four people, though as the original "old Darby" was dropsical, he may have required an exceptionally broad seat. The name arises from a song called "The Joys of Love Never Forgot," that was first published in the "Poetical Essays" section of *The Gentleman's Magazine* for March, 1735. Two characters in that song have their infirmities described with the same sort of frankness that Hogarth used when depicting diseased or decrepit people; and this devoted husband and wife have come down to us as symbolic of long-lasting love and admirable devotion.

> "Old Darby with Joan by his side,
>   You've often regarded with wonder,
>   He's dropsical, she is sore-eyed,
>   Yet they're ever uneasy asunder . . . ."[120]

Another type of seat associated with affectionate devotion was the love seat or courting chair; much narrower than the Darby and Joan chair, and deliberately designed to compel two people to sit very close together. It would be agreeably apposite if the name had a Carolean origin; but although small settees and double chairs were used during the second half of the seventeenth century, the wide-seated chair, or half-settee, did not appear until the early Georgian period, and there are no contemporary references either to love seat or courting chair.

Chairs in common, everyday use, that were neither easy chairs nor designed to perform some special function—the arm chairs and single or side chairs— illustrated the rise, triumphant establishment, and gradual decline of elegance.

An elbow chair with a "bended back," scroll-over arms, cabriole legs, and claw-and-ball feet: an example of early Georgian design, when "the whole chair became a composition of complementary curves." (See page 99.)

From the Puritans, the chair-makers of the Restoration had inherited a tradition of rigidity, which they sought to modify with an abundance of voluptuous ornament and the use of richly decorative fabrics; but although tubby amorini might disport themselves amid fruit and flowers and coiling acanthus leaves on the cresting of backs and on arched stretchers, the basic angularity of the high-backed chairs and settees of Charles II's reign was only disguised. There was no fundamental change of structural character: it was as though an austere man had been clothed in extravagant and costly garments while his bearing and general attitude to life remained unaltered and were incongruously apparent despite his external finery. It was not until the end of the seventeenth century that a new curvilinear conception of chair design melted away the last traces of Puritan severity; and instead of the hard lines of the framework being superficially humanised by the convolutions of carved ornament, the whole chair became a composition of complementary curves. This new approach to design was partly attributable to Dutch influence, which began to affect taste during the reign of William and Mary, and it led to the making of chairs that for comfort and beauty of line have seldom been surpassed. Such chairs, usually made in walnut, with their subtly curved backs and cabriole legs, are associated with the Queen Anne period, which is generally stretched a little beyond the reign of that monarch to cover the first two decades of the eighteenth century. Before that period makers were still apparently regarding chairs primarily as stools, with backs and arms fitted to them. The contemporary name for single chairs strongly suggests this, for they were then known as back stools, a term dating from the sixteenth century which survived as late as the seventeen-sixties, when Ince and

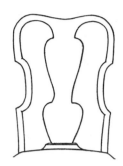

Left: An early Georgian single chair with a fiddle back. A variation of the form is shown above.

Left: An early eighteenth century chair-maker's version of the shapes that were fashionable in London. It is made in beech. Compare this with the chair on the right, which has cabriole legs, shell carving on the knees, and at the junction of the top rail with the back splat. This is an early type, which retains the rather clumsy under-framing.

(*Drawn by Marcelle Barton.*)

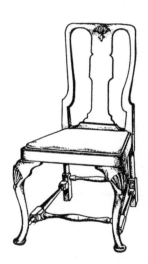

Mayhew and Robert Manwaring all used it for describing single chairs with stuffed backs.[121]

Until the late sixteenth century all chairs were arm chairs, or, as they were sometimes called, "arming chairs." The alternative seat for one person was a stool; and the single chair, without arms, was a comparative rarity until the seventeenth century, when the broad-seated type with the back and seat wholly covered with fabric or leather came into general use, and was known as an upholsterers' chair and sometimes as an imbrauderers' chair. These chairs were made and sold by the dozen, and could be hired from upholsterers for extra

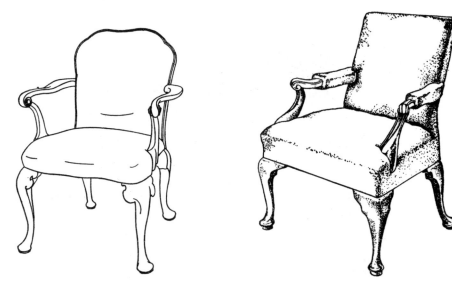

Left: An elbow chair with a stuffed seat and back. An early Georgian type.
Right: An easy chair with open sides, cabriole legs, and a slightly raked
back. Compare this with the design from Chippendale's *Director*, on page
212. (*Drawn by Marcelle Barton.*)

Left: A ladder-back mid eighteenth century chair with scroll carving on
the top rail. Chairs of this type made in mahogany with very simple under-
framing were much in use in the less pretentious town and country houses.
Right: A ladder-back chair with pierced rails sometimes called a fiddle-back,
because the apertures in the rails represented those in the sound holes of a
violin. (*Drawn by Marcelle Barton.*)

Design for a burjair chair, from plate LX of *The Universal System of Household Furniture*, by Ince and Mayhew (1760.) See opposite page.

seating at a dinner party. They provide another example of a fancy name, for they are often described as farthingale chairs, which is not contemporary and, like so many romantic terms, was probably coined by some Victorian writer or furniture dealer who plausibly associated their origin with the need for accommodating the wide fardingale or farthingale worn by fashionable women in the reign of James I.

Sets of side chairs, upholstered in matching material, may have helped to introduce the suite, which consisted of chairs, stools, and couches, sometimes numbering as many as twenty-four pieces. Suites of upholstered chairs had existed in the reign of Elizabeth I, but it was not until the mid seventeenth century that they began to bring into decorative unity all the seats in the salons and drawing-rooms and galleries of the English nobility and gentry. At about the same period, the elbow chair originated, and was probably first introduced to distinguish the arm chair from the single chairs in the dining-room or parlour; and after the Restoration the term begins to appear in inventories. In the second half of the seventeenth century, the contents of the small, unpretentious houses of farmers and superior artisans would occasionally include an elbow chair.[122] The line "He nodded in his Elbow Chair," occurs in *Hans Carvel*, a poem by Matthew Prior (1664–1721). Celia Fiennes, in one of her later journeys (1701–3), describes the house of Mr. Ruths, where one of the bedrooms included "chaires crosstitch, and two stooles of yellow mohaire with crostitch true lover knotts in straps along and a cross, an elbow chaire tentstitch . . ."[123]

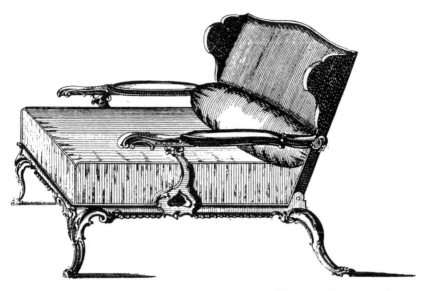

Alternative design for burjair chair, by Ince and Mayhew. These burjairs, as they were called, were the eighteenth century ancestors of the modern bergère chair.

Chair-makers, cabinet-makers and upholsterers used a special nomenclature which described the anatomy of the things they produced; but this body of trade and technical terms was not systematically recorded until Thomas Sheraton published *The Cabinet Dictionary* in 1803, and in that prolix work many of the terms current in the late eighteenth century are unfortunately ignored, for the author may have regarded them as commonplace technicalities, unworthy of mention. Among the obvious terms connected with chairs were arms or elbows, legs, knees, feet, and back, or back rest. Hipping was the term used when a cabriole leg rose above the level of the seat rail. The horizontal members were rails, such as the seat rail and the top rail of the back, and the latter was sometimes enriched with carved decoration, known as cresting, while a shaped, ornamental piece below the seat rail was an apron. The rails that connected the legs of chairs and stools and other seats were stretchers; though as chair design was refined and improved, this form of underframing was discarded. The upright central member of a chair back between the seat and the top rail was a splat or splad, and in the early part of the eighteenth century it often took the form of an elongated vase. For example, the bended-back chair, an early Georgian type, had a vase-shaped splat, gently curved to give comfortable support to the back. Sometimes such chairs were known as fiddle-backed, a contemporary and admirably descriptive term, used when the outer frame of

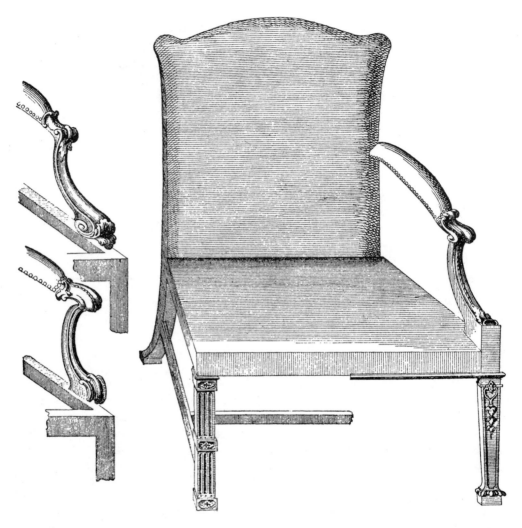

A French chair, from Chippendale's *Director* (3rd edition), showing alternative designs for the arms and legs. "The backs and seats are stuffed and covered with Spanish leather or damask etc. and nailed with brass nails." The term "French" was used to describe not only chairs with upholstered seats and backs, but various kinds of window seats, such as those shown on page 228 and the corner chair on page 229. A bracket foot, used on chests of drawers, which curved outwards, was known as a "French foot," and an example of its use occurs in the chest of drawers on page 242. When the leg of any piece of furniture terminated in an upturned scroll, it was often called a "French scroll foot," as on the chair opposite.

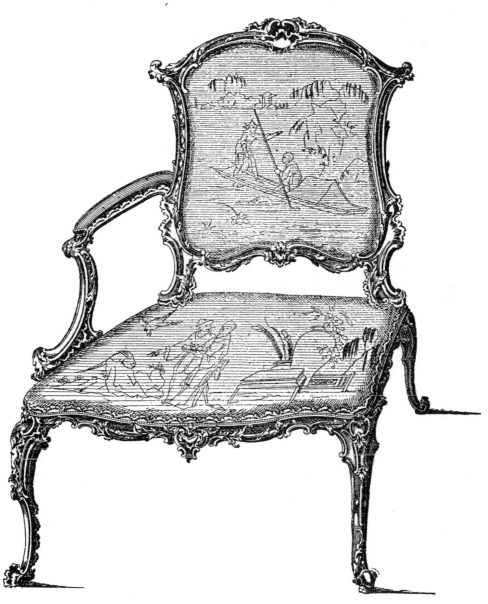

Another type of French chair, from Chippendale's *Director* (3rd edition). This is the type that is open below at the back, which, as Chippendale pointed out, made them "very light, without having a bad effect." He mentioned that "a skilful workman may also design the carving, without any prejudice to the design."

the back curved inwards, producing a waisted effect which resembled the form of a violin, a resemblance that was increased because the spaces between the frame and the splat were shaped like the sound holes. This term fiddle-backed was also used to describe the type of ladder-backed chair which had pierced spaces in the rails or slats, because those piercings again suggested the sound holes of a violin. As its name implies, a ladder-backed chair was formed by horizontal rails between the upright members. (See pages 208 and 209.)

The top rail of a chair-back was sometimes called a yoke, from its resemblance to the yoke used for carrying milk pails; but it may also have been a contemporary name for a cupid's bow cresting. A form of horizontal yoke-back, that is really a curved, continuous arm rail, appears in the reading chair from *The Cabinet Maker's and Upholsterer's Drawing Book*, reproduced on page 198, and this Sheraton describes as the "top yoke." Yoke or yolk-back also denoted a very plain type of cheap chair. Mr. R. W. Symonds has referred to "the retail price of five shillings and sixpence that Chippendale charged for a plain but completed yolk-back chair when he sold a set of eight to Sir Rowland Winn."[124]

A bar back was a shield-shaped open back, with ornamental bars curving upwards from the base of the shield to the top rail. (A bar-back settee from Hepplewhite's *Guide* is shown opposite.) Shield-back chairs were introduced in the latter part of the eighteenth century, and they were also known as camel-back because the convex curve of the top rail in some examples suggested a camel's hump. Within the shield many variations of the splat appeared, in the form of vases and urns and even carved representations of the Prince of Wales's feathers; and occasionally the shield would be filled with gilded canework. (See page 226.)

From the early Georgian period onwards, mahogany was the wood chiefly used by fashionable chair-makers and cabinet-makers; and the first supplies came from Jamaica. Spanish mahogany came from San Domingo. There were several varieties, but the chief source of supply was Jamaica, for the merchants there bought mahogany from Cuba and Honduras and shipped it to England.[125] "The kinds of mahogany employed in chair making," said Sheraton, "ought to be Spanish or Cuba, of a clean straight grain. Wood of this quality will rub bright, and keep cleaner than any Honduras wood."[126]

This strong, ruddy and beautifully marked wood gave chair-makers a superb material, which encouraged their inventive powers. Between the comparatively simple though richly embellished chair forms of the early eighteenth century, and the delicate combinations of carved decoration, gilded cane work, and painted panels, that appeared sixty or seventy years later, there was the great creative period when Chippendale and his contemporaries designed so many variations of the chair.

Chair-makers and cabinet-makers, like all other craftsmen, regulated their designs by earnest and consistent study of the orders of architecture. Thomas

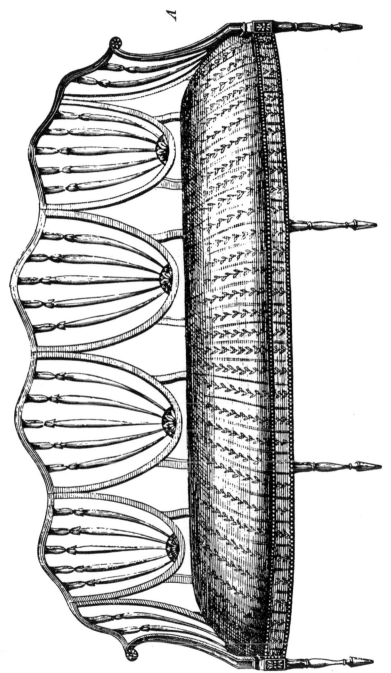

A bar-back settee. (From Hepplewhite's *Cabinet Maker and Upholsterer's Guide*, 1788.)

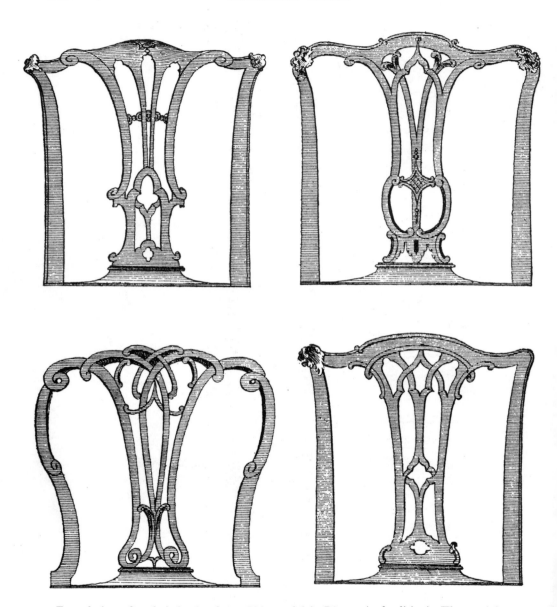

Four designs for chair-backs, from Chippendale's *Director* (3rd edition). These might almost be regarded as basic designs, because they permitted a great number of variations in the ornamental treatment of the pierced splats and the top rail.

Chippendale begins his preface to *The Gentleman and Cabinet Maker's Director* with these words: "Of all the Arts which are either improved or ornamented by Architecture, that of CABINET-MAKING is not only the most useful and ornamental, but capable of receiving as a great assistance from it as any whatever. I have therefore prefixed to the following designs a short explanation of the five orders. Without an acquaintance with this science, and some knowledge of the rules of Perspective, the Cabinet-Maker cannot make the designs of his work intelligible, nor shew, in a little compass, the whole conduct and effect of the piece. These, therefore, ought to be carefully studied by every one who would excel in this branch, since they are the very soul and basis of his art." Robert Manwaring in his preface to *The Cabinet and Chair-Maker's real Friend and Companion* (1765) quoted Chippendale's advice, and also gave examples of the five orders. He began by saying that "The Art of Chair-making, as well as that of Cabinet-making, hath of late Years been brought to great Perfection, notwithstanding which, it will be ever capable of Improvement; and although there have appeared of late several Treatises and Designs for Household Furniture, some of which must be allowed by all Artists, to be of the greatest Utility in assisting their Ideas for composing various Designs; yet upon the whole, the practical Workman has not been much instructed in the Execution of those Designs, which appear before him so very rich and beautiful. The Intent therefore of the following Pages, are to convey to him full and plain Instructions, how he is to begin and finish with Strength and Beauty, all the Designs that are advanced in this Work, by which Circumstances the Author thinks himself sufficiently justified for intitling it, *The Cabinet and Chair-makers' real Friend and Companion*. . ."

Many of the designs for chair-backs in Manwaring's book might have been adapted from Chippendale's *Director*, although in his preface he declared that "they are actually Originals, and not pirated or copied from the Designs and Inventions of others, which of late hath been too much practised."

Chippendale produced certain basic forms of chair back, which allowed an infinitude of variations in the piercing of the splat and the contours and ornamentation of the top rail. The four designs for chair-backs, reproduced on the opposite page from plate XVI of the third edition of the *Director*, and the chairs on pages 220 and 221, exhibit the characteristic framework which Chippendale perfected. Every design he published showed that the style of the chair was determined by the back; for the legs, whether cabriole or tapering, were merely embellished to accord with the type of decoration used on the splat, the uprights, and the top rail. The ribband-back chair, on page 218, from the first edition of the *Director*, has the same basic form of back as the chairs on pages 220 and 221, and three of the designs on page 216; nor did he wholly depart from this form in such exotic examples as his Chinese chairs. Of these he gave nine designs, explaining that they were "very proper for a Lady's Dressing-Room: especially if it is hung with India Paper. They will likewise

A ribband or ribbon back chair, from the first edition of Chippendale's
Director (1754). Despite the intricate character of the splat, the chair-back
has the same basic form as those illustrated on pages 216, 220 and 221.

suit Chinese Temples. They have commonly Cane-Bottoms, with loose cushions; but, if required, may have stuffed Seats, and Brass Nails."

When the cabriole leg was replaced by the tapering, square-sectioned type, legs became less important features of a chair; they were not in such close decorative partnership with the back, nor did they exhibit those complementary curves which made the Queen Anne or early Georgian chair such a boldly harmonious composition. An attenuated form of cabriole leg survived in some types of what were called French chairs, the legs often terminating in a whorl, an upturned scroll that was called a French scroll foot. (See page 213.) The tapering leg of square section, and the tapering turned leg, were used by chairmakers during the second half of the eighteenth century, and in the last decade the Greek revival brought in the swept or sabre leg, derived from classical prototypes, depicted on Greek and Etruscan vases. This was a hollow curved leg of rectangular section, which resembled the curve of a cavalry sabre; and it had much the same complementary relationship to the curves of the back that distinguished Queen Anne chairs. Throughout the Regency the sabre leg gave an elegant lightness to chairs, though, as mentioned in an earlier chapter, that period was the prelude to the downfall of good design. (See pages 134 and 135, also plates 41, 45, and 46.) The refinements of line achieved in the late eighteenth and early nineteenth centuries were consistently illustrated by the slender curves of the arms on elbow chairs, compared with the heavier, scroll-over arms of the early Georgian types. (See page 99.)

Although elbow chair was a term originally used to designate the arm chair in a dining-room set, it was applied also to open-sided arm chairs. Like winged chairs, these arm chairs encouraged an upright and dignified posture; and this is apparent in the portrait of Hayman's client who sits at his ease, a squat, portly figure, in an elbow chair in the artist's studio (see plate 29). Chippendale's designs for French chairs in the *Director* show how a dignified and comfortable compromise had been worked out between the elbow chair and the easy chair.

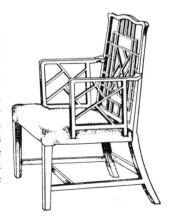

Left: An elbow chair in mahogany, a simplified version of the types in the Gothic taste that were popularised by fashionable chair-makers. The concession to Gothic fantasy appears in the back. *Right:* A mahogany elbow chair in the Chinese taste. Such chairs with variations of Chinese lattice work in the back and sides were illustrated in Chippendale's *Director*. (See pages 222 and 223.)
(*Drawn by Marcelle Barton.*)

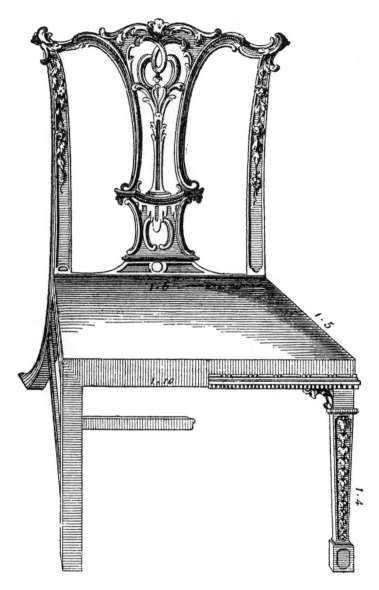

A design for a chair, from Chippendale's *Director* (3rd edition), showing alternative treatments for the leg.

Another chair design, from Chippendale's *Director* (3rd edition), showing the use of cabriole legs and an interlaced back splat.

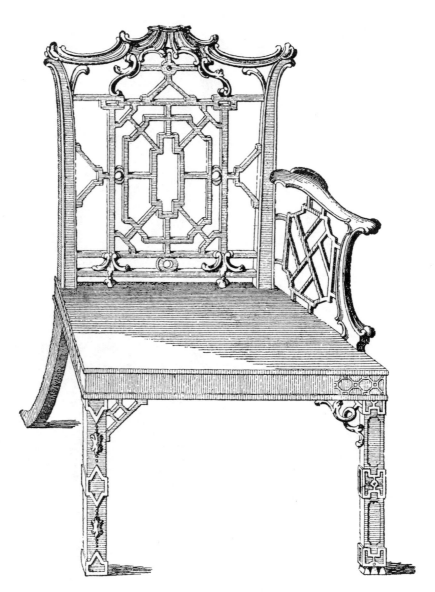

A Chinese chair, showing alternative treatments for the leg, and the type
of arm that would be used. From Chippendale's *Director* (3rd edition).

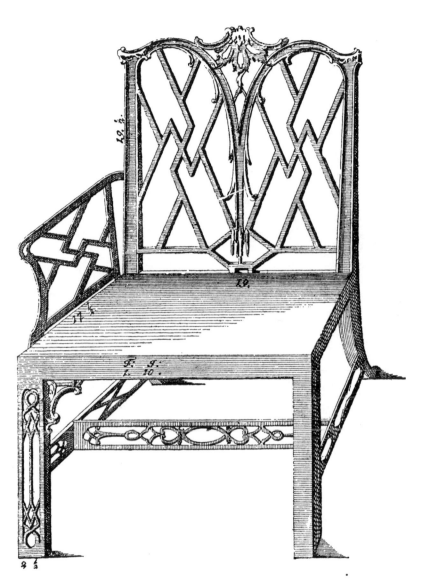

Another design for a Chinese chair, showing the use of open frets in the
leg and stretchers. From Chippendale's *Director* (3rd edition).

Sheraton described, and illustrated, many designs for arm chairs in *The Cabinet Dictionary*, including the tub-backed curricle arm chair whose shape was suggested by the lines of an open carriage (see page 225). For these curricles he claimed "entire originality" and added that they were "well adapted for dining parlours, being of a strong form, easy and conveniently low, affording easier access to a dining table than the common kind."[127] Then there was the bergère chair, which Ince and Mayhew spelt *burjair*, when they illustrated alternative designs in the *Universal System of Household Furniture* (1760). This French name was used originally to describe upholstered arm chairs; but in England it usually denoted an arm chair with an upholstered seat and back, and open sides. The burjairs reproduced on pages 210 and 211 from the *Universal System of Household Furniture* had rudimentary wings. Later the name was identified with an arm chair that had cane-work sides and back; and Sheraton in *The Cabinet Dictionary* describes a bergère as "having a caned back and arms. Sometimes the seats are caned having loose cushions."[128]

There were variations of the chair form, such as the French corner chair which had a broad seat with a back and a curved side, resembling a truncated sofa; and an array of settees, sofas and couches. The terms settee and sofa are almost interchangeable; but generally a settee is a seat with a back and arms, designed to hold two or more people, while a sofa is long enough to allow people to recline. Settees were sometimes little more than a double seat, such as that shown in the reproduction of Hogarth's painting on plate 26; occasionally they were formed from two or more conjoined chair-backs, like the bar-back settee from Hepplewhite's *Guide* shown on page 215. A miniature type of settee, used as a window seat, was known as a French stool. The couch probably evolved from the day bed, and was a long upholstered seat with a back against which the head could rest, sometimes having a side that extended for about half its length. Some types of sofa, such as those with scrolled ends and sabre legs in the Royal Pavilion at Brighton, illustrated on plate 45, were almost identical with couches, and Sheraton in describing what he called a Grecian squab makes it clear—so far as he ever made anything clear—that he regarded sofas and couches as indistinguishable.[129]

Garden chairs were often intended to blend with rural surroundings, and incorporated in their design ornamental renderings of tree trunks and branches, and even fragments of rockeries. Robert Manwaring described them as "rural chairs," claiming that his published designs "for Summerhouses, Gardens and Parks, are entirely new, and are the only ones that ever were published. . . ."[130] Chippendale published a design for a garden chair in which he used stylised representations of gardening implements in the back. (See page 227.) A term sometimes used to describe a rustic seat was forest chair, and it occurs in an advertisement by William Partridge, a cabinet-maker, which includes "Garden Seats, Windsor and Forrest Chairs and Stools, in the modern Gothic, and Chinese Taste. . . ." (*Jackson's Oxford Journal*, July 13th, 1754.)

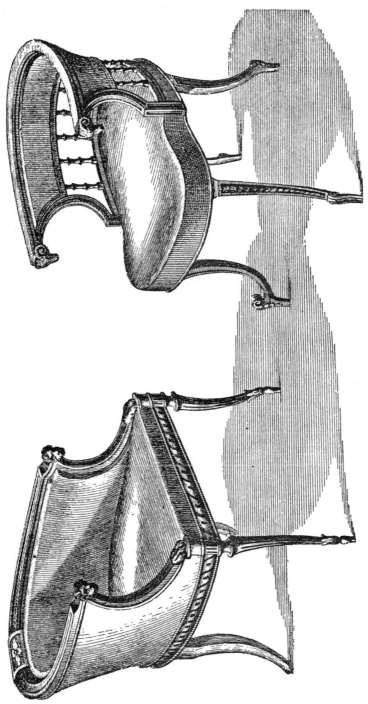

Designs for curricles, from plate 7 of *The Cabinet Dictionary*. (In the text, Sheraton referred to them as appearing on plate 6, but in error his engraver omitted plate 6 and put in two plates both numbered 7.) The lions' masks and paws on the left-hand design show how unimportant such motifs had become, compared with their commanding character in the early Georgian period. The rams' heads in the right-hand design, so often prominent in decoration conceived by the brothers Adam, are here merely vestigial.

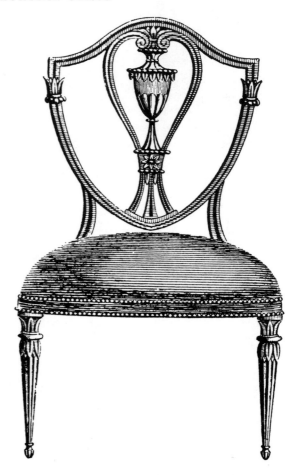

A shield-back chair with a splat
in the form of a vase. (From
Hepplewhite's *Guide*, 2nd edition,
1789.)

These modish and often slightly preposterous experiments in rustic furniture
had no kinship with the work of rural craftsmen, who made their own well-
judged modifications to current fashions, and evolved their own characteristic
types, such as the stick-back Windsor chair. Windsor has now become a generic
name for chairs and seats of stick construction, and Mr Ralph Edwards has
traced it back to 1724. R. W. Symonds quotes a catalogue of the furniture
of Thomas Coke, sold on February 12th, 1728 in the Great Piazza, Covent
Garden. Lot 41 included "Two cane Chairs, a matted Chair, a Windsor Chair,
and a Table. . . .5s."[131] This evidence effectually disposes of the popular
story that George III discovered some stick-back chairs in a cottage in Windsor
where he was sheltering from the rain and, because he found them so comfortable, ordered some to be made for himself, and that thereafter they were
named Windsor in his honour.

It is not known exactly when or where Windsor chairs first originated; but it is probable that various elementary types of chairs in stick construction were developed during the seventeenth century, from the turned or "thrown" chairs which had been made since the Middle Ages. Turning is the craft of shaping wood by using cutting tools upon a rotating surface, the appliance used being called a lathe; and turning had been long-established in England, for drawings of chairs with turned uprights appear in mediaeval manuscripts. Stick construction may have arisen from the experiments of some unknown village craftsman, working with beech spindles. The technique is simple, and consists of socketing turned legs into the underside of a shaped seat of wood—generally elm—and socketing spindles into the top of the seat to form the chair-back, the upper end of the spindles being fitted into a straight or curved rail. There are two main types of Windsor chair: the hoop-backed, with the spindles socketed into a

Left: A Rural Chair, designed for a summer-house. (*Drawn by Marcelle Barton,* from plate 27 of *The Cabinet and Chair-Makers' Real Friend and Companion* (1765) by Robert Manwaring, with the plates engraved by Robert Pranker.) *Right:* A garden seat, from Thomas Chippendale's *Director,* (3rd edition, 1762), which he described as "proper for arbours, or summer-houses."

Window seats which were given the fashionable label of "French stools." (From plate LXI of *The Universal System of Household Furniture*, by Ince and Mayhew, 1760.)

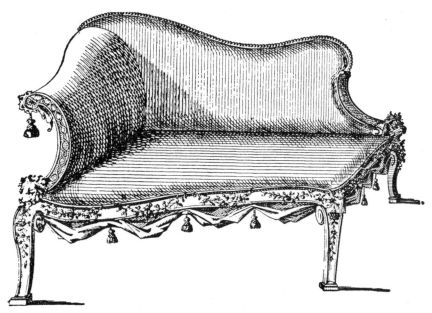

French corner chair. (From plate LVII of *The Universal System of Household Furniture*, by Ince and Mayhew, London, 1760.)

bow, and the comb-back, which has a top rail shaped like a comb. Both types are shown on page 230, and an example of the comb-back with a slender vase splat and cabriole legs appears in Hogarth's drawing of "The Sleeping House-wife," reproduced on plate 33.

During the nineteenth century, the large-scale manufacture of Windsor chairs was established in Buckinghamshire. Legs and spindles were turned by independent craftsmen, called bodgers, who worked in the beech woods that surrounded the market town of Chepping Wycombe, as High Wycombe was formerly called, and were assembled in various workshops in or near the town, which became, and still remains, the centre of a great chair-making industry. The manufacture existed in many other localities, and it seems likely that English Windsor chairs were exported to the American colonies in the opening decades of the eighteenth century, for they were copied there, and American chair-makers gradually formed their own traditions of design, uninfluenced by English developments. In the early years of the nineteenth century the term "White Wycombe" was used for Wycombe or Windsor chairs "in the white," that is unstained and unpolished. They were stacked on farm wagons and travelled through the Midlands and elsewhere, and sold from door to door for a few shillings.

Windsor chairs were to be found in every inn, in every kitchen, in farmhouse

Left: The hoop-back Windsor chair with cabriole legs and a spur stretcher. This type had an infinity of variations, both in England and the American Colonies, where special regional types were evolved by American designers. *Right:* A comb-back Windsor chair with four cabriole legs. This type was commoner in the American Colonies than in England, but English varieties were also developed and the Windsor chair was universally adopted both in town and country houses.
(*Drawn by Ronald Escott.*)

and cottage, and in the luxuriously furnished homes of wealthy people too; for if anything deserved the title of the national chair, it was this characteristically English design, made exclusively from home-grown woods. The elm seat was slightly hollowed to compensate for the absence of a cushion, and to accommodate human contours, and the rake of the back was nicely adjusted to a comfortable sitting position. The bentwood member, the bow, was usually of ash or yew, and the spindles and legs of beech, though yew was occasionally employed. The back splat sometimes took the form of an elongated vase, but was also pierced in a variety of patterns, with wheels or stars or decorative frets like the hoop-back example shown above. Cabriole legs were often used on the more highly finished types, and after the mid eighteenth century the effect of the Gothic taste was marked by the piercing of the splat with cuspings, while the bow of the back sometimes took the form of a pointed arch. The simplest comb-back types are usually classified by the form of the back, and these include stick-back, lath-back, spindle-and-baluster, and Roman spindle, which were made throughout the nineteenth century.[132] In the American colonies the fan-back type was developed, the back spindles fanning out from the seat to the comb-shaped top rail. The first rocking chair was probably a Windsor chair, with the two curved members, called bends, fitted to the feet; and the invention is attributed to Benjamin Franklin, at some unspecified date between 1760 and 1770. Thereafter the rocking chair became an American domestic institution, which still survives in the Middle West.[133]

The Windsor chair is almost the only basic type of furniture that has survived the Industrial Revolution with its design intact and undeformed by the use of mechanical methods. From the earliest days, this branch of chair-making was partly mechanised, so the transition to machine production was easy and obvious. The chair-maker was a highly skilled specialist, generally able, in

A rush-seated, high-backed, country-made chair of the late eighteenth century. The sturdy under-frame resembles that of the elbow chair in the Gothic taste shown on page 219, and any touches of elegance were reserved for the arms and the back.
(*Drawn by Marcelle Barton.*)

Robert Manwaring's words, "to begin and finish with Strength and Beauty" and certainly able to follow, and occasionally to improve, existing fashions in chair design, even when he worked in the comparative isolation of some country town or remote village.

"Chair-making is a branch generally confined to itself," said Sheraton, "as those who professedly work at it, seldom engage to make cabinet furniture. In the country manufactories it is otherwise; yet even these pay some regard to keeping their workmen constantly at the chair, or to the cabinet work. The two branches seem evidently to require different talents in workmen, in order to become proficients. In the chair branch it requires a particular turn in the handling of shapes, to make them agreeable and easy: and the only branch of drawing adapted to assist such, is that of ornaments in general. It is very remarkable, the difference of some chairs of precisely the same pattern, when executed by different chair makers, arising chiefly in the want of taste concerning the beauty of an outline, of which we judge by the eye, more than the rigid rules of geometry. Drawing, in perspective, seems more proper for those who keep to the cabinet branch, which enables them more accurately to judge of a sketch given them to work by, and of the effect of the whole."[134]

Sheraton's reference to the importance of drawing ornaments is suggestive, and it may have a bearing on his complaint that some chair-makers exhibited a want of taste in their rendering of the structural lines of a chair. A preoccupation with ornament certainly led to its excessive use and to a consequent coarsening of detail and the loss of good proportions in chair-making during the first quarter of the nineteenth century; but until the end of the Regency period, most of the Georgian graces were preserved, both in the postures of ladies and gentlemen when seated, and in the lines of the chairs and settees and sofas they used.

Half an hour before Lord Chesterfield died, he was visited by Mr. Dayrolles, and the Earl had sufficient strength to say, in a weak voice: "Give Dayrolles a chair." They were his last words.

Dr. Warren, his physician who was present, said: "His good breeding only quits him with his life."

When Lord Chesterfield died on March 24th, 1773, admiration for good breeding was widely diffused throughout society. The invitation, "pray be seated," still meant that you would be offered a chair that combined elegance with dignity, for appreciation of those qualities in design was one of the Georgian graces that became a man of good breeding.

"Elegance is surely to be desired if it be not gained at the expense of dignity," wrote Dr. Johnson; but a false conception of elegance, arising from an increasingly avid appetite for ornament, led to the sacrifice of dignity in chair design. Only the humble Windsor chair preserved, throughout the nineteenth century, the memory of structural good sense and congruous ornament that had distinguished the great age of English chair-making.

CHAPTER IV

BED AND BEDROOM

F ROM mediaeval times until the middle years of the nineteenth century, fabrics have played a conspicuous part in the design and general character of beds and bedsteads. By the end of the seventeenth century, the bedstead had become little more than a framework for richly decorative materials, brocade, brocatelle, damask, velvet, satin, taffeta, mohair, the fine woollen material known as camlet, or chamlet, and innumerable cotton fabrics, such as chintz. Brocade was also known as brocado, or brocaddo, and according to a contemporary description it was "a stuff of Cloth of Gold, Silver or Silk, raised and enriched with Flowers, Foliages or other Figures."[135] Brocatelle, or brocadella, was a material of cotton or coarse silk, made in imitation of brocade, with a raised design in the warp and a plain weft background. Horace Walpole, writing to Sir Horace Mann, said: "I shall some time hence trouble you for some patterns of brocadella of two or three colours: it is to furnish a round tower that I am adding, with a gallery, to my castle; it is to be a bedchamber entirely hung, bed, and eight armchairs. . . ." (July 7th, 1760.) Damask was described as "fine Silk, Linen, etc., in Flowers or Figures."[136] Chintz, or chints, was sometimes called painted calico. Calico was a generic name for every kind of Oriental cotton cloth, and was sometimes spelt Calicut, which indicates its derivation from that Indian city. All the materials that were "enriched with Flowers, Foliages or other Figures" demonstrated their designers' certitude and fecundity of invention; there were no hesitant experiments, no fumbling search for fresh ideas of form— natural forms and the treasury of classical motifs could inspire an infinity of variations, and colour was used without the nervous frugality of our own century or the dazzling crudity of earlier ages.

The wooden framework of the bedstead—posts, head, and tester—was often covered completely with fabric. A bed was virtually a room within a room; it provided a draught-proof shelter, and when its curtains were drawn at night, it was transformed into a stuffy, compact cabin, with three walls of fabric and one of wood, the head. During the eighteenth century bed curtains were reduced in size; the height of the bed was lowered; the wooden framework reappeared, and its decorative character was reasserted. The tester, or canopy, supported by the head at the back, and by a pair of elegant columns at the

A design for a tent or field bed, from Chippendale's *Director* (3rd edition).

foot, had a frieze and cornice that delicately recalled the proportions of one
or other of the classic orders; so did the columns, albeit in a somewhat
attenuated form. It was in the design of these columns that the Georgian
upholsterers exercised their taste and ingenuity, for upholsterers, and their
dependent craftsmen, the bed-joiners, were as familiar as cabinet-makers and
chair-makers with the orders and their correct proportions: their familiarity
with classical architecture and their skill as craftsmen authorised discreet
liberties. So the bedpost became a decorative feature—slender, but never too
thin; ornamental, but seldom ornate; and exhibiting such a range of delicate
mutations that the bed recovered from the over-dressed appearance it had
acquired during the late seventeenth century when fabrics were used with
opulent extravagance. During the middle years and second half of the eighteenth
century, the bed often afforded an opportunity for a minor exercise in architectural composition; and although its design was influenced by the Chinese
and Gothic taste, and to a lesser extent by the Rococo style, it never became
either uncomfortable or ridiculous in the interests of fashion.

An alternative design for a field bed from Chippendale's *Director* (3rd edition).

Some types, such as tent beds and field beds, demanded a return to an almost complete dependence upon fabrics, their arched or domed canopies being partly or wholly covered with fabric, from which deep valances and curtains hung, almost concealing the framework. (There was a close relationship between the design of valances on beds and those at the head of windows, which concealed the attachment of curtains to the rod.) The terms tent and field appear to have been interchangeable, and Chippendale describes the designs shown on plate XLIX of his *Director* as "Tent, or Field-Beds." Two of the designs from that plate are reproduced above and opposite. Boswell mentions "a handsome tent-bed with green and white check curtains" which "gave a snug yet genteel look to my room, and had a military air which amused my fancy and made me happy."[137] There was certainly nothing military about the designs included in Chippendale's plates, but there were simpler types which could be easily dismantled and packed up for transport; and fifty years later Sheraton called them "camp or field bedsteads," observing that there are a great variety, which we need not to mention, as they have all folding tester laths, either hexagonal or elliptical shaped, and hinged so as to fold close together."[138] Some small travelling variety of tent bed was

A Gothic bed, from Chippendale's *Director* (3rd edition.)

A Chinese bed from Chippendale's *Director* (3rd edition).

Night Table.

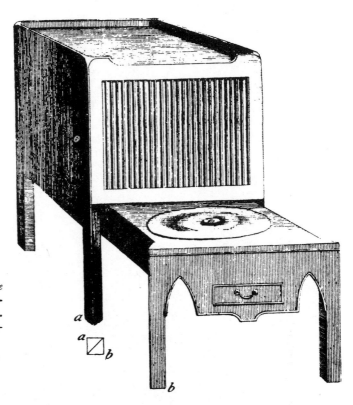

Night table. (From *The Cabinet Maker and Up-holsterer's Guide*, by A. Hepplewhite & Co., London, 1788.)

evidently referred to by Horace Walpole when he described the arrival at Calais of that celebrated beauty, Lady Coventry. "I can't say her genius is equal to her beauty," he wrote: "she every day says some new *sproposito*. She has taken a turn of vast fondness for her lord: Lord Downe met them at Calais, and offered her a tent-bed, for fear of bugs in the inns. 'Oh!' said she, 'I had rather be bit to death, than lie one night from my dear Cov.!'" (Letter to Sir Horace Mann, July 27th, 1752.) Eight years later he described her death. "She lay constantly on a couch, with a pocket-glass in her hand: and when that told her how great the change was, she took to her bed the last fortnight, had no light in her room but the lamp of a tea-kettle, and at last took things in through the curtains of her bed, without suffering them to be undrawn." (Letter to Sir Horace Mann, November 1st, 1760.) Her maiden name had been Maria Gunning, and she was the eldest of two sisters remarkable for their loveliness even in that age of famous beauties. (See appendix 6.)

NIGHT — - BASON STAND

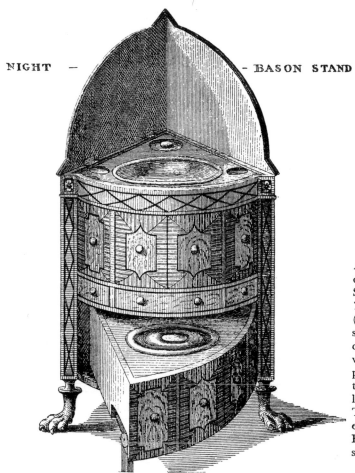

A night bason stand, designed by Thomas Sheraton from plate 12 of *The Cabinet Dictionary* (1803). It is made to stand in a corner, and consists of a night convenience, and the stool part has a hinged foot on the inside which may be let down to support it. This is a much more elaborate design than Hepplewhite's night table shown on the opposite page.

So many types of bed qualified for the description of field or tent; some were almost as impressively monumental as state beds, others had the military air which pleased Boswell, and some acquired names which suggest a military origin. For example, the Marlboro' bed may have been some form of camp or field bed, named after the first Duke of Marlborough, though there is no evidence to confirm this or contemporary illustrations that would reveal its appearance. Possibly the name referred to a bedstead with tapering Marlboro' legs, similar to those used on chairs in the late eighteenth century. (See page 161.) The term occurs in the West Country, and was coined perhaps by some up-holsterer or bed-joiner working in the Wiltshire market town of Marlborough. R. W. Symonds has traced several references to it in advertisements in the

Fig 1

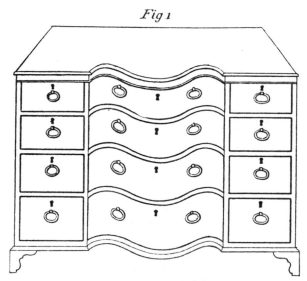

A serpentine-fronted dressing chest with straight wings and bracket feet.
(From *The Prices of Cabinet Work*, 1797 edition.)

Bristol Journal, and one of these, dated September 20th, 1783, offers for sale
"A neat Mahogany Marlboro' Bedstead."

In submitting a design for a state bed "to the Judicious and Candid, for
their Approbation," Chippendale suggested that it embodied "Magnificence,
Proportion, and Harmony."(139) According to Sheraton, the state bed was
"intended for the accommodation of princes and noblemen."(140) But such
designs were certainly not confined to those exalted classes: the state bedroom,
with its towering bed and rich furnishing was to be found in the great houses
of fashionable people. William Whitehead, writing in *The World* in September,
1753, described the excessive elaboration of such an apartment. "The best,
or as my Wife calls it, the state bedchamber," he said, "is furnished in a
manner that has half undone me. The hangings are white sattin, with French
flowers and artificial moss stuck upon it with gum, and interspersed with ten
thousand spangles, beads and shells. The bed stands in an alcove, at the top
of which are painted Cupids strewing flowers and sprinkling perfumes. This
is divided from the room by two twisted pillars, adorned with wreaths of
flowers, and intermixed with shell-work."(141)

This reference to a bed standing within an alcove emphasises the established
harmony between the interior decoration of a room, and the articles that
furnished it: the architect designed such features as alcoves, and often controlled
the work of the upholsterer who supplied the furnishing. Chippendale illustrated
designs for couch beds on plates XLVI and L in the third edition of his *Director*,

Fig 2

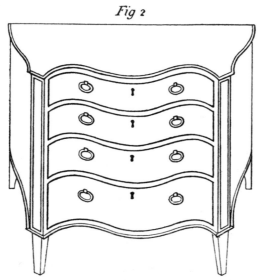

A serpentine dressing chest with ogee ends and taper stump feet. (From *The Prices of Cabinet Work*, 1797 edition.)

both designed for alcoves, one made specifically "for an Alcove in Lord Pembroke's House, at Whitehall." Chippendale described this type of bed as "A couch with a Canopy. The curtains must be made to draw up in Drapery, and to let down, when it is occasionally converted into a Bed. This Sort of Couches is very fit for Alcoves, or such deep Recesses as are often seen in large Apartments. It may also be placed at the End of a long Gallery." Hogarth's painting of the Countess's Dressing Room, in *Marriage à la Mode*, shows a bed standing in an alcove, almost a state bed, with a deep cornice, scrolled at the corners, and a semicircular break in the front acting as a pedestal for the coronet that denotes the rank of the occupants. (See plate 26.) The arched alcove is complementary to the design of the bed.

The canopied bed long remained in fashion, and there were many variations of its form, such as the half-tester, which was sometimes called an "Angel" bed. This type of bed had the canopy bracketed forward from the head, extending partly over the area of the bedstock, which was the old name for the framework that held the mattress and bedclothes. The head and end of a bedstead into which the rails are fixed were often known as a pair of bedstocks. The term half-headed, which frequently occurs in inventories, may have applied both to the half-tester bedstead and to one with a headboard only and no tester. The Angel bed was defined in 1706 as "A sort of open bed, without bedposts," and this definition is included in the sixth edition of *The New World of Words*, by Edward Phillips.[142]

Fig 3

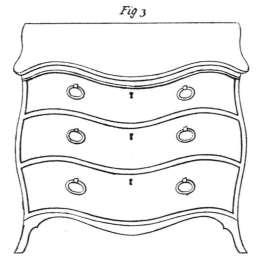

A French commode dressing chest with a serpentine front resting on
French feet. (From *The Prices of Cabinet Work*, 1797 edition.)

Contemporary descriptions of bedroom furnishing often show the extent to
which fabrics were used for decorative effect; and Celia Fiennes gives an
example of this in recording her visit (*circa* 1701–3) to the house of Mr. Rooth
at Epsom where a bedchamber and closet were "hung with very rich tapistry,
the bed crimson damaske lined with white India sattin with gold and crimson
flowers printed, the chaires, one red damaske the other crostitch and tentstitch
very rich, soe round the roome. . . ."[143] Wallpapers did not come into general
use in England until the eighteenth century, and in the seventeen-fifties they
were sufficiently well established to earn an attack from William Whitehead.
"The upper apartments of my house," he complained, "which were before
handsomely wainscoted, are now hung with the richest Chinese and India
paper, where all the powers of fancy are exhausted in a thousand fantastic
figures of birds, beasts, and fishes, which never had existence."[144] Wallpaper
patterns derived much of their decorative character from fabrics. Paper as a
wall covering was not as satisfactory as a textile. Comparatively small pieces
of hand-made paper had to be used, for until the end of the eighteenth century
there was no machinery that could manufacture paper in long strips. The
joining up of innumerable small squares of paper could disrupt the pattern,
as the joints often remained visible.

The bedroom and the dressing-room were occasionally combined in one
large apartment, but generally they were separated. "The lodging-room,"
said Sheraton, "admits of furniture simply necessary, but light in appearance,
and should include such pieces as are necessary for the accidental occasions of

the night. Here should be a small book shelf with such books as should tend to promote our pious resignation of body and soul to the care of the great author of the universe, and divine superintendent of human happiness."[145] It seems incongruous to find such advice tacked on to a recommendation for furnishing; but Sheraton wrote tracts in his spare time, and his suggestion for reading matter would have seemed perfectly appropriate in an age when there was a Bible by nearly every bedside.

Bedroom furnishing included various devices, designed to increase comfort, such as the warming-pan and the bed wagon. The latter consisted of an open wooden framework of four hoops, six lateral slats, braced by four turned spindles, with the space between the inner hoops partly enclosed to form a resting-place for a small charcoal burning-pan. It was a cumbersome appliance, probably used for airing beds and not, like the warming-pan, for taking the chill off linen sheets. Bed steps were often used, as beds were very high above the floor compared with modern beds, and these sets of two or three steps some-times included a cupboard for a chamber-pot or a bidet. Arrangements to cope with "the accidental occasions of the night" were crude, and when any special trouble was taken about their design it excited remark. Horace Walpole, writing to George Montagu on March 27th, 1760, mentioned that he had "breakfasted the day before yesterday at Aelia Laelia Chudleigh's," and observed that "The house is not fine, nor in good taste, but loaded with finery." He gave a detailed list of the articles that offended him, and concluded by saying: "But of all curiosities, are the *conveniences* in every bedchamber: great mahogany projections . . . with the holes, with brass handles, and cocks, &c.—I could not help saying, it was the *loosest* family I ever saw!"

Articles concerned with the toilet, which are the subject of the next chapter, were usually confined to the dressing-room; but chests and tallboys would form part of the bedroom furnishing. In the published works of eighteenth century cabinet-makers and upholsterers the detail and general design of beds and bedroom furniture are clearly shown, although the finely engraved plates often suggest an excessive richness rather than elegance. The absence of perspective, the draughtsman's habit of showing on one plate alternative ways of finishing and decorating an article, so that it appears unsymmetrical, and the occasional crudity of the drawing, militate against a just appreciation of the design. It should be remembered always that Chippendale's *Director*, Hepplewhite's *Guide*, and Shearer's *Designs for Household Furniture* were trades-men's catalogues, primarily intended to suggest ideas to potential customers in the hope that it would lead to an order being placed with an individual or a firm. Sheraton was apparently content to publish designs for other cabinet-makers. Thomas Hope's *Household Furniture and Interior Decoration* (1807) was certainly not a catalogue: it was an illustrated essay on design, a vehicle for conveying its author's ideas about taste to fashionable society, for Hope was not a tradesman. Although contemporary drawings are apt to be misleading, enough original work has survived to show us how, sleeping or waking, the men and women of the Georgian Age were surrounded by furniture of immaculate design.

The bow-fronted and serpentine-fronted chests of drawers of the late eighteenth century, the character of the drawer handles, the mouldings and enrichment, exemplified the operation in detail of the universal system of design, and the affinity with the proportions and ornamentation of the classic orders is discernible. The chest of drawers, which came into general use in the latter part of the seventeenth century, was an excellent labour-saving device, for it facilitated the tidy disposal of household linen and clothes, hitherto stored in deep chests with lids, which gave ample accommodation but could

A bureau-dressing table from Chippendale's *Director* (3rd edition). Chippendale sometimes referred to these as commode bureau tables.

A commode clothes press from Chippendale's *Director* (3rd edition),
showing alternative treatments for the cupboard doors and the bracket feet.
In describing this design, Chippendale states that "the ornament may be
omitted if thought superfluous."

not compare with the convenience of the chest of drawers, or the double chest, that "skyscraper" among pieces of furniture, the tallboy. Tallboy is a contemporary term that appears in the late eighteenth century, and, like its American equivalent, highboy, is most descriptive, and far less clumsy than chest-on-chest, or double chest.

Very often clothes were accommodated in rooms that were specially equipped for hanging dresses or costumes. The word wardrobe, from mediaeval times, was used to denote a special room or closet for clothes, and free-standing cupboards were usually called clothes presses. Chippendale illustrates a form of tallboy on plate CXIII of the *Director* which he describes as "a Chest of Drawers, and a Cloaths-Press, with sliding Shelves." Details are given of the cost and construction of a "Wing Clothes Press" in *The Prices of Cabinet Work* (1797); it was a large piece of furniture, 6 ft. 8 in. long, and 6 ft. 9 in. high to the top of the cornice. The term wardrobe is applied to a free-standing cupboard for clothes in Hepplewhite's *Guide* (1788). These large cupboards were architectural pieces: from base to cornice they were complementary to the character that the architect had impressed upon the interior of the bedroom. The decorative effects might, and indeed did, vary considerably, but the basic proportions remained and were respected and followed alike by cabinet-makers and upholsterers. Sheraton's directions to use "furniture simply necessary, but light in appearance" were not always followed; though bedrooms were seldom overcrowded, and nothing was allowed actively to compete with the bed itself. The dressing-room, which also served as a reception-room, was often far more elaborate than the bedroom, for there the most earnest business of the day began for ladies and gentlemen whose lives were largely dedicated to the pursuit of pleasure and the appreciation of beauty.

CHAPTER V

"THE TOILET STANDS DISPLAY'D"

SHERATON, in concluding the entry on furnishing in *The Cabinet Dictionary*, said: "The dressing-room exhibits the toilet table and commode, with all the little affairs requisite to dress, as bason-stands, stools, glasses, and boxes with all the innocent trifles of youth. . . ."[146] The basin stands were shapely supports for very small basins; the dressing-stools were broad-seated and comfortable, specially designed for use at the toilet, and not just backless chairs, matching the other chairs in the room, and in some the X-shaped underframing of an earlier period was revived. Two examples of such dressing stools by Ince and Mayhew are shown on page 256. As for the glasses and boxes and other receptacles, they were innumerable, and the extent of the silversmith's contribution to the glittering array on the toilet is indicated by contemporary advertisements for new and second-hand plate. In *The Whitehall Evening-Post*, March 8th–10th, 1759, there is an announcement by Stafford Briscoe of silver "To be sold very Cheap" which includes "a Sett of chased Dressing-Plate, and a Number of other curious Particulars; also the very greatest Choice of new and old Plate, either chased or plain, in the newest Taste. . . ."[147]

Another of Briscoe's typical advertisements, September 6th–8th, 1759, offers "A complete Sett of light plain gadroon'd Dressing-Plate for a Lady's Toilet, Second-hand, fashionable, but as good as new, to be sold very cheap, for ready Money."[148]

A satirical account of a fashionable lady's toilet table appears in *The World*, following the description of the state bedchamber that was quoted in the last chapter. "Under a very magnificent Chinese canopy stands the toilette, furnished with a set of boxes of gilt plate, for combs, brushes, paints, pastes, patches, pomatums, powders white grey and blue, bottles of hungary, lavender and orange flower water, and, in short, all the apparatus for disguising beauty. Here she constantly pays her devotions two hours every morning; but what kind of divinity she adores, may be safer for you to guess than for me to tell. By this time I imagine you will conceive my house to be much fuller of furniture than my head. Alas! sir, I am but a husband, and my wife is a woman of quality."[149] The estimate of two hours for toying with such a diversity of preparations seems altogether too modest.

Pope, in "The Rape of the Lock," gave the most engaging details of "all the little affairs requisite to dress," in these lines:

"And now, unveil'd, the toilet stands display'd,
Each silver vase in mystic order laid.
First, robed in white, the nymph intent adores,
With head uncover'd, the cosmetic powers.
A heav'nly image in the glass appears,
To that she bends, to that her eye she rears;
Th' inferior priestess, at her altar's side,
Trembling, begins the sacred rites of pride.
Unnumber'd treasures ope at once, and here
The various offerings of the world appear;
From each she nicely culls with curious toil,
And decks the goddess with the glitt'ring spoil.
This casket India's glowing gems unlocks,
And all Arabia breathes from yonder box.
The tortoise here and elephant unite,
Transform'd to combs, the speckled and the white
Here files of pins extend their shining rows,
Puffs, powders, patches, Bibles, billet-doux.
Now awful beauty puts on all its arms;
The fair each moment rises in her charms,
Repairs her smiles, awakens every grace,
And calls forth all the wonders of her face:
Sees by degrees a purer blush arise,
And keener lightnings quicken in her eyes.
The busy sylphs surround their darling care,
These set the head, and those divide the hair,
Some fold the sleeve, while others plait the gown;
And Betty's praised for labours not her own."

Everybody mastered a set of gestures, appropriate to their taste, figure, and station in the more exalted ranks of society. "Your carriage genteel, and your motions graceful" Lord Chesterfield had advised: the advice was followed. (Reproduced from a print of Aston, published in 1744, by Samuel Nathaniel Buck.)

Toilet preparations were briskly advertised, and no restrictions were placed upon the vendors of ointments and treatments; the public was wholly unprotected, and sometimes the results were fatal. It was said that Lady Coventry, whose death-bed was described in the previous chapter, used such a quantity of paint on her face that it checked the perspiration and was thought to have been the immediate cause of the disorder that led to her death.[150]

Here is a typical advertisement for beauty treatment from the *Whitehall Evening-Post*, June 29th–July 1st, 1758:—

TO THE LADIES

"As the smallest Speck is seen on Snow, so the least Blemish is observed on a Lady's Face; but the most disagreeable are such, as are occasioned by a Superfluity of hairs growing on the Forehead, Temples, round the Mouth, or too large Eyebrows, or such as meet together, all of which are great Enemies to Beauty; but to destroy them, a Gentleman, at the King's Head, near Gray's Inn Gate, Holborn, prepares for that a Compound of that sovereign Virtue, that wherever it is applied, it softens the Roots of the Hair, opens the Pores of the Skin, and instantly takes off thousands of those disagreeable Hairs, Root and Branch, without harming the finest Skin. Attendance from Ten to Three every Day.

"To be sold at the same Place, the Ointment of
Life, and an infallible Cure for the Ague."[151]

The apparatus of the toilet became increasingly complex; the importance of creating the right impression was never forgotten either by ladies or gentlemen, and many young men of fashion took to heart the advice Lord Chesterfield had given to his son when he said "that all the talents in the world will want all their lustre, and some part of their use too, if they are not adorned with that easy good-breeding, that engaging manner, and those graces, which seduce and prepossess people in your favour at first sight. A proper care of your person is by no means to be neglected; always extremely clean; upon proper occasions fine. Your carriage genteel, and your motions graceful. Take particular care of your manner and address when you present yourself in company. Let them be respectful without meanness, easy without too much familiarity, genteel without affectation, and insinuating without any seeming art or design."

Several hours at the beginning of each day were devoted, both by ladies and gentlemen, to preparations for showing themselves to Society. The toilet, or toilet table, sometimes called the toiletta, was frequently adorned with as many frills, flounces and draperies as the lady who ultimately rose from it, and fashionable furniture-makers and upholsterers illustrated in their trade books the most intricate confections, for that is the only word which justly describes such designs. The drapery that is hung round the gilded mirror on the toilet table in the Countess's dressing-room, on plate 26; the even more elaborate drapery of Queen Charlotte's dressing table, on plate 32; and the toiletta from the

STRATAGEM.

The voluminous skirts of the lady, and all the elaborate draperies and the towering head-dress, suggest the hours that were spent at the toilet table, or, as it was sometimes called, the toiletta.

(See opposite page.)

Barralet ad viv. del.   *Walker sculp*

M.ʳˢ LESSINGHAM as M.ʳˢ SULLEN.

Sull. *The Devil take his impudence.*
Act 4

Publish'd. Nov. 16. 1776. by T. Lowndes. & Partners

A lady's toiletta, illustrated in Ince and Mayhew's *The Universal System of Household Furniture* (plate XXXVI), published in London in 1760. The draperies were complementary in form to those affected by the ladies who spent so many hours preparing to show themselves to the fashionable world.

Universal System of Household Furniture, reproduced on page 251, show the important part given to decorative fabrics in the design of the most significant article in the dressing-room.

There were, also, more solid and mechanically adroit designs; and of these a fitted dressing table described in Hepplewhite's *Guide* as a "Rudd's table, or reflecting dressing table," was abundantly equipped with appliances and receptacles for preparing the complexion, adjusting the set of the head-dress, placing the jewels and the patches, and attending to all the delicate details that had to be perfect before a lady could face the world with the confidence that exhaustive care for the demands of fashion bestowed. There were two varieties, and a lighter and simplified version was illustrated in *The Prices of Cabinet Work* (1797). The heavier variety, which is shown opposite, was described in Hepplewhite's *Guide* (1788) as "the most complete dressing table made, possessing every convenience which can be wanted, or mechanism and ingenuity supply." Then follows a mysterious statement, for the *Guide* tells us that Rudd's table "derives its name from a once popular character, for whom it is reported it was first invented."

This vague reference to the identity of Rudd is tantalising; he may conceivably have been the designer of the table, for articles of furniture were occasionally named after their makers. We know that an English cabinet-maker called Rudd lived in the eighteenth century, though there is no record of his work, or his address or the dates of his birth or death. The only reference to his existence is an entry in *The Dictionary of Architecture*, which mentions a Jean Baptiste Rudd, born at Bruges in 1792, and described as the son of an English cabinet-maker who had settled in that city.[152] This Jean Baptiste Rudd ultimately became the city architect of Bruges. The reference in Hepplewhite's *Guide* to "a once popular character" might apply more appropriately to a character who was certainly popular with her own clientele, and, as far as the public was concerned, notorious. This was Margaret Caroline Rudd, whose sprightly exploits led to her trial at the Old Bailey as an accomplice of Robert and Daniel Perreau, who were executed for forgery. Her career was highly successful, as such careers go, and she consorted with the nobility and gentry whose generosity would have enabled her to indulge her taste for commissioning such costly luxuries as the reflecting dressing table. Certainly she made large sums of money, certainly her capacity to continue earning depended upon the preservation of her charms, and when Hepplewhite's book was published in 1788, she had long ceased to be in the public eye. Her trial had taken place in 1775, and the immense interest aroused by the case of the Perreau brothers and Mrs. Rudd, had helped to deflect public attention from the impending loss of the American Colonies, so to some small extent, Lord North and his government may have been grateful to Mrs. Rudd for supplying such a convenient distraction. Although she was as popular as ever with the nobility after her trial, and was seen in the company of Lord Lyttelton, and in the spring

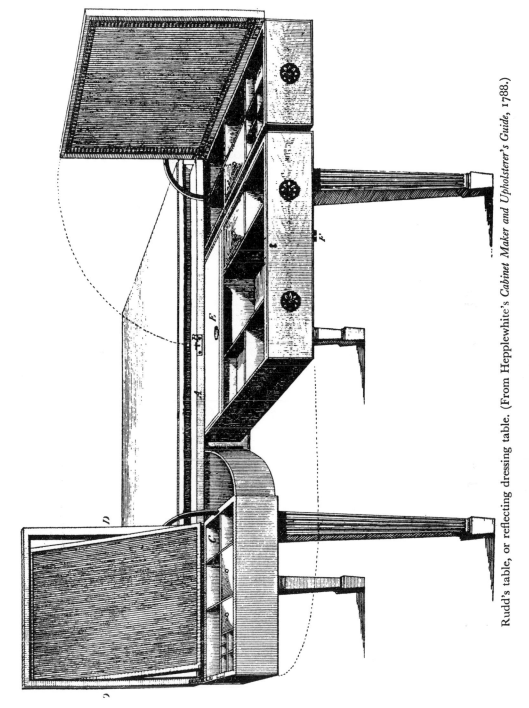

Rudd's table, or reflecting dressing table. (From Hepplewhite's *Cabinet Maker and Upholsterer's Guide*, 1788.)

Fig 4

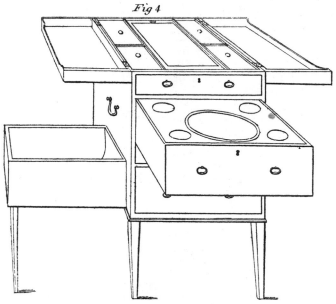

A lady's dressing stand, with folding tops and two drawers. There are three sham drawers in front, to supply depth for the square bidet which pulls out at one side, and the washing stand which pulls out to front. A compact design which shows how much more attention was paid to making-up rather than washing. (From *The Prices of Cabinet Work*, 1797 edition.)

of 1776 was visited by James Boswell, always seeking sensation as well as sexual relaxation, her career soon ended. When she was tried for her life she was only thirty; nearly four years later, in the early summer of 1779, she died in circumstances which suggest that she had not only been discarded by her clients, but was poor and neglected. Still, she does justify the use of the phrase "a once popular character."

The constantly varying fashions and the trouble which ladies took to deck themselves becomingly, provoked admiration, imitation, and mirth. It was frequently suggested, and the meagre appliances for washing certainly reinforce the suggestion, that the fine ladies and gentlemen were careless enough about cleanliness except on those occasions when they displayed themselves to the modish world at some rout or ball. Two "Poetical Essays" published in *The London Magazine* in April, 1762, laugh slyly at the intermittent preoccupation of ladies with their appearance, and deplore the time and attention given, when natural beauty supplied the foundation, to the elaborate disguise of Nature. The first, "On a certain LADY" is an attack on slovenliness, far more detailed and thorough than the comparatively mild reproof quoted from the fable of "The Owl and the Nightingale" in an earlier chapter. (See page 168.)

A dressing commode or dressing chest, designed by Thomas Sheraton, and illustrated on plate 41 of *The Cabinet Dictionary* (1803). He described it as "a small case of drawers, containing four drawers in height, the uppermost of which is divided into conveniences for dressing; hence the name dressing-chest. Or sometimes the top is hinged, and made to rise with a quadrant, and the dressing part is fixed in a wall at the top, and not in the drawer; in which case, a glass is usually hinged to the under side of the top, with a foot to keep it in any position; and there is sometimes a knee hole in the front, but frequently none, when such dressing chests are used by persons who stand to dress. But if they sit to dress, there must either be a dressing drawer to draw out, or a knee hole in the front when the dressing part is in a well under the top."

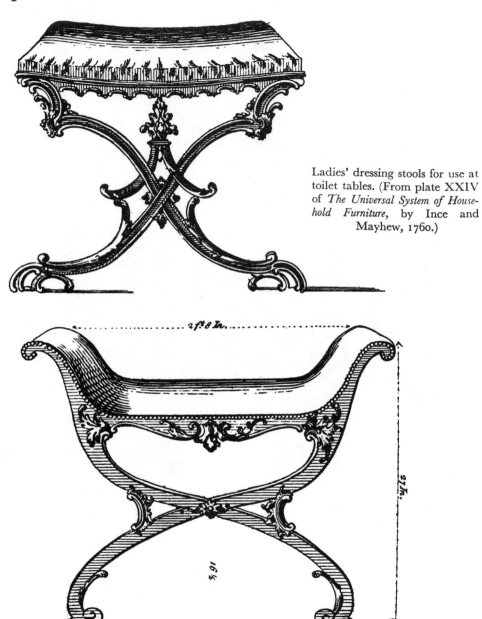

Ladies' dressing stools for use at toilet tables. (From plate XXIV of *The Universal System of Household Furniture*, by Ince and Mayhew, 1760.)

The verses begin after a line that explains: "They only make the satire who apply it."

> At home, when marry'd Lydia fits,
> And only spouse's friends admits,
>   How negligent her airs!
> Quite a-la-mode in dishabille,
> See! snuff her nose and fingers fill,
>   Her hair about her ears.
>
> Her hankerchief and morning-gown,
> About her shoulders loosely thrown,
>   With scarce a single pin in;
> No stays, no hoop, are seen upon her,
> (Those double guards of female honour)
>   And then, ye gods! her linen.
>
> But when a ball, or masquerade,
> Calls her from this domestic shade,
>   In publick light to shine;
> She's drest compleat from head to foot,
> (If jewels, silk, and lace, can do't)
>   No dutchess half so fine.
>
> So flies, when wint'ry seasons reign,
> Obscure in filth and dirt remain,
>   Nor dare to 'tempt the skies;
> Till warm'd by Phoebus' genial rays,
> They bask and wanton in the blaze,
>   And shew a thousand dyes.

The other poem, of which the first twelve lines are quoted below, is entitled "Beauty and Fashion," and is described as "A Repartee."

> "Says Beauty to Fashion, as they set at the toilette,
> 'If I give a charm, you surely will spoil it;
> When you take it in hand, there's such murth'ring and mangling,
> 'Tis so metamorphos'd by your fiddling and fangling,
> That I scarce know my own, when I meet it again,
> Such changelings you make, both of women and men.
> To confirm what I say, look at Phryne, or Phillis,
> I'm sure that I gave 'em good roses and lillies:
> Now what have you done?—Let the world be the judge:
> Why you daub 'em all over with cold cream and rouge,
> That, like Thisbe in Ovid, one cannot come at 'em,
> Unless thro' a mud-wall of paint and pomatum.' "

Everybody had a perfect right to laugh at fashions; but such laughter left the modish world unperturbed; and even the moralists were occasionally indulgent. A very long dissertation on the evils of extravagance in the section devoted to dress in *The Ladies Library* concludes with the admission that "To think there is Merit in rejecting all Gaiety and Expence in Apparel, is as dangerous as to launch out into it."[153] From the same work comes a plea for charitable tolerance about the manners and carriage and dress of gentlemen, which though subdued in tone, is the antithesis of Puritan acerbity. "That may be accounted Pride and Haughtiness, which is perhaps the natural Air and Mien of a Person," it began. Then followed an example: "A Gentleman of good Sense, and Easiness of Conversation, has the Misfortune to have past all his Life-time for a Fop; and asserted, purely because by Nature or ill Custom he has acquir'd such a Gait, that he cannot turn his Head without Trouble to him, thence it is that he is reckon'd stiff and proud; whereas his Conversation, and manner of living with all his Acquaintance, is the freest imaginable. There is a Shiness also in several People which is taken for Contempt of others, and is a very Diffidence of themselves; and there is also a Delicacy and Decency of both Sexes, which is mistaken for Pride: This in all Ages has produced a Set of slovenly Christians, who think 'tis not Saint-like to be neat."[154]

Men did not escape the severe and often brutal comments of caricaturists and critics: the accusation of foppishness would have been difficult to parry, had any gentleman bothered to do so, as a certain stiffness of carriage was requisite in a period when men wore wigs. The voluminous, elaborate wigs of the late seventeenth and early eighteenth centuries became trimmer and smaller, and altogether more manageable by the beginning of the nineteenth century. Sometimes men "wore their own hair" and powdered it, and the powdered wig and powdered hair gave to those clean-shaven Georgian male faces a sedate framework. Consequently the portraits of those masterful-looking men, whether they happened to be soldiers or sailors, statesmen or men of leisure, bore a certain vague resemblance to each other—but remove the wigs, and the powerful individuality of those faces is at once enhanced. The wig made heavy demands upon a gentleman's toilet preparations, particularly when the fashion for powdered heads was introduced. This led to the use of powdering closets, which were flimsy structures composed of paper screens, wherein the gentleman was enclosed so that powder could be puffed on to "his own hair," or on to a wig, without distributing it over the dressing-room. When not in use, the wig rested upon a block or a stand.

The articles that were used by men of fashion in their dressing-rooms were as numerous and varied as those designed for ladies: there were shaving chairs and shaving tables, a variety of adjustable toilet mirrors, and the tall cheval glass, or horse dressing glass as it was sometimes called—the term "horse" being derived from the four-legged frame in which the long mirror was suspended. A shaving chair had a head-rest rising above the top rail and was generally a corner

Brandon Invt.

THE FOLLY OF 1771

Publish'd as the Act Directs April 10. 1771. by W. Darling Engraver in Great Newport Street

A contemporary print that satirised the towering head-dresses of ladies of fashion.

chair, resembling an angle or writing chair. The shaving table could be little more than a bason stand, with a rising glass at the back, like the example from Chippendale's *Director* reproduced on page 263, or it could be as comprehensively convenient as the design on page 262, also from the *Director*, which had "a folding Top, and a Glass to rise out with a Spring-Catch." There were "Places for holding Soap, and other Necessaries, and behind them are Places for Razors" and "Places for Bottles. . . ."[155] Sheraton described the mechanism of the adjustable mirror on the shaving table, which was "made to rise to any height by means of a brass rack and thumb spring, which catches the holes of the rack, and supports the frame to which the glass is hinged."[156]

Dressing glasses, or toilet mirrors, on box stands, with the mirror swinging between two tapering upright standards, were used throughout the eighteenth century; reflecting old or young, freshly beautiful or heavily doctored faces, and framing the reflection in delicately moulded rectangles, ovals or shields. In the seventeen-nineties the box stand with its drawers was occasionally omitted, and the toilet mirror was hinged to a skeleton framework, supported

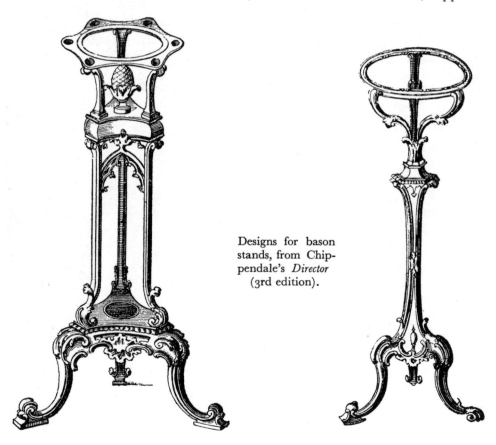

Designs for bason stands, from Chippendale's *Director* (3rd edition).

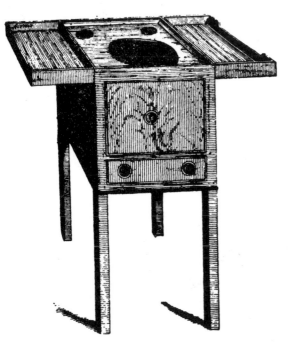

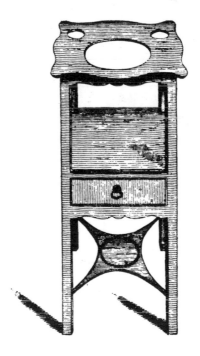

Three bason stands from Hepple-white's *Guide*. The size of the bason these stands could accommodate is a sufficient comment on the amount of washing that was considered necessary for ladies and gentlemen of that period. Compare these examples with the later, more elaborate designs by Sheraton on page 264. The stands have become impressively decorative, but the size of the bason is unchanged. The shaving tables shown on the next two pages are really amplifications of the bason stand. The designs from Chippendale's *Director* on the opposite page are mere excuses for introducing something ornamental to the bed-room or dressing-room: the basons they supported were not very much larger than soup plates.

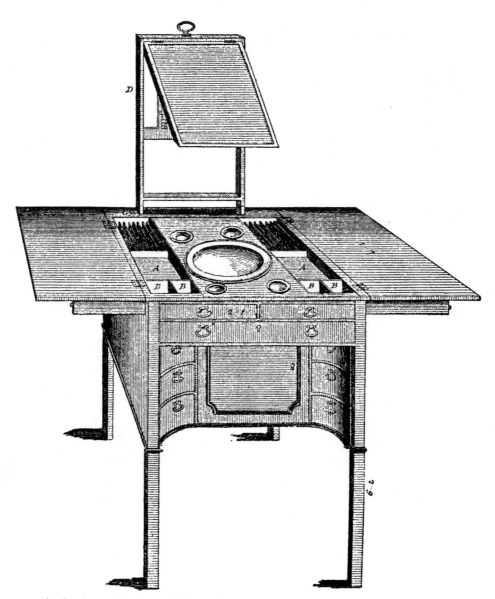

A shaving table from Chippendale's *Director* (3rd edition). This has a
folding top from which a glass rises with a spring catch.

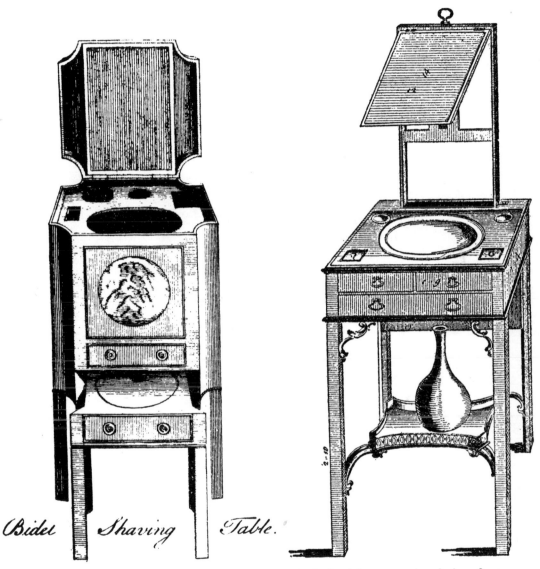

Bidet Shaving Table.

Left: Bidet shaving table, from Hepplewhite's *Guide*. *Right:* A bason stand and glass, from Chippendale's *Director* (3rd edition). There is a rising glass at the back.

Two bason stands designed by Thomas Sheraton, and illustrated on plate 10 of *The Cabinet Dictionary* (1803). The circular tripod bason stand on the left was, said Sheraton, "entirely novel, and is designed for a young lady to wash at. The back, to which the curtains are fixed, is made separate, and turned over in a scroll, where the lights are fixed. To this back must also be fixed a small shelf to hold a soap glass, and to which a face glass is hinged and supported by a small brass wire foot behind, which falls into notches, The bason occupies the whole circumference as is obvious by the design. The curtains are intended not merely for ornament, but to cover the bason, by being brought forward, which, having a small fringe at the bottom, will look handsome. The lower part contains a cupboard for the water jug, and in the lower frieze may be a small drawer, if thought necessary."

On the right, is a more straightforward design, enclosed at the top by a tambour. Of this, Sheraton said, it was "the first of the kind I have seen." Both these examples suggest that washing was still perfunctory, a mere dipping of the fingers and dabbling at the face.

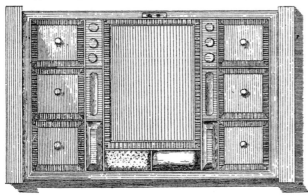

A dressing table designed by Sheraton, and illustrated on plate 40 of *The Cabinet Dictionary*. This table, Sheraton said, was "so constructed as to accommodate a gentleman or lady with conveniences for dressing." He intended this particular design for a lady, and said that it was "so distinct in its parts as to require no explanation." The top is raised and supported on a quadrant stay, and there are two side flaps which may be raised to extend the area of the top.

An early eighteenth century glass with a walnut frame. Mirrors appeared everywhere, so that the work put in at the toilet table could be inspected, and stray curls and wigs straightened. (*Drawn by Marcelle Barton.*)

on four feet like a miniature cheval glass. The appliances and furniture, the bottles, bowls, basons and other articles made to assist ladies and gentlemen in practising the artifice of the toilet, had the same gracious characteristics and the same relationship in terms of design as the furnishing of the drawing-rooms and galleries where people of *ton* displayed the results of their hours in the dressing-room. The manners of those stylish people, as well as the refinement of their toilet, were the result of abundant leisure. They had ample time for living gracefully, and had none of the labour-saving devices which allow men and women of the twentieth century to crowd so much into the day that the need for organised relaxation becomes imperative. It is true that modern people are free from that Georgian complaint, the spleen; nor are they overcome by the vapours; but the overcrowded life of today is not necessarily a full life. So far as men are concerned the time given to the toilet has been cut to the minimum by gadgets like the safety razor and the electric razor, which are intended to save precious minutes. There is no place in the modern world for a man who lingers excessively over his toilet in order to show himself to his fellow creatures as a beautifully finished and even artistic spectacle.

The preoccupation of some Georgian gentlemen with their appearance sometimes overbalanced into absurdity; and when an extravagant effeminacy in male fashions culminated in the preposterous figure of the macaroni, the critics and the caricaturists soon made him a figure of fun. This modish creature was vivisected in the *Town and Country Magazine* in May, 1772. The article, which was entitled "Character of a Macaroni," is a piece of hard-hitting invective, though perhaps the writer is a little too severe on men of fashion, and his words are slightly tarnished with envy. The article, which was illustrated by the engraving reproduced on the opposite page, reads as follows :—

"The Italians are extremely fond of a dish they call Macaroni, composed of a kind of paste; and as they consider this as the *fummum bonum* of all good eating, so they figuratively call everything they think elegant and uncommon *Macaroni*. Our young travellers, who generally catch the follies of the countries they visit, judged that the title of Macaroni was very applicable to a clever fellow; and accordingly, to distinguish themselves as such, they instituted a club under this denomination the members of which were supposed to be the standards of *taste* in polite learning, the fine arts, and the genteel sciences; and fashion, amongst the other constituent parts of taste, became an object of their attention. But they soon proved, they had very little claim to any distinction, except in their external appearance: in their dress, indeed, they were high-finished *Petits Maitres*; in every thing else they were *Coxcombs*. The infection at St. James's was soon caught in the city, and we have now Macaronies of every denomination, from the colonel of the Train'd-Bands down to the errand-boy. They indeed make a most ridiculous figure, with hats of an inch in the brim, that do not cover, but lie upon the head, with about two pounds of fictitious hair, formed into what is called a club, hanging down their shoulders as white as a baker's sack: the end of the skirt of their coat reaches the first button of their breeches, which are either brown striped, or white, as wide as a Dutch-man's; their coatsleeves are so tight, they can with much difficulty get their arms through their cuffs, which are about an inch deep; and their shirt sleeve,

"The Polite Macaroni." (From *The Town and Country Magazine, or Universal Repository of Knowledge, Instruction, and Entertainment*, May, 1772, page 242.) The engraving illustrated an article on the "Character of a Macaroni," and that carefully decorative type was ridiculed for rendering "his sex dubious by the extravegence of his appearance. . . ."

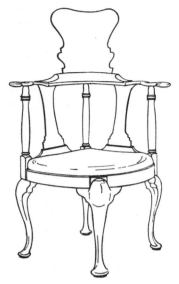

An early Georgian shaving chair.

without plaits, is pulled over a bit of Trolly lace. Their legs are at times covered with all the colours of the rainbow; even flesh-coloured and green silk stockings are not excluded. Their shoes are scarce slippers, and their buckles are within an inch of the toe. Such a figure, essenced and perfumed, with a bunch of lace sticking out under its chin, puzzles the common passenger to determine the thing's sex; and many a time an honest labouring porter has said, *by your leave, madam*, without intending to give offence."

The author, at this point, commends the action of "a great many of the ladies of rank and beauty" who at a masquerade at the Pantheon "chose to adapt the *male* dress in domino, and appeared as *masculine* as many of the *delicate Macarony things* we see swarming everywhere, to the disgrace of our *noble patient British race*. There was this difference, that they looked *lovely* and *charming*, and were justly *admired*, while every person of sense despises the ridiculous *Billy Whiffles* of the present age."(157)

This reference to the account of the masquerade, which appeared a few pages earlier than his article in the same magazine, enabled the author to say "It is pleasant to find that the ladies have turned Satyrists against these Epicene beings, who, with the song, may be pronounced to

" '. . . . answer no end,
And to no sex belong.' "

"Whither," he asked, "are the manly vigour and athletic appearance of our forefathers flown? Can these be their legitimate heirs? Surely no; a race of effeminate, self-admiring, emanciated fribbles can never have descended in a direct line from the heroes of Poictiers and Agincourt. In this free country every one has a right to make himself as ridiculous as he pleases, either in politics or dress; but when a writer tilts against common sense in the papers, or a Macaroni renders his sex dubious by the extravagance of his appearance, the shafts of sarcasm cannot be too forcibly pointed at them. In this opinion we have hung up the subjoined Macaroni—what the world calls the *polite Macaroni* —to the ridicule of our numerous town and country readers, who cannot help smiling, whilst they lament that this nation, in the most perilous times, is to be defended by such *things as these.*"[158]

The writer had reminded his readers that "in this free country every one has a right to make himself as ridiculous as he pleases, either in politics or dress," and William Whitehead had said much the same thing nearly twenty years earlier in *The World*, when he wrote of "our modern idea of liberty, which allows every one the privilege of playing the fool, and of making himself ridiculous in whatever way he pleases."[159] There has never been any shortage of fools in any period of history, but in the eighteenth century when they were rich enough and elected to become macaronis, they did far less damage to society than their more ambitious contemporaries who entered politics. The macaroni was a comparatively harmless dandy, an extreme example of the preoccupation with gracious living which characterised the Georgian Age. No previous period in England's history can bear comparison with the eighteenth century for beauty in costume, care in toilet, elegance in manners, grace in movement, and above all an undeviating sense of style. The spectacle of a fashionable assembly, with men and women arrayed in exquisite clothes, going through the stately movements of a minuet, in a great room gleaming with delicate gilded decor- ation designed according to the taste of the brothers Adam, illuminated by hundreds of wax candles, whose soft yellow flames were sparklingly reflected by crystal chandeliers, had a matchless perfection, and the beauty of the scene was enhanced by the dignity of the participants.

F. Hayman *inv*   C. Grignion *sculp.*

A plate from *Fables for the Female Sex* (London, 1744), illustrating "The Lawyer and Justice" (Fable viii). This shows the miserable sort of lighting available for reading and writing. A solitary candle was often the only source of light in a study or for reading by the fireside.

CHAPTER VI

WRITING AND READING

EDUCATED people two hundred years ago were conscientious and habitual letter-writers, expressing themselves with racy zest, often in dexterous phrases that were spiced with a pungent frankness. "The importance of writing letters with propriety," said Dr Johnson, "justly claims to be considered with care, since next to the power of pleasing with his presence, every man should wish to be able to give delight at a distance." All kinds and conditions of people wrote easily and freely, and without recourse to the clichés and reach-me-down thoughts which come so readily to our more literate and less original age. Letter-writing was not merely a polite obligation; it was an art that was practised with obvious enjoyment; and it engaged the services of many craftsmen, from cabinet-makers to silversmiths, who made the bureaux and writing-tables, the trays, inkpots and candlesticks, and all the other well-designed articles that furnished the desk top. Even without the evidence of the vast amount of correspondence that has been preserved, the innumerable varieties of bureaux, and the numbers that have survived, would afford the most convincing proof of the widespread popularity of letter-writing. In devising ways of increasing the comfort and ministering to the convenience of those who delighted to correspond with their friends and acquaintances, Georgian cabinet-makers, as usual, exercised a consistent ingenuity. They made inventive improvements upon that basic and very old form of furniture, the desk, which by the middle of the eighteenth century had transcended its original simple function, and had become an essential and significant item in the furnishing not only of a library or study, but of the boudoir and dressing-room. Boswell had a bureau put in the dining-room of his London lodgings.(160)

The writing-desk was used in the Middle Ages, and the term desk is of mediaeval origin, denoting a table desk with a sloping lid for writing; it was also the name for the superstructure of a plate cupboard, on which the plate was displayed. Writing-desks and tables were made in many forms, light or massive, and satisfying in design, between the late seventeenth and early nineteenth centuries; and they were usually equipped with a standish, which was a tray of silver or Sheffield plate to hold the ink bottle, sand-box, pens, wafers, sealing-wax, a small candle for heating the wax, and a tinder-box for

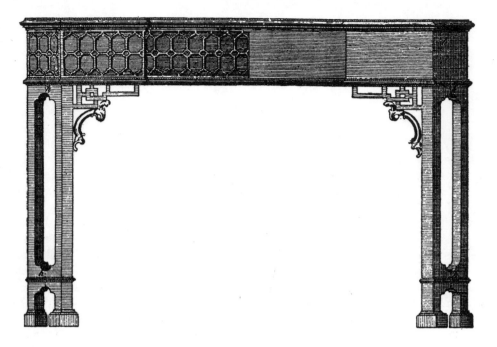

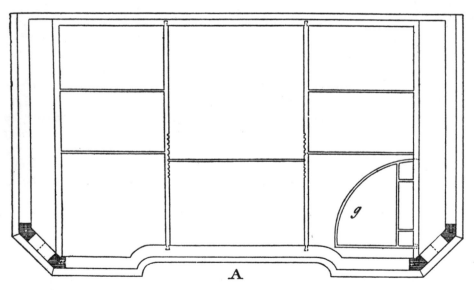

A writing table from Chippendale's *Director* (3rd edition). "Half of the front feet come out with the drawer, which parts at *h, h. A* is the plan of the table with the partitions; *g* is a quadrant drawer for ink and sand."

lighting the candle. In some designs for writing-tables a small quadrant drawer
for ink and sand obviated the need for a standish, and such a design, from
Chippendale's *Director*, is shown on page 272. Originally the term standish
was confined to the inkstand, and as late as 1775, in the twenty-first edition
of Bailey's *Universal Etymological English Dictionary*, it was still defined as "a
standing Inkhorn Glass etc., for a Table." The sand-box was an indispensable
article in the days before blotting-paper was invented, when sand was peppered
over the wet ink from a castor of silver or brass. The comparatively slow speed
of writing has been forgotten in the day of fountain-pens and typewriters, but
the preparation of a quill pen which had to be trimmed with a knife (we still
call a pocket knife a penknife, though the quill has vanished), the constant
dipping of the pen into the inkpot, all took time, and compelled a leisurely
pace and encouraged carefulness of composition. Dr. Johnson observed that
"The mechanical art of writing began to be cultivated amongst us in the
reign of Queen Elizabeth, and was at that time so highly valued, that it
contributed much to the fame and fortune of him who wrote his pages with
neatness, and embellished them with elegant draughts and illuminations; and
it was partly, perhaps, to this encouragement, that we now surpass all other
nations in this art." Immense care was taken to make letters not only interesting
but legible. Ladies and gentlemen were instructed by writing masters, and
letter-writing was not only an exercise in the art of composition, but an exact
and beautiful craft.

The tendency of many people to be untidy when dealing with papers was
tactfully recognised by cabinet-makers, who attempted to correct it by inventing
the bureau, which provided so many convenient places for keeping letters and
stationery; and even if untidiness still prevailed, then the hinged writing-board
or flap could be closed to conceal the interior with its pigeon-holes, drawers,
small central cupboard, and general state of chaos. When the flap lay flat it

Walnut bureau, *circa* 1720 to 1730, with brass drop
handles on the drawers and bracket feet. (*Drawn by
Marcelle Barton.*)

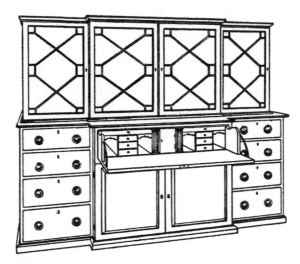

A large bookcase with drawers and cupboards in the base, fitted as an escritoire. These "architectural pieces" as they have since been called, were very popular in the first half of the eighteenth century, but they became large and grandiose before the end of the century, and often bore the burden of expressing some extravagant version of the Chinese or Gothic taste. (See pages 279 and 283.) (*Drawn by Marcelle Barton.*)

rested upon lopers, or sliding rails, that were pulled out from the carcase of the bureau. Narrow pull-out trays, fitted on either side of a bureau, or bureau bookcase, were called candle slides, and they supported a pair of candlesticks.

At night nearly all reading and writing was done by candle-light, for lamps that were safe and practical and capable of giving better illumination than wax or tallow candles were not available in England until the last quarter of the eighteenth century. A Swiss named Ami Argand invented an improved lamp, with a tubular wick placed between two concentric burners, which was patented in 1784, and first made in the Birmingham district by Matthew Boulton at the Soho Foundry. It was one of the many minor activities in which that enterprising manufacturer was engaged, and Argand had intended to "commit to Boulton's care the manufacture of most parts of the lamp. . . ."[161] There were hanging oil lamps in bronze and brass, but until Argand's patent, there was no desk or table lamp that could give a really good light. Candle-light might be brilliant when it emanated from hundreds of wax candles, but it could be depressing when the source was a solitary tallow dip. Horace Walpole, describing his visit to Lady Mary Wortley when she returned to England, said he "found her in a little miserable bed chamber of a ready-furnished house, with two tallow candles, and a bureau covered with pots

Left: A bureau bookcase. The term probably originated in the mid eighteenth century, though a contemporary description, used by Chippendale and Hepplewhite, was "desk and bookcase." *Centre and right:* A mid eighteenth century escritoire, showing the fitted writing drawer open and closed. Both examples have glazed doors with rectangular panes, and these would probably have been described by the contemporary term, "sash doors," which may have arisen from the resemblance of such doors to the proportions and divisions of sash windows. (*Drawn by Marcelle Barton.*)

and pans." (Letter to Sir Horace Mann, Arlington Street, January 29th, 1762.) The tallow candles added to the squalor of the scene.

The bureau probably evolved from the scrutoire, or scriptoire, which was a writing-cabinet with a fall-down front, introduced during the reign of Charles II. The term scrutoire remained in use until the late eighteenth century. In a letter to George Montagu, about his stay in Houghton for the Lynn election, Horace Walpole said: "I have chosen to sit in my father's little dressing-room, and am now by his scrutoire, where, in the height of his fortune, he used to receive the accounts of his farmers. . . ." (Houghton, March 25th, 1761.) The bureau had many different forms and supplementary functions, when for example it was surmounted by bookshelves enclosed by glazed or panelled doors, it became a bureau bookcase. The contemporary description, used by Chippendale and Hepplewhite, was "desk and bookcase." Sometimes the shelves above a bureau were used for the display of china and ornaments, and the article was then a bureau cabinet. The bureau table was a form of kneehole writing-table, with a drawer below the top and drawers on either side of the kneehole space; but this was a flat-topped table and not a true bureau with a hinged flap. Some bureaux had a kneehole space, flanked by drawers, with another set of drawers at the back of the kneehole. The bureau dressing-table, which appeared early in the eighteenth century, was a small

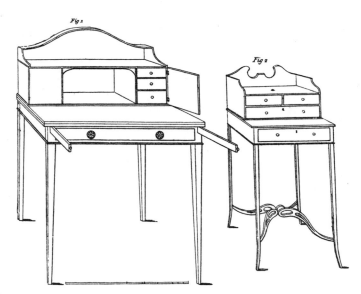

To the left is a sheveret, which is described in *The Prices of Cabinet Work*, 1797 edition, as a lady's cabinet. A lady's work-table is shown on the right, which is really a miniature sheveret. This term occurs in the Gillow records.

bureau on a stand with cabriole legs, two or three shallow drawers below the desk, and a swinging dressing-glass above. This type was designed primarily for ladies. A combined writing- and dressing-table was illustrated by Chippendale in his *Director*, and he devoted two plates of the third edition to four designs of what he called "buroe dressing tables." Each had a recess for the knees, and resembled a small writing-desk.

A compact and convenient piece of furniture, comparable with the bureau, was the escritoire, secretaire, or secretary, which had a writing-drawer with a hinged front that folded down flat and extended the area of the writing-board. The escritoire often had bookshelves above, and is sometimes wrongly described as a bureau bookcase. A writing-drawer was very often fitted to a large bookcase, like the example shown on page 274, or to a tall chest like that on the opposite page.

Writing-tables, library tables, and desks with pedestals and drawers and cupboards had a sombre dignity, as befitted their place in the library or study; the excellence of their proportions was discreetly emphasised by carved decoration; their moulded detail was related to that of the large bookcases which furnished the library, and the panelling on its walls. Writing-desks and tables increased in slenderness and delicacy of detail in the last decades of the eighteenth century, thus following a general trend in furniture design. This new lightness of form was exhibited in such articles as the sheveret, or lady's

A tall chest with one drawer fitted as an escritoire. There was a certain intermingling of articles concerned with the toilet and with writing. (See page 276.) (*Drawn by Marcelle Barton.*)

A kneehole kidney writing-table with a rising desk. Alternative treatments are shown for drawers or cupboards in the pedestals. (From *The Prices of Cabinet Work*, 1797 edition.)

cabinet, which was a narrow writing-desk with tapering legs. An example, described and illustrated in *The Prices of Cabinet Work* (1797), was 2 ft. 6 in. wide and 1 ft. 6 in. deep, with a case at the back, 9 in. wide and 9 in. high, with cupboards at each end. A reproduction of this sheveret (or cheveret), slightly reduced in scale, is given on page 276. The firm of Gillow of Lancaster made many sheverets, and an order for one in satinwood is recorded on July 5th, 1790.[162]

Among the articles for occasional use was the screen writing-table, or writing fire-screen. This was a very shallow writing-desk with a fall front and a cupboard below, with the carcase, which was raised on curved or claw feet, acting as a fire-screen, so it was possible to sit before a fire and write, keeping the feet warm and the complexion unravaged. It was introduced during the late eighteenth century by Thomas Shearer, and was made in two sizes: small for ladies, and a little larger for gentlemen, for both sexes were concerned with protecting their complexions from the melting heat of a roaring coal fire. Both types are illustrated and described in *The Prices of Cabinet Work* and are reproduced on page 279. The lady's screen was 1 ft. 8 in. wide and the gentleman's 2 ft. 6 in.; when closed they occupied little more room than ordinary fire-screens. Among the extras listed in the specification for such designs was lipping the flap for a cloth lining, and supplying "a fix'd case, fitted up for ink, sand, pens, and wafers," also "a paper case made to lift out, with front, back, and one partition with scollop edges."[163]

Shearer's design for this specialised type of writing-table is recorded: there were other designs that we know only by name. For example, there was Cobb's table, named after John Cobb, an upholsterer and cabinet-maker who was in partnership with William Vile. The firm of Vile and Cobb had premises at the corner (No. 72) of St. Martin's Lane and Long Acre, and at the beginning of the reign of George III "held a pre-eminent position among the cabinet-makers to the Royal Household...."[164] We no longer know what Cobb's table was like, though we have, thanks to the irrepressible garrulity of John Thomas Smith, a description both of its purpose and its designer. In *Nollekens and his Times*, Smith portrays Cobb as a foppish and excessively dignified man, who affected the appearance and aped the manners of a macaroni. "He was the person," he wrote, "who brought that very convenient table into fashion that draws out in front, with upper and inward rising desks, so healthy for those who stand to write, read, or draw." The absurdity of Cobb's pomposity is revealed by Smith's account of the occasion when it was neatly punctured by George III. "One day when Mr. Cobb was in his Majesty's library at Buckingham-house, giving orders to a workman, whose ladder was placed before a book which the King wanted, his Majesty desired Cobb to hand him the work, which instead of obeying, he called to his man, 'Fellow, give me that book!' The King, with his usual condescension, arose, and asked Cobb, what his man's name was. 'Jenkins,' answered the astonished Upholsterer.

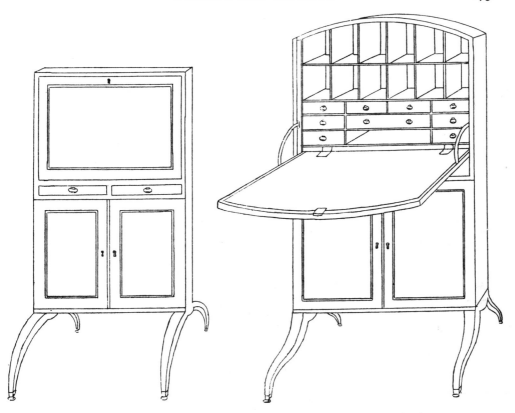

Left: A writing fire-screen for ladies. It was a shallow desk with a fall front and a cupboard beneath. The carcase acted as a screen, so that it would be possible to sit in front of the fire and write, keeping the feet warm and the complexion unravaged. *Right:* A writing fire-screen for gentlemen, which was a more commodious edition of the design for ladies. (From *The Prices of Cabinet Work,* 1797 edition.)

'Then,' observed the King, 'Jenkins, you shall hand me the book.' " This anecdote was culled by Smith from Banks, "the cellaret maker."[165]

The library of a Georgian house was generously planned; books often covered the walls from skirting to frieze, with the chimney-piece, doors and windows alone breaking the continuity of the shelves. In such large, book-lined rooms, there would be reading-desks, a library table, easy chairs, and perhaps a reading-chair. Free-standing bookcases would follow the accepted architectural proportions, and the cupboards in the lower part would correspond to the plinth, and above the bookshelves with their glazed doors would be a frieze and cornice, with perhaps a broken pediment and a pedestal for a bust. The glazing bars on the doors enclosed rectangular panes, and in the early Georgian period they often resembled the general proportions of sash windows,

Glazing bars for bookcase doors, from a plate of twelve designs, reproduced
from *The Prices of Cabinet Work*, 1797 edition. (See opposite page.)

Glazing bars for bookcase doors, from a plate of twelve designs, reproduced from *The Prices of Cabinet Work*, 1797 edition. (See opposite page.)

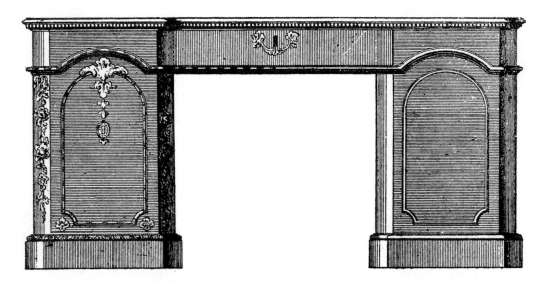

A library table showing front and side views. From Chippendale's *Director* (3rd edition).
It is described as having "drawers in the upper part" which "draw out at each end
of the table. It has doors at both sides, with upright partitions for books, and drawers
on the other side within the doors."

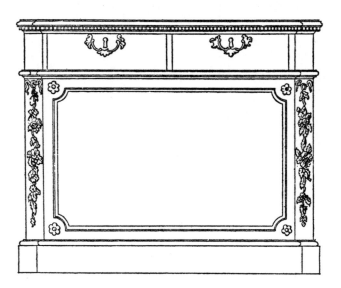

which may have originated the term sash doors in connection with bookcases. After the middle years of the eighteenth century, glazing bars became more decorative, and like the glazing bars of windows were progressively refined in section. This reduction in the size, which was an advantage in windows as it allowed more light to be admitted, was used by cabinet-makers as an opportunity for decoration, and the glazed doors of bookcases were filled with ornamental devices. Two plates giving twenty-four designs for bookcase doors were included in *The Prices of Cabinet Work*, of which twelve are reproduced on pages 280 and 281.

Chippendale included several designs for library bookcases in his *Director*, generally with glazed doors, and one, on plate LXXXVII of the third edition, with a drawer "which may have conveniences for writing or dressing at" and a glass in the upper door, so that the books were concealed by a mirror. There were several suggestions for Gothic bookcases, which were similar in their proportions to the classical designs, and decorated with trefoils, quatrefoils, and other forms of tracery, with pinnacles rising above the cornice. The displaying of well-bound books on shelves was not confined to the library; and in addition to such articles as the bureau bookcase, there were small movable bookcases, and, towards the end of the eighteenth century, revolving

MOVING BOOKCASE

A moving bookcase, designed by Thomas Sheraton, from plate 23 of *The Cabinet Dictionary* (1803). Compare this with the example illustrated on plate 43.

bookshelves. Sheraton described and illustrated "small open shelves for books under present reading, and which a lady can move to any sitting room."[166] One of his designs for such a "moving bookcase" is reproduced on page 283, and should be compared with the example on plate 43. These bookshelves were made "of thin mahogany or satin wood, banded on the edges of the shelves, which are seldom more than two in number, exclusive of the top and bottom. To keep them light, the shelves are often connected together by means of strong brass wire at each corner, and in the centre of the shelves; so they have no need of close ends of wood."[167]

Books were part of the background of polite life; they were clearly printed, often on beautifully made paper, with richly decorative bindings. The paper has lasted well, and is still a pleasure to handle. Comparatively little good white paper had been made in England before the "War of Jenkins's Ear," which began in 1739, for printers had imported from Europe nearly all the paper they used for books; but the war interrupted the supply, and thereafter English manufacturers improved and increased their output,[168] which was about the only benefit the country derived from that foolish and unnecessary war. The taste for displaying books came in for some whimsical criticism in *The World*, and a suggestion for a "Learned" or "Library-paper" was made for the benefit of those who had "a fine taste in books, and not the least relish for learning; and for the convenience of many more, who are fond of the appearance of learning, and can give no other proof of it, than that of possessing so many books. . . ."[169] This wall-paper was to represent classes of books, and the designer would "exert his fancy in so many pretty designs of book-cases, or pieces of ornamental architecture, accommodated to the size of all rooms, in such richness of gilding, lettering and colouring," that the author doubted "whether the CHINESE-PAPER so much in fashion in most of our great houses, must not, to his great emolument, give place to the LEARNED." He added: "I think the LIBRARY-PAPER will look as pretty, *may* be made as costly, and I am sure will have more meaning. The books for a lady's closet must be on a smaller scale, and may be thrown into CHINESE-HOUSES; and here and there blank spaces may be left for brackets to hold real China ware and Dresden figures. It is to be observed that the lettering should not be put on till the paper is hung up; for every customer ought to have the chusing and the marshalling his own books; by this means he may have those of the newest fashion immediately after their publication; and besides, if he should grow tired of one author or one science, he may be furnished with others at reasonable rates, by the mere alteration of the lettering."[170]

No clumsy thing was ever allowed to intrude in the furnishing of any apartment, and the stark function of an appliance, such as library steps, was deliberately concealed by designing the steps to serve two purposes. "Sometimes they are made to appear like a stool," said Sheraton, "and at others as a Pembroke table, or to rise out of a library table."[171] Georgian ladies and

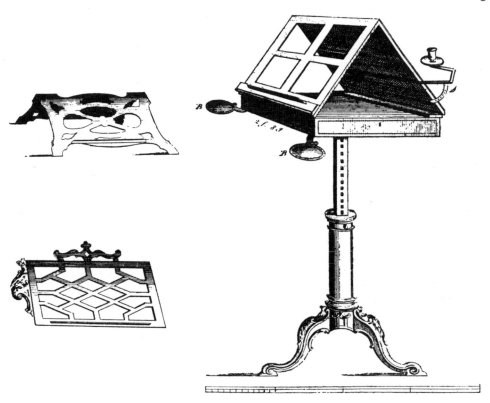

Alternative design for adjustable reading or music desks from plate XXVI
of *The Universal System of Household Furniture,* by Ince and Mayhew (1760).

gentlemen desired to have everything pleasant about them, and their feeling
for style and their respect for common sense never allowed them to accept
ingenious disguise for its own sake: but library steps that sank neatly into a
library table, or folded up and became a useful stool were acceptable, and as
neither designers of furniture nor their patrons regarded frankness about
function as a moral duty, mechanical devices were relegated to the humble
place they have normally occupied in any highly civilised age.

CHAPTER VII

MUSIC IN THE DRAWING-ROOM, FIDDLES IN
THE KITCHEN

WHETHER it took place in the music room of a great house, or in the kitchen of an inn or farm, a musical performance was critically appraised and enjoyed in eighteenth century England, and this widespread delight in music may have come more naturally to people when reading was a comparatively exclusive pastime, and individual talent for entertaining was encouraged. There were fewer professional singers and musicians then, and many competent amateurs. English people are now supposed to be unmusical, a belief that seems to have arisen during the last hundred years; though from the Middle Ages to the early nineteenth century people sang, performed on various instruments, and in every walk of life appeared to be quite unselfconscious about singing or playing in public.

The popular love songs of the Georgian Age had an appealing sweetness and simplicity that never degenerated into the glutinous saccharine cadences of those warbled in the Victorian drawing-room, and were happily free from the tough, slangy endearments which abound in the love songs of the mid twentieth century. Some were frankly hedonistic. One of Macheath's songs in *The Beggar's Opera* extols the charms of women with endearing gentleness.

> "If the Heart of a Man is deprest with Cares,
>   The Mist is dispell'd when a Woman appears;
>   Like the notes of a Fiddle, she sweetly, sweetly
>   Raises the Spirits, and charms our Ears,
>   Roses and Lilies her Cheeks disclose,
>   But her ripe Lips are more sweet than those.
>   Press her,
>   Caress her,
>   With Blisses,
>   Her Kisses
>   Dissolve us in Pleasure, and soft Repose."

This was sung to the air of "Would you have a young Virgin," for the songs in *The Beggar's Opera* were set to popular tunes. Another, sung by Filch in Act I, to the strain of "The bonny gray-ey'd Morn," is as cruel as one of Hogarth's caricatures.

" 'Tis Woman that seduces all Mankind,
By her we first were taught the wheedling Arts:
Her very Eyes can cheat; when most she's kind,
She tricks us of our Money with our Hearts.
For her, like Wolves by Night we roam for Prey,
And practise ev'ry Fraud to bribe her Charms;
For Suits of Love, like Law, are won by Pay,
And Beauty must be fee'd into our Arms."

The practice of writing new verses for old melodies was usual in English ballad operas, and the tradition persisted, and was even honoured in the late nineteenth century by the Salvation Army whose followers sang hymns to popular tunes, which scandalised pious Victorians. Although many of those respectable Victorians abhorred the "pagan century" that had preceded their own, sacred music was not neglected in the Georgian Age, and some of our familiar Christmas carols date from that time. For example, Dr. John Byrom (1692–1763) wrote "Christians awake, salute the happy morn" in 1750, which was set to music by John Wainwright—a carol that has, in common with many of the popular songs, a rousing pace and vitality, which is characteristic of much of the work of such composers as Dr. Thomas Arne (1710–78), and Charles Dibdin (1745–1814). Among the most popular of Dr. Arne's airs was "Rule Britannia," that was included in *The Masque of Alfred*, by James Thomson (1700–48) and David Mallet (?1705–65), for which Arne wrote the music. The words, which seem rather flamboyant today, were almost certainly by Thomson, and they suited the mood of a country that took pride in its past and enjoyed a stout belief in its present and future. There is an enduring freshness about Arne's music, especially in such songs as "Where the bee sucks," and in his settings of "Under the greenwood tree," and "Blow, blow, thou winter wind." (He was the son of Thomas Arne, an upholsterer, whose address was The Two Crowns & Cushions, in King Street, Covent Garden.)

As fresh and melodious today as when it first captivated the public, is Dibdin's "Tom Bowling's Epitaph." It is a forthright sentimental song, spangled with nautical terms, incorrectly used, perhaps, but very appealing to landsmen.

"Here, a sheer hulk, lies poor Tom Bowling,
The darling of our crew.
No more he'll hear the tempest howling;
For death has broached him to.
His form was of the manliest beauty,
His heart was kind and soft,
Faithful below, he did his duty;
And now he's gone aloft."

The titles of the glees and part songs have simplicity and directness and are often coloured by classical allusions. Here are a few titles, selected from the prolific work of Samuel Webb, a most popular song-writer who was born in 1740: "As Nancy danced," "Belinda's sparkling wit," "Bacchus, Jove's delighted boy," "Bid me, when forty winters," "Hither, all ye loves," "Hence, all ye vain delights," "I'll enjoy the present time," "Surely that's a charming maid," "To the festive board," "When innocence and beauty," "When charming Chloe," "When winds breathe soft," "Wine gives the lover vigor," "The death of fair Adonis," and "We our short lives will measure." There were hundreds of others: love songs, drinking songs, hunting songs, patriotic songs, and songs in praise of daring and bravery on land and sea, as welcome in the drawing-room, the dining-room, the kitchen, the inn, or afloat, with or without accompaniment.

The favourite instruments were the fiddle and the flute, and in the drawing-room, the harpsichord, spinet, and, at the beginning of the nineteenth century, the harp after Sebastian Erard had perfected the pedal model. (See plate 47.) The harpsichord had a keyboard resembling that of a piano, but the strings instead of being struck by hammers, were plucked by quills which twanged them when the keys were pressed. It had long been familiar in England and was in use during the sixteenth and seventeenth centuries, and was small, compact, and occupied about the same space as a small sideboard. Some types were designed for travelling with folding underframes. (See plate 36.) The word spinet was formerly a generic name in England for musical instruments with a small keyboard, with one string to a note that was plucked by a quill. Although spinets were in use in the sixteenth century, it was not until the middle of the seventeenth century that the familiar wing shape was introduced.

The pianoforte was invented during the first decades of the eighteenth century by Bartolommeo Cristofori, of Padua, and when it was introduced into England, the word was shortened to piano. Like the harpsichord and the spinet, the piano had a keyboard, but the wires were struck by hammers which were moved by the keys; and the name was derived from the power this instrument gave the performer who could at will play soft (piano) or loud (forte). By the late eighteenth century the grand piano had developed its familiar and beautiful form and there were several accomplished English makers of this instrument. The harpsichord shown on plate 36 and the grand piano on plate 37 were both made by Josephus Merlin of London.

The love of music seldom generated feverish enthusiasm; though Lord Hervey in his Memoirs records the intense, partisan passions aroused at the Court of George II over Handel, who had been singing master to The Princess Royal, and was consistently belittled by Frederick, Prince of Wales, merely in order to irritate his sister. Pro- and anti-Handelists formed two factions at Court, and the affair, according to Lord Hervey, became as important and serious as the rivalry between the Greens and Blues in Constantinople under

Justinian.[172] After a time the anti-Handelists were regarded as enemies of the Court; to say anything against Handel was almost as serious as voting against the Court in Parliament; but such excesses of enthusiasm were exceptional; and people of quality and all ranks of society were content to make and enjoy music.

Horace Walpole described a four-day visit to Chatsworth, and recorded how the old Duchess of Devonshire "stayed every evening, till it was dark, in the skittle-ground, keeping the score; and one night, that the servants had a ball for Lady Dorothy's birthday, we fetched the fiddles into the drawing-room, and the Dowager herself danced with us!" (Letter to George Montagu, September 1st, 1760.)

Naturally, some of the specialists in disapproval were impelled to issue warnings about the dangers of music. In *The Ladies Library*, it was pointed out that music and painting should be approached with caution, as "the Fancy is often too quick in them, and the Soul too much affected by the Senses. Musick especially so softens, that it enervates it, and exposes it to be conquer'd by the first Temptation which invades it. The Ancients were so well convinc'd of its Perniciousness, that they would never suffer it in a well-regulated State. Why are languishing Airs pleasant but because the Soul gives it self to the Charms of the Senses? What is it you mean by Transporting or Moving in Musick, but the Fury or the Softness of Desire? If the wise Magistrate of *Sparta* broke all the musical Instruments, whose Harmony was too delicious and melting, and *Plato* rejected all the softer Airs of the *Asiatick* Musick; what should we Christians do with the *Italian*, as moving as any that ever were known to Antiquity? How can chaste Minds delight in the Languishments of wanton Poetry, made yet more languishing by the Graces of Musick? What great or noble is there in the dying Notes of foreign Strumpets and Eunuchs? The Power of Musick never appear'd more in *England* than it has done of late; we have seen it draw after it numerous Audiences of both Sexes at a very extravagant Expence, who knowing nothing of the Language were bewitched only with the Magick of the Sounds."[173]

This was not only a moral reflection, but was also a typically English expression of disapproval for foreign music. While the fashionable world might be captived by Italian operas, traditional English music never lost its popularity with the country folk, and the less sophisticated townsmen.

There is a discernible affinity between the simple popular airs and the simple satisfying shapes of country-made things. Taste leaves its mark in many ways, and the taste of any period is marked, not only by its architecture and all the things that are used every day by all classes, but by the sounds which please and stimulate people. Certainly the popular tunes of the Georgian Age seemed to match the surroundings in which they were played and sung. The music of the mid twentieth century, stark, powerful, and occasionally discordant, is very obviously related to contemporary sculpture and painting and architecture: the works of Benjamin Britten and Henry Moore, Sibelius and Le Corbusier, are as complementary as the *tum-tum-timmety, jingle-jangle-jee* tunes of the lesser Victorian composers were complementary to the copious vulgarities of Victorian ornamentation and furnishing; but the majestic order of Handel and Purcell, the exquisite melodies of Mozart and Haydn, were akin to the classic orders—they were the aural accompaniment of visual felicities.

The form of various musical instruments has changed very little, and the violin has hardly changed at all. Its elegant shape occasionally inspired some decorative device, and the example of the fiddle-back chair has been given in a previous chapter. The accessories for musical performances were as graceful as the instruments themselves, and such things as music stands, which also served as reading-desks, and the canterburys or small mobile stands for storing music, were light, well-designed articles. The music canterbury, which had its legs mounted on castors, was, according to Sheraton, "adapted to run in under a piano-forte."[174]

Sheraton had some advice to give about the decoration and furnishing of the music room, which, he suggested, should be conducted in a gay style and said that "the paintings or prints of the muses, and masters of music, may consistently make a part of furnishing; and chairs and stools of a richer variety of colours may be admitted with propriety."[175] A "gay style" was appropriate; a musical performance was usually a gay occasion, and not an exclusive and solemn observance; for music, like Georgian architecture, was understood and appreciated as one of the arts of life.

Decoration from the title page of *Fables for the Female Sex*, London, 1744.

CHAPTER VIII

CHIMNEY-PIECE AND CHIMNEY-CORNER

WRITING in 1624 on "chimnies," in his famous essay, *The Elements of Architecture*, Sir Henry Wotton had said that "in the present business, *Italians*, who make very frugal fires, are perchance not the best Counsellers. Therefore from them we may better learn, both how to raise fair *Mantels* within the rooms, and how to disguise gracefully the shafts of the Chimnies abroad. . . ."[176] The first part of this piece of advice was followed for over two hundred years, by framing the fire-place with mouldings whose sections had correct classical affiliations, and treating the chimney-piece as an exercise in architectural composition. Externally the chimneys were often left to take care of themselves, to the great detriment of the skyline, and when they were considered, their graceless sooty fingers were partly hidden behind a high parapet or a balustrade, built above the cornice. In that same essay Sir Henry had referred to Palladio's description of ancient heating systems, praising them for their effectiveness and economy, but with one very English reservation. The antique accomplishment of central heating was, he said, "surely both for thrift, and for use, far beyond the German *Stoves*; And I should prefer it likewise before our own fashion, if the very sight of a fire did not add to the Room a kind of *Reputation*. . . ."[177]

Certainly the open fire gave the rooms of an English house a reputation, not only for visible comfort, but for draughts, which were tolerated, for without them blowing along at floor level, the fire would smoulder and die. The blazing log or sea coal fire was the focal point of social life in the penetrating damp chilliness of an English autumn and winter; it cheered the parlour, the drawing-room, the dining-room and the kitchen. It was occasionally criticised. In *The Spectator* a husband, who describes himself as "one of those unfortunate men . . . married to a woman of quality" complains that his wife's "whole time and thoughts are spent in keeping up to the mode both in apparel and furniture. All the goods in my house have been changed three times in seven years. I have had seven children by her; and by our marriage articles she was to have her apartments new furnished as often as she lay in. Nothing in our house is useful but that which is fashionable; my pewter holds out generally half a year, my plate a full twelvemonth; chairs are not fit to sit in that were made two years since, nor beds fit for anything but to sleep in, that have stood

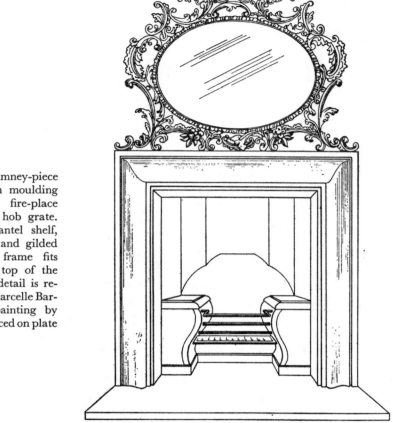

A marble chimney-piece with a bolection moulding framing the fire-place opening, and a hob grate. There is no mantel shelf, and the carved and gilded Rococo mirror frame fits directly on the top of the moulding. This detail is reconstructed by Marcelle Barton from the painting by Zoffany, reproduced on plate 32.

up above that time. My dear is of the opinion that an old-fashioned grate consumes coals, but gives no heat. If she drinks out of glasses of last year she cannot distinguish wine from small-beer. Oh, dear sir, you may guess all the rest."[178]

The letter was written in 1712, and that complaint about the old-fashioned grate devouring coal without heating the room was often justified at the beginning of the eighteenth century; but grates were improved in design and performance by the middle years, and apparently satisfied everybody. The modish enthusiasm for classical forms and usages never led to the approval or adoption of the heating devices perfected in Roman times. *Cali-Ducts*, as Wotton had called them, were never introduced; the Roman system of central heating, perhaps the most efficient ever invented, was not revived; the architecture of Rome might inspire the decoration and determine the proportions of English houses, but the hypocaust could not compete with the chimney-piece and the open fire-place. When heating systems were used at all, they were employed only for conservatories.

The design of many articles of English furniture has been influenced by the habit of sitting round the fire. The phrase "round the fire" recalls the open hearth, placed centrally in the great hall of the mediaeval house, and the "fireside circle" is also a term that survives from the Middle Ages, for since fire-places built against a wall and directly connected with a chimney became common during the latter part of the fifteenth century, the circle has changed to a semicircle; but the English, happily inexact and illogical, could never have brought themselves to speak of sitting "half round the fire," and the "fireside semicircle" or "fireside crescent" would have been unthinkable.

Wherever people sat in winter, there was usually a fire to comfort them. In the great houses servants lived and spent their leisure in the kitchen; in farm houses and cottages the kitchen was the living-room, ample, cheerful, and dependent for comfort upon the dimensions of the fire-place. In the farm-house kitchen the fire-place was almost an additional room, with its own furniture, often built-in, with a warm though usually very hard seat in the chimney-corner. Settles and benches and wainscot chairs would be used in the kitchen.

The chimney-piece flank of an interior, from Isaac Ware's *A Complete Body of Architecture,*
showing alternate treatments for the panelling.

In the dining-room, as we have seen in an earlier chapter, gentlemen might after dinner discuss their port round the table, but were more likely to group their chairs about the fire-place until they joined the ladies for tea or coffee in the drawing-room. The heartiness of the comforts that are associated with the fire-place were not incompatible with gracious form; and easy chairs, from the late seventeenth century to the downfall of design in the eighteen-twenties, preserved their admirable proportions. The chimney-piece was incorporated in the general scheme of interior decoration, and was often a feature of great beauty, giving an opportunity to the architect to indulge his taste for sculptured ornament, and providing accommodation above the mantelpiece for a painting or a looking-glass in a carved frame, or a collection of decorative trifles. Addison tilts at this fashion, so does Swift: the former, in the letter from "Sir John Enville" in *The Spectator*, complaining that Lady Mary Oddly "set herself to reform every room of my house, having glazed all my chimney-pieces with looking-glass, and planted every corner with such heaps of china, that I am obliged to move about my own house with the greatest caution and circumspection for fear of hurting our brittle furniture."[179] Swift in his *Directions to Servants* gives this advice to the chambermaid: "If you happen to break any china with the top of the wisk on the mantle-tree or the cabinet, gather up the fragments, put them together as well as you can, and place them behind the rest. . . ."

The overloaded condition of the mantel-shelf is shown on plate 27, in the interior by Hogarth, and the ability of the architect to make the chimney-piece a dominating feature is demonstrated by the interior at Wanstead House on plate 25. That architects were alert to such opportunities for self-expression is obvious from the following paragraphs of Isaac Ware's *Complete Body of Architecture*. "We are in nothing left so much to the dictates of fancy, under the whole science of architecture, as in the construction of chimney-pieces," he wrote. "Those who have left rules and examples for other articles, lived in hotter countries; and the chimney was not with them, as it is with us, a part of such essential importance, that no common room, plain or elegant, could be constructed without it.

"With us no article in a well-finished room is so essential. The eye is immediately cast upon it on entering, and the place of sitting down is naturally near it. By this means, it becomes the most eminent thing in the finishing of an apartment; and, as fancy is to stand in the place of rule and example in its construction, nothing is more essential than to direct the young architect how he shall employ this wild guide properly: on what occasions he is to give the reins to imagination; and when it is to be limited by method."[180]

Ware classified chimney-pieces under two sections: simple and continued. "In order," he said, "to ascertain the propriety of the peculiar kinds of marble we shall recommend, for it is not every one we can recommend to the architect for his purpose, we shall first consider the chimney-piece as suited to rooms of

The lower part of a chimney-piece, from plate 85 of Isaac Ware's *A Complete Body of Architecture*. A coloured marble was recommended for this design on the grounds that "when so much pomp is intended at so moderate an expense, and the labour of which has contributed in so slight a degree to it, the high colouring and body of the marble will assist the design and serve happily to suit the chimney to the lustre of the other parts of the room."

A design from Isaac Ware's *A Complete Body of Architecture*, of which he wrote, "We will suppose, for the present instance, a room furnished in a moderate degree of elegance, and that the proprietor desires to have a chimney decorated with one of the orders, but not at too great expense. In this case, the furnishings of the room, and the intention of the owner, in point of expense, limit the number of columns. The first thought refers the architect to the Doric order, as by far the least expensive; and both determine against more than one column on each side."

more or less elegance, by placing it before him in the two general conditions, simple, or continued to the ceiling: by simple, we mean a chimney, which terminates at its mantle-piece, or by a pediment, or other such ornament over it: and by this kind of chimney, continued up to the ceiling, we understand an entire work finishing that part of the room, and consisting of the proper or simple chimney and ornaments above correspondent to it in breadth; leaving a pannel for a picture, terminated at the heighth of the room, with sculpture, accommodated, in nature and degree, to that of the lower part."(181)

A parlour chimney-piece, from Isaac Ware's *A Complete Body of Architecture*.
Of this design, Ware wrote that if it be "considered as one of the simple
kinds, a variegated marble would be, at first thought, alloted for it; and in
any of that kind it would make a handsome figure: but if we consider the
dolphins, the faces, the ornament of the sides, and the sculpture allowed
to the walls, we may very properly make the exchange, and prefer a plain
colour."

For both the simple and the continued chimney-piece the most minute
directions were given, not only in Ware's book but in the countless guide
books on building, for the proportions, appropriate introduction and proper
use of the various orders, and even for carefully controlled flirtations with
the Gothic and Chinese styles. For example, in *The Builder's Director, or Bench-
Mate*, Batty Langley announced that he had "given a great Variety of *Gothick*-
Moldings for the *Bases* and *Capitals* of *Columns, Arches, Weatherings, Jaumbs* for
Doors, Windows, Chimney-Pieces, &c. and the Manner of describing them

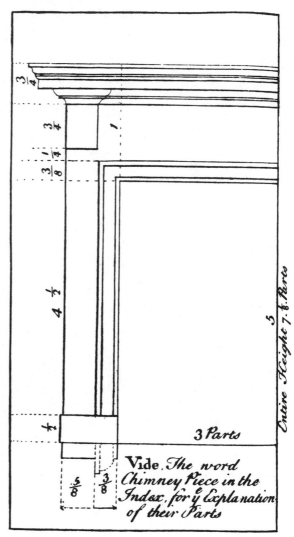

The copy-books supplied sailing directions for the enlightenment of every type of workman, from the rural joiner and carpenter to the well-established town maker. Good classical proportions were thus universally preserved. This and the two examples on the opposite page are from *The Builder's Director or Bench-Mate* by Batty Langley (1751).

geometrically of any Magnitude desired: Which being entirely new, I hope will be favourably received."[182] In some of Langley's designs for chimney-pieces, a distinct anticipation of Victorian Gothic is discernible. (See page 124.)

Isaac Ware was full of fatherly advice about the ornamentation of the chimney-piece, sagely observing that "when the young architect has learned what it will be right to do, the next consideration is how to do it."[183] He knew that sea subjects were popular and he devoted a complete chapter to the marine chimney-piece. "By this term," he said, "is meant a chimney-piece, all the ornaments of which are taken from marine or sea subjects. These are

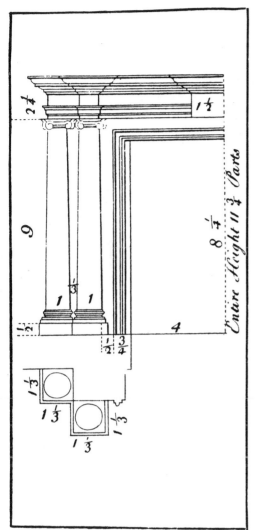

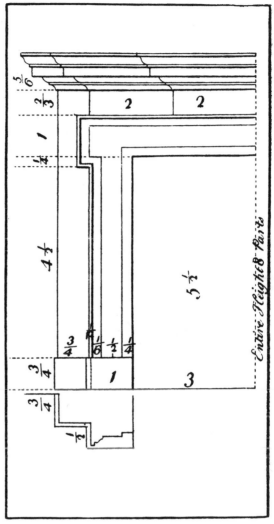

in themselves extremely numerous, full of beauty, and full of variety. The
whole scope and series of them are in the choice of the architect on such an
occasion; and his judgment is to display itself in a proper choice among the
multiplicity of forms, and a just assortment and continuation of those he
chuses. The first direction we shall give the young architect on this head, is to
review the variety of Nature, and take his choice among them. Let him not
limit his fancy by the small number that have been used by others; there are
not only more, but better. The architects of the present time do not sufficiently
study Nature; and it is in the works alone of those who have professedly treated

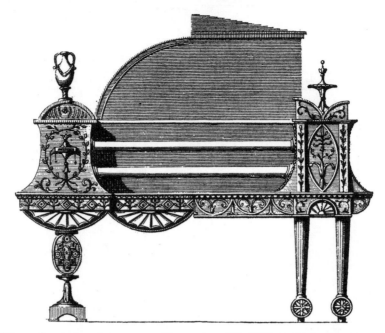

Alternative designs for a grate. (From plate IX of *The Builder's Magazine, or Monthly Companion*, London, 1774.) In the text of this plate, the authors said, in the best tradesmen's English, "As we mean to enrich our Work with every thing that can be found useful to the Architect, Carpenter, Mason, Smith, &c. we hope these designs will be found acceptable."

of these subjects, that he who would be eminent in this part of his business must study the means."[184] (See page 297.)

The framework and the general architectural character of the chimney-piece indicated the Georgian designer's capacity for doing the right thing in the right way; and this same incomparable ability appeared in the accessories of the fire-place—the grate, the fire-place furniture, and the fender. The basket grate and the hob grate, were usually of wrought iron, but when improvements in the smelting of cast iron enabled this malleable material to be used extensively, manufacturers of grates had their products competently designed. Some of the great iron-founding firms like the Carron Company had a close connection with architectural design; and that foundry, established on the banks of the River Carron near Falkirk in Stirling, derived great advantage from its association with the brothers Adam.

"As early as 1764, John Adam was a partner in the Carron Company while carrying on his father's architectural practice; but it was his younger brothers, Robert and James, who were to produce a new and elegant interpretation of the Greek and Roman orders, thus evolving a style that had far-reaching

Design for a stove. (From plate LXXV of *The Builder's Magazine, or Monthly Companion*, London, 1774.)

effects on English architecture. Much of Robert Adam's delicate ornamental detail was especially applicable to cast iron, and where previously railings, gates, verandahs, fire-places, vases and urns had been of wrought iron, Adam used either a mixture of wrought and cast, or cast iron alone, or a mixture of cast iron and steel. It was natural that he should turn to the Carron Company for much of his work, and the influence of the brothers Adam may be traced in the designs of many of the Company's early castings, particularly in panels, grates and fire-places.

"During this period Carron employed as designers the brothers William and Henry Haworth, who had studied at the Royal Academy School during the presidency of Sir Joshua Reynolds. Henry started as a designer and carver at Carron in 1779, and did much good work, but unfortunately died two years later. He was succeeded by his brother William who worked as designer and carver at Carron for the next fifty-six years. The brothers came of an artistic family, their father and grandfather being noted carvers. The father, Samuel Haworth, to commemorate the granting of the Royal Charter in 1773, carved for Carron the famous portraits of King George III and his Queen, which were to adorn so many of the fashionable hob grates of the period. The brothers led a simple life and can hardly be said to have become famous in their day. But, with their father, they created a distinctive style of ornament which has characterised much of Carron's work. They have left much carving

GG—L

A fire-screen or pole-screen, of the type that appears in Hogarth's painting, *Marriage à la Mode*. (See plates 27 and 28.) From the first edition of *The Gentleman and Cabinet Maker's Director*, by Thomas Chippendale, 1754.

in wood of the most delicate order: whether classical figure work, ornamental panels, mouldings, decoration, or balcony and balustrade work, their crafts-manship is faultless, and shows a complete mastery of the casting process."[185]

That the skill of craftsmen like the Haworths was given such liberty for expression, is a tribute to the far-sightedness of eighteenth century industrialists. They shared the universal respect for the principles of architectural design. In pottery, Wedgwood, as we have mentioned earlier, was the shining example of the promising but short-lived partnership between art and industry, and in iron-working the directors of the Carron Company were equally progressive. The gifts and antecedents of the Haworths have been described as follows: "Both brothers were masters of classical figure work, as well as being quite accomplished painters. Understanding of foundry technique ensured for their products beautiful quality and definition, when finished with light black lead. They were of a London family and represented the third generation of craftsmen. Their father, who died in 1779, had a flourishing carving business in Denmark Street, St. Giles-in-the-Fields, employing with his two sons Henry and William, some thirty carvers, many Dutch and Flemish craftsmen among them. His establishment received occasional visits from George III himself."[186]

In common with other industries and crafts, metalworkers had studied the ornamental conventions of the classic orders; and the pierced and engraved fenders of steel and iron and brass, which bordered the marble hearths, and the shovels, tongs and pokers, made in sets from the late seventeenth to the early nineteenth century, showed by their form and decoration how thoroughly those conventions had been mastered, and how ably interpreted. The coal box, scuttle or hod, as it was variously termed, was probably of brass or iron; but the wear and tear to which such articles were constantly subjected led to constant replacements, and no examples have survived from the period. There is reason to believe that these receptacles were sometimes elegantly decorated. John Thomas Smith refers to "a certain created lord, who had his coronet painted upon his coal scuttles."[187]

Coals had to be carried, usually from a cellar, to all the rooms. Swift, in his *Directions to Servants*, suggests to the housemaid that she should "Bring up none but large coals to the Dining-room and your Lady's Chamber; they make the best fires, and if you find them too big it is easy enough to break them on the marble hearth." He advises the chambermaid to "Oil the Tongs, Poker and Fire-shovel up to the Top not only to keep them from rusting, but likewise to prevent meddling people from wasting your master's coals with stirring the fire."

During the summer months, when the fire was not in use, a fire-board or chimney-board was used, which closed the fire-place opening, and was painted or papered to match the interior treatment of the room. It has been suggested that dummy board figures were used for this purpose, and also for fire-screens. The dummy board figure, which is sometimes called a picture board dummy, was fashionable in the seventeenth and eighteenth centuries, and was an essential part of interior furnishing. It was a cut-out flat board, painted in oils to represent human and other figures, and stood either against or a few inches away from a wall. It is quite likely that one or two dummy board figures stood in front of the empty fire-place during the summer. Their owners were very fond of them, and became quite attached to these paintings, which were almost regarded as members of the family. Sometimes they were in miniature, sometimes life size. That they were ever used as fire-screens is most unlikely, for they would never have resisted the heat of a fire. (See plate 37.)

The fire-screen was in constant use to shield complexions. It was an old invention, originating in the Middle Ages. A circular screen on an iron pole is shown in the painting of "The Virgin and Child," by the Flemish artist, Robert Campin (1375–1444), and pole-screens of this type with sliding panels of tapestry, needlework or painted wood were familiar articles of furnishing during the eighteenth century. They could be easily adjusted, and the lady in Hogarth's painting reproduced on plate 28 is nervously making some such adjustment: another screen is shown on plate 27, and an example from the first edition of Chippendale's *Director* appears on page 302. There were other types, folding and sliding, and there were also table fire-screens as well as the specially designed writing fire-screens described in a previous chapter. The illogicality of the English was seldom more agreeably or harmlessly illustrated than by the multiplication of such devices which afforded protection from the otherwise uncontrollable fierceness of the large fires. Stoves were very seldom used, though in the late eighteenth century a cast iron stove might occasionally appear in a hall; but for rooms where people lived, they were never popular. As Sir Henry Wotton had said, the very sight of a fire added to a room "a kind of *Reputation*."

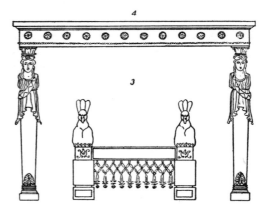

A mantelpiece and grate. (From Thomas Hope's *Household Furniture and Interior Decoration*, 1807.)

CHAPTER IX

"LET US TAKE THE ROAD"

WHEN you "took the road" you also took a good many risks and needed a good many cushions if you travelled by coach. A letter in *The Spectator* describes how a lady kept "her seat in a hackney coach as well as the best rider does on a managed horse. The laced shoe on her left foot, with a careless gesture, just appearing on the opposite cushion, held her both firm and in a proper attitude to receive the next jolt."[188] Unless you were wedged in securely, the jolting was intolerable, for even after springs were improved, it was long before road surfaces were good enough to carry the fast stage coaches that made travel so exhilarating during the last quarter of the eighteenth and the first thirty years of the nineteenth centuries.

The turnpike system, which did much to improve the roads, was a typical piece of English enterprise, sporadic, uncontrolled and unsupervised by government, and highly efficient. It was left to local initiative to provide a few miles of good road surface, and the people who invested their capital received an income from the tolls taken from travellers. The system was excellent, and long stretches of well-made roads were to be found all over the country; but no continuous standardised road surfaces had been known in the island since Britain was a Roman province. There were no hordes of state officials employed to collect the tolls. Collection was local, and the disrespect with which toll-keepers were treated was symptomatic of the widespread and commendable impatience with officials of any kind that once distinguished England and the English.

Whether you travelled in your own fast private coach, a hired coach, or a stage coach, you expected discomfort and danger. The song sung by Matt of the Mint in Act II of *The Beggar's Opera* is full of sinister implications.

"Let us take the Road.
        Hark! I hear the Sound of Coaches!
        The hour of Attack approaches,
To your Arms, brave Boys, and load.
        See the Ball I hold!
Let the Chymists toil like Asses,
Our Fire their Fire surpasses,
        And turns all our lead to Gold."

But you could be robbed courteously. Good manners came to the surface in the most unlikely professions. The following news item appeared in *The General Evening Post*, during October 1736:—

"Last Sunday Mr Hawkins of Battersea going with his Wife in a Chaise to Lambeth, was attack'd in Battersea-Field by a single Highwayman, who robb'd them of between four and five Pounds, and her Wedding Ring, the latter she begg'd to have return'd, which he did, and 6s. to defray the Expences of their Journey, and after returning them Thanks for his Booty, wish'd them a good Morning and rode off undiscover'd."[189]

It made a good news story, though it is worth recalling what Dr. Johnson said about such items and their writers. "In Sir Henry Wotton's jocular definition, 'an ambassador is said to be a man of virtue, sent abroad to tell lies for the advantage of his country.' A *news-writer* is a man without virtue, who writes lies at home for his own profit."

The design of vehicles, public and private, improved considerably during the eighteenth century. The stage coach changed from a ponderous and clumsy box on wheels, to a shapely, well-sprung conveyance, comfortably upholstered within, the seats outside having side rails to which the passengers could cling as the coach swayed and rocked at full speed. These superior coaches were confined to the main roads, and after the middle of the century their journeys were timed, and they arrived and departed to the minute. It was very important not only for travellers to know the correct time, but for the innkeeper and his staff. In the coaching inns a hanging clock of plain design, with a large wooden dial and a short trunk or case below for the weights, became a feature of the coffee-room. Such clocks have been mis-named Act of Parliament clocks, and erroneously connected with Pitt's Act of 1797, which taxed clocks and watches. (See page 307.) Although the speed as well as the general design of stage coaches improved, six miles an hour was seldom exceeded, until the royal mail coaches set a new pace, and ten or twelve miles an hour became possible. (See Appendix 8.) The country stages long retained the cumbersome form that had originated in the seventeenth century, though it was occasionally modified by a few refinements of line, in imitation of smarter vehicles. For example, the coach shown in Hogarth's "Country Inn Courtyard" has slightly curved ends to the body instead of the box-like

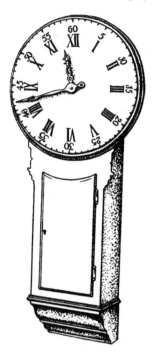

A coaching inn clock. This type of hanging clock was weight-driven, of very plain design, with a large wooden dial, usually japanned black with gilt figures on it, and a short trunk or case underneath. These clocks have been mis-named Parliament or Act of Parliament clocks, and erroneously connected with Pitt's Act of 1797 under which clocks and watches were taxed, but clocks of this design were in use in the coaching inns during the middle of the eighteeenth century. (See page 306.)
(*Drawn by Marcelle Barton.*)

form of earlier types. (See plate 23.) The country stage, crude though it was, was far more comfortable than the lumbering stage-wagon.

The fast, lightly built, brightly painted mail coaches that raced along the high roads during the half-century between 1780 and 1830 prolonged the memory of Georgian grace, and bequeathed some of their structural and decorative characteristics to the first class carriages of the early railways. Some traces of the felicities of Georgian coach-work still survived a hundred years later, and influenced, albeit slightly, the design of motor-car bodies. As late as 1921, Aldous Huxley described in *Chrome Yellow* "a smart, expensive-looking machine, enamelled a pure lemon yellow and upholstered in emerald green leather. There were two seats—three if you squeezed tightly enough—and their occupants were protected from wind, dust, and weather by a glazed sedan that rose, an elegant eighteenth century hump, from the midst of the body of the car."

Every branch of coach-building had, by the beginning of the nineteenth century, attained the same easy mastery of graceful design that distinguished cabinet-making. Even the miniature carriages for children, the forerunners of the perambulator, shared the graces and bright decoration of larger vehicles. In the "Introductory Observations" to the first volume of *A Treatise on Carriages*, which William Felton, the coach-maker, published in 1794, the author could claim that "The art of Coach-Making has been in a gradual state of improvement for half a century past, and has now attained to a very high degree of perfection, with respect both to the beauty, strength and elegance of the machine: the consequence has been, an increasing demand for that comfortable conveyance, which, besides its common utility, has now, in the higher circles of life, become a distinguishing mark of the taste and rank of the proprietor."[190]

He followed his opening paragraph with a few immodest words of praise for the trade he practised. "The superior excellence of English workmanship in the construction of carriages," he said, "has not only been the occasion of a very great increase in their number among the inhabitants of this country, but the exportation of them to foreign nations, in time of peace, is become a considerable and profitable branch of British commerce."[191] Like Thomas Chippendale and Ince and Mayhew and other leading furniture-makers, Felton was advertising his wares and abilities in a glorified trade catalogue, though he presented it primarily as a guide, and illustrated the book with plates which gave constructional details of a variety of private vehicles. He explained his intentions to his potential readers (and customers) without disguise. "The Gentleman whose situation in the world enables him to keep a carriage," he said, "has hitherto been unavoidably deprived of the means of acquiring such a knowledge of the manner of building and repairing carriages, as would enable him to judge when any attempt is made to impose upon him, either in the original price charged for a new carriage, such as his fancy and inclination may lead him to make choice of, or in the necessary expence that may be requisite to repair the damages a carriage may have sustained by time or accident. It is therefore intended, in this Treatise, to exhibit to public view, such a distinct account, not only of the original price of the carriage, and the repairs that may be necessary, but also of the separate prices of the different component parts thereof, as will enable the proprietor effectually to guard against imposition.

"This Treatise will be of equal advantage to the Gentleman who builds a carriage, as the House-builder's Price-book has, by experience, proved to be to him who builds a house; and as there are many more Gentlemen who amuse themselves in getting carriages built than in building houses, the utility of this Treatise will be more general."[192]

He anticipated criticism from his fellow-tradesmen, particularly as he published lists of prices for different types of work. "This Treatise," he asserted, "can by no means injure the fair and honest trader, but will rather be of advantage to him, in so far as he may charge such prices as are fair and reasonable, without the risk of suspicion; and his employer will always have it in his power to have recourse to a regular standard of prices, both for building and repairing. It will, however, prove an effectual check upon the fraudulent and designing: and from that quarter the Author will, no doubt, be loaded with calumny; but he is prepared to meet it, and to refute every

Two early nineteenth century perambulators (*circa* 1810).

Above is a Regency style model in dark blue, with shafts. This would probably be drawn by a donkey or a pony. Below, is an English barouche perambulator in yellow and dark green, with springs. (Formerly in the collection of the late Professor Sir Albert Richardson, P.P.R.A., at Avenue House, Ampthill.) (*From drawings by Marcelle Barton.*)

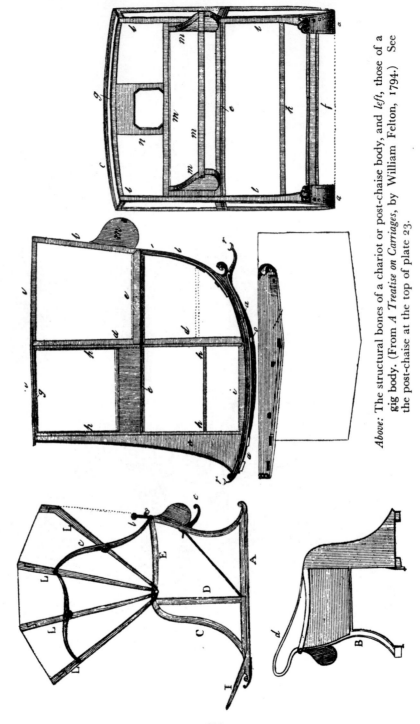

Above: The structural bones of a chariot or post-chaise body, and *left*, those of a gig body. (From *A Treatise on Carriages*, by William Felton, 1794.) See the post-chaise at the top of plate 23.

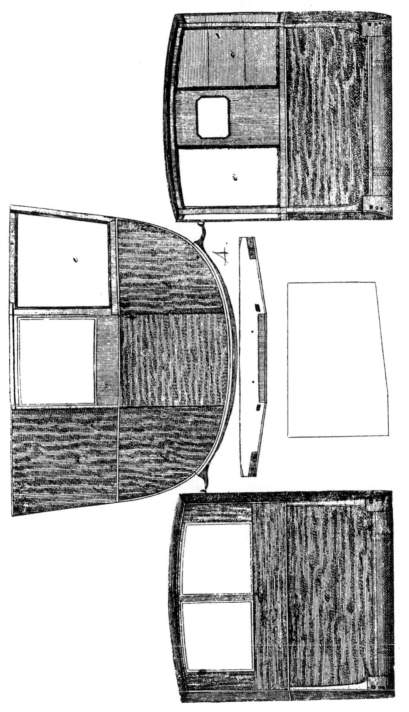

Three views of the body of a coach or chariot. (From *A Treatise on Carriages*, by William Felton, 1794.) These lightly built, elegant vehicles were constructed with a skill comparable to that exercised by the great cabinet-makers of the period.

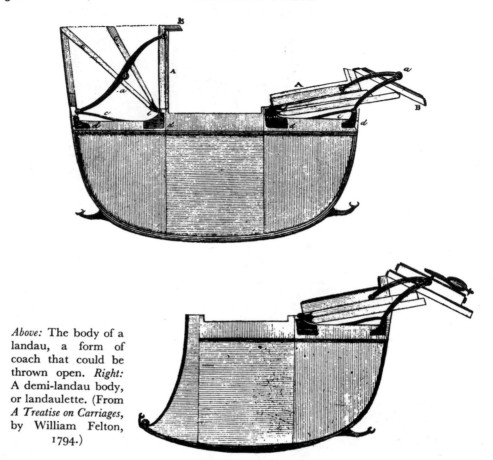

Above: The body of a landau, a form of coach that could be thrown open. *Right:* A demi-landau body, or landaulette. (From *A Treatise on Carriages,* by William Felton, 1794.)

attack made upon the propriety and fairness of the different charges that are stated in this Treatise, either in building or repairing."[193]

Felton's *Treatise* shows how thoroughly every detail in coach-building was considered in terms of materials and design. As much care was lavished on the form and finish of a chariot or a post-chaise (for as Felton said "these bodies differ not in the least from each other") as Chippendale and his contemporaries gave to the form and finish of some exquisite cabinet. All the accessories were well shaped, even such a prosaic thing as a boot or budget (the terms were interchangeable) for carrying luggage. The construction of carriages, phaetons, gigs, or curricles, the method of hanging the bodies, the form of the springs, all contributed to a curvilinear effect in fulfilling various functions. As Felton pointed out: "The bodies of carriages are suspended from the springs by braces; the proper method of executing this, adds much to the elegance of the carriage, and the ease of passengers. . . ."[194]

Lightness was desired, but never at the expense of structural strength. Felton wrote his *Treatise* when the taste for extreme slenderness in furniture design and delicacy in ornamentation had been established by the work and example of the brothers Adam. "The workmanship of a carriage must be particularly firm," said Felton, "and not partially strained in any part, as it is to bear much racking in its use. The timbers throughout are lightened or reduced, for the sake of external appearance, assisted also with moulding edges, and carving in some trifling degree, which greatly helps to ornament the whole."(195)

Felton was sound on ornamental painting which was "merely to beautify the carriage, which it does materially, when it is well executed; but when otherwise, it hurts the appearance of it. This depends on the capacity of the

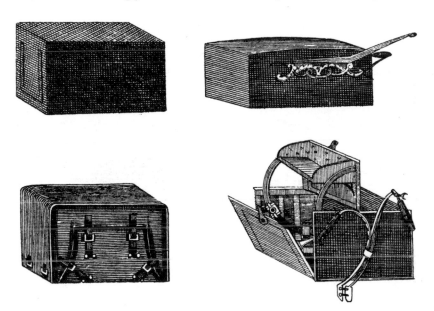

A boot or budget was really a development of the mediaeval travelling chest, and it was not until the Georgian period that the chest became an integral part of the vehicle, designed with it, instead of being an independent object, fortuitously affixed to the framework of a coach. Here are four examples.

Top: Two square japanned boots. These were the most usual types, made in elm, covered with strong russet, and welted round the sides.

Below left: A platform or luggage boot, the sides framed in iron, and provided with straps.

Below right: A boot combined with a coachman's seat, which was hung on springs, the whole construction being much stronger than the other types.

(All from *A Treatise on Carriages*, by William Felton, 1794.)

Above: Two examples of short blocks used for post-chaise carriages.

Left: Raised hind end, having a guard handle which helped the carriage servant up, and also deterred other carriage horses from approaching too near.

Below: Raised fore ends or fore blocks.

All these show the influence of contemporary architectural design, not only in the proportions but in the embellishment of the scrollwork. The ubiquitous acanthus leaf is much in evidence.

Above: Examples of spring blocks of the most elaborate type: these could be reduced to simpler designs.

Left: A footman cushion, which consisted, usually, of a board construction, leather-covered, to provide extra comfort for the servant and to obviate the danger from other carriages colliding.

This is an instance of servants being considered in terms of design— to this extent their accommodation on vehicles was far ahead of the accommodation provided for them in houses, where they were confined to the basements and the attics.

(All from *A Treatise on Carriages*, by William Felton, 1794.)

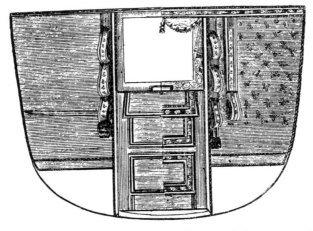

The interior of a coach, showing the upholstery and the various trimmings
and linings. (From *A Treatise on Carriages*, by William Felton, 1794.)

artist; the pannels had better be entirely plain, than daubed as many of them
are in imitation of painting; and in particular that of Heraldry, which requires
some merit to execute properly."[196] He included explicit directions and
plates about the proper use of heraldic devices, and referred his readers to
Edmonson's *Book of Heraldry* which gave "every information necessary on
that subject." (See page 317.) Knowledge of the subject was essential in the
eighteenth century. Every innkeeper who catered for the nobility and gentry
was versed in heraldry. Inn servants could tell at a glance, when an equipage
drew up before the premises, the rank and eminence of the passenger who
would alight when the footman let down the steps. It was usual for the arms
and crests which a family was entitled to bear to be painted on the side panels
of a carriage; not a discreet miniature representation, such as survives today
on a few—a very few—vehicles, but a boldly emblazoned proclamation of
the rank and dignity of the owner. This determined the degree of obeisance
performed by the landlord when he hastened out to assure his lordship that
he would find within everything to his liking. To be associated with the nobility,
however tenuously or doubtfully, was a social ambition. That celebrated
beauty, Mary Robinson (1758–1800) had a light blue carriage, "and upon
the centre of each panel, a basket of flowers was so artfully painted, that as
she drove along it was mistaken for a coronet."[197]

Rivers of colour flowed through the streets of the Georgian city: the traffic
had an iridescence which owed as much to the brightly painted and gilded
vehicles as to the rich uniforms of coachmen and footmen. And here and
there, moving slowly but steadily, would be that most characteristic of Georgian
conveyances, the sedan chair. These chairs were in use during the seventeenth

century, and had been brought to England by Sir Sanders Duncombe in 1634, from Naples, according to John Evelyn, who had observed the streets of that city to be "full of gallants on horseback, in coaches and sedans." (*Diary,* February 8th, 1645.) Duncombe was granted a fourteen years' licence for them by Charles I, and thereafter they enjoyed a great and consistent popularity that lasted until the third decade of the nineteenth century. Very few records exist of seventeenth century types; usually they appear as incidental objects in contemporary engravings of street scenes; though in a set of "Cries of London," issued in 1655, one plate represents "The Siddan Carriers," and furnishes a fairly detailed though crudely drawn example. It was unpretentious, little more than an upright box, rather like a truncated sentry-box, roofed by a shallow dome. The sides were pierced by two glazed windows, one divided by glazing bars into sixteen small panes, through which the seated passenger had a good view, and another with twelve panes, farther forward. There was probably a window in the front, for even at that date the ultimate form of the sedan chair was perceptible.

The history of the design of sedan chairs in England from the end of the Puritan period to the early nineteenth century is comparable with that of English furniture: it is a record of progressive refinement, without marked departure from a basic form. The private sedan chair acquired the status as well as the high degree of finish and ornamentation of a piece of fine furniture, though English chairs seldom displayed the Rococo extravagance of their French counterparts; instead their design usually suggested the air of unpretentious comfort associated with the well-appointed town or country house. The great advantage of the sedan chair was that the passenger could enter it in the hall of the house he was leaving, and be carried through the streets and finally upstairs in his own house and into the bedroom, if he was an invalid or particularly indolent. This was seldom done with a hired chair; but the private chair, conveyed by one's own chairmen, would certainly be carried upstairs, and would rest under cover in the house—probably in a corner of the hall—when not in use. Public chairs, which could be hired, lacked the amenities of the privately-owned vehicle. They were neither capacious nor comfortable, and early in the eighteenth century a skit on their meagre dimensions in *The Tatler,* read as follows:—

"The humble petition of William Jingle, Coach-maker and Chair-maker of the liberty of Westminster; To Isaac Bickerstaff, Esquire, Censor of Great Britain; Showeth, that upon the late invention of Mrs. Catherine Cross-Stitch mantua-maker, the petticoats of ladies were too wide for entering in any coach or chair, which was in use before the said invention. That for the service of the said ladies your petitioner has built a round chair in the form of a lantern, six yards and a half in circumference, with a stool in the centre of it; the said vehicle being so contrived as to receive the passenger by opening in two in the middle, and closing mathematically when she is seated. . . ."[198]

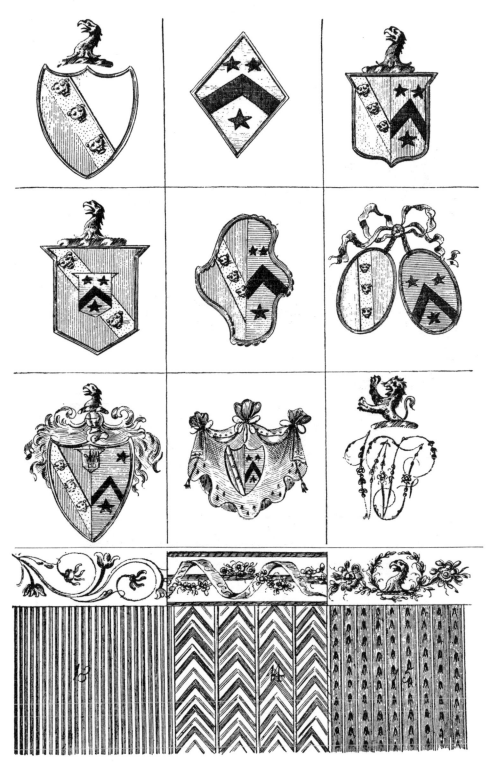

Painted and varnished ornamental heraldic arms: the three lower examples
are of striped and zigzag work. (See pages 313 and 315.) (From *A Treatise
on Carriages*, by William Felton, 1794.)

Rivers of colour flowed through the streets of Georgian London, not only
on the occasion of state processions, but every day. Coaches that had three
windows at the side, and one in front, were sometimes called "glass coaches,"
and there are three examples of them on this page, and two opposite. (From
a contemporary engraving, *circa* 1762–63.)

Two painted and gilded coaches, from a contemporary engraving, *circa* 1762–63. (See opposite page, and compare with the early Georgian type at the head of page 305.)

If public chairs were not parked under shelter, they suffered, for although they were stoutly constructed and covered with leather, they could not resist the effects of continuous exposure to English weather. In *Humphry Clinker*, Smollett's criticism of the Circus at Bath was sharpened by his comment that no proper parking-place had been contrived for sedan chairs. He said: "If, instead of the areas and iron rails, which seem to be of very little use, there had been a corridor with arcades all round, as in Covent-Garden, the appearance of the whole would have been more magnificent and striking; those arcades would have afforded an agreeable covered walk, and sheltered the poor chairmen and their carriages from the rain, which is here almost perpetual. At present, the chairs stand soaking in the open streets, from morning to night, till they become so many boxes of wet leather, for the benefit of the gouty and rheumatic, who are transported in them from place to place." On the lower part of plate 22 a sedan chair is shown parked in the piazza at Covent Garden.

The private sedan chair was a more comfortable and sumptuous vehicle than those that plied for hire, and a well-preserved example is illustrated on plates 20 and 21, dating from the reign of Queen Anne. It is supposed to have been made originally for Charles, the second Duke of Grafton, then a young man in his early twenties. (Formerly in the possession of the late Sir Albert Richardson. The original ash poles and the leather straps used by the chairmen still exist. There are two sets, one 18 ft. long for street use, the other 7 ft. long, for carrying the chair upstairs. Five shallow grooves are cut on the underside at the ends of each pole to give the chairmen a firm grip. The original

Detail of the rear wheel of George III's state coach. (See opposite page and plate 34.)

Detail of the body and decoration of George III's state coach. This is reproduced from an engraving published in *The London Magazine* for December, 1762. The coach was designed by Sir William Chambers, who was the King's architect, for the architect, as the master designer, was the obvious person to call in for the direction of such an imposing work, and he used classical motifs with freedom and imagination. The complete coach is shown on plate 34. (See also opposite page.)

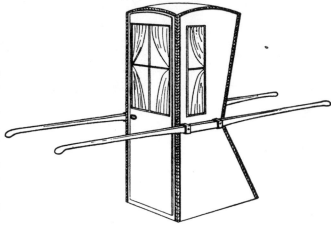

Two sedan chairs, of the type used in Bath in the late eighteenth and early nineteenth centuries. (*Drawn by Marcelle Barton from contemporary prints.*) The left-hand example appears in Thomas Malton's engraving of the Circus at Bath on the upper part of plate 16, and the other in the print of the Pump Room on plate 18.

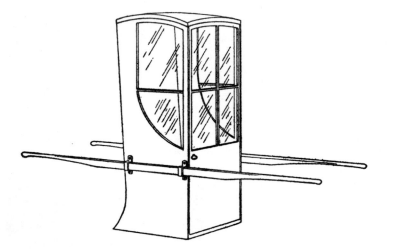

brass links, carried by the link boys to light the chairmen at night, are also preserved and are illustrated on plate 21.

The chair is covered with golden leather which shows very little sign of wear and tear; and the exterior surface is divided into irregular panels by thin strips of brass, ornamented with imitation nail-heads in repoussé, these strips extending over the domed roof, dividing it into eight segments. This roof has marked affinities with the prevailing taste for classical architecture, for the shallow dome springs from a cornice formed by the hammered metal strips, which are upturned at the corners to form acroteria in miniature. The glazing bars of the windows follow contemporary window design and are $\frac{7}{8}$ in. in width, very slightly curved, with surface variation provided by a raised, flat central member $\frac{3}{8}$ in. wide. The same moulded detail appears on both sides of the glazing bars, which still retain traces of gilding. Those bars frame panes of thin, unblemished white glass, beautifully clear, the sight size of each pane being 1 ft. 6 in. wide, by 1 ft. 11⅝ in. deep. The windows slide easily in their grooved frames and may be raised or lowered by straps, which pass over small ivory knobs to allow the window to be adjusted. These straps are of dark red damask with a bright yellow floral pattern.

The internal width of the chair is 1 ft. 10 in. and the depth 2 ft. 5½ in.—not too roomy for ladies and gentlemen wearing the voluminous costume of the period. But once inside it was tolerably comfortable, for the back had a slight rake, an advantage that was absent from the box-like mid seventeenth century types, and this provided a degree of comfort for the passenger comparable with that of a high-backed winged easy chair. The height of the seat from the floor is 1 ft. 6 in. and its depth is 1 ft. 5 in., which accords with the directions given for the height of seats in carriages in Felton's *Treatise*. Felton recommended 1 ft. 2 in. from the floor, exclusive of the cushion. The seat of this chair consists of a well-stuffed damask covered cushion, resting upon a wooden shelf: below, a valance with an embroidered border hangs to the floor. The interior is lined throughout with claret-coloured damask, garnished with lines of dome-headed brass nails, ¼ in. in diameter. The windows are curtained in a plain, dark red material, hanging from brass rings which slide on thin iron curtain rods. At the head of the windows are pelmets with gold fringes and a central tassel. The door is fastened on the outside with an iron hasp.

The design of this private chair is similar to that shown in Hogarth's painting of "The Arrest," in the *Rake's Progress*. The chair from which the unfortunate gentleman is being dragged has a gadrooned and gilded edge to the roof and the glazing bars of the windows are also gilded; but it is basically the same type as the private chair made for the Duke of Grafton; and this basic type persisted, for it appears frequently in paintings and engravings of the second half of the eighteenth century. John Kay's engraving of Edinburgh chairmen, made about 1792, has the same ornamental characteristics, though the inward curve of the back is more pronounced. (See page 327.) In Rennoldson's engraving of John Collet's painting of a scene in Covent Garden, entitled "The Female Orators," a parson is shown emerging from a sedan chair, which is another variation of the characteristic type, but with a flat roof, decorated with turned finials at the corners. Part of this engraving appears on page 325, and the complete scene is reproduced on plate 22.

In Hogarth's "Beer Street" a chair is shown in the background with windows that are glazed with large panes of plate glass, like many of the French chairs of that time. It was clearly a private chair, for plate glass was then costly. The domed top, surmounted by what appears to be a coronet, is supported in front on slender, turned columns, which terminate in finials. (See page 324.) This form of light, open construction increases its resemblance to the ornate French sedan chairs of the Louis XV period, which were not

A section from an engraving of Hogarth's "Beer Street." This shows, above
the fishwives in the foreground, a private sedan chair. The design follows
contemporary French fashions, with three large plate glass windows
instead of smaller windows divided by glazing bars, like the example on the
opposite page. The occupant, who appears to be exasperated because her
chairmen have paused for refreshment, has folded the hoops of her dress on
each side, so she appears to be sitting in a winged chair. (See page 326
and plates 20–21.)

This shows the difficulty of emerging gracefully, or indeed, emerging at all, from a sedan chair. True, the reverend passenger is trying to avoid hearing the remarks of the fishwife on the right, so he is alighting perhaps more awkwardly than usual. This is reproduced from an engraving by Rennoldson published in 1768, of John Collet's painting entitled "The Female Orators." The complete scene, which is in Covent Garden, is reproduced on plate 22.

only profusely decorated with carved and gilded ornamentation, but had the side and front panels below the glazed area elaborately painted with landscapes, classical or floral motifs, and a variety of fanciful subjects. In England a few noblemen might indulge a taste for such embellishment, but the more solidly comfortable type of chair was favoured, whether public or private.

Not that everybody would have agreed about the standard of comfort provided, and that observant critic, Louis Simond, had some hard things to say about sedan chairs, and said them with uncompromising vivacity in the second volume of his *Journal of a Tour and Residence in Great Britain* (1810–11). He implied that although the sedan chair was still in use in the opening decade of the nineteenth century, it was then regarded as an archaic conveyance, used only by ladies and gentlemen of the old school. "The ladies who go to court on the birthday are dressed in the fashion of fifty years ago," he wrote, adding that he supposed this was more suitable to the age of the king and queen. "They are carried there in sedan chairs, which can penetrate further than carriages; and it is really a curiosity to see them as they pass along the street toward the Palace of St. James's. To enable them to sit in these chairs, their immense hoops are folded like wings, pointing forward on each side. The preposterous high head-dress would interfere with the top, and must be humoured by throwing the head back; the face is therefore turned up, kept motionless in that awkward attitude, as if on purpose to be gazed at; and that face, generally old and ugly, (young women not going much there, it seems) is painted up to the eyes, and set with diamonds.

"The glasses of the vehicle are drawn up, that the winds of Heaven may not visit the powder and paint too roughly; and this piece of natural history, thus cased, does not ill resemble a foetus of a hippopotamus in its brandy bottle. The present generation can hardly believe that it was possible to be young and handsome in this accoutrement; and yet it was so. I have seen some of these ladies smile on the wondering spectators as they passed, conscious, I should hope, of their own absurd appearance."[199]

The windows of the chair could be closed at will, and spring curtains could ensure privacy for the passenger. These spring curtains, or blinds as they were subsequently called, were, as William Felton put it, "so convenient, that they are indispensibly necessary to almost every kind of close carriage."[200] They were far easier to manipulate than curtains, and by the end of the eighteenth century were probably adopted as standard equipment both for public and private chairs.

Few changes were made in the general design of sedan chairs after the middle years of the century. About 1770 a wheeled type was introduced, but it never gained the same degree of popularity as the wheel-less sedan. To be trundled along on wheels, like a load on a gardener's or a tradesman's barrow, was to discard any pretentions to elegance; and, apart from the innate conservatism of English society, such a mode of progression may well have offended

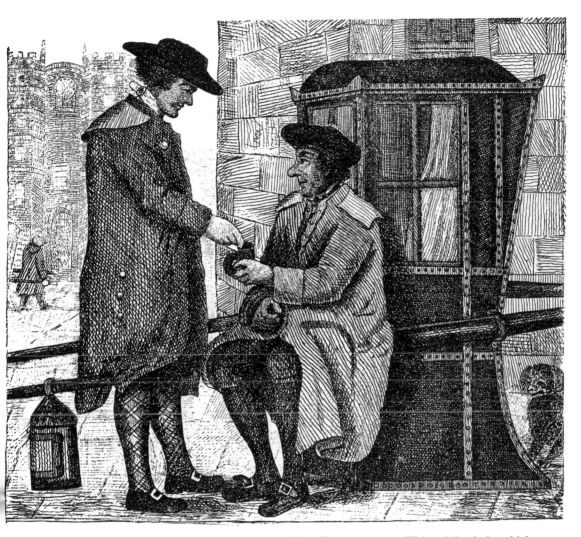

Edinburgh chairmen, from an engraving by John Kay, *circa* 1792. This public chair, which could be hired, retains some of the decorative features of the much more ornate private chair shown on plate 20, though the inward curve of the back is more pronounced, resembling the type illustrated at the top of page 322.

the acute sense of style enjoyed by the Georgian nobility and gentry and all those who imitated their taste, their foibles, and their easy but assured dignity. The prejudice against the wheeled sedan remained, and in contemporary drawings and engravings the original type is almost invariably depicted.

There were two principal varieties of that type, the first derived from the early eighteenth century models, with four-paned side and front windows, and a flat or domed roof; the second having a more pronounced rake to the back, which also splayed out slightly below the seat level, forming a concave line from the roof to the base. This concave line was sometimes repeated in the front of the vehicle, so from the side view it had a slight waist. The side windows were large, without glazing bars or with one horizontal bar, dividing the window into two panes: the top was either slightly domed or flat. Chairs of this kind appear in some of Thomas Shepherd's drawings of Bath, published in 1829 (see plate 18), and an earlier, straight-fronted variety, is shown in an engraving of the Circus at Bath, made in 1784 by Thomas Malton (see plate 16).

There was little difference between these two main varieties of the basic type; but there were innumerable minor variations, created by the form of ornamentation used in private chairs. Both were still familiar though increasingly rare objects during the third decade of the nineteenth century. Phiz illustrates both varieties in the *Pickwick Papers*, though one of them, with four-paned windows, was exceptionally wide, for it had "been originally built for a gouty gentleman with funded property" and could thus accommodate the collective amplitude of Mr. Pickwick and Mr. Tupman. The other, into which Mr. Winkle in his dressing-gown is peering at the horrified Mrs. Dowler, has a moulded cornice, supported at the corners by decorative scrolls, and a pronounced dome with a round knob on top.

Some slight suggestion of the form of the sedan chair was preserved by the body of the hansom cab; but the wheelless vehicle, that was under no obligation to carry a light on the highway and relied entirely on man-power, had disappeared by the beginning of the Victorian era.

CHAPTER X

EPITAPH

EPITAPHS, tombs, and memorial inscriptions reveal almost as much about a period, and the manners, beliefs, habits and spiritual fibre of people, as architecture and the things used in daily life. It is partly the innate kindness of humanity that impels the living to be gentle in the statements cut in stone about their dead relatives or friends, though in the past respect was sometimes tinged with superstitious dread. The Latin tag, *de mortuis nil nisi bonum* was certainly taken to heart by the English. The virtues of the dead were made much of, often in language as florid as the decoration of their monuments, though it is occasionally possible to read between the lines, and even at a distance of two hundred years a faint sigh of thankfulness can almost be detected as we follow the incised Roman and cursive lettering which conveys to us the manifold virtues of an iron-handed father or a trying husband. The lettering used was derived from antique models. Roman capital letters cut on innumerable monuments in Italy supplied the prototypes; and the alphabets used in England during the seventeenth and eighteenth centuries, exhibited many varieties of these basic forms, which were always used with clarity and dignity.

Good lettering was to be found everywhere—on tombs, inn signs and notice boards. Even a country clock-maker like John Godden engraved the brass dial of the clock shown on plate 42 with a beautiful script, and the word Wingham in shaded capital letters of classical type. The use of good letter forms was as universal as the use of the orders of architecture. The types used for printing had the same classical clarity as incised, engraved, or painted letters. Many improvements in the design of types were made, and some of the typefaces have remained in use ever since: for example this book is printed in a type invented by John Baskerville (1706–75) and named after him. As mentioned in an earlier chapter, even the labels on medicine bottles and pill-boxes were distinguished pieces of design, and no matter what the scale was, the letters were clear and invariably legible.

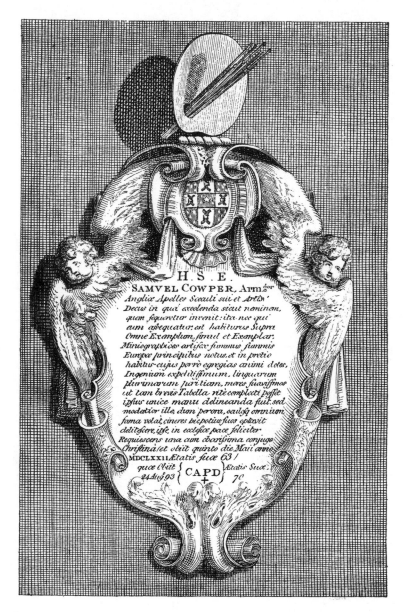

A monument to Samuel Cowper, the miniature painter, in the church of
St Pancras in the Fields. This is a late seventeenth century example, already
foreshadowing the conventional use of classical motifs, and rather puffy
cherubim, which distinguished so many monuments of the Georgian Age.
(Reproduced from *The Antiquities of London*, by John Thomas Smith, 1795.)

The design of memorial tablets and tombs was affected by the influence of the classic orders: the ornamental devices, the inevitable acanthus leaves, the urns, and all the symbols used to perpetuate a note of mourning, originated in Greece and Rome. Frequently such monuments were encumbered by sculptured effigies; and in the late seventeenth century and early Georgian period, cherubs would often adorn with a slightly inappropriate and over-corpulent air of jollity, the framework of a tablet or the pediment of some elaborate canopy. Cherubs may very easily be confused with cupids, and their presence could thus suggest a carnality that was either not apparent or not offensive to Georgian mourners. The angel, lightly draped and heavily winged, did not become popular until Victorian times.

Pains and indeed genius were lavished upon the composition of epitaphs. There was a long-standing controversy, that was never satisfactorily resolved, about the propriety of using Latin rather than English. Boswell records the occasion when, with trepidation, several friends of Oliver Goldsmith ventured to criticise the Latin epitaph that had been written for him by Dr. Johnson. In order to bring it to the Doctor's attention, and to spread the effects of the anticipated storm, they addressed to the Doctor a Round Robin, which read as follows:

"We the Circumscribers, having read with great pleasure, an intended Epitaph for the Monument of Dr Goldsmith, which considered abstractedly, appears to be, for elegant Composition and Masterly Stile, in every respect worthy of the pen of its learned Author, are yet of opinion, that the Character of the Deceased as a Writer, particularly as a Poet, is perhaps, not delineated with all the exactness which Dr Johnson is Capable of giving it. We therefore, with deference to his Superior Judgement, humbly request, that he would at least take the trouble of revising it; & of making such additions and alterations as he shall think proper, upon a farther perusal: But if We might venture to express our Wishes, they would lead us to request, that he would write the Epitaph in English, rather than in Latin: As We think that the Memory of so eminent an English Writer ought to be perpetuated in the language, to which his Works are likely to be so lasting an Ornament, Which we also know to have been the opinion of The late Doctor himself."

The signatories included Edward Gibbon, Edmund Burke, Thomas Franklin, Sir Joshua Reynolds, and Sheridan. Reynolds took it to Dr. Johnson, who received it with great good humour, and desired Sir Joshua to inform the signatories that he would alter the Epitaph "in any manner they pleased as to the sense of it; but he would never consent to disgrace the walls of Westminster Abbey with an English inscription." Johnson, on another occasion, had said:

"The language of the country of which a learned man was a native, is not the language fit for his epitaph, which should be in ancient and permanent language. Consider, Sir; how you should feel, were you to find at Rotterdam, an epitaph upon Erasmus, *in Dutch!*"[201] Nevertheless, Dr. Johnson con-descended to use his mother tongue when he wrote some rather indifferent lines on Hogarth's death in 1764.

> "The hand of him here torpid lies,
> That drew th' essential form of grace;
> Here, clos'd in death, th' attentive eyes,
> That saw the manners in the face."

People who were neither learned nor sufficiently distinguished to merit burial in Westminster Abbey had to be content with English, and nobody seemed to mind, except unusually sensitive critics, like Jonas Hanway who was outraged by the crudities of rustic epitaphs. During his tour from Portsmouth to Kingston-on-Thames he indulged his indignation in a country churchyard. "From RUMSEY," he wrote, "pursuing our journey, we stopt at the little village, I think they called it WHITE PARISH. Whilst the horses were watering I strolled into the churchyard. Whether from the consideration of our common mortality, or only for the pleasure of filling up a vacant moment in any rational way, but I always find myself led, on these occasions, by a kind of instinct. Good God! what nonsense is handed down to posterity, engraved on stone! 'Tis shameful to a nation that any of their clergy should be ILLITERATE OR LAZY. Ought not the vicar or his curate to inform his parishioners, how admirably adapted many passages, in the old and new testament, are to those occasions? We see how the harmony of numbers enchants! These attempts of the unletter'd muse are a proof of it. But poetry does not consist merely in rhyme; and the words of men are not so good as the word of GOD. What think you of this EPITAPH?

> "This world is full of crooked streets;
> Death is a place where all men MEETS:
> If life were sold that men could buy,
> The rich would live, the poor must die."[202]

That atrociously expressed posthumous criticism of the privileged classes, with its sly hint of an ultimate and inescapable equality, would have amused many tolerant and even fastidious gentlemen, for its comic aspect would have been appreciated. The reflections of unlettered bucolic philosophers usually provoked mirth; but Jonas Hanway was without humour and could only feel outraged. Other critics were also mildly outraged by epitaphs, and the motives that prompted their composition were occasionally questioned, their good taste impugned, and their sincerity doubted. For example, the Reverend Richard Warner, in his book, *A Tour Through the Northern Counties of England and the Borders of Scotland*, had some severe strictures to make on Lord Lyttelton's monument to his first wife, Lucy. He said "Of such public declarations of mental anguish it may be remarked, that their foundation is vanity, and their

The tomb of William Hogarth, in Chiswick churchyard, Middlesex. (From *The Antiquities of London*, by John Thomas Smith, 1795.)

super-structure is affectation. The seriousness which embraces the heart, it has been well observed, is not the offspring of volition but of instinct. It is not a purpose, but a frame. The sorrow that is sorrow indeed, asks for no prompting; it comes without a call; it courts not admiration; it presses not on the general eye, but hastens under covert, and wails its widowhood alone; its strong hold is the *heart*; there it remains close-curtained—unseeing, unseen. Delicacy and taste recoil at the publication of internal griefs. They prophane the hallowedness of secret sadness; and suppose selected and decorated expression compatible with the prostration of the soul. No man will give Lord Lyttelton credit for those feelings towards his first love, which the polished lines of his elegy breathe, who adverts to the circumstances and character of his second. But this composition was not the only poetical tribute to the memory of Lucy from the pen of his Lordship."

He then gave the Latin epitaph upon her monument in Hagley Church, also the English epitaph which reads as follows:—

> " 'To the memory of LUCY LYTTELTON, daughter of
> Hugh Fortescue, of Filleigh in the county of
> Devon, esq; father to the present Earl of Clinton,
> by Lucy his wife, the daughter of Matthew Lord Aylmer,
> who departed this life the 19th of January 1746–7,
> aged 29; having employed the short time assigned to
> her here in the uniform practice of religion and virtue.
>
> 'Made to engage all hearts, and charm all eyes;
> Though meek, magnanimous; though witty, wise;
> Polite, as all her life in courts had been,
> Yet good, as she the world had never seen;
> The noble fire of an exalted mind,
> With gentlest female tenderness combin'd;
> Her speech was the melodious voice of love,
> Her song the warbling of the vernal grove.
> Her eloquence was sweeter than her song,
> Soft as her heart, and as her reason strong.
> Her form each beauty of her mind exprest,
> Her mind was Virtue by the Graces drest.' "[203]

When in the course of his travels Mr. Warner arrived at Ripon, he visited the church "to pay a parting tribute to the memory of the late Mr Weddell, and heave a sigh over the monument of departed taste, urbanity, and benevolence. Under his marble bust is a tablet with the following inscription:

> " 'To the memory of WILLIAM WEDDELL, esq; of Newby,
> in whom every virtue that ennobles the mind was
> united with every elegance that adorns it, this

Monument, a faint emblem of his refined taste, is
dedicated by his Widow;

> Whom what awaits, while yet she strays
> Along the lonely vale of days?
> A pang, to secret sorrow dear—
> A sigh—an unavailing tear—
> Till time shall every grief remove,
> With life, with memory, and with love.
>   Obiit 1789.'

"These beautiful lines, you know, are Gray's; but adopted with peculiar felicity by one who has never ceased to feel the severity of a loss as heavy as it is irremediable."[204]

He was greatly impressed by the arrangement of epitaphs and monuments in Lichfield Cathedral. He noted that: "One regulation for the preservation of its walls and the prevention of their disfigurement by bad taste, is an order of the chapter, prohibiting any monuments to be erected within the fabric, and directing that all notifications of the names and ages of persons buried in the cathedral should be inscribed on little tablets of black marble, and inserted in the walls of the southern transept." He observed that a few monuments had been erected and there were three "commemorating remarkable persons," which read as follows:—

" 'Sacred to the memory of the Right Hon. LADY MARY WORTLEY MONTAGUE, who happily introduced from Turkey into this country the salutary art of Inoculating the Small-Pox. Convinced of its efficacy, she first tried it with success on her own children, and then recommended the practice of it to her fellow-citizens. Thus by her example and advice we have softened the virulence, and escaped the danger, of this malignant disease. To perpetuate the memory of such benevolence, and to express her gratitude for the benefit she herself has received from this alleviating art, this monument is erected by Henrietta Inge, relict of Theodore William Inge, esq; and daughter of Sir John Wrottesley, bart. A.D. 1789.'

"Near this tribute to the public spirit of the witty and elegant Lady Mary Wortley Montague, is a testimony of friendship to the memory of Johnson, with these lines:

" 'The friends of SAMUEL JOHNSON, L.L.D. a native of Lichfield, erected this monument as a tribute of respect to the memory of a man of extensive learning; a distinguished moral writer, and a sincere christian. He died 13th Dec. 1784; aged 75 years.'

"Adjoining this monument is another, of equally elegant and simple pattern, the design of Wyatt, and execution of Westmacott, commemorating the friend of Johnson, Garrick; the witty, the pleasant, and the vain. It is inscribed:

WILLIAM WOOLLETT
ENGRAVER to his MAJESTY,
was born at
Maidstone in KENT,
upon the 15th. of August,
MDCCXXXV.
He died the 23. and
was interred in this place,
on the 23. Day of May,
MDCCLXXXV.

The tomb of William Woollett, formerly in the churchyard of St. Pancras in the Fields. (Reproduced from *The Antiquities of London*, by John Thomas Smith, and first published in 1795.) Smith records that "On this tomb were written the following lines with a pencil, which are now defaced:

Here Woollett rests, expecting to be sav'd;
He graved well, but is not well engrav'd.

It is not improbable but these lines gave rise to a noble subscription for erecting a Monument to Woollett's memory in Westminster Abbey, to which Benjamin West Esqr. and Mr. Alderman Boydell were very liberal Contributors."

" 'Eva Maria, relict of DAVID GARRICK, esq; caused this monument to be erected to the memory of her beloved husband, who died the 20th of January, 1779, aged 63 years. He had not only the amiable qualities of private life, but such astonishing dramatic talents, as too well verified the observation of his friend: "His death eclipsed the gaiety of nations, and impoverished the public stock of harmless pleasure." '

"There is an air of *bathos* in this remark, which gives it rather a ridiculous effect, but it certainly has truth for its foundation; for since the death of the inimitable histrionical powers of Garrick, the stage has alike lost its force to charm, and its influence to improve."[205]

In the composition of epitaphs, as well as in the form of the tablets and monuments on which they were engraved, and the lettering which recorded their sentiments, the Georgian sense of style is always apparent; nor was it reserved only for the tombs of noble or distinguished people—it was another example of the instinctive feeling for design and for the right decorative note which guided the choice of words for these miniature biographies, and determined their cadence. In the preface to *A Select Collection of Epitaphs and Monumental Inscriptions*, published in 1806, epitaphs are described as "brief biographical memoirs, the outliness of characters which have appeared in the drama of human life." An admirable definition; admirable too were the reflections that "However amiable the maxim 'speak not ill of the dead;' praise for excellencies never possessed is poignant satire in the eyes of those who are well informed, and culpable imposition on the credulity of strangers. Complimentary Epitaphs, the effusions of courtesy, are far less estimable than those which characterise the wise, the great, and the good."[206]

Sometimes the appraisal of virtues was very short. In the south aisle of the nave of Chester Cathedral, a small stone tablet condenses into four words the qualities that won consistent admiration in the age of reason.

"JOHN VERNON
of BELL HILL in
CHESHIRE
GENTLEMAN,
departed this life Octr. 11th, 1797. Aged 72.
Polite, learned, ingenious, upright, To the *best* of *Husbands*
ANN, his afflicted *Relict*, Erected this.
She departed this life March 23rd 1812.
Aged 88."

Placid recitals of virtues could be dull, as they were in so many Victorian epitaphs, but Georgian composers never allowed epitaphs to be either boring or commonplace, and although the language was enlivened with a brightly ornate phrase here and there, such ornamental flourishes rarely suggested insincerity. Some of the epitaphs to young people had a moving simplicity, and revealed great depth of religious feeling. Here are three examples, the first from a memorial tablet in Stanton Church, near Broadway in Worcestershire.

"Sacred to the memory of Frances, 3rd daughter of
Reginald and Frances Wynniatt, who died
March 12, 1808, aged 19 years.

"Cut off in the morning of her life her many amiable virtues endeared her to all who knew her. Sensible and prudent in all her actions she lived unspotted from the world and untainted with any of its vanities. The qualities of her heart and understanding were alike happy and full of promise. The latter she had improved by diligent cultivation: and the first she exercised by yielding implicitly whenever an occasion presented itself, to the benevolent sympathies of her nature. Her manners were most engaging and bespoke a sweetness of disposition ever studious to contribute to the happiness of those around her. The natural sensibility of her heart was still further refined and exalted by a genuine sense of religion and unfeigned piety, wholly unaffected and unostentatious but visible in its constant influence upon the tenure of her thoughts and actions, upheld by the animating prospect of a future and better state of existence, she supported the lingering illness, which brought her to a premature grave with exemplary patience and cheerful resignation—.
"Her afflicted parents have erected this marble, unwilling that so much unassuming merit should descend to the grave unnoticed and pass away unrecorded."

The second is within the parish church of St. Mary the Virgin, Twickenham, Middlesex, and reads thus:

"Sacred to the Memory
of
an only Daughter
whose virtues and piety
so endeared her to her heavenly Father,
that he was graciously pleased
while her young mind was yet
pure and uncontaminated,
to remove her
from this world of cares,
and
to take her to himself.

"The Honble Caroline Anne Agar Ellis
only Daughter of
Henry Viscount Clifden and Lord Mendir

and Caroline his Wife
eldest Daughter of George Duke of Marlborough,

departed this life
the 12th of May, 1814
in the twentieth year of her age,
and was buried in the Chancel Vault of this Church."

Georgian epitaphs were less impressive in verse, for although the debased doggerel of which Jonas Hanway complained was exceptional, even educated people were prepared to measure out a few yards of fustian in an endeavour to force into rhymed couplets sentiments that would have been more happily expressed in prose. The third example is in verse, and appears on an engraved brass tablet, framed in marble, in St. Michael's Church, Whichford, Oxfordshire.

"Near this place lie the remains of
Henrietta Ingram
3rd daughter of the
Rev Mr. John Ingram & Ann his wife
She died May 7th 1762
Aged 21

"Remember thy Creator in the Days of thy Youth

"Kind stranger stay a moment ere you pass
Attend, and View this Monumental Brass
Which thus indented with a virgin's Name
To Future Ages may record Her Fame.

"If Youth & Innocence can claim a Tear,
Weep, gentle Passenger, for both lie here.
Youth in its prime, with each fair Virtue fraught
And Innocence that scarcely err'd in Thought.
Yet neither Youth, nor Innocence could save
Or Virtue rescue from an Early Grave.

"And Reader know, the Time will come when Thou
Must low in Earth be laid, as She is now!
Perhaps ere Evil Days Arrive, thy Bloom,
To Death may be consign'd, beneath a Tomb!
Or should Old Age o'er take thee thou wilt see
All is on Earth Vexatious Vanity!
So then like Her, in Youth thy God adore,
At whose right Hand are pleasures, evermore!"

Verses of a far more robust kind appear on the memorial tablet to Sir Edward Wynter, in the gallery on the south side of St. Mary's Church, Battersea. (See opposite page.) The splendour of his adventurous career is proclaimed, and although he died in the late seventeenth century, there is a Georgian formality about the design of the tablet and its wording.

"Edward Wynter, died March 2nd, 1686. Aged 64.

"Born to be great in fortune as in mind
Too great to be within an Isle confind
Young, helpless, freindless, Seas unknown he tryd
But English Courage all those wants supply'd
A pregnant wit a painfull diligence
Care to provide & bounty to dispence
Joynd with a Soul, Sincere, plain, open, Just
Procur'd him Freinds & Freinds procur'd him trust
These were his Fortunes rise & thus began
This hardy Youth, raisd to yt happy Man
A rare Example & unknown to most
Where wealth is gaind & conscience is not lost
Nor less in Martiall Honour was his name
Witness his actions of Immortall Fame;
Alone, unarm'd a Tygre He opprest,
And crush'd to death ye Monster of a Beast.
Thrice-twenty mounted Moors he overthrew
Singly on foot, some wounded, some he slew,
Dispersed ye rest: what more cou'd Sampson do!
True to his Freinds, a Terrour to his Foes,
Here, now, in Peace his honour'd bones repose."

.   .   .   .   .   .

"In the same vault lie the Remains of Mrs Catherine Wynter Relict of Wm Wynter Esq. Grand-son of the above Sr Edward Wynter. She died Augst the 20th, 1771, Aged 56. Also her son, Wm Woodstock Wynter, who died Oct. 30th, 1747 Aged 14
"The above Monumt was Re-erected & Repair'd by Edwd Hampson Wynter Esqr Great Grand-son to the above Sr Edwd Wynter

"Edward Hampson Wynter Esqr (1781) Died June the 3rd, 1797."

Although the man of action was occasionally commemorated by a catalogue of the more showy aspects of his valour, very often a plain statement giving the name, date of death, and age, was all that appeared on the tomb of some outstanding soldier or sailor. In the churchyard of St. Peter's, at Petersham

SIR EDWARD WYNTER'S MONUMENT.

On the South Wall, in Battersea Church.

- Alone, unarmed a Tyger he opprest,
- And crusht to death the monster of a beast.
- Thrice twenty mounted Moors he overthrew.
- Singly on foot; some wounded, some he slew;

Publish'd May 1.1794. by N. Smith. G.t Mays Buildings. S.t Martins Lane.

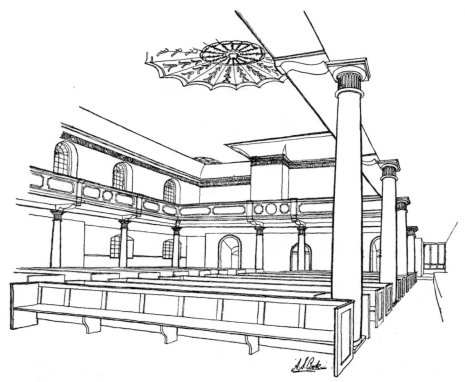

The interior of St. Mary's Church, Battersea, showing the slender, elegant columns that support the gallery. (*Drawn by A. S. Cook.*) In the gallery above the south aisle is the monument to Sir Edward Wynter, reproduced from *The Antiquities of London*, by John Thomas Smith, and shown on page 341.

in Surrey, the tombstone of the discoverer of Vancouver Island, a Captain in the Royal Navy, bears only this inscription:

"CAPTAIN GEORGE VANCOUVER,
DIED IN THE YEAR 1798
AGED 40
Erected by the Native Sons
of British Columbia Post No. 2"

Within the church is a tablet, erected at a much later date by the Hudson's Bay Company, setting forth in dignified and restrained language, and in lettering far inferior to that used on his tombstone, an account of Vancouver's great work as a navigator and explorer.

Epitaphs not only record the virtues of the departed and the esteem in which they were held by their friends and relatives, but very frequently reveal

St. Mary's Church, Battersea, completed in 1777. The design, which is attributed to Joseph Dixon, follows the ground plan of the original church. An interior view is shown opposite. (*Drawn by A. S. Cook.*)

An interior view of St. Peter's, Petersham, Surrey, a Georgian church with gallery and high boxed-in pews where the pew-owners could have the greatest privacy for their devotions, or slumbers. Another view of the interior is shown opposite. (*Drawn by A. S. Cook.*)

some forgotten or neglected aspect of history. The depressing plight of loyal Americans, who were driven from that country and dispossessed of all their property as a result of the War of Independence, is disclosed by an epitaph in St. Philip's Cathedral at Birmingham. Engraved on a tablet crowned by a draped urn, it reads as follows:—

"Near this Place are deposited the Remains of the Hon.ble Peter Oliver, L.L.D., formerly His Majesty's Chief Justice of the Province of *Massachusetts Bay* in *New England*. In the year 1776 on a Dissolution of the Government, He left his native Country, but in all the consequent Calamities His Magnani-

Interior of St. Peter's Church, Petersham, showing the Clerk's desk and the pulpit. (See opposite page.) (*Drawn by A. S. Cook.*)

mity remained unshaken, And (though the Source of his Misfortunes) Nothing could dissolve His Attachment to The British Government, nor lessen his Love & Loyalty to his Sovereign. On *Thursday* 13*th* of *Octr.* 1791 in the true Faith & Hopes of a Christian He resigned this Life. Aged 78."

Another record of the uprooting of an American family and its exile to the Mother Country appears in the South transept of Chester Cathedral. A tablet placed high on the plinth of the west column bears these words:

"Sacred to the
Memory of
"Frederick Philipse Esquire,

late of the Province of New York; a Gentleman, in whom the various social, domestic and religious virtues were eminently united. The uniform Rectitude of his Conduct commanded the Esteem of others; whilst the Benevolence of his Heart, and Gentleness of his Manners secured their Love. Firmly attached to his Sovereign and the British Constitution, he opposed, at the Hazard of his Life, the late Rebellion in North America; and for this faithful Discharge of his Duty to his King and Country, he was Proscribed, and his Estate, one of the largest in New York, was Confiscated, by the Usurped Legislature of that Province. When the British Troops were withdrawn from New York, in 1783, he quitted a Province to which he had always been an Ornament and Benefactor, and came to England, leaving all his Property behind him; which Reverse of Fortune he bore with that Calmness, Fortitude and Dignity which had distinguished him through every former Stage of Life.

"He was born at New York the 12th Day of September in the year 1720; and died in this Place the 30th Day of April, in the Year 1785, aged 65 Years."

A small stone near by, let into the pavement of the south transept, marks his burial-place. The Philipse family manor-house at Yonkers, New York state, still exists and is preserved as an historic monument. (It is described in Appendix 7.)

The tolerance of the age of reason was posthumously tested by John Baskerville. He "died at Birmingham in 1775, and was inurned according to his desire, in a conical building near his late widow's house, in the said town, with the following epitaph, written by himself, inscribed thereon:

> "Stranger,
> Beneath this cone, in *unconsecrated* ground,
> A friend to the liberties of mankind directed
> His body to be inurned.
> May the example contribute to emancipate
> Thy mind
> From the idle fears of *Superstition*,
> And the wicked arts of priesthood."[207]

A nobleman could be buried and entombed in the grand manner; his descendants might honour him with some ambitious architectural gesture, as Earl Fitzwilliam honoured his predecessor, the Marquis of Rockingham, by building a mausoleum in Wentworth Park, which the Reverend Richard Warner described in detail. "It stands on an elevated spot of ground," he wrote, "to the right of the grand entrance into the park from the Rotherham road; is ninety feet high, and consists of three divisions. A Doric basement story, square; another above this of the same figure, but of Ionic architecture; each of its four sides opening into the form of an arch, and disclosing an elegant sarcophagus standing in the centre. This is surmounted by a cupola, supported by twelve columns of the same order, taking a circular arrangement. At each corner of the railing that incloses this superb edifice is an obelisk of great height. But the most interesting part of it is the interior of the lower story; an apartment rising into a dome, ornamentally stuccoed, and supported by eight pillars, encircling a white marble statue of the late Marquis of Rockingham in his robes, as large as life, by the admirable chissel of Nollekens. This stands on a square pedestal, one side of which is inscribed with the titles of this great man. The remaining three form a noble, but just, tribute to his memory, being dedicated to deserved eulogium, and the effusions of disinterested friendship."[208]

The classic orders which played such an influential and consistent part in the design of everything in the Georgian Age, lent dignity to death itself. Through their medium Georgian grace was impressed alike upon the great architectural monument or the modest memorial tablet in a country church. Death afforded the final occasion for using that great system of design which served and is identified with the greatest period of British civilisation.

BOOKS REFERRED TO IN THE TEXT

PART I

CHAPTER I

(1) *Farm and Cottage Inventories of Mid-Essex, 1635–1749.* Edited for the Education and Records Committees of the Essex County Council by Francis W. Steer, F.R.Hist.S., Senior Assistant Archivist. (Essex Record Office Publications, No. 8, 1950.) Pages 239–240.

(2) *Ibid.,* page 231.

(3) *A History of English Furniture,* by Percy Macquoid. In four volumes: I. The Age of Oak. II. The Age of Walnut. III. The Age of Mahogany. IV. The Age of Satinwood. (London: Lawrence & Bullen, 1904–1908.)

(4) *Sylva, or a Discourse of Forest Trees and the Propagation of Timber,* by John Evelyn. (London: Printed for John Martyn, Printer to the Royal Society, 1679. Third, enlarged and improved edition.) Chapter IV, page 35.

(5) *Ibid.,* Chapter V, page 39.

CHAPTER II

(6) *Diary,* November 4th, 1644.

(7) *The Revolutions of Civilisation,* by Sir William Flinders Petrie. (London: Harper & Brothers. Third edition, 1922. First published in 1911.) Chapter III, Section 17, page 74.

(8) *An Essay in Defence of Ancient Architecture; or A Parallel of the Ancient Buildings with the Modern,* by Robert Morris of Twickenham. (London: Printed for D. Browne, at the Black-Swan, without Temple-Bar; W. Bickerton, in Devereaux-Court, near Temple-Bar; J. Pote, at the Golden-Door, against Suffolk-Street, near Charing-Cross; and J. Walthoe, at Richmond. 1728.) Chapter IV, page 34.

(9) *Architecture in Britain, 1530 to 1830,* by Sir John Summerson. (Pelican History of Art. London: Penguin Books, 1953.) Chapter 22, page 219.

(10) *An Essay in Defence of Ancient Architecture,* by Robert Morris. Chapter IV, pages 34–35.

(11) *An Inquiry into the Principles of Beauty in Grecian Architecture,* by George, Earl of Aberdeen. (London: John Murray, 1822.) Page 28.

(12) *The New Practical Builder and Workman's Companion,* by Peter Nicholson, Architect. (London: Thomas Kelly, 1823.) Plate III.

(13) "Three Tiers of Taste," by Paul Reilly. The *Observer,* September 7th, 1952.

(14) *The Decline and Fall of the Roman Empire,* by Edward Gibbon. Volume I, Chapter XIII.

(15) *The Four Books of Architecture,* by Andrea Palladio, literally translated from the Italian by Isaac Ware. (London: Printed for R. Ware, at the *Bible* and

Sun, on *Ludgate-Hill.*) The "Advertisement" follows the dedication page, and is dated June 1737. No date appears on the title page.

(16) *The History of the Royal Society of London, for the Improving of Natural Knowledge,* by Thomas Sprat. (London: the third edition, corrected, 1722.) Part III, Section XXXII, page 394.

(17) *Ibid.,* page 394.

(18) *Glass in Architecture and Decoration,* by Raymond McGrath, B.Arch., A.R.I.B.A., and A. C. Frost. (London: The Architectural Press, 1937.) This advertisement is quoted in Section II, page 97.

(19) *Building for Daylight,* by Richard Sheppard, F.R.I.B.A., and Hilton Wright, A.R.I.B.A. (London: George Allen & Unwin Ltd., 1948.) From the Introductory Historical Note on English Window Design, by John Gloag. Pages 29–31.

(20) *The Journeys of Celia Fiennes,* edited by Christopher Morris. (London: The Cresset Press, 1947.) Section 7. Journey from London to Oxford and thence into Sussex (*c.* 1694). Page 39.

(21) *An Essay Towards the Description of Bath,* by John Wood, Architect. (London: Printed by James Bettenham, in the Year 1749, and Sold by C. Hitch in Pater-Noster Row; and J. Leake at Bath. The Second edition corrected and enlarged.) Volume II, Part III, Chapter I, pages 239–240.

(22) *The Analysis of Beauty,* by William Hogarth. (London: Printed by J. Reeves for the Author, and Sold by him at his House in Leicester-Fields. 1753.) Chapter VIII, page 46.

(23) *Men and Buildings,* by John Gloag. (London: Chantry Publications Ltd., second revised edition, 1950.) Chapter VII, pages 117–119.

(24) *Op. cit.,* page 119.

(25) *The Antiquities of Athens,* measured and delineated by James Stuart, F.R.S. and F.S.A., and Nicholas Revett, Painters and Architects. (London: Printed by John Haberkorn, 1762.)

CHAPTER III

(26) *A Frenchman in England, 1784.* The *Melanges sur l'Angleterre* of François de la Rochefoucauld. Edited from the MS. by Jean Marchand and translated by S. C. Roberts. (Cambridge University Press, 1933.) Pages 42–43.

(27) *Sylva, or a Discourse of Forest Trees and the Propagation of Timber,* by John Evelyn. (London: 1679. Third edition.) Chapter XXXIV, page 240.

(28) *A Frenchman in England, 1784.* Page 45.

(29) *Journal of a Tour & Residence in Gt. Britain, during the years 1810 and 1811,* by Louis Simond. (Edinburgh: Printed by George Ramsay and Company for Archibald Constable and Company, Edinburgh; and Longman, Hurst, Rees, Orme and Brown, London, 1815.) Volume I, page 146.

(30) *Op. cit.,* Volume I, page 152.

(31) *Memoirs of William Hickey,* edited by Alfred Spencer. (London: Hurst & Blackett Ltd. Tenth edition, 1948.) Volume I, 1749–1775. Chapter VII, pages 72–73.

(32) *Op. cit.,* page 75.

(33) *Journal of a Tour & Residence in Gt. Britain during the years 1810 and 1811*, by Louis Simond. (Edinburgh: Printed by George Ramsay and Company for Archibald Constable and Company, Edinburgh; and Longman, Hurst, Rees, Orme, and Brown, London, 1815.) Volume I, page 152.

(34) *Op. cit.*, page 152.

(35) *The Royal Society of Arts 1754–1954*, by Derek Hudson and Kenneth W. Luckhurst. (John Murray, 1954.) Chapter XVI, page 280.

(36) *An Essay Towards a Description of Bath*, by John Wood, Architect. (London: Printed by James Bettenham, in the Year 1749, and Sold by C. Hitch in Pater-Noster Row, and J. Leake at Bath. Second edition, corrected and enlarged.) Volume II, pages 2–5.

(37) *Lord Chesterfield's Letters to His Son.* Letter CCII. November 1749.

(38) *Proportional Architecture; or the Five Orders; regulated by Equal Parts*, by W. Robinson. (London: Printed and sold by W. Dicey at Ye Printing Office in Bow Church Yard, and C. Corbett at Addison's head against St. Dunstan's Church, Fleet Street, 1736.) Second edition.

(39) *The Analysis of Beauty*, by William Hogarth. (London: 1753.) Chapter VIII, page 46.

(40) *Op. cit.*, Chapter X, page 50.

(41) *Op. cit.*, Chapter IX, pages, 48–49.

(42) "The Years of Mahogany: The Early Georgian," by Haldane Macfall. *The Connoisseur*, Volume XXIV, May–August, 1909.

(43) *The Architecture of Marcus Vitruvius Pollio*, translated by Joseph Gwilt. (London: Priestly and Weale, 1826.) Book I, Chapter II, page 11, and Chapter III, page 15.

(44) *Characteristicks of Men, Manners, Opinions, Times*, by the Right Honourable Anthony, Earl of Shaftesbury. The sixth edition, corrected, with the addition of a Letter concerning Design. 1737. Volume III, page 402.

(45) *Op. cit.*, Volume III, Miscellany III, pages 180–181.

(46) *Op. cit.*, Volume III, Treatise VII. *A Notion of the Historical Draught or Tablature of the Judgement of Hercules.* Pages 390–391.

(47) *The Universal System of Household Furniture: Consisting of above 300 Designs in the most Elegant Taste, both Useful and Ornamental*, by William Ince and John Mayhew. The work was first published in parts between 1759 and 1762.

(48) *China and Europe*, by Adolf Reichwein. (London: Kegan Paul, 1925.) Page 20.

(49) *A Voyage Round the World in the years 1740–44.* By George Anson, Esq., afterwards Lord Anson. Compiled from his Papers and Materials by Richard Walter, M.A., Chaplain to H.M.S. *Centurion*. (London: Printed for: W. Strahan, J. Rivington & Sons, J. Robson, G. Robinson, T. Lowndes, T. Cadell, N. Conant, W. Goldsmith, J. Nichols, R. Baldwin, W. Otridge, J. White, E. Johnston and T. King. Fifteenth edition, 1780.) Book III, Chapter X, page 531.

(50) *Op. cit.*, page 533.

(51) *Op. cit.*, pages 529–530.

(52) *The World*, No. 12. March 22nd, 1753. (New edition, 1795. Printed for P. Dodsley, Pall-Mall.) Pages 69–70.

(53) *Op. cit.*, pages 71–72.

(54) *Op. cit.*, page 69.
(55) *Op. cit.*, pages 68–69.
(56) "The Gothick Taste," by J. Isaacs, M.A.(Oxon.), Professor of English Language and Literature in the University of London, Queen Mary College. A lecture given at a General Meeting of the Royal Institute of British Architects, June 17th, 1952. *Journal of the R.I.B.A.*, Volume 59, No. 9. July, 1952. Page 337.
(57) *Poems on Several Occasions*, by W. Woty. (Derby: Printed for the Author, by J. Drewry. M,DCC,LXXX.)
(58) *Travels in Asia Minor, and Greece, or An Account of a Tour made at the Expense of the Society of Dilettanti*, by R. Chandler, D.D. (London: Printed for Joseph Booker, New Bond Street, and R. Priestly, High Holborn. Third edition, 1817.) Volume II, Chapter X, pages 57–58.
(59) *Op. cit.*, Volume I, Preface, page vii.
(60) *The Pleasures of Melancholy*, by Thomas Warton. (Oxford University Press, 1802.) Volume I. Pages 91–92.
(61) "Some Account of the Writings of Edward Gibbon, Esq." Preface to Volume I, of the edition of *The History of the Decline and Fall of the Roman Empire*, published in London, 1807.
(62) *The Discovery of Man*, by Stanley Casson. (London: Hamish Hamilton, 1940.) Chapter III, page 141.
(63) *A Complete Body of Architecture*, by Isaac Ware. (London: 1767. This is not the first edition.) Book I, Chapter I, pages 5–6.
(64) *An Historical Essay on Architecture*, by Thomas Hope. (London: John Murray. Second edition, 1835.) Preface, pages v, vi and vii.
(65) *The Cabinet Dictionary*, by Thomas Sheraton. (London: Printed for W. Smith, King Street, Seven Dials, 1803.) Pages 215–216.
(66) *Memoirs of Adam Black*, by Alexander Nicolson. (A. & C. Black Limited. Second edition, 1885.) Chapter I, pages 32–33.

PART II

CHAPTER I

(67) *The Spleen*, by Matthew Green. Lines 330–331.
(68) *Lord M*, by Lord David Cecil. (London: Constable & Co., 1954.) Prelude, page 6.
(69) *The Character and Conduct of the Female Sex, and the Advantages to be derived by young Men from the Society of virtuous Women.* A Discourse in three Parts, delivered in Monkwell-street Chapel, Jan. 1st, 1776. By James Fordyce, D.D. Reviewed in *The Monthly Review*, February 1776, page 131.
(70) The *Tatler*, No. 205. August 1st, 1710.
(71) *Farm and Cottage Inventories of Mid-Essex, 1635–1749.* (Essex Record Office Publications, No. 8.) August 20th, 1666, page 105, and November 4th, 1678, page 156.

(72) *London in 1710. From the Travels of Zacharias Conrad Von Uffenbach.* Translated and Edited by W. H. Quarrell and Margaret Mare. (London: Faber & Faber Limited, 1934.) Page 57.

(73) *The Life of Samuel Johnson,* the second edition, revised and augmented by James Boswell. (London: Printed by Henry Baldwin for Charles Dilly, 1793.) Volume II, page 574.

(74) *Memoirs of William Hickey,* edited by Alfred Spencer. (London: Hurst & Blackett Ltd. Seventh edition.) Volume II (1775–1782). Chapter VI, page 68.

(75) *The Life of Samuel Johnson.* (Second edition, 1793.) Volume II, page 240.

(76) *A Frenchman in England, 1784,* by François de la Rochefoucauld. (Cambridge University Press, 1933.) Page 29.

(77) *Op. cit.,* page 30.

(78) *Op. cit.,* page 31.

(79) *A Journal of Eight Days Journey from Portsmouth to Kingston upon Thames, with Miscellaneous Thoughts, Moral and Religious; in a series of sixty-four letters; addressed to two Ladies of the Partie,* to which is added *An Essay on Tea.* By a GENTLEMAN of the Partie. (London: Printed for H. Woodfall, 1756.) Letter XIX, page 59.

(80) *Dictionarium Britannicum, or a more Compleat Universal Etymological English Dictionary,* by N. Bailey. (London: Second edition, 1736.)

(81) *The Ladies Library,* Written by a Lady. Published by Sir Richard Steele. (London: Printed for J. and R. Tonson in the *Strand.* The fifth edition, 1739.) Volume I, pages 121–122.

(82) *Fables for the Female Sex.* (London: Printed for R. Francklin, in Russell-Street, Covent-Garden, 1744.) Fable XIII, "The Owl, and the Nightingale." Pages 81–82.

(83) *The Whitehall Evening-Post; or, London Intelligencer.* No. 1642. From Saturday, August 21, to Tuesday, August 24, 1756. Page 3, column 1.

(84) *The General Evening Post.* (London.) From Tuesday, October 19, to Thursday, October 21, 1736. Page 3, column 2.

(85) *Memoirs of William Hickey,* edited by Alfred Spencer. (London: Hurst & Blackett, Ltd. Seventh edition.) Volume II (1775–1782). Chapter XXI, page 286.

(86) *Op. cit.,* page 285.

(87) *London in 1710. From the Travels of Zacharias Conrad Von Uffenbach.* Translated and edited by W. H. Quarrell and Margaret Mare. (London: Faber & Faber, 1934.) Page 130.

(88) *Op. cit.,* pages 130–131.

(89) *London and its Environs Described.* (London: Printed for R. and J. Dodsley in Pall-Mall, 1761.) Volume VI. Pages 214–215.

(90) *Boswell's London Journal, 1762–1763.* (London: William Heinemann Ltd., 1950.) Wednesday, December 15, 1762. Page 86.

(91) *The Adventures of Roderick Random,* by Tobias Smollett. Quoted from the tenth edition. (London: 1778.) Volume I, Chapter XIII, pages 100–101.

(92) *The Whitehall Evening-Post; or, London Intelligencer.* No. 2217. From Saturday, May 31, to Tuesday, June 3, 1760. Page 4, column 2.

(93) *The Torrington Diaries,* edited by C. Bruyn Andrews. (London: Eyre and Spottiswoode (Publishers) Ltd., 1934.) Volume I, page 191.

CHAPTER II

(94) *A Journal of Eight Days Journey from Portsmouth to Kingston upon Thames*, to which is added *An Essay on Tea*. (London: Printed for H. Woodfall, 1756.) Letter III, page 215.

(95) *Memoirs of William Hickey*, edited by Alfred Spencer. (London: Hurst & Blackett Ltd. Tenth edition, 1948.) Volume I (1749–1775). Chapter VII, pages 75–76.

(96) *A Journal of Eight Days Journey from Portsmouth to Kingston upon Thames*, to which is added *An Essay on Tea*. (London: 1756.) Letter III, pages 215–216.

(97) *Op. cit.*, Letter V, page 222.

(98) *Op. cit.*, Letter V, pages 223–224.

(99) *Op. cit.*, Letter VIII, page 244.

(100) *Op. cit.*, Letter VI, page 236.

(101) *Op. cit.*, Letter VIII, page 254.

(102) *The Life of Samuel Johnson*, by James Boswell. (London: 1793). Volume I, page 286.

(103) *State of the Poor, or a History of the Labouring Classes in England*, by Sir Frederic Morton Eden, Bart. (London: Printed for J. Davis, 1797.) Volume I, Book II, pages 496–497.

(104) *Cottage Economy*, by William Cobbett. (London: Printed and Published by C. Clement, No. 183, Fleet Street, 1822.) Pages 19–20.

(105) *The World*, No. 64. Thursday, March 21st, 1754.

(106) *The Cabinet Dictionary*, by Thomas Sheraton. (London: 1803.) Page 320.

(107) *The London Furniture Makers, 1660–1840*, by Sir Ambrose Heal. (London: B. T. Batsford Ltd., 1953.) Page 8.

(108) *A Journal of Eight Days Journey from Portsmouth to Kingston upon Thames*, to which is added *An Essay on Tea*. Letter IX, page 248.

(109) *The Cabinet Dictionary*, by Thomas Sheraton. (London: 1803.) pages 20–1.

(110) *London and its Environs Described*. (London: Printed for R. and J. Dodsley in Pall-Mall. 1761.) Volume V, pages 243–244.

(111) *Evelina, or a Young Lady's Entrance into the World*, by Fanny Burney. (First published 1778.) Letter XII.

(112) *Evelina*. Letter XXIII.

(113) *Memoirs of William Hickey*. Volume I (1749–1775). Chapter XXIII, page 298.

(114) *A Book for a Rainy Day*, or recollections of the events of the last sixty-six years, by John Thomas Smith. (London: Richard Bentley, 1845.) Entry for 1772. Pages 17–18.

(115) *Op. cit.*, pages 14–15.

(116) *Cottage Economy*, by William Cobbett. Page 13.

CHAPTER III

(117) *The Journeys of Celia Fiennes*, edited by Christopher Morris. (London: The Cresset Press, 1947.) Page 364.

(118) *Correspondence of Thomas Gray*, edited by Paget Toynbee and Leonard Whibley.

(Oxford: Clarendon Press, 1935.) Volume II. Letter 231, dated December 29th, 1756. Pages 490–491.

(119) *Op. cit.*, Volume III. Letter 467, dated February 3rd, 1768.

(120) *The Gentleman's Magazine.* March 1735, Volume V, page 158.

(121) *The Universal System of Household Furniture*, by William Ince and John Mayhew. (First published in parts, 1759–1762.) Plates LV and LVI. *The Cabinet and Chair-Maker's Real Friend and Companion*, by Robert Manwaring. (London: 1765.) Plates 22 and 23.

(122) *Farm and Cottage Inventories of Mid-Essex, 1635–1749.* (Essex Record Office Publications, No. 8.) Inventory of the goods of William Eree, of Writtle, dated May 28th, 1677, included in the list of furniture in the parlour "one elbow chair." Page 143.

(123) *The Journeys of Celia Fiennes*, edited by Christopher Morris. (London: The Cresset Press, 1947.) Part IV, Section 10, page 346.

(124) Letter by R. W. Symonds published in the correspondence columns of *Country Life*, October 26th, 1951.

(125) R. W. Symonds writing in the *Connoisseur*. Volume XCIV, July–December, 1934, pages 216–217.

(126) *The Cabinet Dictionary*, by Thomas Sheraton. (London: 1803.) Entry CHAIR, page 146.

(127) *Op. cit.*, entry ARM, page 18.

(128) *Op. cit.*, entry ARM, page 19.

(129) *Op. cit.*, entry GRECIAN COUCH, SOFA, SQUAB, pages 247–248.

(130) *The Cabinet and Chair-Maker's Real Friend and Companion*, by Robert Manwaring. (London: 1765.) Preface.

(131) "The Windsor Chair," first of two articles by R. W. Symonds. *Apollo*, Volume XXII, No. 128, August 1935. Page 69.

(132) *High Wycombe Furniture*, by Sir Lawrence Weaver. (London: The Fanfare Press, 1929.) Detailed descriptions of the nineteenth century varieties of Windsor chair are given in this work.

(133) *The American Nation*, by John and Julian Gloag. (London: Cassell & Company, Ltd. Revised and enlarged edition, 1955.) Section One, Chapter XI, pages 116–117.

(134) *The Cabinet Dictionary*, by Thomas Sheraton. (London: 1803.) Entry CHAIR, pages 145–146.

CHAPTER IV

(135) *Dictionarium Britannicum, or a more Compleat Universal Etymological English Dictionary*, by N. Bailey. (London: Second edition, 1736.)

(136) Bailey, *op. cit.*

(137) *Boswell's London Journal, 1762–1763.* (London: William Heinemann Ltd., 1950.) Wednesday, February 9th, Monday, February 13th, 1763. Pages 185 and 189.

(138) *The Cabinet Dictionary*, by Thomas Sheraton. (London: 1803.) Entry CAMP, page 123.

(139) *The Gentleman and Cabinet Maker's Director*, by Thomas Chippendale. (London: Third edition, 1762.) Description of plate XLVII.

(140) *The Cabinet Dictionary.* Entry STATE BED, page 311.

(141) *The World*, No. 38. September 20th, 1753. (New edition, 1795. Printed for P. Dodsley, Pall-Mall.) Page 243.

(142) *The New World of Words, or Universal English Dictionary*, by Edward Phillips. (London: Sixth edition. Printed by J. Phillips at the King's Arms in S. Paul's Church Yard, N. Rhodes at the Star, Bride-Lane, Fleet Street, and J. Taylor at the Ship, S. Paul's Church Yard. MDCCVI.) Page 31.

(143) *The Journeys of Celia Fiennes*, edited by Christopher Morris. (London: The Cresset Press, 1947.) Part IV, Section 10, page 346.

(144) *The World*, No. 38. September 20th, 1753. (New edition, 1795.) Page 242.

(145) *The Cabinet Dictionary*. Entry FURNISH, page 219.

CHAPTER V

(146) *The Cabinet Dictionary*. Entry FURNISH, page 219.

(147) *The Whitehall Evening-Post: or, London Intelligencer*. No. 2024. From Thursday, March 8, to Saturday, March 10, 1759. Page 2, column 3.

(148) *The Whitehall Evening Post*. No. 2102. From Thursday, September 6, to Saturday, September 8, 1759. Page 4, column 1.

(149) *The World* (London, 1795.) Volume 1, No. 38, Thursday, September 20th, 1753, pages 243 and 244.

(150) *George Selwyn and His Contemporaries*, by John Heneage Jesse (London, 1843). Volume I, pages 162 and 176.

(151) *The Whitehall Evening-Post: or, London Intelligencer*. No. 1915. Thursday, June 29 to Saturday, July 1, 1758. Page 4, column 3.

(152) *The Dictionary of Architecture*, issued by the Architectural Publication Society. (London, 1887). Volume VII, page 81.

(153) *The Ladies Library*, written by a Lady. Published by Sir Richard Steele. (London: the fifth edition, 1739.) Volume I, page 73.

(154) *Op. cit.*, page 73.

(155) *The Gentleman and Cabinet Maker's Director*, by Thomas Chippendale. (London: Third edition, 1762.) Description of plate LIV.

(156) *The Cabinet Dictionary*, by Thomas Sheraton. (London, 1803). Entry SHAVING TABLE, page 304.

(157) *The Town & Country Magazine or Universal Repository of Knowledge, Instruction and Entertainment*. (London: Printed for A. Hamilton, Junr. near St. John's Gate.) Volume IV, 1772. Account of masquerade, April 30th, page 237, column 2.

(158) *Op. cit.*, pages 242–243.

(159) *The World* (London 1795). Volume 1, No. 12, Thursday, March 22nd, 1753, page 69.

CHAPTER VI

(160) *Boswell's London Journal, 1762–1763*. (London: William Heinemann Ltd., 1950.) Entry December 12th, 1762. Page 81.

(161) *An Early Experiment in Industrial Organisation, Being a History of the firm of Boulton & Watt, 1775–1805*, by Erich Roll. (London: Longman, Green and Co., 1930.) Chapter V, page 132.

(162) *The Gillow Records*. These records, which are at the Lancaster branch of Waring and Gillow Ltd., include the Estimate and Sketch Books since 1784. The order for the satinwood sheveret appears under the date quoted in the Estimate and Sketch Book for 1790.

(163) *The Prices of Cabinet Work, with Tables and Designs*, revised and corrected by a Committee of Masters Cabinet Makers. (London: Printed by S. Low, Berwick Street, Soho; and sold by Messrs. Taylors, at their Architectural Library, High Holborn; and E. Booker, New Bond Street. 1797.) Pages 78–80, and plate 6.

(164) *The London Furniture Makers*, by Sir Ambrose Heal. (London: B. T. Batsford Ltd., 1953.) Pages 38 and 189.

(165) *Nollekens and his Times*, by John Thomas Smith. (London: Henry Colburn, New Burlington Street, 1828.) Volume II, pages 243–244.

(166) *The Cabinet Dictionary*, by Thomas Sheraton. (London: 1803.) Entry BOOK-SHELF, page 73.

(167) *Op. cit.*, page 73.

(168) "James Whatman, Father and Son," by Thomas Balston. *The Paper-Maker*, Volume CXXIX, No. 4, April 1955. Pages 292–293.

(169) *The World*, No. 64. March 21st, 1754. (New edition, 1795.) Page 76.

(170) *Op. cit.*, pages 76–77.

(171) *The Cabinet Dictionary*, by Thomas Sheraton. Entry LIBRARY STEPS, page 337.

CHAPTER VII

(172) *Lord Hervey's Memoirs*, edited by Romney Sedgwick. (London: William Kimber, 1952.) Chapter II, page 79.

(173) *The Ladies Library*, written by a Lady. Published by Sir Richard Steele. (London: the fifth edition, 1739.) Volume I, page 17.

(174) *The Cabinet Dictionary*, by Thomas Sheraton. (London: 1803.) Entry CANTER-BURY, page 127.

(175) *Op. cit.* Entry FURNISH, page 217.

CHAPTER VIII

(176) *The Elements of Architecture*, by Sir Henry Wotton. The First Part. *Reliquiae Wottonianae*. (London: Printed by T. Roycroft, for R. Marriott, F. Tyton, T. Collins and J. Ford. 1672. The Third *Edition*, with large *Additions*.) Page 37.

(177) *Op. cit.*, page 39.

(178) *The Spectator*, No. 308. Friday, February 22nd, 1712. Sir Richard Steele.

(179) *The Spectator*, No. 299. February 12th, 1712. Joseph Addison.

(180) *A Complete Body of Architecture*, by Isaac Ware. (London: 1767 edition.) Book VI, Chapter I, page 553.

(181) *Op. cit.*, Book VI, Chapter II, page 555.

(182) *The Builder's Director, or Bench-Mate*, by Batty Langley. (London, 1751.) Introduction, page vii.

(183) *A Complete Body of Architecture*. Book VI, Chapter XXIV, page 601.

(184) *Op. cit.*, Book VI, Chapter XXV, page 603.

(185) *A History of Cast Iron in Architecture*, by John Gloag and Derek Bridgwater. (George Allen & Unwin Ltd., 1948.) Section Two, pages 70, 71.

(186) "Yesterday and Today—Designing for Cast Iron," by Grey Wornum, F.R.I.B.A. *The Official Architect*, Volume VIII, No. 5, Special Cast Iron Number. May 1945, page 243.

(187) *Nollekens and his Times*, by John Thomas Smith. (London, 1828.) Volume I, page 411.

CHAPTER IX

(188) The *Spectator*, No. 454. August 11th, 1711–2. (Sir Richard Steele.)

(189) *The General Evening Post*, No. 478. From Tuesday, October 19, to Thursday, October 21, 1736. Page 2, column 2.

(190) *A Treatise on Carriages*, by William Felton, Coach-Maker, No. 36, Leather-Lane, Holborn. (London: Printed for and sold by the author; by J. Debrett, Piccadilly; R. Fadler, Bond-Street; J. Egerton, Whitehall; J. White, Fleet-Street; W. Richardson, Cornhill; and A. Jameson, Long-Acre. 1794.) "Introductory Observations," page i.

(191) *Op. cit.*, pages i to ii.

(192) *Op. cit.*, pages vi to vii.

(193) *Op. cit.*, pages x to xi.

(194) *Op. cit.*, Chapter XIX, page 234.

(195) *Op. cit.*, Chapter III, pages 56–57.

(196) *Op. cit.*, Chapter XV, page 207.

(197) *A Book for a Rainy Day*, by John Thomas Smith. (London: Richard Bentley, 1845.) Entry for 1781, page 71.

(198) *The Tatler*, No. 113. December 29th, 1709.

(199) *Journal of a Tour & Residence in Gt. Britain, during the years 1810 and 1811*, by Louis Simond. (Edinburgh and London, 1815.) Volume II, page 162.

(200) *A Treatise on Carriages*, by William Felton. Chapter XI, page 160.

CHAPTER X

(201) *The Life of Samuel Johnson*, by James Boswell. (London: Second edition, 1793.) Volume II, pages 448–453.

(202) *A Journal of Eight Days Journey from Portsmouth to Kingston upon Thames*, to which is added *An Essay on Tea*. (London, 1756.) Letter VIII, "Reflections on Tombstones," page 22.

(203) *A Tour Through the Northern Counties of England, and the Borders of Scotland*, by the Rev. Richard Warner. (Bath: Printed by R. Cruttwell, 1802.) Volume I, pages 75, 76, 77.

(204) *Op. cit.*, Volume I, pages 261–262.

(205) *Op. cit.*, Volume I, pages 107, 108, 109.

(206) *A Select Collection of Epitaphs and Monumental Inscriptions with Anecdotes of Distinguished and Extraordinary Persons*. (Ipswich: Printed and Sold by J. Raw;

sold also by Messrs Longman, Hurst, Rees, and Orme, Paternoster Row, London, 1806.) Preface, pages iii–iv.

(207) *Op. cit.*, page 25.

(208) *A Tour Through the Northern Counties of England, and the Borders of Scotland,* by the Rev. Richard Warner. Volume I, pages 221–222.

GENERAL REFERENCES

For quotations from the letters of Horace Walpole, the Toynbee edition has been used. (Published in sixteen volumes between 1903 and 1906.) General reference has been made to the following: *The Dictionary of Architecture* (issued by the Architectural Publication Society between 1852 and 1892); the *Journal of the Royal Institute of British Architects,* and *The Architectural Review.*

Contemporary sources, apart from those specifically cited, include the various writings of Dean Swift and Dr. Johnson; Hester Thrale's *Thraliana*; and *The Letters and Works of Lady Mary Wortley Montagu,* edited by Lord Wharncliffe (London: Richard Bentley, 1837).

APPENDIX I

THE PRINCIPAL ARCHITECTS AND THEIR WORKS

The architect was the master designer, a regulator of taste, whose influence pervaded polite society and inspired the activities of craftsmen and tradesmen. In the brief list that follows, the principal architects and a few of their works are given, also the books that some of them published on architecture. The list is arranged in approximately chronological order, and is followed by a note on the Architects' Club.

SIR CHRISTOPHER WREN (1632–1723)

Wren's architectural career began about 1663 when he became a member of the Commission for repairing St. Paul's Cathedral. In 1666 he was appointed one of the Commissioners responsible for rebuilding London after the Great Fire, and he was directly responsible for the designs of the large majority of rebuilt City churches, as well as contributing much to other rebuilding, and designing and supervising the new St. Paul's Cathedral. He became Surveyor-General of the King's Works in 1668–69: was knighted in 1673; became the Comptroller of Windsor in 1684; and the first Surveyor of Greenwich Palace in 1696. He was put in charge of repairs to Westminster Abbey in 1699. Wren was President of the Royal Society from 1681 to 1683.

Principal Buildings

St. Paul's Cathedral, 1675–1710.
The Library, Trinity College, Cambridge, 1676–84.
Tom Tower, Christ Church, Oxford, 1681–82.
St. James's, Piccadilly, 1682–84.
The Royal Hospital, Chelsea, 1682–91.
The Royal Hospital for Seamen, Greenwich, 1696 onwards.
Marlborough House, London, 1709–11.
52 City churches to whose design and construction he contributed much.

NICHOLAS HAWKSMOOR (1661–1736)

He assisted Wren and Vanbrugh. Clerk of the Works at Kensington Palace, 1689; at Greenwich Hospital, 1698; and at Whitehall, 1715. Was appointed Secretary to the Board of Works when it was established in 1715, and was one of the two Surveyors appointed by the Commissioners for Building Fifty New Churches in London.

Principal Buildings

Greenwich Hospital (as Clerk of the Works, 1698–1736; as Assistant Surveyor, 1705–29).
Clarendon Building, Oxford, 1712–15.
Blenheim Palace (with Vanbrugh).
All Souls College, Oxford, ·1715–40.
St. Mary Woolnoth, London, 1716–27.
St. George's, Bloomsbury, 1720–30.

PUBLICATIONS

Remarks on the Founding and Carrying on the Buildings of the Royal Hospital at Greenwich (1729).
A Short Historical Account of London Bridge, with a Proposition for a new Stone Bridge at Westminster (1736).

SIR JOHN VANBRUGH (1664–1726)

His career as an architect began in 1699 with the design of Castle Howard, and from then until his death he built up a fairly prosperous practice. He was made Comptroller of His Majesty's Works in 1702: in 1703 became a member of the Board of Directors of Greenwich Hospital; and was knighted in 1714. In 1715 he was made Surveyor of Gardens and Waters (the first to hold this official post); in 1716 he succeeded Wren as Surveyor to Greenwich Hospital. He was also made Clarenceux King of Arms in 1704, and for a time (1714–17) he was Garter King of Arms.

Principal Buildings

Castle Howard, Yorks, 1699–1726.
Blenheim Palace, Oxon, 1705–20.
Seaton Delaval, Northumberland, 1720–28.
Greenwich Hospital (Great Hall and King William Block), *c.* 1703 onwards.

COLEN CAMPBELL (?–1729)

He was Chief Clerk of the King's Works and Deputy Surveyor in 1718–19. The Earl of Burlington became his patron, and is believed to have first become interested in Palladian architecture after Campbell's *Vitruvius Britannicus* was published. Campbell was Surveyor to Greenwich Hospital in 1726.

Principal Buildings

Burlington House, London (with the Earl of Burlington), 1718–19.
Wanstead House, Essex, 1715. (Dem. 1824).
Houghton, Norfolk, 1721.
Mereworth Castle, Kent, 1722–25.
Compton Place, near Eastbourne, 1726–27.

PUBLICATIONS

Vitruvius Britannicus (in three volumes), (1715, 1717, 1725).
Edited Palladio's *Five Orders of Architecture* (1729).

THOMAS ARCHER (?1668–1743)

Practised in London and Hampshire: also in Dorset, Derbyshire, Oxon, Northants, Surrey, Bedfordshire and Bucks.

Principal Buildings

Chatsworth House, Derbyshire (north front), 1704–5.
Heythrop House, Oxon, *c.* 1705–10.
Roehampton House, Wandsworth, 1710–12.
Wrest Park, Beds (garden pavilion), 1711–12.
Hurstbourne Priors, Hants, *c.* 1712.
Hale House, Hants. Soon after 1715.
Harcourt (afterwards Bingley) House, Cavendish Square, London, 1722.
Cliveden House, Bucks.
St. Philip's, Birmingham, 1710–15.
St. John's, Smith Square, London, 1714–28.
St. Paul's, Deptford, 1712–30.

JAMES GIBBS (1682–1754)

A Scotsman by birth. From 1713–15 one of the Surveyors to the Commissioners for Building Fifty New Churches in London. Practised in London, Oxford, Cambridge, the Midlands and southern counties.

Principal Buildings

St. Mary-le-Strand, London, 1714–17.
Burlington House, Piccadilly, 1718 (part of the structure).
St. Clement Danes, London, 1719–20.
St. Martin-in-the-Fields, London, 1722–26.
The Senate House, Cambridge, 1722–30.
King's College New Building, Cambridge, 1724–49.
Sudbrooke Lodge, Petersham, Surrey, 1726–28.
The Radcliffe Library, Oxford, 1737–49.

PUBLICATIONS

A Book of Architecture (1728).
Rules for Drawing the Several Parts of Architecture (1732).
Bibliotheca Radcliviana (1747).

WILLIAM KENT (*c.* 1685–1748)

Believed to have been a coach-maker's apprentice. Was sent to Europe by three patrons in 1709, and returned to England in 1719 with Lord Burlington who had met him in 1714–15 in Rome, and who remained his patron for the rest of his life. Kent did not begin his architectural career until the early seventeen-thirties. He became Master Carpenter at the Board of Works in 1726, and in 1735, Master Mason and Deputy Surveyor. He was also Inspector of Paintings in the Royal Palaces from 1727–28. He lived mostly at Burlington House. He designed a great deal of highly decorative furniture. (Portrait on plate 7.)

Principal Buildings

Chiswick House, Middlesex (internal decorations), *c.* 1727.
Esher Place, Surrey (additions), *c.* 1730.
Holkham Hall, Norfolk, 1734 onwards.
Treasury Buildings, Whitehall, 1734–36.
Stowe, Bucks, c. 1736.
Horse Guards, Whitehall, 1750–58.

PUBLICATIONS

Edited *Designs of Inigo Jones*, with some additional designs by Lord Burlington and himself (1727).

GIACOMO LEONI (*c.* 1686–1746)

A Venetian architect, who came to England sometime before 1715–16, when he published an English edition of Palladio, and in order to superintend publication he left the Continent, under the patronage of Henry, Duke of Kent. (*See* Isaac Ware's comments on pages 25 to 26.) In Europe, he had worked for the Elector Palatine. In England he was employed only by private patrons.

Principal Buildings

Wrest Park, Beds, 1715 onwards.
Argyll House, Kings Road, Chelsea, 1723.
Moulsham Hall, Essex, 1729 onwards.
Clandon Park, Surrey, 1731–35.

PUBLICATIONS

The Architecture of Palladio, Revis'd, Design'd, and Published by Giacomo Leoni, a Venetian: Architect to his most Serene Highness, the Elector Palatine. (In 2 volumes, 1715–16. 2nd edition 1721; 3rd edition 1742, with "Notes and Remarks of Inigo Jones now first taken from his original Manuscript in Worcester College, Oxford." French translation 1726.)
A manuscript treatise entitled *Compendious Directions for Builders.*
Translated *The Architecture of L. B. Alberti* (in 3 volumes, 1726. 2nd edition 1739.)

HENRY HERBERT (1693-1751)
Ninth Earl of Pembroke

A famous amateur of the arts, particularly of architecture. His chief collaborator was Roger Morris.

Principal Buildings

White Lodge, Richmond Park, c. 1727.
Marble Hill, Twickenham, 1723-29.
The Column of Victory at Blenheim Palace, 1730-31.
Wimbledon House, Surrey, 1732-33.
The Palladian Bridge, Wilton, 1736-37.
The Water House, Houghton, Norfolk.

RICHARD BOYLE (1694-1753)
Third Earl of Burlington and fourth Earl of Cork

The most significant patron of his time, largely responsible for the introduction of the Palladian style to England. In addition to helping such men as Flitcroft, William Kent, Gibbs and Colen Campbell, all of whom worked with or for him, and by using his influence to place them in important public posts, his wealth enabled him to buy invaluable drawings and documents and to sponsor the publication of important works on architecture. It is believed that he was also a talented practising architect. (Portrait on plate 7.)

Principal Buildings

Burlington House, London (with Gibbs and Campbell).
Petersham Lodge, Surrey, c. 1721. (Dem. 1853.)
Chiswick House, Middlesex (with Kent), c. 1725.
Holkham House, Norfolk (assisted with planning).

PUBLICATIONS

Fabbriche Antiche disegnate da Andrea Palladio Vicentino, e date in luce da Ricardo Conte di Burlington (1730).

THE DANCES—FATHER AND SON

GEORGE DANCE, Senior (1695 or 1700-68)

Practised in London, chiefly the City and East End: also a little in Kent. Clerk of the City Works, 1735.

Principal Buildings

The Mansion House, London, 1739-52.
London Bridge, alterations (with Sir Robert Taylor) 1755-60.
The Corn Exchange, Mark Lane, London, 1749-50.
St. Leonard's, Shoreditch, 1736-40.
St. Botolph's, Aldgate, 1741-44.

GEORGE DANCE, JUNIOR, F.S.A., F.R.S. (1741-1825)

Youngest son of George Dance, senior. Clerk of the City Works, 1768. A member of the Architects' Club. He was an accomplished draughtsman, and contributed many pencil portraits to *A Collection of Portraits sketched from the Life since the Year 1793* (1808–14). Practised in London and the southern counties.

Principal Buildings

All Hallows Church, London Wall, 1765–67.
Newgate Prison, London, 1770–78.
Additions, etc., to the Mansion House, 1775; 1795–96.
Rebuilding and additions at the Guildhall, London, 1777; 1787; 1788–89.
Theatre Royal, Beaufort Square, Bath, 1804–5.
Coleorton House, Leics, 1804–5.
He also planned America Court, The Crescent, The Circus (all in the Minories), Finsbury Square, Alfred Place (off Tottenham Court Road) and Picket Place (Strand).

PUBLICATIONS

Report on Inspection, with a Committee of Aldermen, of several Gaols of this Kingdom (1816).

ROGER MORRIS (1695-1749)

He came from Yorkshire, and his patrons were the Duke of Argyll and the Earl of Pembroke. Morris was Carpenter and Principal Engineer to the Board of Ordnance; and Clerk of the Works at Richmond New Park Lodge in 1727. His work was mainly Palladian, though one or two buildings were in the Gothic taste. (He was related to Robert Morris of Twickenham whose work is quoted on pages 18 to 19.)

Principal Buildings

Whitton Park, Twickenham, Middlesex, 1724–25.
White Lodge, Richmond Park (with Henry Herbert), 1727.
Marble Hill, Twickenham, 1728–29.
Palladian Bridge, Wilton, 1736–37.
Longford Castle, Wilts, *c.* 1742.
Inverary Castle, Argyllshire, 1746–61.
Kirby Hall, Yorks.

BATTY LANGLEY (1696-1751)

Better known as an author than an architect. He and his brother, Thomas, conducted an architectural school in Soho, to which he moved about 1740. He advertised himself as able to carry out the duties of an architect, surveyor, etc., and was in the employ of the Duke of Kent, at Wrest Park, Bedfordshire, about 1735, but it is not known in what capacity.

Practical Geometry, applied to the Useful Arts of Building, Surveying, Gardening and Mensuration (1726, 1728, 1729).

The Builder's Chest Book, or a Compleat Key to the Five Orders of Columns, in Architecture (1727).

New Principles of Gardening; or the laying out and planting Parterres, Groves, Wildernesses, Labyrinths, Avenues, Parks, etc. (1728).

A Sure Guide to Builders, or the Principles and Practice of Architecture Geometrically Demonstrated (1729).

The Young Builder's Rudiments, with the Five Orders of Columns in Architecture (1730, 1736).

Ancient Masonry, both in the Theory and in the Practice (1734 or 1735, 1736).

The Builder's Compleat Assistant (2nd edition 1738?, 4th edition after 1788).

The City and Country Builder's and Workman's Treasury of Designs (1740. Editions with additional plates in 1741, 1750 and 1756).

The Builder's Jewel, or the Youth's Instructor, the Workman's Remembrancer (1746, 1754, 11th edition 1768, 1787, 1808).

Ancient Architecture Restored and Improved by a great Variety of Grand and Useful Designs (1st part 1741). Complete edition with a dissertation "On the Principal Ancient Buildings in this Kingdom" and entitled *Gothic Architecture, etc.* (1742).

The Measurer's Jewell (1742).

The Builder's Director, or Bench-Mate (1746, 1751, 1767).

The Builder's Treasury of Designs for Piers, Gates, etc. (before 1750).

London Prices of Bricklayers' Materials and Work (1747, 1748, 1749, 1750, 1818).

The Workman's Golden Rule for Drawing and Working the Five Orders in Architecture (? 1757).

HENRY FLITCROFT (1697–1769)

A protégé of Lord Burlington. Clerk of Works at Whitehall and St. James's, 1726. Comptroller of the Works, 1758. Practised in London, Yorkshire, and the southern counties.

Principal Buildings

St. Giles-in-the-Fields, London, 1731–34.

No. 10 St. James's Square (Chatham House), London, 1734.

Alterations and additions to Wentworth Woodhouse, Yorks, *c.* 1735 and *c.* 1770.

Various houses in Bloomsbury, Dover Street, Sackville Street and Hampstead.

Woburn Abbey, Beds, 1747–61.

MATTHEW BRETTINGHAM (1699–1769)

The son of a Norwich bricklayer, known chiefly for the controversy over his alleged authorship of the design of Holkham Hall, though it seems likely that Kent was the author of the original designs. Brettingham was retained by the Earl of Leicester to superintend the buildings at Holkham.

Principal Buildings

Norfolk House, St. James's Square, London, 1747–55. (Dem. 1938.)
No. 5 St. James's Square, 1748–51.
Benacre Hall, Suffolk, 1763–64.
Holkham Hall, Norfolk (assisted).
Egremont House, Piccadilly (now the Naval and Military Club), 1756.

PUBLICATIONS

The Plans and Elevations of the late Earl of Leicester's House at Holkham, 1761.

ISAAC WARE (?–1766)

The protégé of an influential nobleman, possibly Lord Burlington. Visited Italy
some time before 1727. Became Purveyor to the Board of Works in 1728; Clerk of
the Works at Windsor Castle, 1729; Clerk of the Works at Greenwich, 1733; Clerk
Itinerant and Draughtsman to the Board of Works *c.* 1733; Secretary to the Board
of Works, 1736. He made the official drawings for Kent's design of the Horse Guards.
He was a Warden of the Carpenter's Company, 1761–62, and Master in 1763.

Principal Buildings

Chesterfield House, London, 1748–49. (Dem. 1937.)
The Lock Hospital, Hyde Park Corner (now St. George's Hospital, as
   rebuilt by Wilkins), 1733.
Wrotham Park, Middlesex, 1754.

PUBLICATIONS

A translation of *Palladio* (The "Advertisement" is dated 1737, but 1738 may be the
   date of publication.)
Designs of Inigo Jones and Others (1st edition, possibly 1735; others in 1743 and 1756).
The Complete Body of Architecture (1st edition, possibly 1735; others in 1756, 1760 and
   1767).
A translation of Sirrigatti's *Practice of Perspective* (1756).
An edition of Brook Taylor's *Method of Perspective* (1766).

JOHN CHUTE (1701–76)

An amateur architect and friend of Horace Walpole.

Principal Buildings

Designed a large part of Strawberry Hill for Horace Walpole, and also
   the Gothic chapel there.
Chalfont House, Bucks.
Considerable alterations at The Vyne, Hants (his own house).
He also prepared designs for Hagley Hall, Worcs, which were not carried out.

THE WOODS—FATHER AND SON

JOHN WOOD, Senior (1704-54)

The son of a builder at Bath. He worked first in Yorkshire, and in Marylebone, London, and by 1727 had established himself. He became interested in the re-planning of Bath, about 1725, and in 1727 he returned there to live, and concentrated upon this work until his death. A financial crisis in the affairs of the project in 1727 was overcome by Wood making himself solely responsible for the planning and construction of Queen Square. His success at Bath brought him further work and he became a fashionable architect.

Principal Buildings

Bramham Park, Yorks, *c.* 1724-25.
Bath: Gay Street, 1727 onwards.
      Queen Square, 1728-36.
      The Royal Mineral Water Hospital, 1738.
      North and South Parades, 1740-43.
      Began work on The Circus, 1754.
Prior Park, near Bath (not the east wing), 1735-48.

PUBLICATIONS

The Origins of Building, or the Plagiarisms of the Heathens Detected (1741).
An Essay towards a Description of Bath (1740, 1749, 1765).
A Description of the Exchange of Bristol (1743).
Choir Gaure, vulgarly called Stonehenge . . . Described, Restored and explained (1747).
A Dissertation Upon the Orders of Columns and their Appendages (1750).

JOHN WOOD, Junior (1728-81)

The son of John Wood the elder, with whom he worked first as an assistant, and then in his own right as an architect and partner. On his father's death, he took over the work of planning in Bath, where he remained for the rest of his life, though he also designed buildings in other parts of the country.

Principal Buildings

Buckland House, Berks, 1755-57.
Bath: Completed The Circus his father had begun.
      Royal Crescent, 1767-75.
      Brock Street, *c.* 1767.
      Rivers Street, *c.* 1770.
      Catherine Place, *c.* 1780.
      New Assembly Rooms, 1769-71.
      The Old Royal Baths, 1773-77.

A Series of Plans, for Cottages or Habitations of the Labourer (1781, 1792, 1806).

RICHARD BENTLEY (1708–82)

Practised in a very limited way in London, Berks, Kent and Bucks. He was never more than a talented amateur, but exerted a notable influence in spreading the Gothic taste.

Principal Buildings

Robert Bateman's villa at Old Windsor, Bucks. (Gothicized this structure in the early seventeen-fifties.)
Gothic monument to Sir Horace Mann's brother, at Linton, Kent.
Gothic stable at Chalfont House, Bucks, c. 1760.
As a member of the "Committee of Taste," he helped to superintend the extensions to Strawberry Hill for Horace Walpole, and his designs for this (1751–61) with others for pavilions, etc., are bound in a volume. The majority were not executed. He illustrated the first edition of Gray's poems (1753).

JAMES STUART, F.R.S., F.S.A. (1713–88)

As a young man, worked as a fan-painter for Lewis Goupy, at the same time studying mathematics, Latin and Greek. Visited Rome in 1742, and Naples in 1748 with Nicholas Revett and others. Stuart and Revett planned to publish a work on the antiquities of Athens, and did so, with the help of the Society of Dilettanti (*see* Appendix IV), the first volume appearing in 1762. Stuart had returned to England in 1755; he became a member of the Society of Dilettanti, and also a Fellow of the Royal Society, and of the Society of Antiquaries. He was Surveyor to Greenwich Hospital in 1758, and Serjeant-Painter in 1764. His private architectural practice, though potentially a very good one, remained small. His main achievement was the work on Athens. (*See* plates 2, 3, and 4.) He designed a large number of monuments and medals and was consulted on matters of design by Josiah Wedgwood.

Principal Buildings

Lichfield House, 15 St. James's Square, London, 1763–66.
Londonderry House, Hertford Street, London, 1760–65.
Portman House, Portman Square, London, 1775–82. (Bombed 1940.)

The Antiquities of Athens measured and delineated by James Stuart, F.R.S. and F.S.A., and Nicholas Revett, Painters and Architects. (1st volume 1762, 2nd volume 1787, appearing in 1788–89, 3rd volume 1795: further supplements in 1816 and 1830.)

SIR ROBERT TAYLOR (1714–88)

He was apprenticed to Henry Cheere, the sculptor, when he was fourteen, and then visited Rome. His father died bankrupt in 1743, but he was given considerable help by influential friends, and soon became well known as a sculptor. He was a member of the Mason's Company. He was appointed Surveyor to the Bank of England in 1765; Architect of the King's Works in 1769; Master Carpenter in 1777; Deputy Surveyor and Master Mason, 1780: Surveyor of Greenwich Hospital in 1788. He had also been Surveyor to the Admiralty, H.M. Customs, the Foundling Hospital, and Lincoln's Inn. He was elected a Sheriff of London in 1782, and knighted the same year. He built up a large and lucrative architectural practice.

Principal Buildings

Stone Buildings, Lincoln's Inn (completed by Hardwick), 1774–80.
Heveningham Hall, Suffolk, 1778–88.
Ely House, 37 Dover Street, London, c. 1772.
Grafton House, Piccadilly.
Asgill House, Richmond, Surrey.

JAMES PAINE (c. 1716–89)

Studied architecture under Thomas Jersey, and built up a large, prosperous practice. Became Clerk of Works at Greenwich in 1744–45; Clerk of Works at Charing Cross Mews, 1746; Clerk of Works at Newmarket, 1750–80; Clerk of Works at Richmond New Park Lodge, 1758. From 1780 to 1782 he was one of the two Board of Works architects. A Director of the Society of Artists of Great Britain, and from 1771–72 was its President.

Principal Buildings

Middlesex Hospital, London, 1755–75. (Dem. 1928.)
Richmond Bridge, Surrey, 1774–77.
Works at Chatsworth, Derbyshire.
Kedleston House, Derbyshire (central block and corridors), 1757–61.

PUBLICATIONS

Plans, Elevations and Sections of Noblemen and Gentlemen's Houses . . . executed in the counties of Derby, Durham, Middlesex, Northumberland, Nottingham and York. (1st volume 1767, 2nd volume 1783, which included other parts of the country.)

LANCELOT "CAPABILITY" BROWN (1716–83)

Began his career as a gardener, and in 1740 became gardener to Lord Cobham at Stowe, thus meeting William Kent, with whom he worked closely. In 1749 he set up on his own as a landscape gardening consultant, working with Robert Adam and Henry Holland. He had a considerable reputation as an architect, and excelled in the designing of such small buildings as gate houses and lodges.

Principal Buildings

Croome Court, Worcestershire (with Robert Adam), 1751–52.
Claremont House, Surrey, 1770–72.

JOHN CARR (1723–1807)

Practised in Yorkshire. At first a builder and mason, he began to design his own buildings about 1754, and became a prosperous and fashionable architect in the North of England. He was one of the original members of the Architects' Club.

Principal Buildings

Built Kirby Hall, Gt. Ouseburn, designed by Lord Burlington, 1750.
The Pikeing Wellhead at York, 1752.
Grandstand at Knavesmire racecourse, York, 1754, his first original design.
Arncliffe Hall, Northallerton.

1759–71:
Harewood House, Yorkshire.
Houses in Harewood village, rebuilt as a model village.
Denton Park, Yorkshire.
Constable Burton, North Riding.
Basildon Park, Berkshire.
Aston Hall, near Rotherham.
Gledhow Hall, near Leeds.
Two houses in Castlegate, York, and one in Skeldergate.

SIR WILLIAM CHAMBERS (1723–96)

He practised chiefly in London and Dublin. Worked for the King and Queen, was Comptroller of the Board of Works and later, Surveyor-General of H.M. Office of Works when this was formed. He designed furniture and interior decoration, and George III's Coronation coach. (*See* Plate 34 and pages 320 and 321.) He was one of the original members of the Architects' Club, founded in 1791. (Portrait on plate 7.)

Principal Buildings

Extensive building and planning at the Palace and Gardens of Kew, including the Pagoda, 1757–62.

After 1762
Stabling at Harewood House, Yorkshire.
Carrington House, Whitehall, London.
House for Lord Melbourne in Piccadilly (now the central building of the Albany).
Wick House for Sir Joshua Reynolds, Richmond Hill, Surrey.
House near Green Park, London.
The Town Hall, Woodstock, Oxon.

Entrance gates and bridge at Blenheim, Oxon.

Entrance Gates at Wilton, Wiltshire.

Bridge at Woburn, for the Duke of Bedford.

Observatory for George III, in grounds between Old Deer Park, Richmond (now Kew Observatory), 1768.

Designed Milton Abbas, Dorset, 1773.

Somerset House, London, 1775–86.

Designs for Trinity College, Dublin, including theatre, chapel, archway and bell tower, 1759 onwards.

Duddingston, near Edinburgh, 1763–64.

PUBLICATIONS

Designs of Chinese Buildings, Furniture, Dresses, Machines and Utensils (1757).

A Treatise on Civil Architecture (1759).

Treatise on the Decorative Part of Civil Architecture (1791).

Plans, Elevations, Sections and Perspective Views of the Gardens and Buildings at Kew in Surrey (1763).

A Dissertation on Oriental Gardening (1772).

HENRY KEENE (1726–76)

Surveyor to the Fabric of Westminster Abbey in 1746. Was a protégé of Lord Halifax, and employed by him at his Sussex house. Practised in London, Oxford and the home counties.

Principal Buildings

The Guildhall, High Wycombe, 1757.

Trinity College, Dublin (west front), 1752–59.

Nos. 17–18 Cavendish Square, London, 1756–57.

Corsham Court, Wilts (rebuilt north front), 1759–60.

Christ Church, Oxford (the Anatomy School), 1766–67.

ROBERT ADAM, F.R.S. (1728–92)

Educated at High School, Edinburgh, and Edinburgh University, he went to Europe in 1754, returning to London in 1757–58. In Rome he was admitted a member of St. Luke's Academy, and in 1757 he explored and measured the remains of Diocletian's Palace at Split, in Dalmatia. On his return, he set up in practice with two of his brothers, James and William. He was a member of the Society of Arts, and became a Fellow of the Royal Society in 1761. In that year he was appointed Architect of the King's Works, jointly with Sir William Chambers; in 1765, he became Surveyor of Chelsea Hospital. (Portrait on plate 7.)

Principal Buildings

Screen wall, at the Admiralty, London, 1760.
Society of Arts, John Adam Street, London, 1772–74. (*See* page 114.)
No. 20 St. James's Square, London, 1772–74.
The Adelphi Buildings, Strand, London, 1768–72. (Dem. 1936.)
Osterley House, Middlesex, 1761–80.
Kenwood House, Hampstead, 1767–69.
Croome Court, Worcs, 1760 onwards.
Luton Hoo, Beds, *c.* 1768–75.

PUBLICATIONS

Ruins of the Palace of the Emperor Diocletian at Spalatro (1764).
Works in Architecture of Robert and James Adam (1773).

JAMES ADAM (1730–1794)

Brother of Robert Adam with whom he collaborated. Travelled in Europe 1761–63. He did not apparently build very much, but some of his designs are included in *The Works in Architecture of Robert and James Adam*. Among them is a small house for Captain Hugh Dalrymple, and a gateway for the Duke of Argyll (1756). The Assembly Rooms in Glasgow were attributed jointly to Robert and James Adam.

PUBLICATIONS

Practical Essays on Agriculture, etc., together with Observations on Inclosures, Fences, Farms and Farmhouses, in 2 volumes (1789; 1794).
Believed to have written *Journal of a tour in Italy* (published in 1831) often attributed to Robert Adam.

ROBERT MYLNE, F.R.S. (1734–1811)

He came from a famous family of Scottish master masons, and was apprenticed in Edinburgh to a mason, and afterwards assisted his father in that trade. In 1754 he went to Europe, and spent four years there, mostly in Rome, with his brother. He was awarded the Silver Medal for architecture at St. Luke's Academy, Rome, in 1758, and in 1759 was elected a member of the Academy. He was also a member of the Academies of Florence and Bologna. He returned to England in 1759. He was an engineer as well as an architect and carried out surveys of bridges and harbours, canals and waterworks, as well as planning the Gloucester and Berkeley Ship Canal and the fen drainage scheme at Eau Brink Cut, Kings Lynn. He became joint engineer to the New River Company in 1767; Surveyor to St. Paul's Cathedral, 1767; Surveyor to Canterbury Cathedral, 1767; Clerk of the Works at Greenwich Hospital, 1775–82; Surveyor to the Thames Commissioners from 1788. He was elected a Fellow of the Royal Society in 1767, and was an original member of the Architects' Club.

Principal Buildings

Blackfriars Bridge, 1760–69. (Dem. 1868.)
Almack's Club, London, 1764–65. (Dem. 1863.)
New River Company's Offices, Clerkenwell, London, 1770.
City of London Lying-In Hospital, 1770–73. (Dem. 1903.)
The Wick, Richmond Hill, Surrey, 1775. (This is adjacent to Wick House, by Sir William Chambers.)

THOMAS LEVERTON (1743–1824)

A builder's son, who started his career in his father's trade, he first exhibited his architectural work at the Royal Academy in 1771. He was closely concerned in the development of Bedford Square, London (*see* plate 15), and was Surveyor to the Phoenix Fire Insurance Company and to the Theatres Royal in London. With his pupil, Thomas Chawner, he was appointed architect to the Land Revenue Apartment. His work was greatly influenced by the brothers Adam.

Principal Buildings

No. 65 Lincoln's Inn Fields, London, 1772.
Phoenix Fire Insurance Office, Charing Cross, 1787. (Dem.)
Watton Wood Hall, Herts (now Woodhall House), 1777–82.
Riddlesworth Hall, Norfolk, 1792.

HENRY HOLLAND, F.S.A. (1745–1806)

Partner and assistant to Lancelot Brown, he was Clerk of the Works at The Mews at Charing Cross, 1775–82. He was district Surveyor of the Liberties of Hatton Garden, Ely Rents, Saffron Hill, St. Mary-le-Strand, the Duchy of Lancaster and Precincts of the Savoy, 1774; and Surveyor to the East India Company, 1799. He practised in London, the southern counties, and Bedfordshire, and was an original member of the Architects' Club. (*See* plate 38.)

Principal Buildings

Brooks's Club, 60 St. James's Street, London, 1776–78.
Claremont House, near Esher, Surrey (in partnership with Lancelot Brown), 1771–74.
The Albany, London, 1803–4 (additions and conversion into residential chambers).
Southill House, Beds (rebuilding), 1795.

PUBLICATIONS

Resolution of the Associated Architects, with the Report of a Committee appointed to consider the causes of the frequent fires, and the best means of preventing the like (1793).
Two papers to the *Communications of the Board of Agriculture*, Volume i, 1797: one on the construction of cottages, and one advocating the use of pisé.

JAMES WYATT, F.S.A., R.A. (1746–1813)

His first commission, the Pantheon in Oxford Street, was so successful that shortly after its opening in 1772 he was well established in practice and had become an A.R.A. (*See* plate 10.) He was appointed Surveyor to Westminster Abbey in 1776; Surveyor of the Ordnance in 1782 or 1783; Surveyor-General and Comptroller of the Works in 1796; F.S.A. in 1797; R.A. in 1785. He was a founder-member of the Architects' Club.

Principal Buildings

The Pantheon, Oxford Street, 1770–72. (Dem. 1936.)
No. 15 St. James's Square. London, 1791–94.
Fonthill Abbey, Wiltshire, 1796–1807. (Tower collapsed, 1807.)
Henham Hall, near Southwold, Suffolk, 1793–97.
Kew Palace, Surrey, 1802–11. (Dem. 1827–28.)

JOHN NASH (1752–1835)

Nash was employed in Sir Robert Taylor's office, and by 1777 had established his own architectural and building practice, but became bankrupt in 1783. He started again in Wales, returned to London in 1796, and went into partnership with Humphry Repton. His connection with the Prince Regent began in 1798, for whom he designed a conservatory, and the drawing of it was exhibited at the Royal Academy. Nash became architect to the Department of Woods and Forests in 1806; Surveyor-General in 1813; one of the three "attached architects" directing royal works in 1815. He was dismissed from this post in 1830, when on the death of George IV, Nash was left without a patron. He worked mainly in London, but also in Wales and the provinces, and was one of the first architects to experiment with the large scale use of cast iron in building.

Principal Buildings

Buckingham Palace, London, 1825–30.
The Royal Pavilion, Brighton, 1815–21.
Regent's Park and adjacent terraces, and Regent Street.
All Souls Church, Langham Place, London, 1822–25.
Clarence House, London, 1825.
Carlton House Terrace, London, 1827–33.
United Service Club, Pall Mall, London, 1827.

HUMPHRY REPTON (1752–1818)

He began his career in business, but failed, and after studying botany and gardening, became a landscape gardener. He worked in collaboration with John Nash, and later with his own sons, in order to carry out commissions which involved architectural as well as landscape planning.

The majority of these, devoted to landscape gardening, were published with a memoir
by John Claudius Loudon, in 1840, under the title *The Landscape Gardening and
Landscape Architecture of the Late Humphry Repton.*

SIR JOHN SOANE, R.A. (1753–1837)

John Soane worked at first in the office of George Dance the younger. He was
admitted to the Royal Academy Schools in 1771, and awarded the Silver Medal in
1772 and the Gold Medal in 1776. From 1772 to 1778 he was one of Henry Holland's
assistants, and was then awarded the King's Travelling Studentship, and visited
Italy. By 1784 he established his own private practice, and became Surveyor to the
Bank of England in 1788, a post that led to many important contacts, and he soon
became one of the busiest, best known, and most prosperous architects in the
country. Other official posts which he held were: Clerk of the Works at Whitehall,
Westminster and St. James's (1790); Deputy-Surveyor of H.M. Woods and Forests
(1797); Clerk of the Works to Chelsea Hospital (1807); one of the three "attached"
architects to the Board of Works (1814). He was elected A.R.A. in 1795, and R.A.
in 1802, becoming Professor of Architecture at the Royal Academy in 1806. In
1834 when the Institute of British Architects was founded, Soane was presented
with a Gold Medal, for, owing to his position at the Academy, he was not free to
accept the Presidency of the Institute which had been offered to him. Soane showed
his appreciation of the Gold Medal by presenting (among gifts to other bodies) the
Institute with £750 with which the Soane Medal was founded. He left his house
and the collections it contained to the nation: it is now the Soane Museum in
Lincoln's Inn Fields. (Portrait on plate 7.)

Principal Buildings

Pitzhanger Place, Ealing, 1800–3. (*See* plate 18).
Bank of England (rebuilding), 1788–1833.
Nos. 12, 13 and 14 Lincoln's Inn Fields, 1792–1824.
No. 18 Park Lane, London, 1812.
Holy Trinity Church, Marylebone, London, 1824–28.
St. John's, Bethnal Green, London, 1824–28.

PUBLICATIONS

*Designs in Architecture, consisting of Plans, Elevations and Sections for Temples, Baths,
    Casines, Pavilions, Garden-Seats, Obelisks, and other Buildings* (1778).
Plans, Elevations and Sections of Buildings erected in the Counties of Norfolk, Suffolk, etc.
    (1788).
*Sketches in Architecture, containing Plans and Elevations of Cottages, Villas and other Useful
    Buildings* (1793).
Designs for Public and Private Buildings (1828).
Description of the House and Museum on the North Side of Lincoln's Inn Fields (1832; 1835–
    36). (Privately printed.)
Memoirs of the Professional Life of an Architect (1835). (Privately printed.)

THOMAS HOPE (*c.* 1770–1831)

He was brought up in Holland, and travelled widely in Europe and the Near East during his youth. He was a wealthy connoisseur and collector of antique sculpture, and pottery, who had a great influence on contemporary taste. Apart from making additions to his London house in Duchess Street, Portland Place, and at his country house at Deepdene in Surrey, he did not practise architecture, and is best known as a writer on the subject, and on furniture and costume.

PUBLICATIONS

Observations on the Plans and Elevations designed by James Wyatt, Architect, for Downing College, Camb; in a letter to Francis Annesley Esq. M.P. (1804).
Household Furniture and Interior Decoration executed from designs by Thomas Hope (1807).
Costumes of the Ancients (1809).
Designs of Modern Costume (1812).
An Essay on the Origins and Prospects of Man (1831).
An Historical Essay on Architecture by the late Thomas Hope, illustrated from Drawings made by him in Italy and Germany (published posthumously in 1835).
Anastasius, or Memoirs of a Greek written at the close of the Eighteenth Century (1819). (A novel, which Hope published anonymously.)

SIR ROBERT SMIRKE, F.R.S., R.A., Hon.F.I.B.A. (1781–1867)

Smirke was for a very short time a pupil of Sir John Soane, then of a surveyor named Bush. He was admitted to the Royal Academy Schools, 1796: gained the Silver Medal that year and the Gold Medal in 1799. From 1801 to 1805 he was in Italy, Sicily and Greece. He became Architect to the Board of Trade in 1807; in 1813 was one of the three Board of Works Architects; 1814 Surveyor to the Inner Temple. He was knighted in 1832. Elected A.R.A. in 1808, R.A. in 1811, and was Treasurer to the Academy from 1820 to 1850. He was a Fellow of the Royal Society and of the Society of Antiquaries, and an Hon. Fellow of the Institute of British Architects. His work carried the classical tradition of design far into the nineteenth century. His private work began about 1806, and he built up a very large and extremely prosperous practice.

Principal Buildings

British Museum, 1823–47.
Custom House, London, 1825–26.
Royal Mint, Tower Hill, London, 1807–9: 1815.
Oxford and Cambridge Club, Pall Mall, London (with Sydney Smirke), 1836–37.
General Post Office, St. Martin's-le-Grand, 1824–29. (Dem. 1912–13.)
Royal College of Physicians, Trafalgar Square, 1824–25.

PUBLICATIONS

Specimens of Continental Architecture.

DECIMUS BURTON (1800–81)

He practised chiefly in London and the home counties, particularly in Kent and Sussex, and was greatly helped by the influence of his father (James Burton the builder) and John Nash. He is said to have designed Cornwall and Clarence Terraces, Regent's Park (built by his father), but probably he merely assisted John Nash. He helped to preserve the purity of classical architecture, and was one of its last distinguished exponents.

Principal Buildings

Screen at Hyde Park Corner.

Lodges at Cumberland, Grosvenor, Chesterfield and Prince of Wales Gates, Hyde Park, 1825–46.

Archway on Constitution Hill, Buckingham Palace, 1828. (This was moved in 1883 to the position it now occupies: it was originally the north entrance to the Palace.)

Buildings and gardens for Zoological Society, Regent's Park, 1826–41.

Athenaeum Club, London, 1827–30.

Royal Naval Club, London, 1828–31.

Charing Cross Hospital, London, 1831–34.

THE ARCHITECTS' CLUB

In 1791 The Architects' Club was founded by S. P. Cockerell, George Dance, junior, Henry Holland, and James Wyatt. The original members included Robert Adam, Sir William Chambers, Robert Mylne, and John Soane. No one was eligible for membership who was not an R.A., an A.R.A., or Gold Medallist, or a member of the Academies of Rome, Florence, Bologna, Parma, or Paris. It was a dining club, but acquired a sense of collective responsibility about the architectural profession, and attempted to define the professional activities and qualifications of an architect. Its exclusive character limited its activities and influence, but it lasted until the eighteen-twenties.

FURNITURE-MAKERS AND DESIGNERS

Three names are popularly associated with English furniture of the eighteenth century: Chippendale, Hepplewhite, and Sheraton. Their general familiarity arises largely from the published records of their designs, for no work executed by Hepplewhite or Sheraton has been traced. Less familiar are the names of Shearer, Manwaring, Lock, Ince, Mayhew, Vile, Seddon, and the Gillows. Chippendale, Hepplewhite, and Sheraton have become identified with certain styles of furniture, delineated in their books, though it cannot be assumed that they originated those styles, which were also practised by their contemporaries. There were thousands of cabinet-makers, chair-makers, upholsterers, carvers and gilders at work throughout the country in the Georgian period. In Sir Ambrose Heal's comprehensive book, *The London Furniture Makers, from 1660 to 1840*, he lists 2,500; in Sheraton's *The Cabinet Dictionary*, published in 1803, a list of 253 names is given "of most of the Master Cabinet-makers, Upholsterers, and Chair Makers, in and about London." There were innumerable provincial makers, established in cities and towns and country districts. Of these there are sporadic records, mostly in the form of newspaper advertisements, but few names have come down to us. The furniture-making family of Gillow of Lancaster kept records, which still exist at the Lancaster branch of Waring & Gillow Ltd. Receipted bills, the maker's label pasted on a piece, and trade cards, supplement our knowledge of the extent of the trade, and suggest the capacity of the Georgian makers, and the trade cards, beautifully engraved, are often illustrated advertisements for variously designed articles of furniture.

There were many architects who influenced furniture design, or actually designed pieces which were executed by makers. It is known that Thomas Chippendale worked for the brothers Adam; that William Kent designed furniture, and so, occasionally, did Sir John Soane. Kent and the brothers Adam had a profound influence on the style of furniture, and much of the work in Sheraton's published plates was originated by Robert Adam. Thomas Hope, in the early nineteenth century, also exerted a far-reaching influence on furniture design. Some architects, like Batty Langley, included designs for furniture in their published works, which did not always have the merit of originality. In his book, *Furniture-making in 17th & 18th century England*, R. W. Symonds has illustrated two designs by Batty Langley, of a marble-topped console table and a draped dressing table, side by side with the original designs from which they were copied without acknowledgment. The designer of the console table was Nicholas Pineau, and the dressing table was by Johann Jacob Schübler. (The architects mentioned above are included in Appendix I.) The short list that follows includes a selection only of the more familiar names of makers.

THOMAS CHIPPENDALE (1718–79)

Cabinet-maker and chair-maker. Baptised at Otley Parish Church, Yorkshire, on June 5th, 1718. Died 1779, and buried in St. Martin-in-the-Fields, London, on November 13th of that year. He was the first cabinet-maker to publish a book of designs. Entitled *The Gentleman and Cabinet Maker's Director*, the first edition was issued in 1754; the second, with the same contents, in 1755; the third, much enlarged, in 1762. It is not known when he first came to London; but in 1745 he was living in Conduit Court, Long Acre, and in 1752 at Somerset or Northumberland Court in the Strand. He moved to St. Martin's Lane in 1753 or 1754, where his shop sign was *The Chair*, and he may then have taken into partnership James Rannie, a cabinet-maker. Rannie died in 1766, and Chippendale continued his business alone until 1771, when Thomas Haig joined the business, which then became known as Chippendale, Haig and Company. Sheraton, in the list of makers at the end of *The Cabinet Dictionary* (1803), gives the address of Thomas Chippendale, upholsterer, at 60 St. Martin's Lane. The business was carried on by his son, Thomas Chippendale, junior (1749–1822), in partnership with Haig.

JOHN COBB (—— d. 1778)

Cabinet-maker and upholsterer. He was in partnership with William Vile, and remained in the business after Vile's retirement. He lived in Long Acre from 1751 onwards. His business was prosperous and included Royal clients and members of the nobility. He made some of the furniture for the Holbein Chamber at Strawberry Hill, for Horace Walpole. He is reputedly the inventor of Cobb's Table—a kind of writing-desk—of which only a description (but no drawing) exists, given by J. T. Smith in *Nollekens and his Times*. (*See* page 278.)

HENRY COPLAND

Copland worked with Matthias Lock, at *Ye Swan*, Tottenham Court Road, London, and was primarily a designer, interested chiefly in ornament, and probably the earliest exponent of the Rococo style in England. Very little is known about him, but in *The London Furniture Makers*, Sir Ambrose Heal records that Copland's name appeared on engravings of bookplates, invitation cards, and trade cards as early as 1738. With Lock, he was probably responsible for some of the designs in Chippendale's *Director*.

THE GILLOWS

The firm of Gillow was founded by Robert Gillow, a joiner, at Gt. Singleton in the parish of Kirkham-in-the-Fylde, but in 1695 he removed to Lancaster, and set up in business there as a carpenter. He became a freeman of the borough of Lancaster, and in 1728 and thereafter practised as a cabinet-maker. The firm's records begin in 1731. He had three sons, Richard, Robert junior, and Thomas, and in 1757 Richard, who had been trained as an architect, was taken into partnership. He was the designer of the Customs House at Lancaster. (*See* page 40.) Some time in the middle years of the eighteenth century the Gillows began trading in London, and about 1761 premises were established by the firm in Oxford Street, on the site of those now occupied by Waring and Gillow Ltd.

GEORGE HEPPLEWHITE (―― d. 1786)

All that is known about his life is that he was apprenticed to the firm of Gillow of Lancaster, and later came to London and opened a shop in Red Cross Street, St. Giles's Cripplegate. His book of designs, *The Cabinet Maker and Upholsterer's Guide*, was published after his death: the first edition appeared in 1788, and a second in 1789. His name is sometimes spelt Heppelwhite, and is entered thus in connection with his designs in *The Cabinet-Makers' London Book of Prices*.

WILLIAM INCE

Cabinet-maker and upholsterer, who was in partnership with John Mayhew, and lived and worked in the second half of the eighteenth century. With Mayhew, he was joint author of *The Universal System of Household Furniture*, which first appeared in parts, between 1759 and 1762. The firm of Ince and Mayhew was established at Broad Street, Golden Square, Soho, and was still in existence during the first decade of the nineteenth century. The address given in *The Cabinet Dictionary* (1803) is 47 Marshall Street, Carnaby Market.

MATTHIAS LOCK

A carver and designer of furniture who worked during the middle and late eighteenth century, and was employed by Chippendale. He may have been responsible for some of the plates in Chippendale's *Director*, and was one of the English interpreters of the Rococo style, when it was introduced from France. He published several books on ornament and furniture, and the earliest, in which the plates are dated 1740, was entitled *A New Drawing Book of Ornaments*. Some of his books were produced in collaboration with Henry Copland, and both worked at *Ye Swan*, Tottenham Court Road, after 1725, though Lock's address in 1746 was Nottingham Court, Castle Street, near Long Acre.

ROBERT MANWARING

Cabinet-maker and chair-maker, and a contemporary of Chippendale. In the seventeen-sixties he was established in the Haymarket. He produced work both in the Chinese and Gothic manner, but some of his designs were heavy and ill-proportioned, but this impression is often created by the crudity of the drawing, and many of his chair designs had distinct and pleasing originality. In 1765 he published two books, *The Cabinet and Chair-Makers' Real Friend and Companion; or the Whole System of Chair-Making made Plain and Easy*, and *The Carpenter's Complete Guide to Gothic Railing*. In 1766 he published *The Chair-Maker's Guide*, to which Copland contributed some designs.

JOHN MAYHEW (——— d. 1811)

In partnership with William Ince as a cabinet-maker and upholsterer. Joint author of *The Universal System of Household Furniture*. (See Ince.)

GEORGE SEDDON (1727–1801)

He was the founder of a properous cabinet-making business that was still in existence in the mid nineteenth century, in which his sons, George and Thomas, and his son-in-law, Thomas Shackleton, were partners. About 1750 he established his business at London House, Aldersgate Street, and the firm of Seddon became one of the most famous for furniture during the late eighteenth century, not only in Britain but abroad. In 1791 William Hickey describes in his *Memoirs* the furnishing of the house he took jointly with Mr. Shaw in Garden Reach, Calcutta. For the billiard room "a very capital billiard table, made by Seddons, was purchased at the price of one thousand sicca rupees." (Volume IV, Chapter III, page 26.) Some of the furniture made by the firm has survived.

THOMAS SHEARER

A furniture designer, to whom the design of the sideboard in the form now familiar, has been attributed. Little is known about him, though he was responsible for many of the plates in *The Cabinet Makers' London Book of Prices* (1788), and most of the plates in that book were re-issued in the same year under Shearer's name as *Designs for Household Furniture*.

THOMAS SHERATON (1751–1806)

Cabinet-maker and furniture designer. Born at Stockton-on-Tees, he came to London about 1790, after being a journeyman cabinet-maker for many years. In London, he settled in 106 Wardour Street, Soho, where he taught drawing and architecture. At a later date he moved to 8 Broad Street, Golden Square. He published many designs for furniture, and his principal works were *The Cabinet Maker's and Upholsterer's Drawing Book* (published in parts between 1791 and 1794), and *The Cabinet Dictionary*, published in 1803. His final work, *The Cabinet Maker, Upholsterer and General Artists' Encyclopaedia*, was incomplete when he died, and about a quarter of it was published. In 1812 a posthumous work appeared, consisting largely of plates from his previous books, and entitled *Designs for Household Furniture, by the late T. Sheraton, cabinet maker*. Apart from John Cobb, Sheraton is the only furniture designer of the period about whom we have any revealing personal details. A description of his circumstances and frugal way of life occurs in the *Memoirs of Adam Black*, which is quoted on page 140, and his gentle and unambitious acceptance of poverty is apparent from a sentence in *The Cabinet Dictionary*, which follows his recommendation for setting up a public wood yard in London. "I mention these things," he wrote, "with a view to national credit, and not from my own desire to recommend any extravagant steps in the purchase of grand furniture; for I can assure the reader, though I am thus employed in racking my invention to design fine and pleasing cabinet work, I can be well content to sit on a wooden bottom chair myself provided I can but have common food and raiment wherewith to pass through life in peace." (Entry CABINET, page 118.)

WILLIAM VILE (—— d. 1767)

At the beginning of George III's reign he was cabinet-maker to the Crown; later, he entered into partnership with John Cobb, an upholsterer. Together they rented premises on the corner of St. Martin's Lane and Long Acre, London, where they first paid rates in 1751. Vile's will was made in 1763 and there is no record of his accounts to the Royal Household after 1764–65. He was not a chair-maker.

BOOKS ON FURNITURE
PUBLISHED BETWEEN 1660 AND 1830

CHIPPENDALE, THOMAS. *The Gentleman and Cabinet Maker's Director* (1754).

COMMITTEE OF MASTERS CABINET MAKERS. *The Prices of Cabinet Work* (1797).

DARLY, M. *A New Book of Chinese, Gothic and Modern Chairs* (1751).

HEPPLEWHITE, A., & Co. *The Cabinet Maker and Upholsterer's Guide, or Repository of Designs for Every Article of Household Furniture* (1788).

HOPE, THOMAS. *Household Furniture and Interior Decoration Executed from Designs by Thomas Hope* (1807).

INCE, WILLIAM, and MAYHEW, JOHN. *The Universal System of Household Furniture: Consisting of above 300 Designs in the most Elegant Taste, both Useful and Ornamental* (1759–60). First published in parts.

LANGLEY, BATTY. *The City and Country Builder's and Workman's Treasury of Designs: Or the Art of Drawing and Working and Ornamental Parts of Architecture* (1739).

LONDON SOCIETY OF CABINET MAKERS. *The Cabinet-Makers' London Book of Prices* (1788).

MANWARING, ROBERT. *The Cabinet and Chair-Makers' Real Friend and Companion: or the Whole System of Chair-Making made Plain and Easy* (1765).

MANWARING, ROBERT, and others. *The Chair-Maker's Guide* (1766).

NICHOLSON, MICHAEL ANGELO. *The Carpenter and Joiner's Companion in the Geometrical Construction of Working Drawings. Improved from the Original Principles of P. Nicholson* (1826).

NICHOLSON, PETER. *Practical Carpentry, Joinery and Cabinet-Making* (1826).

NICHOLSON, PETER and MICHAEL ANGELO. *The Practical Cabinet-Maker, Upholsterer and Complete Decorator* (1826).

SHEARER, THOMAS. *Designs for Household Furniture* (1788).

SHERATON, THOMAS. *The Cabinet Maker's and Upholsterer's Drawing Book* (1791–93). Originally published in parts.

  The Cabinet Dictionary (1803).

  Designs for Household Furniture, by the late T. Sheraton, cabinet maker (1812).

SMITH, GEORGE. *A Collection of Designs for Household Furniture* (1808).

  The Cabinet-Maker and Upholsterer's Guide (1826).

SOCIETY OF UPHOLSTERERS, CABINET-MAKERS, ETC. *Household Furniture in Genteel Taste for the Year 1760.* (1760).

STALKER, JOHN, and PARKER, GEORGE. *A Treatise on Japaning and Varnishing* (1688).

THE SOCIETY OF DILETTANTI

The Society of Dilettanti was founded in 1734 by a few wealthy noblemen and gentlemen who had travelled widely in Europe, particularly in Italy and Greece, and also in Asia Minor. They were generous-minded men, with a taste for the antique, who were anxious to share the pleasure that they had derived from their expeditions in search of architectural and artistic treasures, and to foster a wider interest in architecture and archaeology at home. The Society began as little more than a dining club and until 1736 no regular records were kept. It is even likely that some preliminary meetings were held as early as 1732.

The original 46 members were nearly all young men and the most active, probably the original founder, was Sir Francis Dashwood (1708–81), later notorious for his peculiar and profligate practices. Other famous founder members included: Charles Sackville (second Duke of Dorset), 1711–69; Simon Harcourt (second Viscount Harcourt), 1714–77; Sir James Gray, and his brother, Colonel George Gray; William Ponsonby (Viscount Duncannon), 1704–93; Richard Grenville (Earl Temple), 1711–79; John Howe, 1707–69; Thomas Archer, d. 1768; General William Strode; Sewallis Shirley, 1709–65; Sir Henry Liddell, Bt. (later Baron Ravensworth); William Fauquier (Secretary of the Society, 1771–74), d. 1788; Henry Harris (acted as High Steward of the Society from 1736); Sir Charles Hanbury Williams; Thomas Villiers (later Baron Hyde and Earl of Clarendon); Arthur Smyth (later Archbishop of Dublin and Primate of Ireland); and Robert Hay (later Archbishop of York).

The first official meeting took place at the Bedford Head Tavern in Covent Garden on March 6th, 1736. Meetings were held on the first Sunday of each month between December and May, and for a short period (1781–84) two meetings a month were held. Later still, the period of the year was changed from February to July, and this remained the rule. In 1743 the Society contemplated erecting its own house, and bought a site in Cavendish Square, deciding that the building should be a model of the Temple of Pola in Dalmatia; but the scheme was abandoned in 1756. The main purpose of the Society was to encourage, foster, and maintain interest in and knowledge of classical art and taste in England. Much the most important of its activities were concerned with the exploration and recording of ruins in Greece, and the first volume of *The Antiquities of Athens*, measured and delineated by James Stuart, F.R.S. and F.S.A., and Nicholas Revett, painters and architects, published in 1762, was financially sponsored by the Society. Stuart and Revett planned the expedition and made all their own arrangements for the work, and their first volume had a considerable effect in reviving taste for classical studies, and was the starting-point of the Greek revival. When they visited Athens, the Acropolis was not as it is today—a cleared, open space with the Parthenon and other buildings standing independently,

free from all obstructions and splendidly visible. A squalid Turkish village then
occupied most of the site and the Parthenon and other temples were incorporated
with and surrounded by miscellaneous buildings. (See plate 3.)

Stuart and Revett first became known to the Society through their meeting with
Sir James Gray, in Venice, and in 1755 they were elected members, and were
apparently the first members who were not men of leisure. The success of their first
volume of *The Antiquities* was spectacular. The year after its publication, in 1763, the
Society decided to organise and finance another expedition: this time to Asia Minor,
with the object of investigating ruins and ancient monuments. Those who were
sent included Nicholas Revett, William Pars, and Mr. Richard Chandler, of Magdalen
College, Oxford. They departed in 1764, returning two years later, after visiting
Greece and Turkey. They handed over to the Society all the drawings they had made,
inscriptions they had copied, and marbles they had acquired, together with Chandler's
journal of the expedition. Much of this formed the material for *Ionian Antiquities*,
published by the Society in 1769. Chandler later published the inscriptions, and the
first and second parts of his journal, dedicating all these to the Society. The Society
helped Stuart financially in the publication of the second volume of *The Antiquities
of Athens* (1787), by having certain engravings made, and lending drawings. A
third volume was issued in 1794, and a fourth in 1814, though Stuart had died in
1787, just before the second appeared. The second volume of *Ionian Antiquities* was
published in 1797 by the Society, who had by then appointed a Committee of
Publication to deal with it. In 1784 the marbles were given to the British Museum,
and later, the drawings also. A portion of the Parthenon frieze was first presented
to the Royal Academy, and in 1817 went to the British Museum.

In 1786 the Society printed and published *An Account of the Worship of Priapus,
lately existing at Isernia in the Kingdom of Naples; in Two Letters; one from Sir William
Hamilton, K.B., His Majesty's Minister at the Court of Naples, to Sir Joseph Banks, Bart.,
President of the Royal Society; and the other from a Person residing at Isernia; To which is
added, A discourse on the worship of Priapus, and its Connexion with the Mystic Theology of
the Ancients by R. P. Knight Esq.* This publication, which got the Society into a lot of
trouble, originated in some discoveries of Sir William Hamilton, which came before
the Society in the form of a letter to Sir Joseph Banks in 1781, describing a form of
phallic ritual then still existing at Isernia, and carried on side by side with Christian
worship. These rites had previously been investigated—among other archaeological
researches—by Pierre François Hugues (D'Hancarville), whose work had fascinated
some members of the Society, particularly Payne Knight, so that they were rather
innocently enthusiastic for the publication of Hamilton's letter. The nature of the
subject gave widespread offence, and was considered by many people to be an
unpardonable breach of good taste; the fact that it was of great antiquarian interest
was no excuse for delving into such matters; so many copies were called in, and the
work is now extremely rare.

In 1799 a new Committee of Publication of the Society was formed, which produced *Select Specimens of Ancient Sculpture, Aegyptian, Etruscan, Greek, and Roman: selected
from Different Collections in Great Britain.* This was published in 1809.

In 1803 the Society lost an opportunity of investigating and bringing to light the
treasures of Herculaneum, when notes and drawings on these were presented to it by
Sir William Hamilton. All they did was to thank him politely, and there the matter

rested. Early in the nineteenth century they missed another opportunity over the Elgin marbles, for they gave no support to Lord Elgin in his task of removing and preserving the marbles from destruction, although several individual members appear to have been sympathetic to him. The marbles were eventually bought by the Government for £35,000—a little more than half Lord Elgin's expenses in connection with their preservation.

The Society is still active, and meets at the St. James's Club to dine on five Sundays in each year. In recognition of that privilege the Society has housed its collection of pictures on the walls of the Club. In 1955 there were 40 members.

A History of the Society of Dilettanti, compiled by Lionel Cust and edited by Sidney Colvin was published in 1898 by Macmillan & Co.

THE SOCIETY OF ARTS

The Society of Arts was founded in 1754, with the object of promoting the arts, manufactures and commerce of the country. Its formation was inspired by William Shipley, a Northampton drawing master, who after failing to obtain local support for his idea of a fund to be distributed in premiums for promoting improvements in the liberal arts and sciences and manufactures, came to London and secured the support of several influential people, of whom the most important were Viscount Folkestone and Lord Romney. These two noblemen were present with Shipley and eight others at a meeting on March 22nd, 1754, when the Society of Arts was founded. Within eight years its members numbered over 2,500, and included many famous people. Among them were the architects Robert Adam, Sir William Chambers, and George Dance the Elder; John Baskerville the printer, William Caslon the type founder, Thomas Chippendale, Benjamin Franklin, Edward Gibbon, David Garrick, William Hogarth, Dr. Samuel Johnson, James Boswell, Sir Joshua Reynolds, who was elected in 1756 before he was knighted, Samuel Richardson the novelist, and Horace Walpole. The Society of Arts was indirectly responsible for the foundation of the Royal Academy, following a decision to sponsor the first art exhibition in 1760.

Consistently active for over two hundred years, the Society celebrated its bicentenary in 1954. Under the patronage of King Edward VII, it was allowed to use the prefix "Royal" in 1908. Two authoritative accounts of the Society and its work have been written: *A History of The Royal Society of Arts*, by Sir Henry Trueman Wood, Secretary of the Society (London: John Murray, 1913), and *The Royal Society of Arts 1754–1954*, by Derek Hudson and Kenneth W. Luckhurst, Secretary of the Society (London: John Murray, 1954).

THE GUNNING SISTERS

Maria and Elizabeth Gunning were the daughters of an Irish gentleman, and related through their mother to Viscount Mayo. Born in Ireland in 1733 and 1734 respectively, they came to London with their mother and younger sister about 1751. The sisters were practically penniless, but fabulously beautiful and their mother obviously intended to arrange profitable marriages. She was brilliantly successful, for in 1752 Maria married the sixth Earl of Coventry, and Elizabeth the sixth Duke of Hamilton, within a few weeks of each other. Elizabeth, widowed in 1758, married the seventh Duke of Argyll in 1759.

The sisters seem to have been quite unalike in character and appearance. Horace Walpole considered the Countess of Coventry was the lovelier of the two: she was dark, while her sister was fair, and though good-natured and warm-hearted, she seems also to have been ill-educated and almost brainless. The Duchess of Hamilton played a leading part in founding the Select Society of Edinburgh for encouraging the Arts and Manufactures of Scotland, in 1754, and although this was not connected with the Society of Arts in England, it was probably the forerunner of the English Society's Scottish branch, and the two bodies corresponded with each other. The Select Society ceased to exist about 1762.

The Countess of Coventry died in 1760, of what was obviously consumption. The Duchess of Argyll lived until 1790. Horace Walpole and Mrs. Montagu refer to the sisters in their letters, and there is a full account of them in *George Selwyn and his Contemporaries*, by John Heneage Jesse (London: 1843), pages 162 to 176.

GEORGIAN GRACE IN THE AMERICAN COLONIES—THE PHILIPSE MANOR HALL AT YONKERS, NEW YORK

The urbanities of Georgian England were reproduced in the American colonies, where a deep reverence for classical architecture, and all that such reverence implied, moulded the taste of the wealthy colonial families. Many examples of the great country houses of colonial days still survive. For example, on Warburton Avenue and Dock Street in the city of Yonkers, New York State, a spacious and mellow building of brick and stone still stands. It was once the property of the Lords of the Manor of Philipsborough, and is now preserved as an historic monument. Since the beginning of the last century, when just over a score of buildings adjoined the site of the Philipse Manor Hall, the city has devoured the open spaces; the River Nepperhan which once flowed by the manor grounds into the Hudson, when the river bank was only three hundred feet from the house, now flows beneath Dock Street; and Yonkers within a hundred years had become a city of 80,000 inhabitants, its present population being over 110,000. Standing amid the rather squalid building developments of this nineteenth century city, and by comparison with the comely, white-painted timber-framed houses that adorn the residential suburbs of cities in the Eastern states, the Philipse Manor has an air of serene stability and solid endurance.

The house is built of rough rubble with squared-up patches of brickwork, some six courses deep, below the window-sills; but the east front, which presents its twin porches to Warburton Avenue, is of red brick. Until 1911, when the Manor Hall was taken over by the American Scenic and Historic Preservation Society, this brickwork had been hidden by yellow paint, and the stone sides by stucco, which have been removed to restore the original appearance of the Hall. Today the red bricks have the light, rosy hue that distinguishes some of the old brick buildings of Boston, such as the South Meeting House. The plan is L-shaped, the eastern front, over ninety feet long, being the long arm of the L. A string course runs along this front, its deep cornice linking the tops of the ground-floor window architraves, and breaking forward to rest upon the fluted Doric columns of the two porches.

The sash windows are double squares, each square divided vertically by three glazing bars, and horizontally by two, giving twelve panes to each square and twenty-four in all to each window. The glazing bars are heavy, and in section resemble English types common in the late seventeenth century. The ground-floor windows have external shutters. The dormer windows in the roof are casements and they light the great attics, where in Colonial times a large staff of black slaves and white servants was housed. A balustrade surrounds the upper slopes of the roof above the dormers.

On the south front there is another porch, but here the columns support a deep entablature, and the improved proportions obviate the suggestion of exaggerated width that makes the two east front porches seem squat. The south porch has a heavy panelled door, constructed to allow the upper part to remain open while the lower half is closed. Behind it lies the south hall, from which a staircase with slender balusters of pine ascends in two turns to the first floor. On the left hand is the west parlour; on the right, the east parlour. The west parlour is a pleasant room, with a chimney-piece flanked by closets which minimise the forward break of that feature. The mantelpiece is ornamented by a simple flower pattern of unusual character; it might indeed have been inspired by the Morris school of the late nineteenth century instead of being at least one hundred and sixty or seventy years earlier. This is an agreeable example of those occasional, vivid expressions of individual ornament that appear in the conventional classical framework of American Colonial decoration. A fireback bearing the Royal Arms was discovered in 1911 when the fire-place opening was restored to its original dimensions.

The east parlour corresponds closely in size to the west, but it is an elaborate room, with a deep cornice, a heavily carved overmantel with a broken pediment, and a ceiling enriched by ornate flower and bird motifs and two portrait medallions, which are presumed to be likenesses of past Lords of the Manor. There is a closet on the left of the chimney-piece, on the right a doorway leading to the east hall. This hall, although it is entered from a porch less imposing than the south porch, is far more decorative than the south hall. It has a heavy cornice with dentils, a panelled dado, and a mahogany staircase, with twisted balusters, and the handrail sweeps round in a scroll to the newel-post at the foot of the stairs. Here hangs a portrait of Mary Philipse, sister of the third Lord of the Manor, whose beauty and accomplishments attracted young Colonel Washington in the seventeen-fifties, a partiality which endured and may have affected the survival of the Manor Hall during the War of Independence.

On the right of the east hall is the dining-room, where some of the woodwork is old and the mantelpiece and fire-place have been returned to their original positions; for this part of the ground floor was extensively altered in 1868, when the Manor Hall was acquired by what was then the village of Yonkers for $44,000. The village authorities removed the fire-place wall of the dining-room, also the partitions that divided the kitchen from the larder beyond the dining-room, and created one large apartment north of the east hall, which was used as a Court Room.

On the first floor the most interesting room is the west chamber, where there is some of the earliest woodwork in the house. It has a large open fire-place, formerly lined with blue and white Dutch tiles illustrating Biblical scenes. Some of these remain and have been supplemented with modern copies.

It is believed that the south part of the Manor was built in the late seventeenth century, and that the northern addition was made about 1745. During the eighteenth century, before the revolutionary war, the Manor was the background of gracious, comfortable and occasionally sparkling social life. A horde of servants simplified the daily round of the Philipse family. Some of the earlier peculiarities of the family's prosperous condition were preserved in the attenuated form of local legends about the first Lord's traffic with pirates; and the inevitable story of a secret passage from the house to the river still survives. In the closet of the east parlour a stairway once led to the cellar: it was open during the years when the Manor served the village as a hall and court house, but was closed during the work of restoration. The secret way to the river, although believed in for generations, has never been discovered. Colonel Frederick Philipse, the last Lord of the Manor, was, in the felicitous words of the tablet erected to his memory in Chester cathedral where he is buried, "a Gentleman, in whom the various social, domestic and religious Virtues were eminently united." (See page 346.) That tablet records the passing of the Manor from the Philipse family, for its last Lord "opposed, at the Hazard of his Life, the late Rebellion in North America; and for this faithful Discharge of his Duty to his King and Country, he was Proscribed, and his Estate, one of the largest in New York, was Confiscated, by the Usurped Legislature of that Province." Although the Manor was abandoned by the family after 1777, they confided it to the care of their steward; and neither the British nor Washington's forces occupied it, so it escaped damage. Colonel Frederick Philipse was a loyal Tory; Mary Philipse, who in 1758 was married in the east parlour of the Manor Hall to Captain Roger Morris—an A.D.C. to the unfortunate General Braddock—might at one time have become Mrs. George Washington.

In 1779, an act of attainder and confiscation was passed which outlawed the Philipse family, and the sale of their property was conducted by the Commissioners of Sequestration and Forfeiture. The Manor was sold in 1785 for £14,520 to Cornelius P. Low of New York City. Before the end of the eighteenth century it had changed hands twice, and after 1800 it survived the architectural whims of several owners in the sixty-eight years that passed before it became a municipal property.

Today it marks a phase of American life that has vanished so completely that it is historically incomprehensible to most of the visitors who inspect the spacious, white-painted rooms, which exhibit the airs and graces of early Georgian England. The collection of family portraits shows a purposeful race of men and women. Outstanding among them is that of Mary Philipse, a girl with kind eyes but a determined mouth. Had she married Washington, she would hardly have been content with a mere President—she might have been the first American Queen.

COACHES FROM LONDON TO YORK AND NEWCASTLE

Extract from *The Whitehall Evening-Post; Or, London Intelligencer.* From Thursday, June 26th to Saturday, June 28th, 1760. (No. 2228), page 4.

LONDON, YORK AND NEWCASTLE

MACHINES, from London to York in Three Days, and so on from York to Newcastle in Two Days; to begin on Monday the 30th of June 1760. Sets out from the White Swan Inn, Holborn Bridge, London, every Monday, Wednesday, and Friday, and goes to Stilton the first Day, to Barnbymoor the Second, and to the Black Swan in Coney-Street, York, the Third; and returns from York every Tuesday, Thursday, and Saturday; and from Newcastle every Tuesday.

Any Persons applying to the Places aforesaid, may be accommodated with good Machines and able Horses, allowing each Passenger twenty Pounds Weight; all above to pay Threepence per Pound.

N.B.—Sets out from London at Five o'Clock, and from York at Six in the Morning.

Perform'd (if God permits) by

    { ROBERT BIRCH
    { WILLIAM CARTER
    { JOHN BARNES
    { THOMAS BOND

N.B. The Masters will not be accountable for Money, Plate, Jewels, Watches, Rings, or Writings, without they be entered as such, and paid for accordingly.

Advertisements extracted from the back page of *The Whitehall Evening-Post; Or, London Intelligencer*. From Thursday, March 8th to Saturday, March 10th, 1759. Printed for C. Corbett, at the State Lottery-Office, opposite St. Dunstan's-Church, Fleet-Street.

CHARLES COOPER, at the Strafford

Arms in Wakefield, begs Leave to inform the Nobility, Gentry, Tradesmen, and Others, that he carries on the Business of the said House since his Father's Decease, and hopes for the Continuance of their Custom, where they may depend upon the best Entertainment.

From their most humble Servant,

CHARLES COOPER.

To be SOLD,

A Freehold House, with all convenient Offices, thereto belonging, situate on the North Side of St. James's-Square, late the Right Hon, the Earl of Pembroke's, containing, in Front to the Square, 38 Feet little more or less, and 203 Feet in Depth, terminating in a Mews, where is a convenient Way for Carriages. For further Particulars enquire of Mr. Evans, in Farm-Street, near Hill-Street, Berkley-Square.

To be Lett, and enter'd upon forthwith.

Pleasantly situated on the River Trent, five Miles from Nottingham, and twelve from Derby, in a Sporting Country,

A Very good Mansion-House, eight or ten Rooms on a Floor, with convenient Offices of all Kinds, a Dove-house, and Stables for fifteen or twenty Horses, with a Coach-house and Barn. The Gardens and Orchards walled in, and well planted. The Royalty of the Manor, and a Fishery, sufficient for the Family all the Year; with or without twenty or thirty Acres of exceeding good Meadow Land. For further Particulars enquire of Mr. Chappel, of Bridle Smith Gate, Nottingham; or of Mr. Baskerville, of Nag's Head-Court, Gracechurch-Street, London.

To be SOLD,

AN Estate, call'd Sedgwick Park, in the Parishes of Nuthurst and Horsham in Sussex, lying all together, and consisting of Arable, Meadow, Pasture, Wood and Coppice Lands, with a Mansion-House (lately inhabited by Henry Lintott, Esq; deceas'd) new fronted, commanding a fine Prospect to the South Downs, with Stables, Coach-houses, and other necessary Offices; an Orchard, Gardens, Bowling-Green, and two large Fish-ponds.

To be sold also, a Farm, at Slaugham, three Miles from Sedgwick Park, lett at 22l. a Year. The Whole being Freehold, and upwards of 330l. a Year.

Enquire of Mr. Geekie, No. 14, in the Paper Buildings, Inner Temple, London; or of Mr. Buckner, at Chichester in Sussex.

To be SOLD,

Pursuant to a Decree of the High Court of Chancery, before William Spicer, Esq; one of the Masters of the said Court, some Time in April next,

A Freehold Messuage in Dover-Street, Piccadilly, now in the Possession of Sir William Stanhope. A Messuage in the same Street, late in the Possession of Sir Clement Cotterel Dormer, and now lett to Lady Curzon, and a Ground Rent of 18l. per Annum for ever, well cover'd, with a large House belonging to Lord Thomond in the same Street; and also a Freehold Farm and Lands, with some Copyhold Lands thereto belonging, at Dullingham, in the County of Cambridge, late the Estates of Sir Jermyn Davers, deceas'd. Particulars whereof may be had at the said Master's Chambers in Lincoln's Inn; and further Enquiry may be made of Messrs Dighton and Bonnin, at their Chambers, No. 5, Lincoln's Inn New-Square.

AT EYRE's Original Mineral Water Warehouse between the Two Temple Gates, Fleet-Street, just arrived fresh Spaw, Pyrmont, &c. and Selters Water, with Bourn, Brue, Harygate, Scarborough, and Bristol Waters. Where may be had, as usual, all other Mineral and Purging Waters in the greatest Perfection, delivered to any Part of the Town gratis.

N.B. Bath, Cheltenham, Holt, Tilbury, the Original Jessop's Well, Sea, Tar, Acton, fresh every Week.

Hungary and Lavender Waters.

On reading in the Magazine of Magazines, for January, 1759, a Panegyrick Ode on S. RAMBO, High German Hair-Dresser and Tireman.

> INgenious Rambo! Rambo, Genius rare,
> What Albion Artist can with thee compare:
> Or vie, upon the Rolls of Fame,
> To be recorded with thy Name.
> Thou, dextrous, to the human Face,
> Can'st add inimitable Grace.
> Into a Beau transform a Clown:
> Make Blouze a Lady of the Town:
> Ye more, thy artful Fingers rare
> Can so transpose, and form the Hair,
> Beauty to Ugliness impart;
> And Age to Youth transform by Art.
> But Rambo, say! What Creature has the Skill,
> To work the Hair to ev'ry Form, at Will:
> To Squares—to Rounds—to Ovals—and to Hearts:
> To Letters—Cyphers—Sprigs—and Flowers—and Darts:

To various Forms, beyond what is exprest!
To be admired when we are gone to Rest:
To be admir'd by Ages yet unborn!
And, by the prime Nobility be worn.
This Art, from every Mortal else confined,
To MONDET and his Family consign'd.
Oxford-Street, St. James's,
Feb. 3, 1759.   BELGAE. HIB. BRITANICUS. M.

This Day were publish'd,
PROPOSALS for ENGRAVING by SUBSCRIPTION,
THREE Historical PRINTS, from the Original Paintings of Dominichino, Guido, Rheni, and Nicholas Poussin. By ROBERT STRANGE.

A Drawing from the Dominichino, and Specimens of the Work may be seen at the Golden Head, Henrietta-Street, Covent-Garden, where the Subscription is opened, and will be continued till the End of May.

This Day was publish'd,
In ONE Neat POCKET VOLUME,
(Price 6s. sew'd, bound 7s.)
A POLITICAL and SATIRICAL HISTORY of the Years 1756 and 1757. In a Series of Seventy-five Humorous and Entertaining PRINTS. Containing all the most remarkable Transactions, Characters, and Caricaturas of those two memorable Years. To which is annexed, An Explanatory Account, or Key, to every Print, which renders the Whole full and significant.
N.B. This Book sold for 1.l. 17s. 6d. on Cards.
Sold by J. Scott, at the Black Swan in Pater-noster Row.

In a few Days will be publish'd
In ONE VOLUME, OCTAVO,
Illustrated with a general Map of Senegal, Goree, &c.
A VOYAGE TO SENEGAL, the ISLAND OF GOREE, and the River GAMBIA, performed during the Years 1749, 50, 51, 52, and 53; giving an exact Description of the Navigation of the River Niger; the natural History and Commodities of the Country; the Customs and Manners of the Inhabitants; with a full State of the French Factories before their late Reduction to the Crown of Great-Britain. By Mr. ADANSON, Correspondent of the Royal Academy of Sciences.
Printed for J. Nourse, in the Strand; and W. Johnson, in Ludgate-Street.

Till the first of April, and no longer, will be SOLD,
By T. OSBORNE, in Gray's-Inn, who having purchased,
THE very few Remaining Copies of STEPHEN's LATIN THESAURUS, Four Volumes in Folio, of which there are no more than twenty-five left, offers them to the Public at Two Guineas a Sett in Sheets, formerly sold for Four Guineas in Sheets,

after which Time, if any Books remain unsold, the Price will be advanced One Guinea.

N.B. At the abovesaid T. Osborne's is daily selling, the Libraries of the late Hon. Sir LUKE SCHAUB, Bart. and Others. Where may be had Money for any Library or Parcel of Books, Prints, and Manuscripts.

This Day was publish'd, Price 1s. 6d.
In OCTAVO,
CYMBELINE: A TRAGEDY. Alter'd from SHAKESPEAR. As it is now Acted at the Theatre Royal in Covent-Garden.
By WILLIAM HAWKINS, M.A.
Late Fellow of Pembroke College, and Professor of Poetry in the University of Oxford. Printed for James Rivington and James Fletcher, at the Oxford Theatre in Pater-noster-Row.
Where Mr. Hawkins's Works, in Three Vols. 8vo. may be had.

This Day was publish'd,
The FOURTH VOLUME of
THE HISTORY OF THE POPES, from the Foundation of the See of Rome to the present Time.
By ARCHIBALD BOWER, Esq;
Printed for the Author; and to be had at W. Sandby's, at the Ship, opposite St. Dunstan's Church, Fleet-Street; at Z. Stuart's, at the Lamb, in Pater-noster-Row; at Mr. Frith's the Corner of the Old Jewry in the Poultry; and at the Author's, opposite the Duke of Grafton's in old Bond-Street.

PARLIAMENTARY HISTORY OF ENGLAND.
The Authors return their hearty Thanks to the Public, for the generous Encouragement they have given to that Work, whereby the First Thirteen Volumes (from the Conquest to the Battle of Naseby in 1645 are now out of Print: And take this Opportunity of assuring them, that as the INDEX is under the Care of a very able Hand, and in great Forwardness, the Whole will be compleated against the next Winter. In the mean Time the Seven Volumes last published, of which there are but few Copies left, may be had of William Sandby, Bookseller, in Fleet-Street, London; and of Cæsar Ward, York.

This Day were publish'd,
VOLUME the SECOND (Price bound 3s.) of
MADAME de MAINTENON's
LETTERS.
"The victorious Mad. de Maintenon gained such an Ascendant and inspired Lewis XIV, with so much Fondness, that he secretly married her without the least Contract or Stipulation. There are Letters of Her's remaining written with surprising Elegance. &c."   VOLTAIRE.

GG—O

"These Letters give us quite a new Idea of Mad. de Maintenon. In the agreeable and submissive Companion of Lewis XIV we are charmed with the faithful Friend, the prudent Counsellor, the tender Wife, the sincere Christian; in a Word, the Mistress of every oeconomical Virtue." Monthly Review.

Printed for L. Davis and C. Reymers, against Gray's Inn, Holborn. By whom were lately published,

1. The Second Edition of Volume the First. Price 3s.
2. Memoirs of Mad. de Maintenon, 5 Vols. 15s.
3. M. Crebillon's Letters of the Marchioness de M****. Price 3s.

L. DAVIS and C. REYMERS, against Gray's-Inn, Holborn, having just purchased the very few remaining Copies of the following Work, in One Volume, Folio, first published in 1747, at a Guinea in Sheets; propose to reduce the Price to Fourteen Shillings, neatly bound and letter'd.

TRAVELS in TURKEY; and back from Adrianople to Holland, and thence to England. By the Rev. EDMUND CHISHULL, B.D. Chaplain to the Turkey Company at Smyrna. Publish'd from the Originals; with a Preface by the late very eminent Dr. RICHARD MEAD.

*** A few Copies also remain of the Author's Antiquitates Asiaticae, printed uniformly with his Travels in Turkey.

Very soon will be published, in Two Volumes, Octavo, Travels through Part of Europe, Asia Minor, several Islands of the Archipelago, Syria, Palestine, or the Holy Land, Mount Sinai, &c. By John Aegidius Van Egmond, Ambassador Extraordinary from the States-General to the King of Naples and Sicily; and John Heyman, Professor of the Oriental Languages at Leyden. With Plates.

This Day were publish'd, in Quarto.

Beautifully printed and illustrated with upwards of ninety Views and Plans, engraved by Paul Fourdrinier, Price in boards 19s. bound 1.l. 1s.

ANTIQUITIES of the County of LOUTH in IRELAND. Containing the principal Ruins and curious Remains, antient Dwellings, and other Curiosities of the Druids, Danes, English, &c. With proper Explanations and Illustrations, divided into three Books, and taken upon the Spot by THOMAS WRIGHT, Author of the Physical and Mathematical Elements of Astronomy, &c. The Second Edition, revised and corrected, with Additions by the Author.

> "High Towers, fair Temples, goodly Theatres,
> "Strong Walls, rich Porches, princely Palaces,
> "Large Streets, brave Houses, sacred Sepulchres,
> "Sure Gates, sweet Gardens, stately Galleries,
> "Wrought with fair Pillars, and fine Imageries,
> "All these (O Pity) now are turn'd to Dust,
> "And overgrown with black Oblivion's Rust."
> SPENDER'S Ruins of Time.

Printed for T. Payne, next the Mews-Gate, in Castle-Street, St. Martin's.

This Day was publish'd, in 8vo. Price 4s. bound.

THE LAWS of CHANCE: or A Mathematical Investigation of the Probabilities arising from any proposed Circumstance of Play, applied to the Solution of a great Variety of Problems relating to Cards, Bowls, Dice, Lotteries, &c.

By SAM CLARKE, Teacher of Mathematicks.

Printed for Thomas Payne, next the Mews-Gate, in Castle-Street, St. Martin's.

Where may be had

1. The Art of Painting, with the Lives and Characters of above three hundred of the most eminent Painters, containing a complete Treatise of Painting, Designing, and the Use of Prints, with Reflections on the Works of the most celebrated Masters, and of the several Schools of Europe, as well antient as modern. Translated from the French of Monsieur de Piles. To which is added, An Essay towards an English School, and the Life of Sir Godfrey Kneller, by Benjamin Buckeridge, Esq., 8vo. Price bound 5s.

2. The Lives of the most eminent modern Painters who have lived since, or were omitted by Monsieur de Piles. By J. B. 8vo. Price sewed 2s.

3. Euclid's Elements of Geometry, the first Six, the Eleventh and Twelfth Books, translated into English from Dr. Gregory's Edition; with Notes and Additions for the Use of the British Youth. By E. Stone. Note, The Figures are upon the same Page as the Propositions, 8vo. Price bound 6s.

This Day was published,

A SERMON, preached before the HOUSE of LORDS in the Abbey Church of Westminster, on Friday, Feb. 16, 1759; being the Day appointed by his Majesty's Royal Proclamation for a General Fast.

By ROBERT Lord Bishop of St. ASAPH

Printed for C. Bathurst, opposite St. Dunstan's Church, Fleet-Street.

Where may be had,

Dr. Ross's before the House of Commons, Jan. 30, 1759.

Delivered gratis, at R. FRANCKLIN's, in
Russel-Street, Covent-Garden,

A Short State of the Case, with Relation to a Claim made by RICHARD FRANCKLIN, Bookseller on DAVID MALLET, Esq. on Account of some Copies which are inserted in the Works of the late Lord Bolingbroke, published by Mr. Mallet, and which were originally printed by R. Francklin. Of whom may be had, in Three Volumes, 8vo. Price 15s. or separately 5s. each.

1. A Dissertations upon Parties. 2. Remarks on the History of England. 3. A Collection of Political Tracts.

These are the Works on which the Claim was founded.

This Day was publish'd

In TWO VOLUMES, OCTAVO,

Illustrated with Eight Copper-Plates, Price bound 12s.

A TREATISE on the EYE: the Manner of Phaenomena of Vision

By WILLIAM PORTESFIELD, M.D.

Fellow of the Royal Colledge of Physicians, Edinburgh.

Printed for A. Millar, in the Strand; and G. Hamilton and J. Balfour, at Edinburgh.

This Day were publish'd Price sew'd 2s.

AN Enquiry in the Causes of the Alienation of the DELAWARE and SHAWNESE INDIANS from the British Interest; and into the Measures taken for recovering their Friendship. Extracted from the public Treaties, and other authentic Papers relating to the Transactions of the Government of Pensylvania, and the said Indians, for near forty Years; and explain'd by a Map of the Country. Together with the remarkable Journal of Christian Frederic Post, by whose Negotiations among the Indians on the Ohio, they were withdrawn from the Interest of the French, who thereupon abandoned the Fort and Country. With Notes by the Editor, explaining sundry Indian Customs, &c.

Written in PENSYLVANIA.

Printed for J. Wilkie, at the Bible in St. Paul's Church-Yard.

This Day was publish'd, Price 4s.

(Neatly bound in Calf,)

A TREATISE of FEVERS; wherein are set forth the Causes, Symptoms, Diagnosticks, and Prognosticks, of an 1. Acute Continual. 2. Intermitting. 3. Slow Nervous. 4. Military. 5. Malignant. 6. Scarlet. 7. Erysipelatose. 8. Hectic Fever; or Consumption. 9. Small-Pox. 10. Measles. 11. Pleurisy. 12. Peripneumony, Pleuroperipneumony; and 13. The Spurious Peripneumony. Together with the Method of Cure according to modern Practice.

By JOHN BALL. M.D.

Printed for the Author, and sold by J. Scott, at the Black Swan, in Pater-noster-Row. Where may be had, by the same Author, Price 1s. 6d. sew'd and 2s. bound, PHARMACOPEIA DOMESTICA NOVA.

This Day was published, Price 1s. 6d.

To which is prefixed an exact Representation of the dreadful Execution of the Conspirators, drawn on the Spot.

A Full, Clear, and Authorised Account of the late CONSPIRACY and Horrid Attempt upon the Life of the KING of PORTUGAL; brought about principally through the Machinations of the Jesuits; the Motives that led thereto, Discovery of the Plot, and the dreadful Execution of the Conspirators. In a Letter from a Minister of State in Portugal to the Envoy of a foreign Court to that of Great-Britain. Translated from the original Portuguese: with Notes by the Translator. Also a concise, yet entertaining History of Portugal, and particularly of the raising the present Royal Family to the Throne.

Printed for Robert Stevens, at Pope's Head in Pater-noster-Row.

Note, Be careful to have that printed for R. Stevens, being the only full and authentic Account of that horrid Conspiracy, and worth every Person's Perusal who is desirous of seeing a true Relation of the Affair.

This Day was publish'd,

Beautifully printed in TWO large VOLUMES Folio, Illustrated with 180 Copper-Plates, finely engraved, exhibiting the Buildings, Antiquities and Curiosities of the Countries described, and accurate Maps,

(Price Only Three Guineas, neatly bound)

A DESCRIPTION of the EAST, particularly EGYPT, JUDEA, SYRIA, MESO-POTAMIA, ASIA MINOR, GREECE, CYPRUS, CANDIA, and the Islands of the ARCHIPELAGO; with their Antiquities, Works of Art, Natural History and Inscriptions.

By RICHARD POCOCKE, LL.D. F.R.S.

Now Lord Bishop of Ossory.

Printed for D. Browne, T. Osborne, A. Millar, J. Whiston, and B. White, P. Davey, and B. Law, and R. and J. Dodsley.

N.B. Those Gentlemen who have only the First Volume, may now have the Second in Sheets for 1.l. 11s. 6d.

Where also may be had, in Folio, Price 18s. sewed,

1. Bishop Pococke's Inscriptiones antiquae collectae.

2. ——his large Map of Egypt, and the Course of the Nile, on eight Sheets, in Boards and Coloured.

By the KING's AUTHORITY.

This Day was publish'd,

(Price Three Pounds Fourteen Shillings bound and letter'd)

Dedicated to the Right Hon. the Earl of MACCLESFIELD,

The Second Edition, in Two Volumes, Folio,

Illustrated with One Hundred and Six Folio-Copper-Plates, engraven by the best Hands, Eleven of which, relating to Natural History, are finely colour'd.

A NEW and UNIVERSAL DICTIONARY of ARTS and SCIENCES. Containing not only an Explanation of the various Terms made Use of in the several Arts and Sciences; but also, whatever else is requisite to render those Branches of Literature themselves easy and familiar to the meanest Capacities. With an Introductory Preface, tracing the Progress of Literature from the earliest Ages, and enumerating the various Improvements made therein at different Periods of Time. Extracted from the best Authors, Translations, Memoirs, &c. in several Languages.

Printed only for J. Hinton, at the King's Arms in Newgate-Street, London; and sold by all the Booksellers of Great-Britain and Ireland.

The Dictionary, in One Volume, Folio, may be had alone neatly bound and letter'd, Price 2l. 10s. The Supplement, neatly bound and letter'd, Price 1.l. 4s.

N.B. Those Persons who chuse to take in the same in single Numbers, may begin with No. I and continue the same Weekly, the Whole to make Ninety Numbers, Three Sheets in a Number, at 6d. each; containing Sixty-two Copper-Plates, neatly engraved, and given gratis.

Be careful to ask for the Dictionary published by Authority.

Advertisements extracted from three columns on page 3
of *The Norwich Mercury*, printed by Chase and Co. in the
Cockey-Lane, for Saturday, February 23rd, 1788.

HOLT Third Subscription BALL, will be
on TUESDAY the 26th Inst.
Mr. WM. BRERETON ⎱ Stewards
Mr. JOHN MANN ⎰
Tickets to be had at the Feathers Inn, at 3s. 6d. each

AT the THEATRE ROYAL, by his Majesty's Servants, on Saturday, Feb. 23,
1788, will be presented a Comedy, call'd,
The BELLE's STRATAGEM.
DORICOURT, by Mr. BARRETT
And LETITIA HARDY, by Miss TITTER, being her
third Appearance on this Stage.
End of Act III, a Song by Mr. EDWARDS.
In Act IV, a Masquerade, in which a Minuet will be danced by Mr. STRETTON
and Miss TITTER, and a Cotillon by the Characters.
End of the Play a Dance, by Mr. and Mrs. STRETTON.
To which will be added a Farce, call'd
THE FIRST FLOOR.

THEATRE ROYAL, NORWICH
MISS TITTER respectfully begs leave to inform her Friends and the Public, that
her Night is fixed for THURSDAY, the 6th of March, when a favorite COMEDY
will be presented, in which she will perform a principal Character.
Tickets to be had of Miss TITTER, at Mr. Staff's, White Friar's Bridge; Chase
and Co. Crouse and Stevenson; and of Mr Rivett, at the Theatre.

MR. SHARP's CONCERT of VOCAL
and INSTRUMENTAL MUSIC, will be on WEDNESDAY
March the 5th, 1788, at Chapel-Field-House.
ACT I.
New Grand Overture, PLEYEL.
Song, Miss BUTCHER.
New Concertanti, two Violins Obligat. Messrs SHARP and RICHARDS
Song, Miss LEAK, "Angel ever bright and fair."
Solo Concerto, German Flute.

ACT II.
Solo Concerto Violin, Mr. RICHARDS.
Song, Miss BUTCHER.
Quartett, PLEYEL.
Song, Miss LEAK, Son. Regina.
Solo Concerto Oboe, Mr. SHARP.
To begin at Half past Six o'Clock.
Tickets, 2s. 6d. each, to be had of Mr. SHARP, St. Faith's Lane.

WHEREAS JAMES BULMAN, who
travelled for Messrs. Workman, Brumell, and Co. Linen Drapers, Milk-street,
London, hath not been heard of since he left BRANDON on Monday the 14th of
January last; and it is supposed he is detained in some part of the Counties of Suffolk,
or Norfolk by Sickness or some unforeseen Accident: The Information of any Person
to the Parties above-mentioned, where the said Bulman can be found, will be
esteemed a particular Favour.

February 21, 1788.
THOMAS GOSNOLD, of the City of
Norwich, Tailor, having made an Assignment of his Effects for the equal Benefit
of his Creditors; Notice is hereby given to all Persons who stand indebted unto the
said Thomas Gosnold, to pay their respective Debts unto Messrs. Schuldham and
Parker, of this City, Drapers, within one Month from the Date hereof, or they will
be sued to recover the same without further Notice.

BREWERY.
WANTS Employ, a MAN, who by many Years Experience is thoroughly acquainted
with every Stage of the Brewery and Malting, having instructed many capital
Houses in the Brewery Line, both in Town and Country.—Any one whom this may
suit, he flatters himself he can render peculiar Service, in making fine Ale.
N.B. Letters (Post-paid) addressed to A. B. at the White Hart Inn, Wisbech,
Cambridgeshire, will be duly attended to.

A ROBBERY.
WHEREAS some Villain or Villains, on Thursday Night last, or early on Friday
Morning, entered the Tenter Ground between St. Martin's at Oak Gates and the
Gildencroft, belonging to Messrs. GEORGE MANN, and Co. and cut off from one
of the Tenters about Thirteen Yards of fine 6–4th DRAB CLOTH: Whoever will
give Information of the Person or Persons who committed the said Robbery, shall
receive, upon Conviction of any of the Offenders, TEN GUINEAS reward.
GEORGE MANN, and Co.

To be LET, and entered upon immediately.
ALL that MESSUAGE, together with large Workrooms (capable of being altered
for any other Purpose) situate in the Parish of St. Gregory, in Norwich, late in the
Occupation of Samuel Owers, deceased. For Particulars inquire of Sarah Owers

and Benjamin Hugman, Executrix and Executor of the said Sam. Owers, or of
Mr. Copping, Grocer.

The said Sarah Owers and Benjamin Hugman take this Opportunity of informing
their Friends and Customers, that the Combing Business is conducted by them at
their Warehouse in Heigham.

An APPRENTICE wanted immediately,

AN active LAD, of reputable Connections, as an Apprentice in a Retail Shop,
in the several Branches of a Coppersmith, Brazier, Tinplate-worker, and Cutler.—
As there is an extensive Manufactory carried on in the three first Branches, he will
be fully instructed in the Nature of it.—A Premium will be expected.

Inquire of Ralph Ward, Yarmouth, by Letter, post paid.

ADVOWSONS.

WANTED to purchase, the perpetual Advowsons of two Livings, of about the
annual Value of 200l. each, situate either in the Counties of Norfolk or Suffolk,
the Incumbents not less than 70 years of Age.

An immediate Resignation would be preferred.

Applications to be made to Thomas Holloway, of Bream's Buildings, Chancery-
lane, London; or to Mr. Holman, Attorney at Law, Downham-Market, Norfolk.

To the LADIES.
HENRY WALLER,
STAYMAKER, WYMONDHAM,

RETURNS his most grateful Acknowledgements for the great Encouragement he
has already met with, from his Friends and Customers; and further begs Leave to
assure the Ladies, that his utmost Endeavours shall be used to merit their further
Approbation.

N.B. Also a JOURNEYMAN is wanted; one that is a good Hand, may have
constant Employ and good Wages.

To the LADIES.
T H A I N,
STAY-MAKER, NORTHWALSHAM,

BEGS Leave to return his most sincere Thanks to the Ladies of Northwalsham and
its Environs, for the very great Encouragement he has received; and to inform them,
that he is just returned from Town with the newest Fashions of French and Italian
Stays, Corsetts and Riding Stays. Those Ladies who intend honouring him with
their Commands, may depend on having the best of Materials, and their Orders
executed in an Height of Taste not inferior to the first Shops in London, by their
most obedient humble Servant,   R. THAIN.

At SWAFFHAM ACADEMY,

Young GENTLEMEN are conducted through a regular Course of Literature, and
prepared for the University, Sea, Accompting House and Trade, by
J. KING,
And proper Assistants, on the following Terms:

BOARDING and LODGING (including the English Language grammatically, Writing, Arithmetic, Merchant's Accompts, and Mensuration) at Twelve Guineas per Annum, &c. One Guinea Entrance; Algebra, Geometry, Trigonometry, Navigation, and other Branches of Mathematical Learning, Half a Guinea per Quarter; the Latin, Greek, &c. Languages at One Guinea per Quarter; The Rev. Mr. WALKER, Rector of Shingham, and resident Assistant, who has been many Years engaged as a private Tutor, teaches the Classes.

Dancing, &c. by Proper Masters.

J. K. Begs his Friends will accept his most grateful thanks for their many obliging Favours, and hopes his future Exertions to discharge his Duty in his Profession, will merit the Patronage of the Public.

Architecture.
HENRY DOBSON,
ARCHITECT and BUILDER,
No. 7, ST. GILES'S HILL, NORWICH,
IMPRESSED with Gratitude for the Liberal

Patronage of his Friends, begs Leave to return them his most grateful Acknowledgments, and wishes to inform them, and the Public, that he undertakes to execute Buildings of every Description, on the most reasonable Terms. Determined to exert every Endeavour to merit their Approbation, he submits the following to their Attention.

BUILDINGS surveyed or measured.
DRAWINGS for the Direction of Workmen, executed with
Neatness, Precision, and Dispatch.

Also ORNAMENTAL DRAWINGS for finishing ROOMS in the most elegant and approved modern Taste.

Perspective Drawings of any Kind of Mechanical Engines, furnished on moderate Terms, and the strictest Attention paid to their Minutiae.

H.D. respectfully informs such Gentlemen as the following Article may concern, that he executes BECKS and CASKS for Stores of any Dimensions, on the same Terms as in London.

To Gentlemen GRAZIERS
TO be shewn for Sale, on Monday the 3rd of March next, at the Magpye, in Harlaston, a capital Drove of Galloway SCOTS and HEIFERS, by their humble Servants,
WILLIAM SMITH.

Hundreds of TUNSTEAD and HAPPING
THE Directors and acting Guardians of the Poor within the said Hundreds, are desired to meet at the Poor's House in Smallburgh, on Tuesday the fourth Day of March next, at Ten o'Clock in the Forenoon, in order to take into Consideration the placing or apprenticing out such Children maintained in the said House, as are fit for that Purpose.   By Order of this Day's Meeting,
Poor's House,   HENRY BARNARD, clerk,
Feb. 19, 1788.

NORTH ERPINGHAM.—TUNSTEAD and HAPPING

February 20, 1788.

NOTICE is hereby given, that the yearly Meeting of the Members of the Association for prosecuting and convicting HORSE STEALERS, within or near the said Hundreds, will be held at the Angel in Northwalsham, on Monday the 3rd of March next.

DINNER at Two o'Clock.

THE Creditors of the Rev. WILLIAM ARMINE STORY, of Shipdham, are requested to send in an exact Account of their Demands immediately to Mr. Charles Bringloe, Attorney, Hingham, Norfolk.

THE Creditors of Mr. ISAAC JACKSON, Beer Brewer, a Bankrupt, are particularly requested to meet the Assignees on Thursday next, the 28th of February, Instant, at the White Swan Inn, in Norwich, precisely at Four o'Clock, to see a State of his Affairs, to consider of the same, and to advise with the Assignees on what is proper to be now done to bring the Business to a Conclusion.

THIS is to give Notice, that all Persons that stand indebted to the late WILLIAM FITT, Plumber and Glazier, in St. Saviour's, in the City of Norwich, are forthwith desired to pay their respective Debts to Mr. James Meek, Plumber and Glazier, in Magdalen street; and all Persons to whom the late William Fitt stood indebted to at the Time of his decease, are desired to send their Accounts to the said Mr. James Meek, that they may be discharged immediately.

ALL Persons any way related to Mr. HENRY TILLEY, who heretofore was a Sadler in Bond-Street, in the City and Liberty of Westminster, and County of Middlesex, but late of the Assembly-Row, in Mile End Old Town, and now deceased, are hereby requested forthwith to call on Mr. Trumball, Attorney at Law, in Grange Court in the Parish of St. Clement Danes, in the said County of Middlesex, to explain to him their respective Degrees of Kindred, or by letter addressed to him to state the same.

ROYAL EXCHANGE ASSURANCE

(Established by Royal Charter in the Reign of King George the First) for Assuring Houses, Buildings, Goods, Corn, Hay, Live Stock, &c. and also for the Assurance of Lives.

THE CORPORATION of the ROYAL EXCHANGE ASSURANCE have conducted and appointed Mr. HOLMAN, of Downham Market, in the County of Norfolk, Attorney at Law, their Agent and Receiver for Downham Market aforesaid and Parts adjacent, in their Business of Assuring from Loss or Damage by Fire; and also for the Assurance of Lives.

Persons Assured by this Corporation, do not depend upon any uncertain Fund or Contribution, nor are they subject to any Covenant or Calls to make good Losses which may happen to themselves or other; the capital Stock of this Corporation being an unquestionable Security to the Assured, in case of Loss, or Damage by Fire; and in case of Dispute, the Assureds have a more ready and effectual Method of Recovery, than be had against any Societies who do not act under a common Seal.

This Corporation will in cases of Fire allow all reasonable Charges attending the Removal of Goods, and pay the Sufferer's Loss, whether the Goods are destroyed, lost, or damaged by such Removal.—And as an Encouragement to Persons Assuring, all Cities and great Towns may receive Assistance for purchasing Engines, and proper Implements to prevent the Progress of Fire, in Proportion to the Number of Assurances made in such Places.

N.B. All Payments for Losses or Damages by Fire, are made by this Corporation without Deduction.

Policies allowed free of Expence upon Removal from other Offices.

The Corporation have likewise appointed Mr. ROBERT JOHNSON, of Upwell, in the Isle of Ely, and County of Cambridge, their Agent for that Place and Places adjacent; and Mr. Holman's Connections in his Profession frequently calling him to Upwell and that Neighbourhood they have mutually agreed to consolidate the Profits of their respective Agencies; therefore the Favors of the Public to either of them will be a mutual Obligation to both.

Printed Proposals may be had by applying to Johnson and Holman, or either of them.

To be LET, at Lady Day next,

PART of a HOUSE and SHOP, at the Back of the Inns, next Door to Mrs. Key, Hatter.—Inquire of Thomas Gibbon, Lower Close.

To be SOLD

A Large Collection of PRINTS (by Wooller, Strange, Vertue, Hollar, Smith, Lambowm, and other eminent Engravers), late the Property of a Gentleman, deceased, by EDMUND GILLINGWATER, Bookseller, Harleston, Norfolk.

The Engravings are excellent Impressions, and in fine Preservation. The Prices marked in the Catalogue.

Catalogues may be had of Shave, Ipswich; Kendall, Bury; Chase and Co. Norwich; March and Downes, Yarmouth; Millar, Bungay; and at the Place of Sale.

To be SOLD,

ALL that Copyhold MESSUAGE, TENEMENT or DWELLING-HOUSE, with the Yard, Garden, and Blacksmith's Shop thereunto belonging, situate in the Mill-street, in Loddon, in Norfolk, now in the Occupation of Mr. John Edging, at the yearly Rent of 7l. but underlet.

N.B. The above Premises are well situated for a Whitesmith and Blacksmith.

Also all those three Copyhold TENEMENTS or DWELLING-HOUSES, adjoining to the above Premisses, with the Yards and Gardens thereunto belonging, now in the several Occupations of — — Newson, Jeremiah Roberts, and Thomas Foulger, at the yearly Rent of 8l. 1s.

Also all that Freehold TENEMENT or DWELLING-HOUSE, with the Yard and Appurtenances, thereunto belonging, situate in the Mill-street, in Loddon aforesaid, now in the Occupation of Henry Butcher, at the yearly Rent of 2l. 5s.

For further Particulars apply to Mr Robert Holmes, or Mr. Wm. Cole, Attorney, both of Loddon aforesaid.

All Persons who stand indebted to the said Robert Holmes, are requested immediately to pay their respective Debts to the said William Cole; and all Persons to whom he stands indebted, are desired to deliver Accounts of their Demands within one Month to the said W. Cole.

To be SOLD by AUCTION,

At the Custom-House in Yarmouth. on Tuesday the 26th of Feb. 1788, at Two o'Clock in the Afternoon, for private Use only,

ABOUT two Thousand Gallons of Foreign

GENEVA, BRANDY and RUM, which will be

put up in various small Lots to accommodate the Purchasers, who will have an Opportunity of purchasing for their Use any Quantity not exceeding Sixty-three Gallons.

This Day is published, Price Sixpence,

THE RAM'S HORN sounded seven Times.

PART II.

Giving a true Account of what passed at a Meeting of Conference upon WATER BAPTISM, between J. PROUD and the AUTHOR, the 25th of 10th Mo. 1787.—Also an Answer to JOHN HUNT'S Pamphlet, written from a Dream. Also a Message, from the Word of the Lord, to the Teachers among the People called Baptists; likewise a short Reply to JOHN THEOBALD, with some Remarks on J. PROUD'S Pamphlet.

by JOHN BOUSELL,

Of the City of Norwich, a Disciple of Jesus Christ, and an

Offspring of the Primitive Quakers.

Shortly will be published,

A Pamphlet, under the Title of The TRUMPET sounded out of SION upon the Mountains of those Merchants of Babylon, who have taken upon themselves the Office of Teachers to the established Church, to those under the Name of Presbyterians, Independents and Methodists, with Remarks on the present and primitive State of the People called Quakers.

This Day is published, Price 1s.

WHILST we Live let us Live. A Short View of the Competition between the MANUFACTURER and LAND-WORKER. Occasioned by a late Publication, entitled, "Live and let Live."

Norwich: Printed by J. Crouse and W. Stevenson; and sold by Messrs Scatchard and Co. Ave Maria Lane, London; R. Beatnisse and W. Stevenson, Norwich; Messrs Downes and March, Yarmouth: Mr. Marshall, Lynn; Shave, Punchard and Jermyn, Ipswich; Rackham, Bury; Keymer, Colchester; and Dybal, Bungay.

TWO NEW MONTHLY MAGAZINES
On the First of February were published,
Price Six-pence each;

I. THE FAMILY MAGAZINE, or a Repository of Religious Instruction and Rational Amusement. Designed to counteract the pernicious Tendency of immoral Books, &c. which have circulated of late Years among the Inferior Classes of People, to the Obstruction of their Improvement in Religion and Morality.
For January, 1788.
By Mrs. TRIMMER.
Ornamented with a Plate.

II. THE JUVENILE MAGAZINE; or, an Instructive and Entertaining Miscellany for YOUTH of both Sexes:
For January, 1788.
By the Author of The Six Princesses of Babylon
Ornamented with Two neat Plates.

The Contents as follow,—The Editor's Address to her Young Readers.—An Easy Introduction to Geography.—The School Boy.—L'Enfant Docile.—A Fireside Dialogue: the Silly Boy.—Familiar Letters on various subjects.—The Young Miser.—The Little Boy who behaved like a Man.—Instructive Puzzles.—Notes to the Instructive Puzzles: The Little Foreigner; a Drama in One Act.—Poetry.—Monthly Occurrences.

Printed and published by and for J. Marshall and Co. Aldermary Church Yard, Bow-Lane, Cheapside, London; and sold by Chase and Co. Norwich.
Where may be had

Great variety of NEW PUBLICATIONS for the Improvement and Entertainment of YOUNG MINDS.

To be had also of the Booksellers and News Carriers throughout the Kingdom.

THE PLATES

The subjects on the forty-eight plates have been chosen, and their captions written, to illustrate as a consistent story the theme of this book. The chapters have suggested the obligation, recognised by all Georgian designers and artists, to study the classical orders of architecture, and all that they implied; and have shown the influence exerted by the leaders of taste whose knowledge of architecture and its rules was as thorough as those who practised the art. The character of architectural design from the late seventeenth to the early nineteenth century determined, directly or indirectly, the proportions and ornamentation of nearly everything that was made; and the antiquarian studies of men of fashion who led taste and criticised every aspect of it, occasionally changed the character of design, and set designers off in fresh directions. It is possible to follow this story of the Georgian preoccupation with taste in the visual arts, by studying the forty-eight plates that follow.

PLATE I

GEORGIAN WORSHIP OF THE ORDERS OF ARCHITECTURE

Left: Frontispiece from *An Essay in Defence of Ancient Architecture*, by Robert Morris of Twickenham, published in London in 1728. A clumsy allegorical composition inspired by an exaggerated reverence for the classical orders.
Right: The frontispiece from *A Complete Body of Architecture*, by Isaac Ware, the edition published in 1767. The figure in the helmet, presumably the spirit of architecture, is holding up the Orders before the young practitioner, who is apparently overcome by the sight of them. Classical ruins are a feature of the background, suggesting the importance of studying the antique sources. (See Appendix I, page 367.)

PLATE 2

THE INFLUENCE OF RUINS

Piranesi depicted the awful pathos of ruins; he made the decay and neglect of ancient Rome seem agonising. Above, he shows the temple of Antonius Pius, with the column of Marcus Aurelius on the extreme right. Stuart and Revett, in their drawings of Greek ruins, dramatised their occupation and desecration by the infidel Turks. Below is a general view of Athens, from the first volume of *The Antiquities of Athens*, which was published in 1762. The columns in the foreground are part of a Roman ruin: in the distance on the right is the Acropolis.

PLATE 3

THE INFLUENCE OF RUINS

Above: The eastern portico of the Parthenon at Athens, reproduced from Volume II of *The Antiquities of Athens*, by Stuart and Revett, published in 1778. Greek ruins, neglected and despoiled, became associated with anything Turkish, and this habit of thought spread, and affected many branches of design, even the labels used by apothecaries, like these two early nineteenth century examples for Turkey Rhubarb. (See pages 165 and 167 for other examples of labels.)

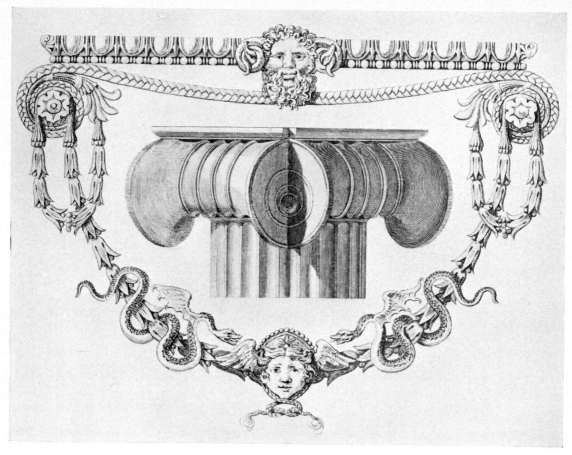

PLATE 4

THE INFLUENCE OF RUINS

Above: An Ionic capital and examples of ornament, used as a tailpiece on page 11 in Volume I of *The Antiquities of Athens*, by Stuart and Revett (1762).

Below: The ruins of Glastonbury Abbey, from an engraving by Samuel and Nathaniel Buck, published in 1733. The influence of Bucks' views of mediaeval ruins had a powerful and stimulating effect upon the Gothic taste, long before Horace Walpole's villa at Strawberry Hill became famous. (See pages 122 and 123.)

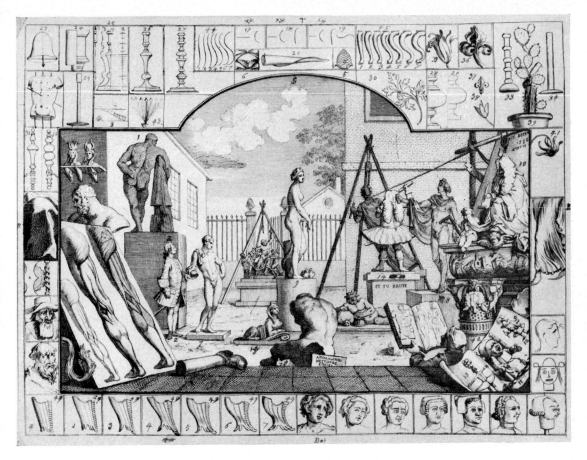

PLATE 5

The first plate of the *Analysis of Beauty*, by William Hogarth. (Reproduced by courtesy of the Trustees of the British Museum.) This was one of the preliminary engravings, and the key numbers are lightly indicated on the proof. In attempting to isolate the "one precise line, properly to be called the line of *beauty*," he illustrated various examples, and chose one from each that expressed this line. For example, at the top of the plate, at 44, there are seven waving lines, of which he selects the fourth from the left as the ideal line of beauty. He uses another illustration at the bottom of the plate to convey "A still more perfect idea of the effects of the precise waving-line, and of those lines that deviate from it, may be conceived by the row of stays, figure 4, where number 4 is composed of precise waving-lines, and is therefore the best shaped stay. Every whale-bone of a good stay must be made to bend in this manner: for the whole stay, when put close together behind, is truly a shell of well-varied contents, and its surface of course a fine form; so that if a line, or the lace were to be drawn, or brought from the top of the lacing of the stay behind, round the body, and down to the bottom peak of the stomacher; it would form such a perfect, precise, serpentine-line, as has been shewn, round the cone. . . ." The cone referred to is shown at the top of the plate, and numbered 20. Hogarth's fanciful capital, composed of three-cornered hats and wigs, appears in the right-hand lower part of the plate, and is numbered 42. (See pages 87 and 90.)

PLATE 6

LEADERS OF TASTE IN THE
GEORGIAN AGE

Above: Alexander Pope (1688–1744) who consistently defended good design and attacked extravagance. (From the painting by C. Jervas. Reproduced by permission of the Trustees of the National Portrait Gallery.) *Above (to the right):* Horace Walpole, the 4th Earl of Orford (1717–97). From an engraving based on a drawing by Sir Thomas Lawrence. *Right (below):* Richard Boyle, 3rd Earl of Burlington (1695–1754), who revived and stimulated interest in the work of Palladio. (Reproduced by courtesy of the Royal Institute of British Architects.)

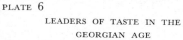

William Kent (?1685–1748)

Sir William Chambers (1723–96)

Robert Adam (1728–92)

Sir John Soane (1753–1837)

PLATE 7

ARCHITECTS WHO PROFOUNDLY INFLUENCED GEORGIAN TASTE
(These portraits are reproduced by permission of the Trustees of the National Portrait Gallery.)

PLATE 10

"WHERE TASTE MUST STOP"

Two interior views of the Pantheon as it was rebuilt by James Wyatt in 1770. Horace Walpole considered that this building by "uniting grandeur and lightness, simplicity and ornament, seems to have marked the medium, where Taste must stop." (See page 102.) *Above:* a Masquerade scene, engraved by Charles White, 1775. (Reproduced by courtesy of the Trustees of the British Museum.) *Below:* an original water-colour drawing in the possession of W. & A. Gilbey Ltd., by whose courtesy the illustration is reproduced.

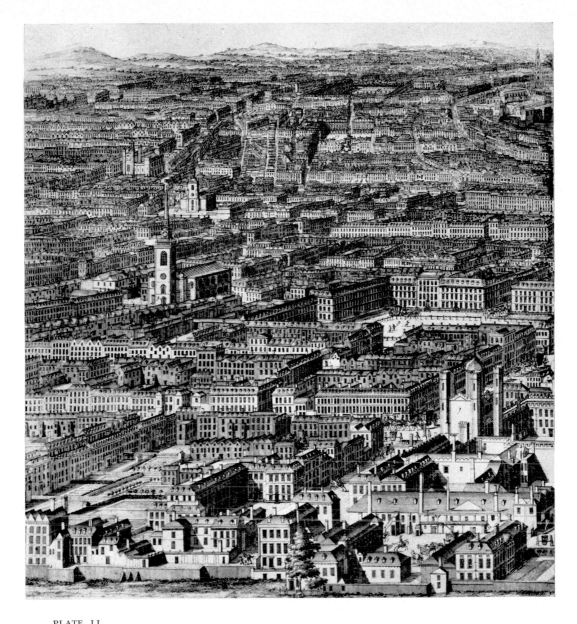

PLATE 11

The western portion of Kip's bird's-eye view of London in 1710. St. James's Palace is in the foreground on the right, and at that date sash windows had been fitted to replace the mullioned windows of the Palace. St. James's, Piccadilly, is to the left and in the centre of the view, with St. Anne's, Soho, beyond. The regular, orderly appearance of early eighteenth century London was created largely by the proportions and placing of the windows in the façades of houses. Even when the horizontal lines of buildings were broken, like the east side of St. James's Square which is shown in the view, the good proportions of the windows still preserved the gracious characteristics of a street or a square.

PLATE 12

Left: Richmond in Surrey, about 1726. This view shows part of the Green and the Parish Church, and the irregular streets of the little riverside town with their orderly buildings. From a print published by Henry Overton and J. Hook. (Reproduced by courtesy of the Richmond Public Library Committee.)

PLATE 13
Right: This continues the view of Richmond, completing the Green and
showing Maids of Honour Row on the right (see illustration on page 29),
with part of the old Palace on the extreme right. This view was depicted
fifty-one years before Richmond Bridge was opened. (See pages 68 and 69.)

PLATE 14
Left: A view of Richmond Hill from the Earl of Cholmondely's, in 1749.
Right: The villa built at Richmond for Sir Charles Asgill by Sir Robert Taylor, during the seventeen-sixties. (See page 70.)

The Thames near Mr. Smith's house at Battersea, looking upstream, by J. Boydell, 1752. The building on the extreme right in the distance is probably York House, where Stephen Theodore Jannsen, one time Lord Mayor of London, founded the Battersea Enamel Works, about 1750. (From a print in the author's possession.) See page 73.

PLATE 15

Residential development in the eighteenth and early nineteenth centuries was consistently well designed, although planned in a piecemeal fashion. *Above:* The river front of the Adelphi, the great residential scheme by the brothers Adam built on the site of Durham House, between 1768 and 1772. (From a contemporary print in the author's possession.)

Left: Houses in Bedford Square built during the seventeen-eighties. Some are attributed to Thomas Leverton. (Reproduced by courtesy of F. R. Yerbury and the Architectural Association.) *Right:* No. 19 Portland Place (originally No. 65) built by Joseph Rose, a plasterer employed by the brothers Adam. This house was part of the development scheme planned by Robert Adam. (Reproduced by courtesy of the Glass Manufacturers Federation.)

PLATE 16

The Circus, Bath, 1784. From an engraving by Thomas Malton.

The circus, originally called the King's Circus, was designed by John Wood the elder
and built between 1753 and 1768. This view of it, as it is today, is reproduced by
courtesy of the National Buildings Record. (See pages 80 and 319.)

PLATE 17

Queen Square, Bath, is shown above, and below, South Parade.
(From engravings by Thomas Malton, Junr., 1775.)

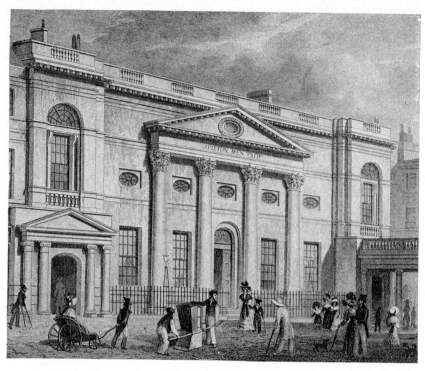

PLATE 18

Two totally different approaches to the use of the classical orders. *Above:*
The King's Bath and the Pump Room at Bath. (From an early nineteenth
century drawing by Thomas H. Shepherd.) *Below:* Pitzhanger Place at
Ealing, designed by Sir John Soane. (From an original drawing made by
Soane's office. Reproduced by courtesy of the Sir John Soane Museum.)

PLATE 19

Two extremes of taste. *Above:* Castle Howard, built at the beginning of the eighteenth century for the third Earl of Carlisle from the designs of Sir John Vanbrugh. (Reproduced by courtesy of F. R. Yerbury.) *Below:* The south-west view of Fonthill Abbey, Wiltshire, designed by James Wyatt for William Beckford, and built between 1796 and 1807. It was fashionable, "gentleman's" Gothic, much larger in scale than the little, jewel-like architectural experiment that Horace Walpole made at Strawberry Hill. (Reproduced from the frontispiece of John Rutter's *Description of Fonthill Abbey.* Third edition, 1822.)

PLATE 20

A sedan chair in gold and leather, presumed to have been made for the second Duke of Grafton in the reign of Queen Anne. The carriage clock at the back is in brass and black, *circa* 1800. (Reproduced by courtesy of the late Sir Albert Richardson, P.P.R.A.) The chair is described in detail on pages 322 and 323. See also plate opposite.

PLATE 21

Above: Back and front views of the sedan chair shown on plate 20. To the right, below, the original brass links used with the chair, and carried by the link boys to light the chairmen at night. *Below:* A London street scene with a sedan chair of the type that could be hired (see page 328 and plates 16 and 18).

A section from a print, in the author's possession, showing a view of St. Mary's in the Strand, published in 1749.

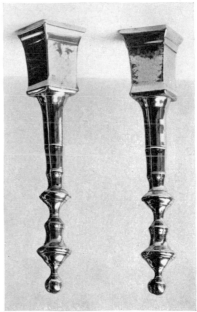

THE FEMALE ORATORS.

Engraved from an Original Picture Painted by Mr John Collet.

PLATE 22

Two scenes in Covent Garden in which sedan chairs appear.

Above, is an engraving by Rennoldson, from the painting by John Collett entitled *The Female Orators*. The engraving was published in 1768. (See page 325 for an enlarged detail of the sedan chair.)

To the right, is a view inside the piazza at Covent Garden, where a country visitor is being cajoled by one lady of the town, and having his pocket picked by another. A sedan chair is parked close by, in which another lady is no doubt awaiting an appropriate victim. (From the frontispiece of *Squire Randall's Excursion around London: or A Week's frolic in the year 1766*.)

PLATE 23
Above: A post-chaise, late eighteenth century.
Right: A private coach driving up Fenchurch Street
(mid eighteenth century).
Below: A country inn courtyard, by William Hogarth.

PLATE 26

THE COUNTESS'S DRESSING-ROOM

Marriage à la Mode, by William Hogarth. (Reproduced by courtesy of the Trustees of the National Gallery, London.)

Key: 1 and 2. Chairs with cabriole front and back legs of the type shown in plate 29. 3. A bed with a fabric-covered tester and elaborate cornice, in an alcove. 4. A toilet mirror, mounted on a dressing table, draped like the mirror that appears on plate 30. 5. A painted leather screen. 6. A double seat or settee with cabriole legs.

PLATE 27

SHORTLY AFTER MARRIAGE

Marriage à la Mode from the painting by
William Hogarth. (Reproduced by courtesy of
the Trustees of the National Gallery, London.)
This is the second of the series.

Key: 1. Chair with carved cabriole legs, about
1720. 2. Carved and gilded chandelier.
3. Card table with cabriole legs, of the same
type that appears in plate 28. 4. Coupled Ionic
columns with angular capitals. 5. Tripod tea-
table (see claw tables on page 191). 6. Chimney-
piece of the type associated with the work of
William Kent. 7. Chair with cabriole legs and
carved knees, about 1720. 8. A low stool with
cabriole legs and claw feet. 9. An ornate
girandole, incorporating a clock.

PLATE 28

The Lady's Last Stake, or *Picquet*, or *Virtue in Danger*, 1761, by William Hogarth. (Reproduced by courtesy of the Trustees of the British Museum.)

Key: 1. Venetian window (see page 41). 2. A card table with cabriole legs: 1720–30. 3. A chair of the same period with cabriole legs. 4. A fire-screen or pole-screen, a simplified version of a type that appears in the first edition of Chippendale's *Director*, 1754. 5. A decorative marble chimney-piece, rather earlier in period than the date of the picture—somewhere about 1730–40. 6. A basket grate. 7. An ornate clock, probably of French design. 8. A picture frame with sconces. Branching arms for candles spring from the lower corners of the frame.

PLATE 29

Francis Hayman, in his studio with a client (? Dr. Martin Folkes). (Reproduced by permission of the Trustees of the National Portrait Gallery.)

Key: 1. A side table with cabriole legs, supporting a marble slab, sometimes known as a marble table. Chippendale uses the word "frame" in his *Director* to describe these tables and calls them "frames for marble slabs." 2. A single chair with interlacing splats and cabriole legs. Only the back legs are visible, but presumably the front legs match them. 3. A low-backed elbow chair with cabriole legs front and back. (See pages 209 and 219.)

PLATE 30

Queen Charlotte at her dressing table, from a painting by Zoffany, in the Long
Gallery at Windsor Castle. (Reproduced by gracious permission of Her Majesty
the Queen.)

This was painted about 1765 in old Buckingham House, and shows Queen Charlotte
with her two eldest children, the Prince of Wales and the Duke of York, both in fancy
dress. The toilet table is draped, so too is the dressing-glass that is set upon it. Compare
this draped toilet table with the designs shown on page 251 and plate 26. The chairs
and the other articles of furniture that appear in the the painting suggest the work of
William Kent.

PLATE 31

Frederick, Prince of Wales, and his sisters, by J. F. Nollekens. From the painting at
Windsor Castle. (Reproduced by gracious permission of Her Majesty the Queen.)

The music desk is supported on a circular base from which a slender, tapering
shaft ascends to support the adjustable desk. Compare this with the design by Ince and
Mayhew shown on page 285.

PLATE 32

The country squire could have his moments of magnificence. Charles Reinhold, in the part of Hawthorne in Isaac Bickerstaff's comic opera, *Love in a Village*. (From a painting by Zoffany in the Garrick Club. Reproduced by courtesy of the Committee.) See pages 9 and 292.

PLATE 33

The Sleeping Housewife from a drawing by William Hogarth. (Reproduced by courtesy of the Trustees of the British Museum.) Compare this highly detailed interior with Hogarth's engraving of "The Farmer's Return" on page 144. In this drawing, which is done with pen with grey and brown washes over slight pencil, the background and the furniture are taken from different periods. The windows on the left, with the mullions and transomes and diamond-shaped panes, are sixteenth or seventeenth century; but the wall terminates in a cornice with a cyma recta or ogee moulding in the upper part, a conscientious piece of classical design. On the right of the chimney-breast the wall is panelled above a dado. On either side of the fire-place are comb-back windsor chairs with cabriole legs, one occupied and largely obscured by the housewife. A table with a drawer and square-sectioned legs of mid eighteenth century design, provides a resting-place for one of the cats, and the bottle; while above, between the windows, is an early eighteenth century glass with a moulded frame and a semicircular head. The clock is a weight-driven type, probably Dutch, and dating from the early part of the eighteenth century. Some doubt has been expressed about the authorship of this drawing, but the cats are indisputably Hogarthian.

PLATE 34

TWO ROYAL VEHICLES

Left: The state coach de-signed by Sir William Chambers for George III. Reproduced from *The London Magazine*, December 1762. Details on a larger scale are given on pages 320 and 321.

Above: A wine fountain in the form of a miniature barrel for use on a large dining table. This regal design, with its resemblance to a state coach, is said to have belonged to Queen Anne, and was an elaborate forerunner of the coaster. (See page 163.) It is in the possession of W. & A. Gilbey Ltd., by whose courtesy the illustration is reproduced.

PLATE 35

The dining-room at Belgrave Hall, Leicester. The hall was built between 1709 and 1713; those dates appear on the lead water heads, and the date 1710 is worked into the brickwork of the stable block; but the style of the Hall suggests that it may be of slightly earlier date. The panelling of the dining-room may be ascribed to the second decade of the eighteenth century, though it has since been repaired in places. The room has been furnished with examples of mid and late eighteenth century designs. The chairs are of the type made by Chippendale and his contemporaries, and the design of the backs may be compared with the examples reproduced from *The Gentleman and Cabinet Maker's Director* on pages 216 and 221. The sideboard has a serpentine front, and above the decanters on it is hung, rather appropriately, a portrait of a local rake, who is said to have shot himself because he was insufferably bored by the task of continually dressing and undressing. His name was Charles Boothby Skrymshire (1740–1800); the portrait is by Sir Joshua Reynolds, and was painted when the sitter was eighteen.

(Reproduced by the courtesy of the City of Leicester Museum and Art Gallery.)

PLATE 36

Square piano by Josephus Merlin, 1784: this was a type designed for travelling, and the legs folded up. To the left is a Chippendale fire-screen. The portrait above the harpsichord is of Janet Hunter, painted by David Martin: it is flanked by a pair of Bristol candlesticks (1775) standing on a pair of Adam brackets. (In the collection of the late Sir Albert Richardson, P.P.R.A., at Avenue House, Ampthill.)

PLATE 37
Above: A Chippendale gilt mirror, flanked by a pair of gilt sconces of carved wood with crystal drops (*circa* 1795). The grand piano is in dark satinwood by Josephus Merlin, London 1786. Two Battersea enamel candlesticks are used to light the keyboard and music (1770). The music stand is of the Regency period in black and gilt, and the music canterbury behind it is painted and ornamented with flower decoration (*circa* 1800). A "dummy board" of a dog is in the foreground. (In the collection of the late Sir Albert Richardson, P.P.R.A., at Avenue House, Ampthill.)

PLATE 38
A gilt chiffonier designed by Henry Holland for the Duke of Bedford, for his temporary residence at Oakley, 1794. (In the collection of the late Sir Albert Richardson, P.P.R.A., at Avenue House, Ampthill.)

PLATE 39

Ladies and gentlemen sat upright: their clothes, and the straight-backed elegance of the chairs they used, demanded that posture; but there is a hint of lounging in the attitude of the gentleman in the lower illustration.

Top left: Mrs. Baddeley in the character of Mrs. Strickland in *The Suspicious Husband.*

Top right: Mr. Wilson and Mrs. Mattocks in the characters of Ben and Miss Prue in *Love for Love.* (From contemporary prints published in 1766.)

Bottom right: From an engraving by Bartolozzi of a painting by W. Hamilton, published in 1793.

PLATE 40
Right: On the left is an early eighteenth century country-made chair in walnut with cabriole legs, turned stretchers and a rush seat, *circa* 1720. On the right a writing-chair in oak, of the same period. The vase form of the back splats in both chairs is similar.

To the left: A wheatsheaf back mid eighteenth century elbow chair.
To the right: A single chair with a pierced back. Both are country-made versions of types usually associated with the designs of Chippendale and his contemporaries. Both chairs have yoke tops.
Below: A late eighteenth century satinwood table, with oval top and drop leaves and a Regency chair with turned front legs.

PLATE 41

Above: Two late eighteenth century elbow chairs. The chair on the left is japanned black and decorated in gold, the other is painted and decorated with floral motifs. Although the details differ the character of these arm chairs is akin to some of Sheraton's designs in *The Cabinet Dictionary*. (See illustrations on page 141.)

Two of a set of six small chairs with backs in the form of reversed semicircles. They are in mahogany with ormulu mounts and have sabre legs back and front. In the King's Library of the Royal Pavilion at Brighton. (Reproduced by courtesy of the Brighton Art Gallery.)

PLATE 42

Left: A long case clock in mahogany, by John Godden of Wingham. This is probably the John Godden of Town Malling (Wingham is a few miles away), a clockmaker who worked in that part of Kent in the late eighteenth century. *Centre:* A detail of the hood and face of the clock by John Godden. Chinese motifs are engraved on the brass face. (See page 118.) *Right:* A long case clock in mahogany with the hood surmounted by a swan-neck pediment. Like the clock by Godden, this was probably made at some time during the last three decades of the eighteenth century.

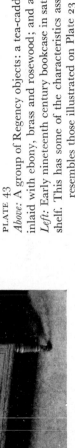

PLATE 43

Above: A group of Regency objects: a tea-caddy in rosewood; a sewing-case in birdseye maple, inlaid with ebony, brass and rosewood; and a silver christening mug, *circa* 1808.

Left: Early nineteenth century bookcase in satinwood with a gilded brass gallery on the upper shelf. This has some of the characteristics associated with Sheraton's published designs, and resembles those illustrated on Plate 23 of *The Cabinet Dictionary.* (See page 283.)

PLATE 44

Above: A large library table in dark mahogany cross-banded, with box lines, and five drawers, on end supports. *Circa* 1800. A gilt scroll-back chair, decorated with carved acanthus leaves; the front legs are turned and reeded, the back legs are swept. *Circa* 1810. On the table are a pair of candlesticks, each in the form of a winged sphinx, seated on a base of ormulu and opal glass. *Circa* 1810. (In the collection of the Royal Pavilion at Brighton, in the King's Bedroom. Reproduced by courtesy of the Brighton Art Gallery.)

Right: A circular library table in mahogany on a fluted stem, decorated in gold, resting on a triangular base, with carved and gilded paw feet. (In the King's Library at the Royal Pavilion, Brighton. Reproduced by courtesy of the Brighton Art Gallery.)

PLATE 45

Right: A sofa in black and gold, with a scroll end, covered in peach velvet. *Circa* 1805. This is in the South Drawing Room at the Royal Pavilion, Brighton, and is in the Royal Pavilion Collection. This is a refined version of the design for a Grecian squab, shown on plate 49 of Sheraton's *Cabinet Dictionary* (1803).

Below: A similar design, produced ten years later (*circa* 1815) in the King's Library, at the Royal Pavilion, Brighton.

(Reproduced by the courtesy of the Brighton Art Gallery.)

PLATE 46

Left: A long case clock in mahogany, stamped George Augustus, and probably made for one of the Royal Palaces. *Circa* 1810. The chair is of the same period, and the sphinx motifs that support the elbows suggest the influence of Thomas Hope.

Above: A Regency chair in mahogany, and a small tripod table, with brass mounts on the feet and at the base of the column, of the same period.
Below: A Regency low chair in black and gold.

PLATE 47

Above: Grand piano in the Music Room at the Royal Pavilion, Brighton. (Presented by Her Majesty Queen Mary in 1930.) The case is in rosewood, inlaid with brass; and the instrument is inscribed "Patent Sostenente Grand. I.H.R.Mott, J. C. Mott and Company, Makers to His Majesty. Patented 1817." In both illustrations carved and gilded seats are shown in the shape of a shell, supported by a dolphin. These seats were probably part of the original furnishing of the Royal Pavilion, *circa* 1805.

To the left: A harp by Erard, *circa* 1815.

(Reproduced by courtesy of the Brighton Art Gallery.)

PLATE 48

The last phase: extravagance in design, barely under control. The Banqueting Room at the Royal Pavilion, Brighton. The twenty-four chairs are reproductions of Regency dining chairs, in mahogany inlaid with yew, with lattice design in the back rails, sabre legs, and seats upholstered in pink velvet. (Reproduced by courtesy of the Brighton Art Gallery.)

INDEX

References in captions are shown by figures in brackets;
quotations are shown in italics.